FILM DIRECTING FUNDAMENTALS

Film Directing Fundamentals

Third Edition

See Your Film Before Shooting

Nicholas T. Proferes

Focal Press
Taylor & Francis Group

NEW YORK AND LONDON

First published 2013 by Focal Press
70 Blanchard Road, Suite 402, Burlington, MA 01803

Simultaneously published in the UK
by Focal Press
2 Park Square, Milton Park, Abingdon, Oxon OX14 4RN

Focal Press is an imprint of the Taylor & Francis Group, an informa business

Notices
Knowledge and best practice in this field are constantly changing. As new research and experience broaden our understanding, changes in research methods, professional practices, or medical treatment may become necessary.

Practitioners and researchers must always rely on their own experience and knowledge in evaluating and using any information, methods, compounds, or experiments described herein. In using such information or methods they should be mindful of their own safety and the safety of others, including parties for whom they have a professional responsibility.

Product or corporate names may be trademarks or registered trademarks, and are used only for identification and explanation without intent to infringe.

Library of Congress Cataloging-in-Publication Data
Proferes, Nicholas T.
      Film directing fundamentals : see your film before shooting / Nicholas T. Proferes. — 3rd ed.
          p. cm.
      Includes bibliographical references and index.
      ISBN-13: 978-0-240-80940-3 (pbk. : alk. paper) 1. Motion pictures—Production and direction.
      I. Title.
      PN1995.9.P7P758 2008
      791.4302'33—dc22

                                              2008004594

ISBN: 978-0-240-80940-3 (pbk)

Typeset by Charon Tec Ltd., A Macmillan Company.

To Frank Daniel
A great teacher,
a generous colleague,
a delightful friend.

CONTENTS

FOREWORD

How do you teach film directing? Nick Proferes's book, *Film Directing Fundamentals*, answers the question perfectly by providing a clear and concise methodology to the directing student. It is the only book I know of that addresses both the art and craft of directing. It not only offers a step-by-step process to follow, but it engages the reader as if you are sitting in Nick's class. His language is accessible, and he uses wonderful examples and clear, in-depth analysis that inspires you to the highest kind of effort.

When I first started teaching at Columbia University, I looked through many texts to find one to recommend to film students who wanted to become directors. Some books were informative but extremely technical and hard to follow; others were oversimplified, or were anecdotes by a particular director. None offered the students a concrete, organic approach. At Columbia, Nick addressed this problem by teaching a lecture course for all beginning students in our graduate film program. His focus is on training directors to engage their audience emotionally by first of all becoming clear on their story (detective work), then helping the director to orchestrate the progression and dramatic escalation of that story. The organization of action through dramatic blocks, narrative beats (director's beats), and a fulcrum around which a dramatic scene moves are categories Nick identifies for the first time.

Film Directing Fundamentals also provides a close analysis of three feature films to give the reader a chance to look at and understand how to use the dramatic elements as tools in their own work. The book leads us through an almost shot-by-shot discussion of dramatic structure and narrator's voice in Hitchcock's *Notorious*, Fellini's *8½*, and Peter Weir's *The Truman Show* and examines style and dramatic structure in 11 other feature films.

The third edition's addition of two new significant sections, "Organizing Action in Action Scenes" and "Organizing Action in Narrative Scenes," extends the book's methodology to these other forms of cinematic expression. Likewise, the inclusion of two new films, *In the Mood for Love* and *Little Children*, offers an insightful comparison of their styles and dramatic structures.

Although I have been an artist and a director for a number of years, it wasn't until I started teaching that I truly began to understand my own process. To have a book that tracks the process so precisely is invaluable to me as a teacher and as a filmmaker. I consulted this book before, during, and after my last film project, and it is certainly a book I will use again and again.

—*Bette Gordon*
Chair and Directing Supervisor of Columbia University Film Division
Director of the feature films *Variety*, *Luminous Motion*, and *Handsome Harry*

ACKNOWLEDGMENTS

This book could not have been written without feedback from the hundreds of students who attended my directing workshops at Columbia University. Their probing questions and impassioned work forced me to constantly clarify my teaching to better serve them, and I thank them one and all. I am also immensely grateful to my colleagues for their support, especially Bette Gordon and Tom Kalin, and for any of their wisdom that I may have purloined without attribution.

I owe sincere gratitude to the director James Goldstone for his valuable professional suggestions, and to Andy Pawelczak, Branislav Bala, and my son Ted Proferes for their astute editorial contributions; to Sonny Quinn for the *The Piece of Apple Pie* story-boards, Greg Bunch for the diagrams, and Patrick O'Connor for digitizing the artwork; to my publisher, Marie Lee, who made this happen, and to my wonderful editor, Terri Jadick.

For the second edition I sincerely thank my new editor Elinor Actipis, who has been a godsend, Branislav Bala and Pedja Zdravkovic, for the *Notorious* diagrams and artwork, and Professor Warren Bass for his close reading and invaluable suggestions throughout the entire process.

For this third edition I must again express my gratitude to Elinor Actipis and Warren Bass; augmented by the professional and academic insights of Bruce Sheridan, Phil South, and David O. Thomas; the shepherding of this edition by Associate Editor Michele Cronin; my storyboard artist, Jorge Alexeis Reyes; and to Cecil Matthai Esquivel-Obregón for his technical support.

For all three editions I am deeply grateful to the directors and writers whose films I have relied on for their masterful demonstration of the directing craft.

INTRODUCTION

Excitement, passion, beauty, surprise, laughter, and tears—these are some of the things we might think about when planning a film, but they cannot be realized unless the director's vision is wedded to a firm grasp of the directing craft. With that end in mind, this book sets out to introduce you to the conceptual aspects of this craft and to offer a step-by-step methodology that will take you from the screenplay to the screen. This methodology is based on the experiences of my own professional career as a director, cameraman, film editor, producer, writer, and graduate filmmaking teacher for 23 years at Columbia University in the School of the Arts' Film Division. I have taught more than 100 semester-long directing workshops where students have made countless hundreds of films, and I have directly supervised well over 100 thesis films. It was as a teacher that I realized the need for an organic, comprehensive text on directing. To put off the job of writing such a text, I developed a series of lectures that I delivered at Columbia and at seminars in Europe. Still my students wanted a book. I began with a 30-page handout that has evolved over the years into this third and final edition. The emphasis throughout is on the *craft* of narrative storytelling in the "classical" sense. The goal is to offer a toolbox that is fully equipped with every essential tool that can then be used to craft any kind of story. To use another metaphor, I want to develop all of the student's directorial muscles.

I make an assumption about the audience for this book—that they will want to engage *their* audience in a cinematic story. Everything contained in this book is aimed at that goal, which I believe is a laudable one. Human beings are in need of narrative and always have been. It has played a significant part in all the diverse cultures of the world, and perhaps even in development of the species itself. Out of concern for survival, our brains are constructed to make sense of incoming stimuli. Given any three facts or images, I, we, all of us, including our ancestors from 40 thousand years ago, are on our way to making sense of these facts: in other words, to making a story. A movement in the grass, birds taking flight, an unnatural stillness, and a Cro-Magnon might begin concocting a scenario of a leopard stalking him.

When I first began teaching, students asked me what books they should read about filmmaking, and I told them *Dear Theo*, Vincent van Gogh's letters to his brother. I still think anyone aspiring to be a film director should read this book—not for the craft of filmmaking, obviously, but for the inspiration to pursue the creation of art through the painstaking development of craft. For years van Gogh drew with charcoal. He spent countless hours drawing potato farmers digging in the fields, his eyes burning through their clothing to imagine the bones and muscles underneath. He built an unwieldy perspective device he would carry for miles to develop this invaluable skill of the representational artist.

After many years, another painter mentioned to van Gogh that he had surely done enough drawing and should begin to work with color. Van Gogh's response: "The problem with most people's color is that they cannot draw."

The point I wish to make is that although every one of you is in a hurry to "use color," it would behoove you to first learn to draw well. And that is where we will start. The "drawing" or methodology in this book is based on the proposition that the screenplay—the blueprint of a film—informs everything the director does. We will begin by focusing on four areas: detective work on the script, blocking actors, the camera as narrator, and work with the actors.

Do all good directors follow this methodology? I believe they do, whether they know it or not. For some it proceeds from an innate dramatic instinct. For others it is forged in the fire of experience. Most likely it is a combination of both. But I also know from my years at Columbia that it is possible to teach these principles. And I know that it is nearly impossible to engage an audience fully, to pull them into your story and keep them there, eliciting their emotions—which is, after all, the main power of film—if the steps called for here are not paid attention to *on some level*.

There are many attributes that are necessary for a good film director: imagination, tenacity, knowledge of the craft, knowledge of people, ability to work with others, willingness to accept responsibility, courage, stamina, and many more. But the most important attribute that can be taught, the one that if missing will negate all the rest, is *clarity*—clarity about the story and how each element in it contributes to the whole, and then clarity about what is conveyed to the audience.

In this third edition I have added new sections on "Organizing Action in an Action Scene" and "Organizing Action in a Narrative Scene" to complement the first two editions' emphasis on dramatic scenes. These new sections offer a more comprehensive view of the diversity to be found in narrative–dramatic films and how we might apply aspects of our methodology to these areas. Outside of a directing textbook these distinctions might have little use, but in a teaching environment they can help us to identify more clearly what might be particular to each, and most importantly, how we might go about rendering each type of scene most effectively.

A key ingredient in learning how to draw is to study drawings done by master artists. It is not only inspirational, but if we look closely we can see what aspects of craft the artist has used to create her effect. The same process is necessary in becoming an accomplished film director. We must study films, and we must study them closely. We must study them until we understand precisely how the various parts fit together, how each discrete element adds to the cumulative effect of the whole. To that end, Part Five, "Learning the Craft Through Film Analysis," which explores various visual styles to help inform our own visual storytelling, has been expanded.

This third edition also includes an instructor's manual that offers instructors a medley of curricula options including a week-by-week "Introductory Directing Workshop" and an "Advanced Directing Workshop," complete with field-tested exercises designed to facilitate the student's mastery of the methodology offered in this book. Qualified instructors can access the manual by signing up at www.focalpress.com/9780240809403.

Alfred Hitchcock said that if he were running a film school, he would not let students near a camera for the first two years. In today's world that film school would soon find itself bereft of students, for the camera serves as a validation that one is indeed pursuing the art of filmmaking. But nevertheless, there are things one should be aware of before picking up a camera, so we will begin our journey in Part One with an introduction to film language and its grammatical rules, then move on to explore the dramatic elements embedded in the screenplay.

P A R T   O N E

FILM LANGUAGE AND A DIRECTING METHODOLOGY

It is important in learning any language to understand its grammar, and it is no different for film language. This is covered in Chapter 1. Chapters 2 through 6 introduce the bedrock of this book's methodology: a journey of discovering answers to questions such as How do I stage a scene? Where do I put the camera? and What do I tell an actor? The answers, I believe, are to be found in your screenplay; therefore, much of our time will be spent on the "detective work" needed to uncover these answers.

In June 2007 Frances Ford Coppola visited Columbia and talked candidly about himself and the influences on his work. Prior to going to film school, he studied theater for four years, and at Columbia he stated categorically that for him the two most important aspects of a film are its text and the actors; this from a director who is supremely cinematic.

However, Mr. Coppola made another important disclosure. When asked what his greatest asset was, he responded without hesitation, "my imagination." Unfortunately this is not an ingredient any book or any teacher can impart, but my hope is that you will be encouraged by the methodology offered in this book to recognize and unleash your own wellspring of imagination. As we begin the introduction of this methodology, please keep foremost in your mind that its sole intention is to support, empower, and embolden your own unique vision.

C H A P T E R   1

INTRODUCTION TO FILM LANGUAGE AND GRAMMAR

THE FILM WORLD

The first dramatic films were rendered as if through a proscenium. The camera was placed in position, and all the action in the scene took place within that camera frame. The audience's view was much the same as a theater audience sitting front row center. The American director D. W. Griffith was one of the first to move the audience onto the stage with works like *For Love Of Gold* (1908), *The Lonely Villa* (1909), *The Lonedale Operator* (1911), and the highly influential, but strongly racist, *Birth of a Nation* (1915). "Look here!" he said to the audience with his camera—"Now here!" Griffith was not only moving the audience *into the scene*, he was then turning their seats this way and that—moving them into the face of a character, then in the next instant pulling them to the back of the "theater" to get a larger view of the character in relation to other characters or showing the character in relation to his or her surroundings.

The reason for putting the audience into the scene is that it makes the story more interesting—more dramatic. But by moving the audience into the action and focusing their attention first here, now there, the director can easily confuse and disorient the audience. The geography of a location or the wholeness of a character's body becomes *fragmented*. Whose hand does that belong to? Where is character A in spatial relationship to character B? Usually the director does not want to cause confusion. Rather, she wants the audience to feel comfortable in this film world—to be spatially (and temporally) oriented—so that the story can take place unimpeded. Usually the director wants the audience to know, "That hand belongs to Bob, and Bob is sitting to the right of Ellen" (even if we haven't seen Ellen for a while). There are times, however, when we will use this possibility for confusion and disorientation to our advantage to create surprise or suspense.

FILM LANGUAGE

When film became a series of connected *shots*, a language was born. Every shot became a complete sentence with at least one subject and one verb. (We are talking about an *edited shot* here, as opposed to a *camera setup*, which can be cut into a number of edited shots.) Like prose, a film sentence/shot can be simple, with only one subject and one verb, and perhaps an object; or it can be a compound sentence/shot, composed of two or more clauses. The type of sentence/shot we use will first depend on the *essence of the moment* that we wish to convey to the audience. Secondarily, that sentence/shot will be contained in a *design of the scene*, which can be an ingredient of an overall *style*. In Alfred Hitchcock's *Rope* (1948), where there are but nine sentences, each one 10 minutes long (the length of a film roll), each sentence contains many subjects and a host of verbs and objects.

Let us look at a simple sentence/shot: a wristwatch lying on a table, reading three o'clock. Without a context outside of this particular shot, the sentence reads, "A wristwatch lying on a table reads three o'clock." The significance of this film sentence, its specific meaning in the context of a story, will become clear only when it is embedded among other shots (sentences); for example, a character is someplace she is not supposed to be, and as she leaves we cut to the very same shot of the wristwatch on the table reading three o'clock. Now the shot—the sentence—is given a context and takes on a specific significance. Its meaning is clear. The character is leaving behind *evidence* (that could cause her trouble). The fact that it is three o'clock might very well have no significance at all.

The necessity of context in interpreting a particular shot applies to the camera angle also. *No camera angle—extreme low, extreme high, tilted to left or right, etc.—in and of itself contains any inherent dramatic, psychological, or atmospheric content.*

SHOTS

Professionals in the film industry don't usually refer to a shot as a sentence. But in learning any foreign language, we have to think in our native language first to clearly formulate what it is we want to say in the new language, and the same principle applies to learning to "talk" in film. It can be extremely helpful before you have developed a visual vocabulary to formulate the content of each shot into a linguistic analogue (the prose and syntax of your native language) to help you find the corresponding visual images. At the same time, it is important to keep in mind that film, unlike the words of the screenplay, is rendered on the screen in a series of images that, when combined in a sequence, gives a meaning that goes beyond mere words. The late Stefan Sharff, a former colleague of mine at Columbia, in his book *The Elements of Cinema*, wrote:

> When a proper cinema "syntax" is used, the viewer is engaged in an active process of constantly "matching" chains of shots not merely by association or logical relationship but by an empathy peculiar to cinema. The blend so achieved spells cinema sense—a mixture of emotion and understanding, meditative or subliminal, engaging the viewer's ability to respond to a structured cinema "language." . . . A cinematic syntax yields meaning not only through the surface content of shots, but also through their connections and mutual relationships.

FILM GRAMMAR

Film language has only four basic grammatical rules, three of which are concerned with spatial orientation as a result of moving the audience into the action. The fourth also deals with space but for a different reason. All of these rules must be followed most of the time, but all can be broken for dramatic effect.

THE 180-DEGREE RULE

The 180-degree rule deals with any framed spatial (right-to-left or left-to-right) relationship between a character and another character or object. It is used to maintain consistent screen direction between the characters, or a character and an object, within the established space.

When a character is opposite another character or object, an imaginary line (*axis*) exists between that character and the other character or object. The issue is most acute in the sight lines between two characters who are looking at each other (Figure 1-1). As long as A and B are contained in the

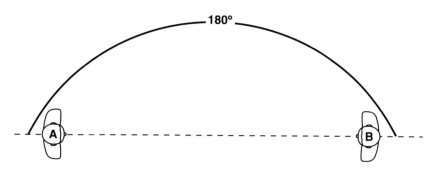

FIGURE 1-1

Axis between two subjects.

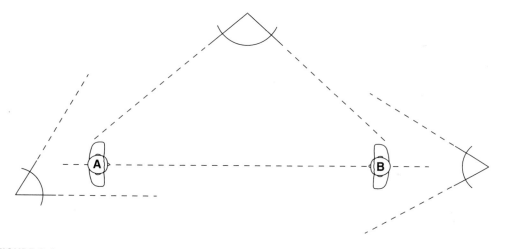

FIGURE 1-2

A and B both contained in three shots from different angles.

same shot, there is no problem (Figure 1-2). (The axis exists even if the characters do not look at each other.)

Now let's place a camera between the two characters, facing toward A, who is looking, not at the camera, but at B, who is *camera right* (Figure 1-3). (Characters almost never look into the camera except in very special situations, such as an object of a point of view (POV) shot, a comic take, or a reflexive moment that recognizes the presence of the camera.)

Let's now turn the camera around toward B who will now be looking *camera left* (Figure 1-4).

If we were to shoot separate shots of A and B then cut them together so that one would follow the other, what we would see on the screen is the two subjects looking at each other. In other words, their sight lines would be correct, and the audience would understand the spatial relationship between the characters. What happens to the sight lines if we *jump the axis* during a scene (Figure 1-5)?

Still shooting in separation, we have moved the camera across the axis for shooting A while leaving the camera on the same side of the axis for B. Subject A will now be looking camera *left*. B will *also* be looking camera *left*. When the two shots are cut together, the result will be that the subjects/characters will be looking in the opposite directions, and the audience will become

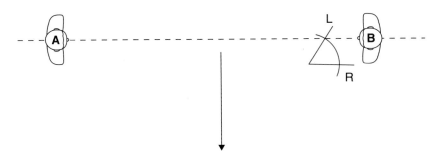

FIGURE 1-3

A looking camera right at B.

FIGURE 1-4

B looking camera left at A.

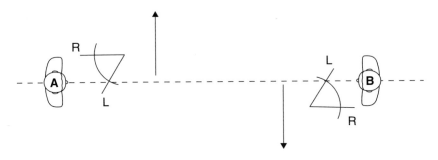

FIGURE 1-5

Jumping axis by moving the camera and shooting A across the 180-degree line.

confused as to spatial positioning between them, the dynamics of the dramatic moment thereby broken.

It is possible to *cross the axis* with impunity as long as we keep the audience constantly apprised of where the characters are in relation to each other. We could dolly across or around. Or we could cut to a *two-shot* from the opposite side of the axis. Other than the fact that character A will jump to the left side of the frame, whereas B will jump to the right side, the audience will still be correctly oriented (Figure 1-6). This "flip-flopping" of characters to opposite sides of the frame, at the right dramatic moment, can be another powerful dramatic tool.

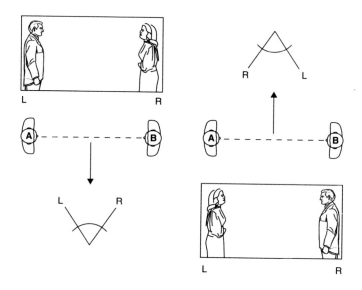

FIGURE 1-6

Jumping the axis with both subjects in the frame.

Having characters change sides within the frame is also a *staging* technique often used by directors, and it is one that is highly effective in punctuating a moment. This is made even more powerful if, say, the position of characters A and B within the frame is changed forcefully. A good example of this exists in Roman Polanski's *Chinatown* (1974), the highly memorable scene in which Evelyn Mulwray (Faye Dunaway) exclaims to the private detective, J. J. Gittes (Jack Nicholson), "She's my sister, she's my daughter!" At the start of this hysterical outburst, Dunaway is on the right side of the frame. Nicholson tries to calm her down. He fails until he slaps her hard, sending her reeling from screen right to screen left. This change in their positioning vis-à-vis the frame serves to end that dramatic "stanza" and announces the arrival of a new one. Another good example of flip-flopping of characters to the opposite side of the frame is in *Taxi Driver* (Martin Scorcese, 1976) as Betsy (Cybill Shepherd) makes her way to a taxi pursued by Travis (Robert De Niro) after a disastrous date at an X-rated movie. Keeping both in the frame, the camera crosses the 180-degree line four times, dramatically punctuating Betsy's exit.

Can we ever jump the axis between our characters while they are in separation? The 180-degree rule often terrifies the beginning director, and so much heed is paid to not breaking this rule that it rarely is. But we can break it—jump the axis between characters—with great dramatic effect *if we do it on an act of energy*: This act of energy can be either psychological or physical. We will see an example of this when we add the camera to a screenplay in Chapter 8.

[handwritten margin note: jumping 180° rule]

THE 30-DEGREE RULE

If we are going from one shot of a character or object (Figure 1-7) to another shot of the same character or object without an intervening shot of something else, the camera angle should change by at least 30 degrees.

The effect of disobeying this rule is to call undue attention to the camera; it seems to leap through space. If the rule is obeyed, we do not notice this leap. But in some instances, disobedience can be dramatically energizing. In *The Birds* (1963), Hitchcock ignores the rule to "punch up" the discovery of the body of a man with a series of three shots from the same angle, each shot coming

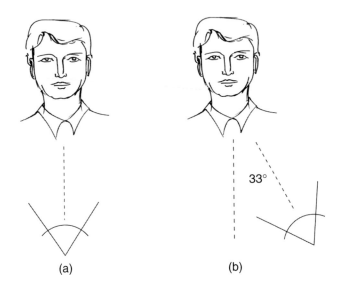

(a)   (b)

FIGURE 1-7

Initial camera angle on character A and camera angle changed by 30 degrees on same character B.

dramatically closer: medium to medium close-up to close-up. (Three is the magic number in this style of *elaboration*, as well as in other stylistic and dramaturgical aspects of film. Given any two types of patterns we anticipate the third, creating dramatic tension.)

Sometimes, because of the geography of the set or other limitations, we have to cut to the next shot from the same angle. We see it done successfully fairly frequently, but the reason it works is because of one of the following mitigating factors: the subject is in motion, the second shot includes a foreground object such as a lamp shade, or the change in image size from one shot to the next is substantial.

SCREEN DIRECTION

The sections that follow explore various aspects of screen direction.

LEFT TO RIGHT

If a character (or car, or anything else) exits a frame going from left to right (Figure 1-8), he should enter the next frame from the left if we intend to convey to the audience that the character is headed in the same direction.

If we disobey this simple rule and have our character or car exit frame right (Figure 1-9), then enter the second frame from the right, the character or car will seem to have made a U-turn.

This rule can be broken if the time period or distance (which can be synonymous) is protracted as with a covered wagon going from New York to California or an ambulance speeding to a hospital. In fact, it can help to elaborate the sense of distance traveled, or in the latter case to increase the dramatic tension through a sequence of shots that reverse the screen direction (right, left, right, left). Each succeeding shot, besides reversing the screen direction, should be varied as to angle and length of time on the screen. The last shot in the sequence should then pay heed to the grammatical rule. That is, if the covered wagon or ambulance exits the starting point going from left to right, it should enter the frame of its destination going from left to right.

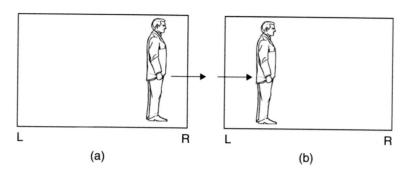

FIGURE 1-8

Character moving left to right and exiting frame right (a) and character entering frame left, moving left to right (b).

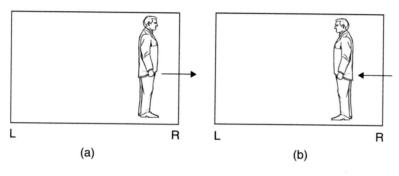

FIGURE 1-9

Character moving left to right and exiting frame right (a) and character entering frame right, moving right to left (b).

RIGHT TO LEFT AND UP

Psychologists have told us that those of us who grew up moving our eyes from left to right when we read find it is more "comfortable" for us when a character in a film moves from left to right. When they go from right to left, a tension is created. Maximum tension is created when the character moves right to left and up. I suspect Hitchcock was aware of this psychological effect on an audience when in the final bell tower scene in *Vertigo* he had Jimmy Stewart climb up the winding staircase right to left.

APPROACHING AND RECEDING

A character approaching the camera and exiting the frame camera right (Figure 1-10) should enter the following frame camera left.

FILM-TIME

Our stories *unfold* in time as well as space, and the ability to use both in service of our stories is of paramount importance. A simplistic view of the use of time in film—but one that contains much storytelling savvy—is that we shorten (compress) what is boring and lengthen (elaborate) what is interesting.

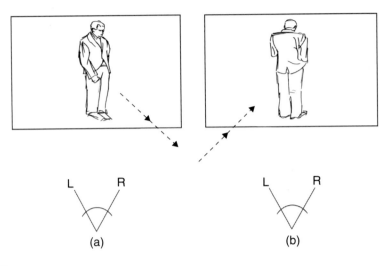

FIGURE 1-10

Character approaching camera and exiting frame camera right (a) and character entering frame camera left and receding from camera (b).

COMPRESSION

We are not talking here about the compression that takes place in the screenplay—a year, or even 10 years, played out in five minutes of film time (an absolutely essential component of nearly all screenplays). And we are not yet talking about transitions between scenes: the "what" that happens between the end of one scene and the beginning of another. What we are talking about here is the compression of time that takes place within a single scene.

In what we might call "ordinary compression," to distinguish it from an *ellipsis* (a cut that makes it obvious to the audience that a jump in time has occurred), we will often be dealing with compression that the audience will accept as real time. A more accurate appellation would be *film-time*. The following example will clarify this.

A MAN enters a large space that he must cross to get to his destination. We have determined that there is no dramatic reason to show every step he takes. In fact, it would be boring, so we compress the distance traveled. How can we accomplish this? Have the MAN enter the first shot and exit it, then enter a second shot already at his destination. This will give the semblance of real time to the audience. The jump across the space will have been made gracefully and will go unnoticed.

ELABORATION

Here we want to take a moment and make it larger, to stretch time. Large elaborations often occur at the end of films, as in, for example, the staircase scene at the end of Alfred Hitchcock's *Notorious* (1946), or Marlon Brando walking through the crowd of dockworkers at the end of *On the Waterfront* (Kazan, 1954). But elaboration occurs with regularity throughout a film. The two instances just mentioned rely on a *series of shots* to achieve this purpose, and that is most often the case. But elaboration can also be a single camera movement, such as the end of *The Godfather Part II* (Francis Ford Coppola, 1987), where the camera moves into a "tight" close-up of the tortured face of Michael (Al Pacino). The movement gets us into Michael's head and allows us to be privy to his thoughts—his realization of what he has become.

Elaboration can also be used to *prepare* the audience for what will happen next, and, at the same time, create *suspense* about just what it will be. In Eric Rohmer's film *Rendezvous in Paris* (1997, French), the artist/protagonist in one of the three stories is seen walking back to his studio in a protracted series of shots. This *undue attention to the ordinary* sets up an expectation, hence suspense, in the audience. The payoff of this elaboration happens when the female antagonist enters the film by passing the artist going the other way. (This is a good example of suspense versus surprise. Suspense has a duration to it and is much more useful and prevalent in cinematic storytelling than is surprise, which comes out of nowhere and is over in an instant. Still, surprise has its undeniable place in cinematic storytelling, and many times a surprise is embedded in a suspense sequence. How many times have we seen a bird fly out unannounced or a cat hiss unexpectedly and jump toward the camera?)

Elaboration can also be used to elicit a mood, as in the comedy *Starting Over* (Alan J. Pakula, 1979). A long, slow tracking shot over the participants of a divorced men's workshop while they listen to an older member's grievances about growing old elaborates the depressive pall that is cast over the entire group.

FAMILIAR IMAGE

A familiar image can reverberate with the harmonics of a previous moment, making the present moment larger. Scharff, in *The Elements of Cinema*, explains:

> We know that cinema thrives on repetition and symmetries. The familiar image structure provides symmetry in the form of a recurrent, stable picture that "glues" together scattered imagery, especially in scenes that are fragmented into many shots or involve many participants. . . . Normally, the familiar image is "planted" somewhere in the beginning of a scene, then recurs several times in the middle, with resolution at the end.

Scharff mentions an image from *Lancelot du Lac*, Robert Bresson (1975, France):

> A solitary shot of a small gothic window flashed periodically on the screen means volumes, since the lonely queen lives behind it. All the emotions, struggles, drives, and fanaticisms of the knights, their whole philosophy of life, are tied to this little window.

A strong image need not appear more than once to become familiar, so that the next time we see it we immediately recognize it, as in, for example, the front entrance to the Nazi spy's mansion in *Notorious* (see Part Five, Chapter 15). When Alicia (Ingrid Bergman) arrives at the front door for the first time, the job of setting up the geography goes unnoticed by the audience because it is integrated with the action of the moment, and we are as curious about the house as Alicia is. But if we had not been privy to the imposing grandeur of the front of the house before the climactic ending of the film, which takes place within a similar framing, we may well have been thinking to ourselves at the moment when the final dramatic resolution is occurring, "Wow, what a big door that is." In addition, Hitchcock uses the same prolonged tracking shot, but in reverse, to enter the mansion and then to exit it—a familiar note that reverberates within the audience's psyche, bringing them an aesthetic pleasure in the director's orchestration of such symmetry.

Familiar images can be incorporated with familiar staging to orient the audience to geography that is less imposing, less memorable—say, an ordinary living room that is going to be used in more than one scene. To orient the audience, it is desirable to decide on an angle that says "this is the same room." An angle that has the characters approach a couch from the same screen direction can give the audience all the information they need. On the other hand, an angle that has the characters approaching the couch from the opposite screen direction than it was approached in a previous scene might confuse the audience to the point that it intrudes on the dramatic moment.

A strong image exiting a frame can make the audience anticipate the return of that image, and this phenomenon can be used to create tension—even if this expectation in the audience is on the subconscious level. Think of the yellow barrel being pulled out of the frame in *Jaws* (Spielberg, 1975) after the first harpoon has been planted in the shark. Later, when that familiar frame is repeated, we find ourselves expecting the barrel to return into the frame—and to our great satisfaction and pleasure, it does.

There is yet another value to the familiar image: *dramatic economy,* a key ingredient of dramaturgy from its inception, starting with Aristotle's *unity of action.* The concept of economy is mostly the purview of the screenwriter, but it also relates to staging, camera, props, and so on. In short, every time a director considers adding a new element to do a narrative, dramatic, or even atmospheric job, she should first ask this question: "Can I do it with what I've already got?"

CHAPTER 2

INTRODUCTION TO THE DRAMATIC ELEMENTS EMBEDDED IN THE SCREENPLAY

We talked in Chapter 1 about elements that appear on the screen, but there are many elements embedded in a screenplay that, if unearthed by the director, will help supply clarity, cohesion, and dramatic power to what appears on the screen.

SPINES

There are two categories of spines we will deal with. The first is the spine of your film, or its main action. Before we get to the dramatic definition of a film's spine, an analogy using representational sculpture might be helpful. When working in clay, a sculptor first builds an armature (i.e., a skeleton, usually of metal) to support the clay. This armature determines the parameters of the final work. If the armature is designed to represent a man standing, it will be impossible for the artist to turn it into a man sitting, no matter how much clay she applies to it. Even without this exaggerated example, a poorly designed armature of a man standing, one that does not take into account the anatomy and proportions of the human skeleton, will still fall far short of supporting the artist's intent. The analogy implies that there is a scientific component to our task, and that is exactly the case. It is called dramaturgy, and *the armature of dramaturgy is the spine—the driving force or concept that pervades every element of the story, thereby holding the story together.*

Stage director Harold Clurman comments in *On Directing*: "Where a director has not determined on a spine for his production, it will tend to be formless. Each scene follows the next without necessarily adding up to a total dramatic 'statement.'"

After the film's spine has been determined, it is necessary to determine the spine of your characters—their main actions. It is the goal that each character desperately desires, aspires to, yearns for. It should be extremely important, perhaps a matter of life and death. The character must save the farm, win her love, discover the meaning of life, live a life that is not a lie, or any of the countless wants we humans have. And the more a character wants something, the more the audience will care about whether or not she gets it. Moreover, the character's spine should be contained under the umbrella of the film's spine. Clurman comments: "The character's spine must be conceived as emerging from the [screen] play's main action. Where such a relation is not evident or non-existent, the character performs no function in the [screen] play."

When Clurman directed Eugene O'Neill's *Long Day's Journey into Night*, he came up with the following spines. For the play, "to probe within oneself for the lost something"; for Tyrone, "to maintain his fatherhood"; for Mary, "to find her bearings, her home"; for Edmund, "to discover or understand the truth"; and for Jamie, "to free himself from guilt."

Elia Kazan, one of America's premier theater and film directors, was a member of the Group Theater in the 1940s and 1950s and shared the same methodology with Clurman. Kazan's *Director's Notebook* for *A Streetcar Named Desire*, published in *Directors on Directing*, edited by Toby Cole, gives us an invaluable look at Kazan's thorough and insightful detective work. Kazan's spine for Blanche, the protagonist, is to "find protection"; for Stella, it is to "hold onto Stanley"; for Stanley, it is to "keep things his way"; and for Mitch, to "get away from his mother."

Federico Fellini said that making a film was, for him, as scientific as launching a space rocket. But he most likely did not make conscious use of a spine for the film or for his characters. Nevertheless, there is an organic artistic unity present in his masterpiece, *8½* (1963, Italian), (analyzed in Part Five, Chapter 17). In other words, Fellini, on some level, paid attention to this important piece of dramaturgy.

The following are spines for Fellini's *8½*:

- Film's spine: to seek an authentic life
- Guido's spine: to live a life without a lie
- Guido's wife: to have a marriage that is not a lie
- Carla: to be loved (by Guido and her husband)
- Mezzabota: to deny an authentic life (by seeking escape in an inauthentic relationship)
- Gloria: to seek salvation in abstractions
- Screenwriter: to seek meaning in art
- Cardinal: to seek union with God through the church (the only authentic path)
- Woman in white: to seek the true, the good, the beautiful

Because the spines of the major characters can all be subsumed under the umbrella of the film's spine, the film achieves the thematic unity that is a basic requirement of art.

The spine is such a powerfully organizing tool that when we apply it after our first readings of the text, it might cause us to rewrite. We might find that the spines of our characters do not fit under the umbrella of the film's spine. Does this mean that we have a film that will not engage an audience? Not necessarily—but it would be more engaging if it were an organic whole. (Other directors might use other words to identify similar categories that serve as a unifying function, such as *premise* and *through-line*.)

WHOSE FILM IS IT?

Most successful films have a protagonist, and *the first question in our detective work on the screenplay is: Who is the protagonist in our film?* Another way of asking the same question, one I believe is more helpful for the director, is: Whose film is it? Which character do we go through the film with? Which character do we hope or fear for—hope that she will get what she wants, or fear that she will not?

I have not included as the primary criterion for a protagonist that he or she be the one who *drives the action* throughout the entire film. Not that it's a bad idea. Quite the contrary; it is one of the key tenets of most dramaturgy. However, there are just too many successful films where that is not the case; for example, with Ingrid Bergman's character Alicia in *Notorious*. Also, there are many fine films where there is no central protagonist at all, or possibly multiple or serial protagonists, such as Robert Altman's *Nashville* (1975), Kenji Mizoguchi's *Street of Shame* (Japanese, 1956), Woody Allen's *Hannah and Her Sisters* (1986), Jonathan Dayton's and Valerie Faris' *Little Miss Sunshine* (2006), or Todd Field's *Little Children* (2006).

CHARACTER

Paul Lucey, in his very fine book on screenwriting, *Story Sense*, states that one of the main tenets of his dramaturgy is, "Write simple stories and complex characters."

Although film takes place in the present, character is created in the past. Character is everything that has gone into the making of our characters before they stepped into our film: genetic inheritance, family influence, socioeconomic conditions, life experience, and on and on. Of course, some influences are more relevant to our stories than others, and we should limit ourselves so that we do not become bogged down with the nonessential. Keep this analogy in mind: *A film is like a train ride in which characters embark on their journey with just enough baggage for that trip.*

There is an often-told story concerning character that bears repeating here. A frog was sitting by a river swollen by a recent flood, when a scorpion came up to him. "Mr. Frog, the river is much too wide for me to cross. Could you please take me across on your back?"

"Oh, no," replied the frog, "when we get to the middle of the river, you will kill me with your sting."

"Why would I do that?" asked the scorpion. "If I killed you, you would sink to the bottom and I would drown."

The frog had not thought of that scenario, but it made perfectly good sense. "Okay," said the frog, "hop on."

"Thank you so much, Mr. Frog," said the scorpion as he hopped on the frog's back.

The frog was a strong swimmer, and in no time at all they reached the middle of the river, but still much too far for the scorpion to walk to the other side. Nevertheless, the scorpion stung the frog with his stinger. As the frog began to die from the poison, and the scorpion began to drown because he had lost his ride, the frog asked incredulously, "Why? Why did you sting me?"

The scorpion replied, "It's my character."

We are familiar with complicated film characters: Guido in *8½* (Fellini, 1963), Charles Foster Kane in *Citizen Kane* (Orson Welles, 1941), Rick in *Casablanca* (Michael Curtiz, 1942), Michael in *The Godfather* (Francis Ford Coppola, 1972), Blanche and Stanley in *A Streetcar Named Desire* (Kazan, 1951), John Forbes Nash Jr. in *A Beautiful Mind* (Ron Howard, 2001), Fiona in *Away From Her* (Sarah Polley, 2006), and Pierre Peders and Katya in *Interview* (Steve Buscemi, 2007).

The character studies in Kazan's *Director's Notebook* on *A Streetcar Named Desire* are brilliant not only in going to the central core of the character but in uncovering the undulations and modulations of that core that make the characters so compelling to watch. This psychology unearthed by Kazan prior to working with the actors points the way to behavior that will ultimately make the psychology available to the audience. This point is made paramount in Kazan's first note to himself: "*A thought*—directing finally consists of turning Psychology into Behavior." The most complicated character in the play/film is Blanche, and Kazan pushes himself in the *Notebook* to discover all of the varied layers of her personality. "Try to find an entirely different character, a self-dramatized and self-romanticized character for Blanche to play in each scene. She is playing 11 different people. This will give it a kind of changeable and shimmering surface it should have. And all these 11 self-dramatized and romantic characters should be out of the romantic tradition of the Pre-Bellum South."

No director has ever been more attuned than Kazan to the idea that everything the director does is aimed at affecting the audience. Again, his *Notebook*:

> The audience at the beginning should see her [Blanche's] bad effect on Stella, want Stanley to tell her off. He does. He exposes her and then gradually, as they [the audience] see how genuinely in pain, how actually desperate she is, how warm, tender and loving she can be . . . how frightened with need she is—they begin to go with her. They begin to realize that they are sitting in at the death of something extraordinary . . . colorful, varied, passionate, lost, witty, imaginative, of her own integrity . . . and then they feel the tragedy.

Kazan's exhaustive investigation of character not only deals with the past; he also projects (in the case of Stanley) into the future: "He is adjusted *now* . . . later, as his sexual powers die, so will he: the trouble will come later, the 'problems.' He's going to get very fat later."

CIRCUMSTANCE

Circumstance is simply the situation the characters find themselves in. It can be, from the character's perspective, objective or subjective—real or imagined. In a feature-length screenplay, the circumstances, especially for principal characters, are more often than not made explicit in the screenplay. They are not up for grabs. But in short films the full circumstance of the character might not be contained in the text.

DYNAMIC RELATIONSHIP

The relationship we are referring to here is not the societal relationship; that is, husband/wife, boyfriend/girlfriend, father/son, mother/daughter, and so on. These static relationships are facts of the story and will come out in exposition. What we want here is to find the ever-changing dynamic relationship that exists between any two characters—the one that supplies what I call the *dramatic juice*. And where do we find it?

The dynamic relationship is found in the present moment, in the "now." It is always established by looking through the eyes of the characters. It can be objective or it can be entirely subjective. The important point is always how one character "sees" another character at the present moment. For example, a bride on the day of the wedding might see the groom as her "knight in shining armor." Seven years later she might see him as her "ball and chain." Or, on the day of the wedding, the bride, instead of seeing "my knight in shining armor," sees "my ticket out of town." A father might see his son as a "disappointment," while the son might see his father as his "boss." That very same father might change during the course of the film and begin to see his son as "his own drummer," while the son might now see his father as his "Rock of Gibraltar."

WANTS

Wants differ from the spine in that they are smaller goals (objective *is another term sometimes used*) *that must be reached before the larger goal of the spine can be achieved.* For example, in 8½ the protagonist's spine is "to lead an authentic life"—a life that is not a lie—but he also wants to make a great film and be a good husband. There are also smaller (but not unimportant), more immediate wants that occur in individual scenes and are called *scene wants*. For the protagonist, Guido, there are scenes in which he wants to escape, to placate, to deflect. Also, these "smaller" wants can conflict with the larger goal of the spine, and as far as dramatic purposes are concerned, it is better if they do. For example: an Ethical Man wants to live his life ethically—his spine, or sometimes called *life want*—but his wife and children are hungry. He wants to feed them, but he can only get sustenance for them by committing an unethical act.

Synonymous with want in drama is the *obstacle* to obtaining that want. This is what elicits the struggle—the dramatic journey. It is what supplies the conflict.

"Hey, will you love me for the rest of my life?"

"Of course I will."

End of film.

If, instead of acquiescence, there is rejection—"Get lost, jerk!"—we have the obligatory obstacle that sets up the obligatory conflict, but only if the character truly "wants."

There are three possibilities concerning a character's want: the character will succeed in obtaining the want, will fail, or will be sidetracked by a new, more urgent want.

It is important to make a distinction between wants and needs. To paraphrase Mick Jagger: "You can't always get what you want, but if you try, you might get what you need." This distinction often supplies the basis for irony in our stories—another very powerful tool used by storytellers since the time of the ancient Greeks.

EXPECTATIONS

Characters might want something, but do they expect to get it? Are they afraid of what might happen, or are they confident? This psychological state is important for the audience to know so that they can more fully access the particular moment in the story. In a scene where each characters' expectations are opposed, and we know about it, dramatic tension is created. (There will be more discussion later on about what the audience should know and when.)

ACTIONS

Drama is told through the actions of your characters. These actions must be conveyed to an audience for them to fully appreciate, as well as understand, the story.

Characters perform actions to get what they want. That seems rather obvious, doesn't it? But what might not be so obvious is that characters rarely perform actions that aren't related to attaining what they want. They almost never voluntarily take their eyes off the prize, but exceptions do occur! Sometimes characters will commit actions that are not related to their immediate wants but instead are generated by their innate characters—like the scorpion.

A character can perform only one action at a time! Sandy Meisner, the famous acting teacher, constantly encountered beginning actors who thought this was not so. Perhaps they thought that it was too limiting. Meisner asked the Doubting Thomas to stand up. Then he barked out, "Turn on the light and open the window!"

Another common misunderstanding is that actors act emotions. They do not. Then where does the emotion come from? The emotional life of the actor/character comes primarily from actions that are wedded to wants that are contextualized by—embedded in—dynamic relationships and circumstance.

Dialogue is action! If I say "hello" to you, it might be a greeting, but if you come into my class a half-hour late it might very well be a reprimand. Only by fully understanding the circumstances and the wants can we arrive at the true intent of the action.

ACTIVITY

It is important to distinguish between action and activity. Suppose you are sitting in your dentist's reception area reading a magazine. Are you waiting or reading? Most likely you are waiting. As soon as the dentist is ready for you, you will drop the magazine. So what is the reading, in dramatic terms? It is an activity that accompanies the action of waiting.

ACTING BEATS

An *acting beat* (also referred to as a *performance beat*) is a unit of action committed by a character. There are literally hundreds of these acting beats in a feature-length film. Every time the action of a character changes, a new acting beat begins. Each acting beat can be described by an action verb.

In the example of the student coming late to class, my action verb, "to reprimand," was an acting beat. Before that beat could take place there had to be at least one acting beat that preceded it, no matter what the circumstance or wants attendant to this particular story. What is that acting beat that must precede any exchange between characters? Awareness! For me or anyone else to reprimand someone—or to greet them—we must first become aware that they are present.

In addition to the narrative/dramatic elements already introduced, are there others that would be helpful? There are, and they go to the heart of the methodology that is offered in this book. I have found them imbedded in hundreds of dramatic scenes in films of every genre and culture. Directors who can identify these elements will obtain a clarity about their scenes that will inform their work with actors, their staging, and not least, their camera.

The three additional elements I have identified and given labels to are dramatic blocks, narrative beats, and a scene's fulcrum. Each of them has to do with the organization of action within a scene.

DRAMATIC BLOCKS

A *dramatic block* can be likened to a paragraph in prose: it contains one overriding dramatic idea. Keeping our dramatic ideas separated gives them more force and power and makes them clearer to the audience. As in prose, when we move on to another idea, we begin a new paragraph, acknowledging to the reader the progression of thought, or in the case of a dramatic film, acknowledging narrative or dramatic change and/or escalation. Acknowledging change gives the audience a sense of forward momentum—of narrative thrust.

Identifying our dramatic blocks will help us to incorporate *spatial renderings* into our staging: "geographical paragraphs" that will contain a single strong "idea" (one *main* action). For example:

REASON   SEDUCE   THREATEN   BEG

If we give each of the above dramatic blocks a significantly different spatial rendering, the series of actions will *unfold* in a more powerful way because the character's intent and increasing desperation will be made clearer—more *palpable*—to the audience. The clarity we see in the above schematic will be helpful in working with our actors, and, of course, must be taken into account when we block them and add the camera.

NARRATIVE BEATS

Why does a director move a camera or cut from one shot to another? Why does a director have a character move from one side of the room to the other? Is what they do random, or can it be explained? If it cannot be explained, it cannot be taught. I believe it can be explained, and not just for some films but for all dramatic/narrative films.

For nearly a century the concept of a beat has been used in acting as a unit of action or nuance from the perspective of a character. However, it is also possible to think of beats from a director's perspective as units that progress the narrative.

The majority of director's beats—or as I have labeled them, *narrative beats*—are acting beats that are articulated ("framed") by the director. All narrative beats contain a heightened "story moment" (such as a significant escalation of action or changes in its direction) or render plot points essential to the story. The latter is an example of a narrative beat, which is separate from an acting beat.

Narrative beats are articulated through staging and/or camera, and the editing process acknowledges this articulation. The director, using staging and camera, either separately or in combination, indicates to the audience that something significant has happened or foreshadows that something significant is about to happen. Whether or not an acting beat is also a narrative beat depends on the style with which each director articulates his or her story. Some will affirm more narrative beats than others.

FULCRUM

In a dramatic scene, a scene where the *character whose scene it is* wants something that is difficult to obtain, often the most important narrative beat is the *fulcrum*—the moment in the scene where things can go either way for that character. One could call this the turning point, but I prefer to use that term in regard to the film's overall dramatic structure (*turning point* is often used to denote the plot point that occurs at the end of the first and second acts). In a feature film with, say, six dramatic scenes, there might be two turning points but six fulcrums.

In the next chapter we will explore how all of the various elements introduced in this chapter are put to use in a dramatic scene by a master director.

C H A P T E R   3

ORGANIZING ACTION IN A DRAMATIC SCENE

What distinguishes a dramatic scene from other scenes? An important difference is that in a dramatic scene one character always has a strong want that the other character or characters in the scene are opposed to. I often liken dramatic scenes to a tennis match or an arm wrestling contest. In an effective dramatic scene a question is raised—will such and such a character get what they want, or will they be defeated? This leads to conflict, the essence of drama. Much of the action in such a scene is usually contained in dialogue, though there are exceptions, and much of the character's reactions are psychological (taking place inside the character's head). Therefore it is important that the *articulation* of action in these scenes makes the interior life of the characters available to the audience.

A proper organization and articulation of a dramatic scene will not merely make it more interesting, but even more importantly, it will assure that the psychology of each moment is made available to the audience.

The Patio scene that follows is from *Notorious*. It was chosen because it is a clear, unambiguous example of a dramatic scene, rendered by a master director whose methodical preparation before shooting is reflected in his staging, camera, and editing, allowing us to fully explore the dramatic elements introduced in Chapter 2, and how they can help to render the text fully.

DRAMATIC ELEMENTS IN ALFRED HITCHCOCK'S *NOTORIOUS* PATIO SCENE

The scene occurs early in the second act, and the synopsis of the story to this point is: Devlin (Cary Grant) is an American intelligence agent who has recruited Alicia (Ingrid Bergman), a woman who likes to drink and has had more than a few lovers. Neither one has any idea what the agency is planning for them, and before they discover what the assignment is, they fall in love.

CIRCUMSTANCE

In the scene just prior to the Patio, Devlin has received his instructions from the agency. He is to inform Alicia, the woman he is deeply in love with, of her first assignment: seduction of the German arms dealer Sebastian for the purpose of gaining information.

WHOSE SCENE IS IT?

To fully appreciate this scene, we have to be in Alicia's head—to be privy to her psychology moment by moment. We will discover in later chapters how Hitchcock assists us in gaining this access—in making Alicia's psychology available to us by his exquisite staging and his use of the camera as narrator.

EXPECTATION

Alicia's expectation is conveyed from the beginning of the scene. There is an excitement in her voice as, preparing dinner, she unself-consciously rambles on about domestic, "wifely" concerns and her thought that "marriage must be wonderful." Devlin, on the other hand, who an hour ago was on the verge of letting his guard down with Alicia, has now raised it higher than ever because he expects to be hurt. He expects that she will take the job and give herself to another man.

SCENE WANTS

Alicia's wanting a romantic evening—just the two of them dining alfresco over a home-cooked meal—indicates her ardent desire to *escalate* the relationship with Devlin. After this evening they will be a couple. Before his meeting with Prescott, Devlin would have wanted the same thing. Now he wants Alicia to refuse the assignment—to refuse to seduce the Nazi. He will not give his love to her unless she does.

DYNAMIC RELATIONSHIPS

For Alicia, Devlin is still the *knight in shining armor*: the man she has stopped drinking for; the man she will change her life for; the man who has rescued her from a meaningless existence. For Devlin, Alicia has returned to an earlier incarnation: *temptress*—or as Alicia herself suggests in the scene, *Mata Hari*—a woman who can hurt him if he lets her get too close, if he lets his guard down. He suggests as much to Alicia earlier in the film in response to her asking, "Are you afraid of falling in love with me?" Devlin's response: "It wouldn't be hard."

(Part of the following takes place in the kitchen and living room, and technically they would be labeled as separate scenes, but I am including them as part of the patio location because they are spatially and temporally continuous. The director must regard them as a dramatic whole to integrate them seamlessly into an overall dramatic arc that contains a beginning, middle, and end—one of the defining characteristics of a dramatic scene.)

NOTORIOUS PATIO SCENE ANNOTATED

The following is the annotated Patio scene with the dramatic blocks, acting beats, narrative beats, and fulcrum identified. Acting beats appear in lower case type on the right. Narrative beats appear in UPPER CASE type.

BEGINNING OF FIRST DRAMATIC BLOCK

LIVING ROOM/ALICIA'S APARTMENT - NIGHT

Devlin enters and walks through the living room to the patio.

ALICIA (o.s.)

Dev, is that you?   to greet

DEVLIN

Ahuh.   to reply

                              ALICIA (o.s.)
I'm glad you're late. This   to share
chicken took longer
than I expected.
What did they say?   to inquire

KITCHEN/ALICIA'S APARTMENT - NIGHT

Alicia cutting the chicken.

                              ALICIA
Hope it isn't done too . . .   to excuse
too much. They caught   (lack of response)
fire once.

LIVING ROOM/ALICIA'S APARTMENT - NIGHT

                              ALICIA (o.s.)
I think it's better if I cut   to relate
it up out here. Unless you
want a half of one yourself.
We're going to have knives and
forks after all. I've decided
we're going to eat in style.

Alicia enters with two dinner plates and moves to the patio where she
sets one of the plates on the dining table.

                              ALICIA
Marriage must be wonderful with   to speculate
this sort of thing going on
every day.
(She kisses Devlin,   to connect
then sets the second plate
on the table.)
I wonder if it's too cold out   to question
here. Maybe we should eat inside.
(She turns to Devlin and puts   to greet
her arms around him.)
Huh?   to persist

SECOND DRAMATIC BLOCK

PATIO/ALICIA'S APARTMENT - NIGHT

Alicia kisses Devlin. He is unresponsive.

                              ALICIA
Hasn't something like this   to search
happened before? What's the   (for a reason)
matter? Don't look so tense.

Troubles? Well, handsome, I
think you better tell Momma
what's going on. All this secrecy
is going to ruin my little dinner.
Come on, Mr. D, what is darkening
your brow?

                              DEVLIN
After dinner.   to delay

                              ALICIA
No, now. Look, I'll make it   to draw (him) out
easy for you. The time has
come when you must tell me
that you have a wife and two
adorable children, and this
madness between us can't go
on any longer.

                              DEVLIN
I bet you heard that line   TO ACCUSE
often enough.

                              ALICIA
Right below the belt every time   TO PROTEST
. . . Oh, that isn't fair, dear.

                              DEVLIN
Skip it. We have other things   TO ANNOUNCE
to talk about. We've got a job.

                              ALICIA
Oh, so there is a job.   TO CONFIRM

                              DEVLIN
You ahh . . . you remember a man   TO QUESTION
named Sebastian?

                              ALICIA
Alex Sebastian?   TO CLARIFY

                    DEVLIN (O.S.)
Yes.   to affirm

                              ALICIA
One of my father's friends, yes.   to explain

                              DEVLIN
He had quite a crush on you.   TO IMPLY

                              ALICIA
I wasn't very responsive.   TO DENY

                              DEVLIN
Well he's here. The head of a   TO INFORM
large German business concern.

ALICIA		to state (a fact)
His family always had money.		
DEVLIN		to explain
He's part of the combine that built up the German war machine and hopes to keep on going.		
ALICIA		to inquire
Something big?		
DEVLIN		TO DISCLOSE (nature of job)
It has all the earmarks of being something big. We have to contact him.		
(Alicia takes that in and turns away from Devlin.)		TO DETACH

BEGINNING OF THIRD DRAMATIC BLOCK

Alicia moves to a chair and sits.	TO DISTANCE
ALICIA	to submit
Go on, let's have all of it.	
DEVLIN	to order
We're meeting him tomorrow. The rest is up to you. You've got to work on him and land him.	
ALICIA	TO DENIGRATE (HERSELF)
Mata Hari. She makes love for the papers.	
DEVLIN	TO TAKE (COMMAND)
There are no papers. You land him.	
Find out what's going on inside his house, what the group around him is up to, and report to us.	to instruct
ALICIA	TO ACCUSE
I suppose you knew about this pretty little job of mine all the time.	
DEVLIN	TO DENY
No. I've only just found out about it.	
ALICIA	TO INQUIRE
Did you say anything? I mean that maybe I wasn't the girl for such shenanigans.	

DEVLIN	
I figured that was up to you. If you'd care to back out.	TO CHALLENGE

ALICIA	
I suppose you told them, Alicia Huberman would have this Sebastian eating our of her hand in a couple of weeks. She's good at that! Always was!	TO ATTACK

DEVLIN	
I didn't say anything.	TO STATE A FACT

ALICIA	
Not a word for that . . . that little love sick lady you left an hour ago.	TO DECLARE (HER LOVE)

DEVLIN	
I told you that's the assignment.	TO REJECT

FULCRUM

At this point, the scene could go either way. Alicia could accept Devlin's last words and let it kill her want. But because her want is strong and all-embracing, she cannot give it up without a fight. Alicia still has hope that she can win Devlin's heart; to make everything like it was a few hours ago. (This fulcrum is also the beginning of the fourth dramatic block.)

BEGINNING OF FOURTH DRAMATIC BLOCK

ALICIA	
Well now, don't get sore, dear. I'm only fishing for a little bird call from my dream man.	to appease
One little remark such as, how dare you gentlemen suggest That Alicia Huberman, the new Miss Huberman be submitted to so ugly a fate.	to protest
(Alicia stands.)	TO CHALLENGE

Alicia's challenge is the apex of this fulcrum, and she will now go on the offensive to pursue her want.

DEVLIN	
That's not funny.	to rebuke
(Alicia approaches Devlin.	TO PURSUE (her love)
Devlin puts a cigarette	TO FEND OFF
into his mouth and lights it.	
Alicia stops her advance.)	TO BACK OFF

ALICIA	
You want me to take the job?	to question

                              DEVLIN
You're asking for yourself.   to reprimand

                              ALICIA
I am asking you.   to insist

                              DEVLIN
It's up to you.   to refuse (help)

                              ALICIA
Not a peep.   to criticize
Oh, darling, what you didn't   TO IMPLORE
tell them, tell me - that you
believe I'm nice, and that I
love you, and I'll never
change back.

                              DEVLIN
I'm waiting for your answer.   TO CUT OFF

BEGINNING OF FIFTH DRAMATIC BLOCK

Alicia turns from Devlin.   TO CONCEDE (defeat)

                              ALICIA
What a little pal you are.   to denounce
(Alicia begins exit from patio.)   TO RETREAT
Never believing me, hmm?   to rebuke
Not a word of faith, just
down the drain with Alicia.
That's where she belongs.
Oh, Dev . . . Dev . . .   to relinquish
                                                     (her hope)
(Alicia pours alcohol into   to seek solace
glass and drinks.)
When do I go to work for   to accept (job)
Uncle Sam?

                              DEVLIN
Tomorrow morning.   to inform
Alicia looks at the food on the dinner table.

                              ALICIA
Oh, we shouldn't have   TO COMPREHEND
had this out here.   (the enormity)
It's all cold now.   TO CONCLUDE
(Devlin looks around.)   to search
What are you looking for?   to question

                              DEVLIN
I had a bottle of   to answer
champagne. I must have
left it somewhere.
Fade out:

To proceed in our investigation it will be necessary for you to acquire a videotape or digital disc of
Notorious. Watch the film from its beginning through the end of the Patio scene.

Watch the Patio scene again. The acting beats, now available to us in the performances of the two actors, should become clear to you. Hopefully you will begin to see how the dramatic blocks are embedded in Hitchcock's "geographical paragraphs"—his use of different "stages" within the one location. And the concept of narrative beats—the director's tools for the articulation of a scene—might begin to make sense now that you see them rooted in Hitchcock's staging, camera, and editing. Hopefully the dramatic function of the fulcrum will be understood—reaching its full dramatic strength in this scene when Alicia stands and faces Devlin.

In the next two chapters you will be introduced to the narrative/dramatic functions of both staging and camera before we discuss in detail how they were used by Hitchcock to enhance the text for the Patio scene.

C H A P T E R   4

STAGING

Unlike the theater, we are not staging (also called blocking) for a proscenium, which has the audience outside of it. Nor are we staging for a theater in which the audience surrounds the action in two-, three-, or four-sided arenas or might actually sit on the stage. In each of these cases each member of the audience has but one point of view from a static position. In film, we are staging for an audience that can be anywhere because the camera can be anywhere. Therefore, as you become more visually proficient, you will move toward an integration of staging and camera. Often you will visualize a shot, then stage the action to get it. However, for teaching the craft of staging, I have found it best to keep it as a separate process—just as long as we bear in mind that in film we are *staging for the camera!*

Staging has eight main functions:

1. The most obvious job of staging is that it *accomplishes the functional and obligatory physical deeds of a scene*. In other words, it *renders the action*, as in, for example, "Jack and Jill go up the hill. . . . Jack falls down. . . . Jill comes tumbling after," or (in Shakespeare's *King Lear*) "Lear dies."

2. *Staging makes physical what is internal.* When staging is used in this way, it helps make the psychology of a character more available to the audience. In an overt action scene, or even in an entire action film, there might be very little need for this kind of staging, but the more psychological the scene—the more *inside the head of the characters*—the more a director will call upon this function of staging.

3. *Staging can indicate the nature of a relationship*, and it can do it quickly and economically, as in, for example, a man sits behind a large desk while another man stands in front of it. Coming upon this staging without knowing anything about the two characters, we would very likely assume that the man standing in front of the desk is a subordinate. Now, if we came upon a different staging—a man sits behind a large desk, another man sits *on* it—we would not so readily assume that the man sitting on the desk is a subordinate. Hitchcock uses this latter staging in *Vertigo* (1958) to help make us aware that the man behind the big desk in this big office with the big windows is a close friend of Jimmy Stewart's character. A great deal of backstory is accomplished very quickly by beginning the scene in this manner.

4. *Staging can orient the viewer.* It can familiarize us with a location or point out a significant prop. One way of doing this is to stage the action so that our character's movement in the space reveals the relevant geography of the location. In this way the viewer can be apprised of a window that our character will later jump from or a door that someone will enter, or they can discover a prop that will have a significant bearing on the plot. An example of this is the hypothetical rifle hanging above the mantel, which Chekhov referred to in discussing dramatic

craft. In Lina Wertmuller's *Swept Away . . . by an unusual destiny in the blue sea of August* (1974, Italy), the director introduces the varied geography of a deserted island while keeping the narrative thrust of the story continuing unabated so that the audience receives the expository information (location geography is most often expository information) without realizing it. "Oh, the island has high cliffs, and sand dunes, and look, there's a tidal pool!" Later, when these various locations are used, this expository information will not get in the way of the drama because the audience has already digested it.

5. *Staging can resolve spatial separation.* "Separation" occurs when a character is shot within a frame that does not contain the other characters (or objects) in a scene. To "resolve" this separateness—to define, clarify, or reaffirm for the audience where a character is spatially in relation to another character or object—a shot that places the disparate characters/objects in the same frame is needed. Staging can be used to create this shot as in character A walking into character B's frame.

   Resolution of spatial separation can also be accomplished with the camera, without a change in staging, by cutting to a two-shot or group-shot that includes character A or B, or a group, or an object. It can also be accomplished with a camera movement; the camera pans from character A to character B. Although each character remains in separation, the "linkage" established by the pan will satisfy the audience's need for spatial clarification.

6. *Staging can direct the viewer's attention.* It can make the viewer aware of essential information. Hitchcock uses staging for this purpose in the *Vertigo* scene mentioned in function 3. To force us to concentrate on the intricate and essential plot points—facts the audience *must* be aware of to understand and enjoy the story—Hitchcock does exactly the opposite of what you might expect. Instead of the "expositor" planting himself in close proximity to Stewart, Hitchcock has him begin to roam. In fact, he roams into another room of the very large office suite so that Stewart *and the audience* are forced to concentrate their attention on what is being said.

7. *Staging can punctuate actions.* It can be used as an exclamation mark, but it can also be used to formulate a question or to supply a period in the middle of a shot. In *Gandhi* (1982, Britain/India), director Richard Attenborough uses staging to emphasize the action contained in Gandhi's (Ben Kingsley) dialogue during a political meeting among different factions of India's elite. The meeting takes place in a large living room, and everyone is sitting comfortably in a horseshoe-shaped pattern. A servant enters with a tea service, and Gandhi stands, moves to the servant, and takes the tea service from him. Gandhi proceeds to talk and serve the teacups. The punctuation through staging goes like this:

   Political point/teacup served/period
   Political point/teacup served/period
   Political point/teacup served/exclamation mark

8. And of course, *staging is used in "picturization"*—in helping to create a frame for the camera to render. An example of this is the tableaus of Yasujiro Ozu in *Tokyo Story* (1953, Japan), which is analyzed in Chapter 18.

   When staging is used to accomplish the functions discussed in points 4 and 5, that staging must be in accordance with points 1 or 2. If they are not, the character's movement will be arbitrary because it is unmotivated. In film, no one sits, no one stands, no one moves a step, unless they are fulfilling the dictates of the story's overt action or are making physical that which is internal.

   What about using staging to liven up a scene—to get the characters off their duffs? True, it often does liven up a scene to have our characters get up and move around, but only if we can justify the motivation for that movement. *The greatest anathema to dramatic tension is arbitrary behavior!*

PATTERNS OF DRAMATIC MOVEMENT

Dramatic movement occurs when there is a change in the dynamic relationship between characters, as when an *ally* becomes a *foe*, or a *knight in shining armor* becomes a *ball and chain*. When there is no change in the dynamic relationship—when there is stasis between characters—it is not dramatic. That is not to say that these relationships of stasis do not exist in film; they are common, but they do not contain the *essential* dramatic movement of the scene or film.

It is helpful in staging to be aware of this change in dynamic relationships and to realize that there are only two overall *dramatic movements* possible between characters, and both can be expressed spatially.

CHARACTERS A AND B ARE APART AND THEY COME TOGETHER

Many films exhibit this pattern, but Wertmuller renders it exquisitely in *Swept Away*. In the beginning the male protagonist, Gennarino (Giancarlo Giannini), and female antagonist, Raffaella (Mariangela Melato), are worlds apart. There is no way these two will ever come together (difficulty). Wertmuller physicalizes this relationship—makes it palpable to the audience—by the spatial separateness between the two as they explore the island. This separateness is highlighted by a pan from the protagonist on top of the highest cliff on the island to the antagonist far below on the beach, while they are screaming obscenities at each other. It seems as if no two people on earth could be further alienated from each other. The relationship, so powerfully embodied in the staging at this point, is in direct contrast to where the two will end up at the end of the second act, when they "marry." Here the bodies of the two are so intertwined with each other that nothing in the world could come between them at this moment, either dramatically *or* physically.

CHARACTERS A AND B ARE TOGETHER AND THEY COME APART

In the Patio scene in *Notorious*, we have a clear example of this dramatic pattern. The scene starts with the two lovebirds together, she throwing her arms around him. She talks of love, but something in him has changed since she last saw him. He is cold and insulting. He offers her a job assignment, one in which she is expected to seduce a former admirer of hers who is a Nazi spy. Psychologically, this drives her away from him. Hitchcock makes this palpable to the audience by having her walk away from the embrace.

A spatial rendering often used (it is used in the continuation of this same scene) has characters A and B apart, then they come closer to each other, then apart again—giving us an accordion pattern. This pattern can also exist as the superstructure of an entire film plot, which is a staple among romantic comedies: boy meets girl, boy loses girl, boy gets girl. In *In the Heat of the Night* (Norman Jewison, 1967), a black policeman from Philadelphia, Virgil Tibbs (Sidney Poitier), and a redneck police chief, Bill Gillespie (Rod Steiger), are a huge distance apart when they first encounter each other. But circumstances force them to work with each other to solve a murder, and in that collegial atmosphere they begin to close the distance that separates them. That resulting closeness sets up an "explosion" that drives them apart. Then, once again, the sharing of experience brings them ever closer, the culmination occurring in the last scene of the film when the redneck police chief carries the black man's suitcase to a waiting train.

There is one final point in this area. Dramatic movement and the spatial movement that makes it physical are always relative to the starting point. Sometimes very small movements can be exceedingly powerful.

CHANGING THE STAGE WITHIN A SCENE

At times, the director will need to create a different atmosphere for the next dramatic block to occur. It could be as simple as moving the actors from a lighted area to one that is darker, or from a table to a couch. The main concept here is that a particular part of the location is saved for this particular part of the scene. We might be aware, tangentially, that this other stage exists, but its evocative power is not used up. A good example of changing the stage can be found in Hitchcock's *Vertigo*, when Madeleine Elster/Judy Barton (later) (Kim Novak), tells John "Scottie" Ferguson (Jimmy Stewart) of her fear of losing her mind. This part of the scene takes place beside a gnarled, twisted, "tortured" tree that reflects the tortured emotions being expressed by Novak, adding a powerful resonance to the moment. Then the stage changes abruptly when Novak runs from the tree to the rocks abutting the ocean below. Will she try to kill herself again? Stewart pursues her, grabs her, and takes her in his arms. As they look into each other's eyes, the crashing of the waves against the rocks creates the atmosphere for another kind of emotion to emerge: love—passionate, urgent love. They kiss for the first time.

When Mitch takes Blanche on a date in *A Streetcar Named Desire*, the stage changes from a public space (dance hall) to an intimate space (small table with two chairs) until it finally ends up at the end of a pier, surrounded by mist, creating an atmosphere that allows the director to take us inside Blanche's head.

STAGING AS PART OF A FILM'S DESIGN

In the theater the director is more likely to work out her staging with the actors present on the set, or a facsimile thereof, and rely heavily on the actors' input. This makes good sense on the stage, but I do not recommend it for the film director. This is in no way meant to imply that the film director does not listen to suggestions from the actors, the director of photography, the dolly grip, or his or her mother for that matter. On the contrary, the director should encourage participation from everyone on all aspects of the production. It does mean, however, that she is the only one fully capable of integrating staging and camera. Only she knows, or should know, what job the staging must accomplish at any particular moment, how that moment fits into the overall design of a particular scene, and how that scene fits into the overall design of the entire film.

A caution about staging and movement on the screen in general: Even though the action might seem to proceed with sufficient alacrity on the set, you should understand that when that same action appears on a screen and receives the concentrated attention of the viewer, it will often seem to be slower.

WORKING WITH A LOCATION FLOOR PLAN

A floor plan is simply an overhead or bird's-eye view of the location. Although some locations do not lend themselves to working with a floor plan, most do. The floor plan helps you to "choreograph" a scene before rendering it with the camera. It allows you to work out staging for the actors that takes into account not only their characters' actions but all of the story or plot requisites of the scene, and it allows you to do this with pencil and paper on the kitchen table.

FLOOR PLAN FOR *NOTORIOUS* PATIO SCENE

This is an elegantly designed scene in which Hitchcock uses staging and camera to render the full dramatic power of the text. It is Alicia's scene, in that she contains the answer to the dramatic question the scene raises: Will this romance blossom or will it be nipped in the bud? We have to be "in Alicia's head" to appreciate the moment-to-moment unfolding of the scene, and Hitchcock uses the staging to make physical what is internal in her, making her psychology fully available to us moment to moment. Of course, we understand much of Alicia's interior life through the wonderful acting of Ingrid Bergman, but Hitchcock's "framing" of the narrative beats, manifested in the staging and camera, makes that psychology more palpable to the audience. He does the same with Cary Grant's impeccable performance, but to a lesser degree, because we understand better where he is coming from and where he is at each moment.

When Alicia reaches the patio, she puts her arms around Devlin, starting the scene "together." The scene ends with them "apart," both at the farthest edges of the French door frame. However, the scene is dramatically more complicated than that, and when Alicia attempts to regain her *want*, Hitchcock has her stand (fulcrum) and then move closer to Devlin. This "pursuing her love" is made much more palpable to the audience in this way than if she had continued to sit, or even if she had stood but did not make the move. This "pursuing" and the subsequent "retreat" makes for an overall accordion pattern that articulates the dramatic pattern of the scene: together/apart/together/apart.

FIRST DRAMATIC BLOCK

Staging in this block (Figure 4-1) "merely" renders the action. It needn't do more. Devlin enters, and through his laconic replies and body language we understand that his expectation for the evening has undergone a huge transformation. On the other hand, Alicia's expectation for the dinner has not changed at all and is readily available to us. Hence, all Hitchcock has to do in this first dramatic block is bring the two expectations *together*.

SECOND DRAMATIC BLOCK

This block (Figure 4-2) starts with *together* and continues to the end with this spatial relationship, even though the psychology between the two changes drastically after Devlin "accuses." (Hitchcock chooses to acknowledge the remainder of the narrative beats in this block with the camera, which we will explore in Chapter 6.)

THIRD DRAMATIC BLOCK

In this third dramatic block (Figure 4-3), because of Devlin's attitude and the job he proposes that Alicia undertake, she "detaches" then "distances" herself from Devlin and sits (*apart*). Devlin moves behind Alicia to "take command." They are no longer looking at each other, increasing the feeling of *apart*. This is a good example of staging for picturization—staging to create a frame for the camera that articulates the dramatic circumstance of the moment or create an atmosphere for that moment to happen in.

FOURTH DRAMATIC BLOCK

There is a huge dramatic arc in this block (Figure 4-4), and Hitchcock articulates many of the narrative beats through staging. Devlin is still hanging tough, and it looks as if Alicia will not obtain her want: intimacy with Devlin. But she does not give up! This is the key to all drama. Alicia's want is great. She will not be defeated without a fight. She stands and CHALLENGES Devlin, "how dare you gentlemen suggest." This is the apex of the fulcrum of this scene. Here, Alicia goes on the offensive to win Devlin over. She PURSUES him, and her internal action is made physical by her movement toward him, only to have him FEND [HER] OFF. Alicia BACKS OFF, articulated in the staging by her turning sideways from him. But Alicia has not yet given up. She attempts one last desperate action, TO IMPLORE, and this action too is made physical by Alicia once again facing toward Devlin with her body. When he CUTS [HER] OFF, she realizes she has lost and turns from Devlin, CONCEDING DEFEAT. (You could get a clear idea of the overall arc of this scene by watching the actors move through it without dialogue. We could even go a step further and put masks over the actor's faces. We would still have a pretty good idea through the staging that for Alicia things started off good, got worse, she tried to make them better, then failed.)

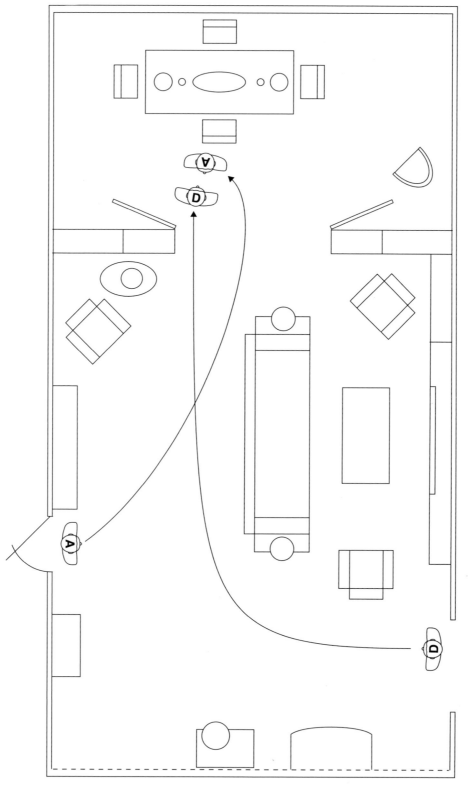

FIGURE 4-1

Staging for first dramatic block of *Notorious* scene.

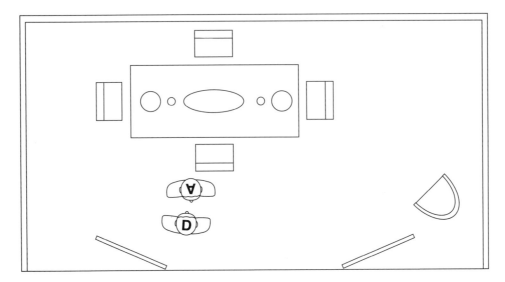

FIGURE 4-2

Staging for second dramatic block of *Notorious* scene.

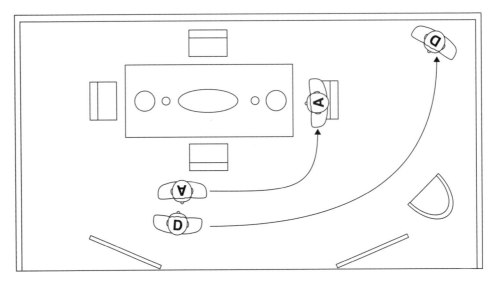

FIGURE 4-3

Staging for third dramatic block of *Notorious* scene.

FIFTH DRAMATIC BLOCK

In the fifth dramatic block (Figure 4-5), Alicia *RETREATS* in defeat, exiting from the patio, and seeks solace in alcohol. Devlin leaves the patio to *RECONNECT* with Alicia as her new boss. The final staging shouts out *"apart,"* as both Alicia and Devlin end up at the farthest edges of the frame—a far cry from where they began.

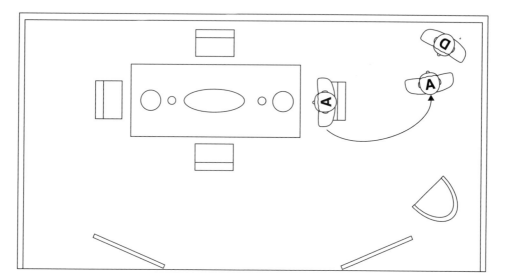

FIGURE 4-4

Staging for fourth dramatic block of *Notorious* scene.

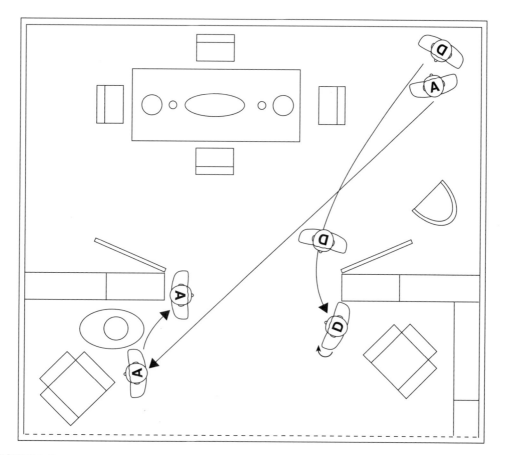

FIGURE 4-5

Staging for fifth dramatic block of *Notorious* scene.

C H A P T E R 5

CAMERA

THE CAMERA AS NARRATOR

Film is a language used to tell stories, and the narrator of those stories is the camera. Yes, the director is the ultimate storyteller, but the "voice" she will use is that of the camera.

There are six variables a director can control with the camera. In all six, composition within the frame is a primary factor.

1. Angle
2. Image size (which affects scale and field of view)
3. Motion (up, down, track, pan)
4. Depth of field (normal, compressed or deep, affected by focal length of lens and *f* stop)
5. Focus (selective within the frame)
6. Speed (normal, fast, or slow motion)

The director will manipulate and integrate these possibilities to create the sentences used to tell the cinematic story and will then organize the sentences into "paragraphs"—complete narrative or dramatic blocks that will rely heavily on compression, elaboration, and a third extremely powerful narrative/dramatic element, the *reveal*.

REVEAL

The reveal is a narrative/dramatic element so pervasive that its power can be underestimated by the beginning filmmaker because, in a sense, each shot reveals something. However, what we are interested in here is the *dramatic* reveal—a reveal that has impact, that carries dramatic weight. Examples of this are the horse's head in *The Godfather* (Francis Ford Coppola, 1972); the spaceship behind Richard Dreyfus's pickup truck in *Close Encounters of the Third Kind* (Steven Spielberg, 1977), or the smaller, but effective, reveal of the final form of the clay mountain that the Dreyfus character finally succeeds in rendering in the same film; the powerful, heartbreaking reveal of the young girl in the grasp of the monster in *The Host* (Junho Bung, 2006, Korea); or the wonderful reveal of the protagonist's face for the first time in 8½ (Federico Fellini, 1963, Italy).

ENTRANCES

Entrances of characters into a film share some of the same duties as reveals, but they have a specific job to do: that of introducing characters to the audience, presenting a "sketch" of who they are—personality, social/economic group, and so on—or a hint of the characters' psychology, such as whether they are happy or sad, or their dramatic function—friend or foe. The entrance also announces to the audience whether or not the character is someone who will play a significant role in your story. *You do not want your principal characters to "slide" into the film. Announce them!*

OBJECTIVE CAMERA

Most of the time the narrator will be speaking with an "objective" voice—as in "Bob is walking down the street. He sees Linda. Linda turns away from him." In prose, it would be called the third person.

The personality of the narrator and the style in which the story is told are introduced at the beginning of a film. Is the camera curious, playful, omniscient, lyrical? Will it use extreme close-ups or stay distant from the characters? Is the camera kinetic or static? Will it make use of a visual motif, such as the closed-down frame (through a doorway) of John Ford's *The Searchers* (1956) or the spotlight in *8½*? (Any repeated visual or audio element can be a motif.) Will the narrator take an active role in *interpreting* the meaning or consequences of an action for us or perhaps take pains to point out a plot point that is integral to understanding the story? Or will it remain stand-offish and let the audience fend for themselves?

It can be helpful for the beginning director to view the narrator as one who must take the audience in a headlock, which is not relinquished until the film is over. With this headlock, the narrator directs the audience's attention wherever the needs of the story dictate. I believe you will discover for yourselves that the audience prefers to be in the hands of a strong, authoritative narrator, rather than a weak, tentative one.

SUBJECTIVE CAMERA

Sometimes a subjective voice is desired. It is not altogether analogous to the first person voice in prose, but it shares that narrative function by allowing the audience to participate more fully in the *interior life or perceptions* of a character. The subjective camera allows us to see what our subject is actually experiencing. An example of this occurs in *Notorious*, when Alicia wakes from a drunken sleep to see Devlin at an angle in the doorway, watching him turn completely upside down as he comes closer to her bed.

The subjective camera should not be confused with simply using a *point of view* (POV) shot, which is an *approximation* of what a character is seeing. The POV contains the dynamics of the spatial relationship, thereby conveying an awareness in the audience that this is indeed what the character is seeing, but there is no shift in voices. It is altogether analogous to a novelist writing in the voice of the third-person narrator, "She sees him," rather than the first-person voice of the character, "I see him." However, the POV can have a high potential for "sharing" the perception of a character, and it can be an important tool in building a subjective voice. (In Part II, Chapter 8, I will introduce the concept of the *strong POV*.)

(The subjective camera should also be distinguished from the *flashback*, a narrative dimension that can be rendered, and often is, with an objective camera, as are other modes of reality, such as dreams, memories, and hallucinations.)

Overusing the subjective narrator can minimize its dramatic power. One way of overusing it is to assign it to more than one person. That one person is usually the protagonist.

The distinctions between subjective and objective camera will become clearer as we proceed through this book, especially in our thorough analysis of *Notorious* (Part V, Chapter 15), in which Hitchcock uses an active (interpretive) camera as well as a subjective voice.

WHERE DO I PUT IT?

There are five questions to answer that will help us determine where to put the camera, and all of them can be subsumed under one general question: What jobs must be done?

1. *Whose scene is it?* This is not always the same as whose film it is. The late Frank Daniel, a great dramaturge and my former colleague at Columbia, told me the following story. The director Frank Capra (*It's a Wonderful Life*, 1946) was holding a question-and-answer session with students and faculty at the American Film Institute, where Mr. Daniel was then dean. Mr. Daniel asked Mr. Capra, "Could you tell us something about the concept of 'whose scene is it?'" Capra, obviously never having been asked this question, shot back, "You've stolen my secret!"

   The most useful factor in answering the question of whose scene it is—the one that will help you most as directors—is, *Whose head does the audience have to be in* to fully appreciate the scene?

   Here is an illustration of how awareness of this question can help you with your camera design. It is from a simple exercise that was done for my first semester directing class at Columbia. In the scene prior to the one we are going to examine, the protagonist, a young man, is preparing to leave his apartment to go out on the town to try to pick up a lover. It is his first time, and he is nervous. In the second scene, our protagonist returns home with another young man—the antagonist. The director chose to capture the beginning actions of this second scene by placing the camera behind the stereo (Figure 5-1). From this long shot we see the two men enter. The protagonist stops near the door as the antagonist continues toward the camera and stands in front of the stereo, inspecting it. After he is finished, the antagonist turns toward the protagonist.

   This is an instance in which the scene belongs to the protagonist, yet the director chose not to be in his head, but instead, to merely render the action. What is actually required in this scene is an interpretation by the narrator/camera as to what is going on emotionally inside the protagonist. In a novel, we could have been helped either by a first-person interior monologue or a third-person rendering of a character's interior state, but because of where the camera is placed, the protagonist's anxiety and yearning are obfuscated by the dynamics of the shot. Yes, we know from the

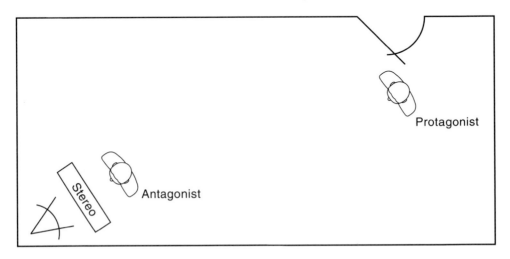

FIGURE 5-1

Camera outside the protagonist's head.

previous scene that the protagonist is anxious, tentative, and wants so much for everything to go right—and yes, all of this is in the actor's behavior—but it is *tangential* information. As narrators, we are obliged to make that anxiety, that yearning, palpable to the audience.

How can we do that with the camera? One way is to get the camera inside the dynamics of what is actually going on. We can do that if we place the camera so that the angle on the antagonist at the stereo is from the protagonist's point of view (Figure 5-2). The audience can then more closely align itself with what he is feeling when he looks at the antagonist's back, which is turned to him. Because a POV should be preceded or followed by a close-to-medium shot of the character whose POV it is, I would choose to start with a fairly close shot when the two enter the apartment, but then the audience won't get a good look at the antagonist. Exactly! I would make sure they did not! It would be effective to see just a hint of someone else, such as a shoulder moving through the frame. The protagonist would behave the same as in the first shot—his yearning and anxiety would be the same—but because we have now made them the essence of this moment, they have become more significant and therefore more powerful.

The preceding design not only allows the audience to be where they should be in this scene—in the head of the protagonist—but it prolongs the reveal of the antagonist. It makes us curious about him. It raises a question. We already know the antagonist has the upper hand when he walks "deep" into the apartment, and when he does turn, he is revealed through the dynamics of the protagonist. Suppose he turns with a drop-dead smile? Or a scowl? Whatever the case, the audience will feel its impact on the protagonist because it has impinged on them!

2. *What is the essence of the moment that I have to convey to the audience?* Vincent van Gogh wrote to his brother, Theo, that what he had come to realize in his work was that if he concentrated on the essence, the ordinary would take care of itself. Not only will the ordinary also take care of itself in film, but we must be exceedingly careful that it does not overwhelm or even bury our essence. It can do so very easily. That is why our headlock on the audience is so extremely useful. In the foregoing student exercise, the second camera design serves to capture the essence of the moment. The ordinary in the scene is that the protagonist has returned with a man (even though this is the first time the protagonist has brought a man home). The essence is what is going on inside of him.

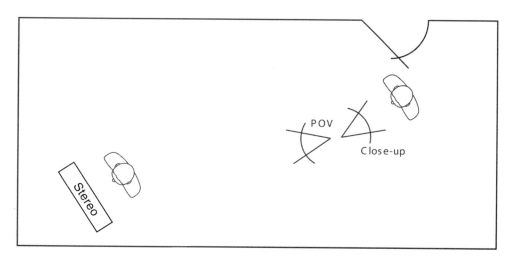

FIGURE 5-2

Camera inside the protagonist's head.

3. *What story points, location, character, or props must be introduced or kept alive?* What essential ingredients of the story must the audience be apprised of, not only to fully appreciate what is happening in the present but to be prepared for what will happen in the future? Is it important to show that there is an elephant in the room, or if it was introduced earlier, should that elephant be kept alive—shown again? Look at the many characters in a film such as *The Godfather* and how they are all kept alive in scenes that do not feature them so that they can be brought to the forefront when needed. Look at the introduction of the staircase in the protagonist's apartment in *All That Jazz* (Bob Fosse, 1979), which works such that when it is used dramatically later on we are prepared for it.

4. *What stylistic elements or motifs must be introduced?* At the beginning of a film, any "special" camera style—such as slow motion, *fragmentation* (visual dissecting of objects or persons), hand-held camera, jump cuts, and so on—should be introduced. An example of this is the slow-motion shot of Jake LaMotta (Robert De Niro) shadow boxing in a boxing ring, accompanied by classical music, that begins Martin Scorsese's *Raging Bull* (1980). Aside from the shot's powerful contrast with the music, portending the thematic elements of the story, the shot prepares the way for the narrator to use slow motion to convey the intensity of LaMotta's first glimpses of the girl of his dreams, then later on to convey the physical violence and exaltation of the boxing ring. In Jean-Luc Godard's *Breathless* (1959, French), the director introduces the jump cut as narrative punctuation in the first few minutes of the film. Had he waited much longer, the jump cut would have been perceived as a mistake, or at the very least, jarring, by the audience.

5. *Is it necessary to resolve the spatial separation between characters or otherwise orient the audience to location or time?* In the earlier example of the two men coming into the apartment, it will be necessary to resolve the spatial separation between the protagonist and the antagonist (if we choose the second design) at some point in the scene. It should be done not only to apprise the audience of their spatial relationship but also to acknowledge a narrative beat. In *Vertigo* Hitchcock holds off on resolving separation for more than three minutes in the scene where Madeline exits Scottie's bedroom in a bathrobe and sits in front of the fireplace. By holding off the resolution, by keeping them in separate frames, the psychological separation between these two strangers is highlighted. For this to work for such a long time—so that the audience doesn't begin to feel nervous or spatially confused—Hitchcock, just previous to Madeline's entrance into the living room, takes great pains to set up the geography of the room so that when the extended separation occurs, the audience is comfortable with the spatial dynamics.

VISUAL DESIGN

A film's design, or even the design of a single scene, is a melding of all the various narrative and dramatic elements. Although we will concentrate on staging and camera—because this is a book about the fundamentals of directing, and because staging and camera are the core elements of design—we should not forget the importance of production design, lighting, costume, setting, props, sound design, and music.

In searching for a film's design, always remember that we are working with pictures. *Look for ways to tell your story visually!* A good question to keep in mind is: What does the picture tell you? Look at the shot of Guido in *8½* as he floats over the traffic jam in the beginning sequence of the film. It is an image of freedom that, once seen, never goes away. Or consider the freeze frame of the young protagonist that ends François Truffaut's *400 Blows* (1959, France). It stays with you for years, perhaps your whole life.

A conscious design can be seen in *Raging Bull*. The boxing sequences are staccato in rhythm, while LaMotta's private life, especially the early courtship of his future wife, has longer shots (in time) with "lyrical" camera movement. There is a short but significant scene fully rendered by one beautifully choreographed shot, in which LaMotta brings his future wife to his bedroom for the first time. It is a textbook example of the wedding of staging to camera movement, using both to acknowledge the narrative beat and, simultaneously, to create an atmosphere in which romance can flourish. The lingering camera (staying with a photo on top of the dresser well after the two soon-to-be-lovers have exited the frame for the bed) is also a masterful example of the *power of dramatic economy*.

STYLE

Design and style are overlapping categories, and it is possible to have an effective design without a distinctive personal style. Style is primarily dependent on the needs of the story being told (tone is a large component) wedded to the director's vision of the world or his or her personal relationship to it. This second ingredient of style is rare, but examples can be noted in the differing visions of the world expressed in the most personal films of Fellini or Ingmar Bergman. Fellini embraces the world, while Bergman seems alienated from it, and each director's worldview is imbued in all of the major stylistic elements, including camera, lighting, staging, and music (or lack thereof).

Style can also be a product of an artistic or political agenda such as Dogme 95, which mandated the hand-held camera style and use of only available light for the Danish film *The Celebration* (1998), directed by Thomas Vinterberg.

Most films do not have a distinctive style, and directors known for a certain style in their early work often change as they evolve. Some of the change is due to differences among the types of stories tackled. For example, Fellini's neorealistic film *La Strada* (1954, Italian) is very different in style from his later work. Misoguchi, known for his long takes, uses significantly more *multi-angularity* (cutting from one shot to another) in *Streets of Shame* (1956, Japanese). Eric Rohmer's *Rendezvous in Paris* (1996, French) uses an extremely fluid camera, whereas up until this film his camera had always been "conservatively" fixed on a tripod. In *Jules and Jim* (1961, French), François Truffaut uses a very kinetic camera for the first part of the film—when all three characters are young and free and unfettered. Then when they become "adults," the camera becomes rock solid, sober, even stodgy in comparison.

Does every instance of stylization (and by that I mean anything that differs from the norm, whatever norm has been introduced at the beginning of the film) have to be introduced early? No. There are some moments in film that are so appropriate to a certain style that no preparation is needed. A good example of two stylistic devices used without prior introduction can be found in *8½*, in the scene where the prostitute dances at the beach for the young Guido and his school chums. Their enjoyment is interrupted by the arrival of the schoolmaster and another priest. Young Guido flees from the schoolmaster's clutches by running toward the camera and exiting the frame. On the cut to the reverse angle, young Guido is already in the middle of the next frame, running away from the camera. This results in a "jump" in real time—an ellipsis. Also, the camera speed goes from normal to fast motion—entirely appropriately—because of the farcical nature of what is happening. The audience finds nothing jarring in this unexpected rendering. It accepts the dramatic punctuation because it is integral to the dramatic moment. (In comedies it is easier to use a new style without preparation than it is in a drama, where the effect can be disruptive to the narrative flow, as if Hemingway all of a sudden threw in a sentence with Faulknerian syntax.)

COVERAGE

Coverage is a term used to express the number of camera setups covering the same moment (additional angles that may or may not be used when the project reaches the editing stage). I consider it to be a dangerous word, especially at this point in a director's development, because it can imply that there is a safety net—a generic solution to every scene—and interfere with the pursuit of a design that is unique and original. The old adage of "wide, medium, close" (referring to filming at each image size) is a prescription for mediocrity. *Just thinking "coverage" can prevent a true investigation into the syntax and grammar of each shot needed for each particular moment occurring in the context of an overall design.*

A good example of a design that is not generic can be found in the lunch scene in Coppola's *Apocalypse Now* (1979) between Captain Benjamin Willard (Martin Sheen) and the general. By not rendering the "normal" action of the scene, by going beneath the surface of it, a close-up of a fork digging into a plate of crawfish, close-ups of three hands in sequence, an isolated shot of a reel-to-reel tape recorder spinning out Colonel Walter E. Kurtz's (Marlon Brando) madness, Coppola creates an atmosphere filled with foreboding that came out of opening himself to the scene in ways that perhaps cannot be taught. Each director who is reading this book is encouraged to pursue this more intuitive, more visceral mode of relating to each and every scene.

Having said this, there are times when some of the "generic" aspects of coverage might be the most effective solution, such as a static scene in which two people are sitting at a table having an extended conversation, or a multicamera setup to ensure coverage might be necessary when there is a complicated action scene that would be difficult or impossible to restage, or where the interplay between actors could not be easily captured in separate takes. (Milos Forman used a two-camera setup to capture that sublime scene in *Amadeus* [1984], in which Mozart is dictating his *Requiem* to Salieri.) Sometimes we choose to be ordinary when we could have used pyrotechnics. The fact is, most often, for most stories, we will choose to be ordinary, and our story will be better off for it. But bear in mind that *most often* does not mean *always*.

CAMERA HEIGHT

"Is there any constant I can use?" you might ask. "Anything that will make my job easier?" Yes, there is—sort of. The camera is always at eye level . . . except when it's not. This is, of course, in relation to our actors. The question then becomes, When is it not? Extreme low or high angles have to be justified by the essence of the moment that must be conveyed while at the same time paying heed to the overall design and style of the film. The "eye level constant" can itself be a variable. Edward Dmytryk was a director with more than 50 films to his credit, among them *The Caine Mutiny* (1954). In his book *On Screen Directing*, he takes a very strong view on the subject:

> The dullest possible shot is one made at eye level. It adds absolutely nothing new to the picture. Unless one is Wilt Chamberlain [a seven-foot tall former basketball player] or a Munchkin, it is the everyday point of view of every person over the age of sixteen. It is preferable to position the lens either somewhat below or somewhat above eye level. The variation from normal should not be too obvious, but it should be offbeat enough to give the viewer a subconscious nudge. . . . Normally, the low setup is preferable for close group shots or close-ups. . . . The high setup is especially useful for long shots. . . . It must be emphasized that there are exceptions to these generalizations, even in respect to the eye-level shot, which can, of course, be useful. But when an exception is made, it should be for a very positive reason.

A point that Dmytryk makes for the slightly lower angle is that it allows the camera to get a better look into the actor's eyes, which is, in film, a powerful way of communicating. (For the same reason, Dmytryk dislikes the profile shot.) Orson Welles, in *Touch of Evil* (1958), used the low angle on his character and on "other men capable of evil," to create a sense of menace. He did not use this low angle on the women in the film.

In *Making Movies* Sidney Lumet talks about camera height as part of his design for *12 Angry Men* (1957):

> I shot the first third of the movie above eye level . . . the second third at eye level, and the last third from below eye level. In that way, toward the end, the ceiling began to appear. Not only were the walls closing in (due to progressively longer lenses) the ceiling was as well. The sense of increasing claustrophobia did a lot to raise the tension of the last part of the movie.

Whatever your constant, and I suggest you begin at eye level, you should have a good reason for moving the camera from it—up or down.

LENSES

The use of various lenses can modulate the narrator's voice and help tell the story more powerfully, so that even a modicum of familiarity with what the lenses can do will add a tremendous boost to your cinematic storytelling. No lens sees what the eye can see, but in whatever format you are shooting in (video, 16 mm, 35 mm), there will be a "normal" that will serve as your constant. On one side of this norm you have wide-angle lenses, which have a greater depth of field—the distance in which objects will stay in focus in relation to the background—and on the other you have "long" (or telephoto) lenses, which compress space. Objects moving toward or away from the camera will appear slower in telephoto and faster in wide-angle. I suggest three films to see for a better understanding of the aesthetic and dramatic power that the various focal lengths can bring to your work.

Citizen Kane (Orson Welles, 1941) uses extreme depth of field—a function of using a wide-angle lens and a lot of light (depth of field being a function of focal length and *f* stop). An actor could stand in the foreground of the shot, and another actor could be in the extreme background, and both would be in sharp focus.

The second film I recommend does just the opposite: Fellini's *La Dolce Vita* (1960, Italy) has no wide-angle shots. In his book *Fellini*, John Baxter writes:

> In this film which Fellini shot in CinemaScope, he told his director of photography to abandon his wide-angle lenses and use mainly the longer 75 mm, 100 mm, and occasionally the 150 mm lens. These gave a shallow depth of field, throwing foreground and background out of focus. *La Dolce Vita* has no panoramas. The characters seem to carry their own private Romes around with them . . . the overall impression is of lone figures in empty landscapes. "Fellini said that we should have the air of castaways on a raft," said Mastroianni, "going where they were driven by any puff of wind, totally abandoned."

The third film is Lumet's *12 Angry Men*, mentioned earlier in relation to camera height. Lumet explains the effect of what he calls his "lens plot":

> One of the most important dramatic elements for me was the sense of entrapment those men must have felt in that room. . . . As the picture unfolded, I wanted the room to seem smaller and smaller. That meant that I would slowly shift to longer lenses as the picture continued. Starting with the normal range (28 mm to 40 mm), we progressed to 50 mm, 75 mm, and 100 mm lenses. As the lenses became longer the walls seemed closer to the men because of the decrease in the depth of field. The sense of increasing claustrophobia did a lot to raise the tension of the last part of the movie. On the final shot, an exterior that showed the jurors leaving the courtroom, I used a wide-angle lens, wider than any lens that had been used in the entire picture. I also raised the camera to the highest above-eye-level position. The intention was to literally give us all air, to let us finally breathe, after two increasingly confined hours.

COMPOSITION

There was a director of photography at the Prague Film School many years ago who taught composition. A slide of a landscape or a person or a group of persons would be projected on a screen. A movable frame, controlled by the student, was used to crop the picture with the camera's aspect ratio (the ratio of width to length of the camera frame). As the student moved the frame over the picture, searching for the "right" composition, the professor would yell out when he was getting close, "Do you feel it? Do you feel it?"

For those of you who feel deficient in this area, I suggest you start watching films with composition in mind. Also, you can go to art museums to see how the masters handled representational framing, or go to photo exhibits. Additionally, of course, you should begin to shoot your own short exercises, looking through the camera while the scene is progressing. I don't recommend you serve as cameraperson for any of your significant films. There your attention must be focused on the actors. However, before the camera rolls, you as director should always set up the shot and check out any staging and camera movements that will occur.

When not shooting, you can walk around with a cardboard cutout of the aspect ratio you will be shooting in (television/16 mm/video format or 35 mm format), viewing the world through this restricted frame. I made one for Kazan and he used it during the filming of *The Visitors* (1972). Better still is a director's viewfinder in which you can change the focal length. They are expensive, but if you can manage to acquire one, it is an invaluable tool for visualization. It is comforting to have a director of photography who has a great eye, but the DP's main function is to light, a huge job in itself. *Choosing the frame comes under the director's job description, and it goes to the heart of what a film director is—so start "seeing."*

WHERE TO BEGIN?

Assuming you have done the detective work and the blocking, the next step is to add the camera to the floor plan shot by shot, incorporating the answers to the five questions that opened this chapter. During this process we must move constantly from the overall *arc* of the scene to the individual beat. Just imagine Michelangelo painting the Sistine Chapel. He is lying on his back, very close to the ceiling, painting the nose of an angel. All his attention is gathered at this tiny spot in a huge "canvas." No matter how beautiful the nose, it will be for naught unless it fits the face aesthetically, and the face fits the body aesthetically, and the body is positioned aesthetically among all of the heavenly hosts in the entire ceiling.

WORKING TOWARD SPECIFICITY IN VISUALIZATION

The first version of your film began the first time you read the screenplay, or perhaps, if you were the author, while you were writing. Another version was born after the detective work, and perhaps the latest version was born after the staging. There will be more versions—or maybe we should start calling them revisions—as we begin to explore the best way of rendering each moment within the context of the entire film. The Russian director Sergei Eisenstein, in a lecture to film students (published as a booklet entitled *On the Composition of the Short Fiction Scenario*), read a short screenplay by L. Leonov, *The Feast at Zhirmuna*, as an example of an exemplary scenario. Then he asked the students to think about how they would shoot it. It is instructive how Eisenstein suggested they go about this visualization.

We liked two details which very strongly revealed the personalities of the main characters. I'll read them to you again: "Oneisim mechanically peels off a thin strip of chipped paint and crushes it between his fingers. Pensively: 'Always meant to re-do this porch. My nephew promised to send us some whitewash, but I guess he forgot'. . . . OK, afterwards!" And also: "The old woman picks a wild flower on the path and trudges back to the house." I ask you to think of how you would direct and shoot these two scenes (their length, shooting angle, etc.), taking into account the psychological loading of these details and their significance in the general development of the action. You should also try to imagine how the old man should be standing over the body of the old woman when he says "lioness," how the door is closed in the kindergarten, how the German would stick his knee in the cracked door, and how near and from which side it should be shot.

Don't concern yourself with complex stylistic questions, don't struggle with graphic problems of the shots. Set up the shots so that the meaning of the inner-shot action is clear. *A shot should be like a line in a poem—self-contained, with its idea crystal clear.*

LOOKING FOR ORDER

Look for order or design that is already present in the blocking. This makes it more likely that, when you add the camera, you will enhance whatever that design is meant to express rather than obfuscate it. A common example of the latter is when the director places two characters a good distance apart, then "hides" this staging by the use of close-ups instead of emphasizing the space between the characters by showing it.

DRAMATIC BLOCKS AND CAMERA

Because you have already identified these dramatic groupings, you must now be sure you keep each intact while rendering them fully and clearly. Each block will usually inhabit a specific geography, so you will be looking for "conjunctions" (connecting shots) from one dramatic block to another because unlike prose on a page, a film scene is usually rendered on the screen seamlessly, without the audience being aware of the indentations of the "paragraphs."

SHOT LISTS, STORYBOARDS, AND SETUPS

What we want to end up with is a list of camera setups for each scene. (A camera setup is when the camera is moved from one position to another, most likely requiring a lighting change. As mentioned earlier, more than one edited shot can be taken from a single camera setup.)

Storyboards are drawings of each individual shot. They are a visual manifestation of a long investigative journey and can be very helpful in communicating the director's vision to others. However, the beginning director should be warned. Storyboards should be the end of the process: annotations of moments in an overall orchestration. Because they are static renderings of moments, they often prevent the beginning director from seeing the flow of the scene and realizing the *connecting tissue* between each of these moments. When the director's journey has been made a number of times—from the detective work on the page, to shooting on the set, to the edited version—the storyboards will begin to be more relevant to the final outcome.

Some directors employ storyboard artists to draw preliminary storyboards to explore the visual renderings suggested by the screenplay, with and/or without the director's initial input. This can be fruitful in exploring possibilities in the previsualization of action sequences.

There are software programs available that can render three-dimensional storyboards on your computer with virtual cameras that pan, tilt, dolly, zoom, and crane while enabling you to choose specific focal lengths for each shot. Other programs can put your characters into motion.

This ability to explore various possibilities for rendering your scenes can be very helpful, allowing the director to *see her film before shooting*. Remember, *the storyboard is the end of a process*, and these electronic bells and whistles will not release you from that obligation.

THE PROSE STORYBOARD

Prose storyboards can be especially effective in locations that do not lend themselves to floor plans, and they are very helpful in spotting errors of omission—missing beats—even if we then go on to visual boards. Let's see how this type of investigation might work with the following text.

```
Jack and Jill go up the hill,
to fetch a pail of water.
Jack falls down and breaks his crown.
Jill is happy.
```

To shoot the preceding scene using the methodology set forth in this book, we would first apply our "detective work" to unearth whose scene it is, as well as the circumstance, dynamic relationships, and wants. Also, we would determine the dramatic blocks, the fulcrum, and the major narrative beats. (We'll assume that this scene is part of a larger film, and the determination of film and character spines have been made, and there has been an investigation of character.)

Supplying my own backstory, my detective work has come up with the following answers: It is Jill's scene. The circumstance is that they are brother and sister whose chore it is to bring home water. He sees her as an "albatross," a burden. She sees him as "a show-off." He *wants* to "put her in her place," which is in the home. She *wants* to "prove that she is his equal and deserves to be treated as such."

PROSE STORYBOARD FOR *JACK AND JILL*

Each sentence is a shot.

```
Moving rapidly,
an empty pail,
being carried by a Young Man.
```

The syntax of the above sentence indicates the varying emphasis in the shot. We start with rapid forward movement of an empty pail being carried by someone—which introduces the chore—and then pan up to that person for his entrance into the scene. We would find him confident, determined, and perhaps discover a hint of maliciousness.

```
Trying to keep the pace,
a Young Girl
```

Jill would be equally determined but obviously not equipped for this arduous trek.

```
A brother/sister estranged,
going UP.
```

Here we would have a two-shot that would resolve the spatial separation between our characters. It would also be wide enough for us to see the slope of the terrain—the UP. The fact that they are brother and sister could be intimated by age difference and attitude.

SECOND DRAMATIC BLOCK

```
Jack going HIGHER.
Jill struggling to go HIGHER.
(Repeat above two times)
```

The "repeating" would be an example of *elaboration* and would be accomplished with multiple angles, creating the idea of danger and its inherent suspense.

```
Distance between the two increases
```

The above implies a two-shot, which again resolves spatial separation while letting us in on the plot-point.

```
Jill, exhausted, stops to rest.
```

A question is raised here. Will the objective of Jill's want be won or lost?

FULCRUM AND BEGINNING OF THIRD DRAMATIC BLOCK

```
Jack realizes Jill has stopped,
smiles.
```

Jack believes he has won, but in his exultation he loses his concentration.

```
Jack takes a step,
loses footing.
Jack loses pail.
Jill startled.
Pail falling.
Jack struggling to gain footing.
Jack losing his footing and falling,
DOWN.
```

FOURTH DRAMATIC BLOCK

```
Jill looks DOWN.
Jack with broken crown.
Jill smiles.
```

The benefit of a prose storyboard is that it gets you thinking about the visual aspects of your film without making a big deal out of it, and it tends to be very accurate in indicating the essential ingredients—the essence of each moment—that must be conveyed to the audience so that they can appreciate the unfolding of the story. In Part V of this book I analyze three films in depth and interpret some of the "visual" scenes with a prose storyboard that, of course, was arrived at *after the fact*. However, I maintain that they can also be arrived at *before* you bring in the camera. The following is a portion of one of the scenes from Peter Weir's *The Truman Show*. It takes place in a dance hall:

Truman is having a good time.

Dream-girl is there.

Truman spots dream-girl.

She spots him.

He can't take his eyes from her.

She can't take her eyes from him.

What the previous scene does that inexperienced directors might not get to with visual storyboards alone is to indicate clearly the narrative beats that each shot conveys. They jump out at you. If you discover a missing beat, it is easy to fix.

The prose storyboard does not necessarily indicate image size or composition, but my teaching experience has taught me that beginning directors must first "get the action right" before going on.

Two examples from *Notorious* that might help you to "see" the evocative effect of prose can be found on page 226, EXT RIDING PATH, and page 232, a 14-minute suspense sequence, MAIN HALL/ADJACENT ROOMS/WINE CELLAR/GARDEN/MASTER BEDROOM.

C H A P T E R   6

CAMERA IN *NOTORIOUS* PATIO SCENE

Hitchcock "covers" the scene economically, using 13 camera setups to obtain 32 shots constituting the edited scene. We will discover that each shot has a specific function—from "merely" rendering the action to articulating it.

There are two camera setups in the first dramatic block (Figure 6-1): one to take Devlin to the Patio, the second to take Alicia. Looking at the film, it might seem as if the camera was in the same position for each shot because both end their panning with an almost similar frame. But if you look closely, the camera for Alicia has been moved to create an angle that supplies more energy to her entrance. She "bursts" into the living room, reflecting her enthusiastic expectation. This contrasts sharply with Devlin's more "solemn" entrance, reflecting his lack of enthusiasm for the job at hand. Also, the final framing of Devlin on the patio is wider, creating more space around him, reflecting his "forlornness."

Camera setups are prefaced by the number sign (#1, #2), while the edited shots are prefaced by the letter E (E-1, E-2).

FIRST DRAMATIC BLOCK

LIVING ROOM/ALICIA'S APARTMENT

E-1, from camera setup #1, MLS: sound of door shutting as Devlin enters frame right. Pan left with him to center of room, revealing patio through open French doors in the background. He rubs his forehead (Figure 6-2).

KITCHEN/ALICIA'S APARTMENT

E-2, MS: (I did not assign this a camera setup): Alicia cutting chicken. This shot (Figure 6-3) locates Alicia geographically and shows how determined she is to overcome her ineptness with domestic duties. She is making every effort to make herself into something she has never been—all for the love of this man.

LIVING ROOM

E-3, from camera setup #1: turns into a long shot as Devlin continues through the double doors to the outside patio and stops, hands in pocket. He hunches his shoulders (Figure 6-4).

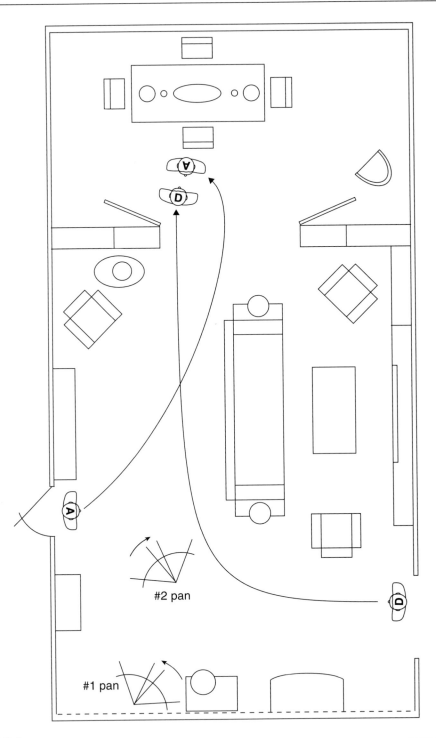

FIGURE 6-1

Camera setups imposed on floor plan for first dramatic block of *Notorious* Patio scene.

FIGURE 6-2

Shot E-1 from camera setup #1.

FIGURE 6-3

Shot E-2.

E-4, from camera setup #2, MS: Alicia enters frame left carrying two dinner plates (Figure 6-5). Camera pans with her into LS as she enters patio, sets down the plates on the table, and hugs Devlin (Figure 6-6).

Because Alicia's physical action of hugging overlaps from one shot to the next, there is a seamless cut that serves as the *connecting tissue* between the first and second dramatic blocks.

FIGURE 6-4

Shot E-3 from camera setup #1.

FIGURE 6-5

Shot E-4 from camera setup #2.

It is minimal to be sure, but nevertheless it does its job of bridging the movement to a new *geographical paragraph*, which in turn alerts the audience to the escalating action. This new paragraph comes about because of the substantial change in camera angle rather than a change in staging.

FIGURE 6-6

Continuation of shot E-4.

   The job of the staging up until now has been only to render the action of the scene—to get them both onto the patio. Now Hitchcock sets in motion the use of proximity as a way of making physical what is going on internally by starting the second dramatic block with them together. (Remember the two patterns of dramatic movement: together/apart, apart/together.)

SECOND DRAMATIC BLOCK

PATIO

You will find Hitchcock to be very economical in the number of camera setups he uses to render this scene. In this second dramatic block (Figure 6-7) he uses three (#3, #4, #5).
   E-5, #3, M2S: (profiles): Hugging action begun in previous shot is completed (Figure 6-8). Alicia kisses Devlin. He is unresponsive. Hitchcock relies solely on the acting beats (the action/reaction between Alicia and Devlin) to carry the first portion of this block.
   Alicia attempts to coax Devlin to tell her what's wrong. She places his arms around her waist. To draw him out, she says, "The time has come when you must tell me that you have a wife and two adorable children, and this madness between us can't go on any longer." Devlin replies with an accusation, "I bet you heard that line often enough." This is a punch in the solar plexus to Alicia, and to articulate that blow, Hitchcock collides two performance beats by cutting from the two-shot (Figure 6-8) to a close-up of Alicia (Figure 6-9); that is, from Devlin's "to accuse" to Alicia's "to protest," E-6, from camera setup #4. This collision emphasizes Devlin's low blow, making it palpable for the audience, and it is a prime example of a narrative beat.
   Hitchcock continues in separation, cutting 11 times between the close-up of Alicia and the close-up of Devlin (Figure 6-10), camera setups #4 and #5, edited shots E6 through E16. Each of these edited shots articulates a narrative beat, starting with Alicia and alternating between her and Devlin: TO PROTEST, TO ANNOUNCE, TO CONFIRM, TO QUESTION, TO CLARIFY, TO

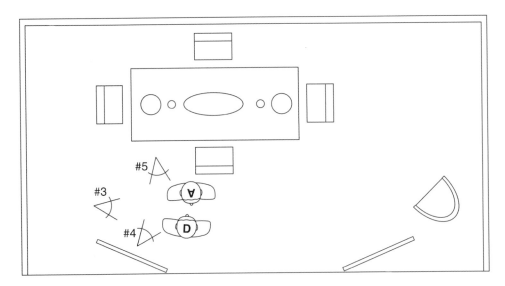

FIGURE 6-7

Floor plan for second dramatic block.

FIGURE 6-8

Shot E-5 from camera setup #3. First shot of second dramatic block.

IMPLY, TO INFORM, TO MAKE SENSE (this narrative beat is not contained in the dialogue but in Alicia's behavior), TO DISCLOSE, and TO DETACH (Alicia moves away from Devlin). This action/reaction—this "volleying across the net" as in a tennis match—heightens dramatically the tension between the two.

FIGURE 6-9

Shots E-6, -8, -10, -12, -14, and -16 from camera setup #4. Acting beats turned into narrative beats.

FIGURE 6-10

Shots E-7, -9, -11, -13, and -15 from camera setup #5. Acting beats turned into narrative beats.

(Separation shots, such as these mentioned previously, that contain an out-of-focus portion of another character or object, are often referred to as a "dirty single.")

When Devlin says, in his close-up, "We have to contact him," Alicia, in her close-up, turns away from Devlin. Her DETACHING herself is an example of a narrative beat articulated through staging, as indicated on the floor plan for the third dramatic block (Figure 6-11). It also serves as

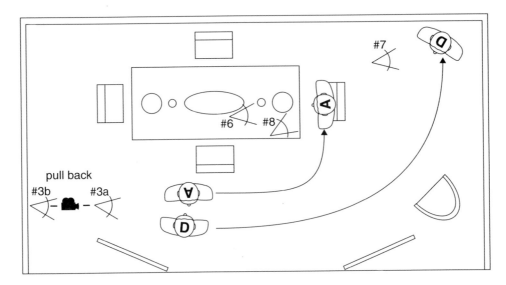

FIGURE 6-11

Floor plan for third dramatic block.

FIGURE 6-12

Shot E-17, from camera setup #3. Alicia *DETACHING*. Connecting tissue between second and third dramatic block.

connecting tissue to the third dramatic block, where Alicia begins the move away from Devlin (Figure 6-12).

The camera pulls back a bit (#3b) to accommodate Alicia's movement to the chair and sitting down. This camera move conveys the emotional as well as the physical distancing of the two characters (Figure 6-13).

FIGURE 6-13

Shot E-17 continued. Shot widens to a two-shot.

FIGURE 6-14

E-18, camera setup #6.

THIRD DRAMATIC BLOCK

Hitchcock makes physical Alicia's internal state by having her move away from Devlin then sit down due to the "weight" he has placed on her shoulders. Hitchcock then cuts to a medium shot of Alicia (Figure 6-14) to articulate her narrative beat, TO DENIGRATE (HERSELF) with these words, "Mata Hari. She makes love for the papers."

FIGURE 6-15 ——

Shot E-18 continued.

FIGURE 6-16 ——

Edited shots E-19, -21, -23, and -25 from camera setup #7.

In this same shot, Hitchcock has Devlin move to a position behind Alicia, *TO TAKE COMMAND* (Figure 6-15), an example of using staging for picturization—to set up a frame that posits the question, What does the shot tell you? However, Devlin's move has no initial motivation and would seem mechanical if our attention was called to it. To mask the beginning of the move, Hitchcock has Devlin begin it off-screen. As Devlin moves behind Alicia, the camera tilts up to a medium two-shot to accommodate his arrival in the frame.

FIGURE 6-17 ───

Edited shots E-20, -22, and -24 from camera setup #8.

Hitchcock turns Alicia's performance beat, "to accuse," into a narrative beat, TO ACCUSE, by cutting immediately after the line, "I suppose you knew about this pretty little job of mine all the time," to a close-up of Devlin's (Figure 6-16), escalating his performance beat into a narrative beat, TO DENY. The cut heightens the dramatic power of Alicia's line. The close-up of Devlin heightens his reply, and with this cut, Hitchcock goes into separation again (for seven shots) back to the volleying across the net between Devlin and Alicia (Figure 6-17)—turning seven perform- ance beats into seven narrative beats. Take note of the dialogue. See how it has heated up and how this rendering through separation articulates that escalation. (*The first and last lines of dialogue in a paragraph of dialogue make the strongest impression on an audience. Likewise for edited shots.*)

Beginning with Devlin's close-up and alternating with Alicia's, the following narrative beats are articulated: TO DENY, TO INQUIRE, TO CHALLENGE, TO ATTACK, TO STATE A FACT, TO DECLARE (HER LOVE), and TO REJECT.

FOURTH DRAMATIC BLOCK AND FULCRUM

Hitchcock announces the fourth dramatic block (Figure 6-18) by cutting from Devlin's close-up to the medium two-shot, the same shot that prefaced the separation "phrase"—in effect bookending the extended separation. The shot E-26, camera setup #6a (Figure 6-19), "releases" us from the intensity of the separation phrasing and prepares us for something new to happen.

At this point, the fulcrum, the scene could go either way for Alicia. A question is raised in the audience's mind. She could accept Devlin's last words and let it kill her want, but because her want is so strong and all embracing, she cannot give it up without a fight. Alicia still has hope that she can win Devlin's heart; to make everything like it was a few hours ago. She goes on the offensive and CHALLENGES Devlin. Hitchcock articulates the apex of the fulcrum by having Alicia stand, changing the direction the scene was headed. As she walks toward Devlin, a possibility is raised along with a question: Will Alicia attain her want?

When Alicia stands TO CHALLENGE Devlin, the camera tilts up with her and tracks in with her to a tighter two-shot as she approaches Devlin TO PURSUE (HER LOVE).

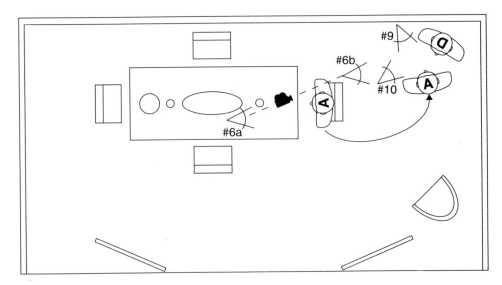

FIGURE 6-18 ────────────────────────────────

Floor plan for fourth dramatic block containing fulcrum.

FIGURE 6-19 ────────────────────────────────

Short E-26, from camera setup #6a-b. Contains fulcrum of the scene.

The ability of the camera to move has been introduced in the very first shot of the film.

The camera movement in shot E-26 emphasizes Alicia's intent by emphasizing her movement toward Devlin. The four narrative beats contained in the shot are articulated through staging, as is the fulcrum: Alicia CHALLENGES (stands), Devlin FENDS OFF (lights cigarette), Alicia BACKS OFF (stops advance, turns sideways) then OFFERS HERSELF (faces Devlin). Now that Hitchcock has cleaned our palate with this extended take, he goes back to separation to articulate the last

FIGURE 6-20

Shot E-27 from camera setup #9. Narrative beat, TO IMPLORE.

FIGURE 6-21

Shot E-28 from camera setup #10. Narrative beat, TO CUT OFF.

two narrative beats of this dramatic block: shot E-27, from camera setup #9 (Figure 6-20), and E-28, from camera setup #10 (Figure 6-21).

This close-up of Devlin (Figure 6-21) is the end of the fourth dramatic block. There is connecting tissue between blocks, articulated through staging by Alicia turning from Devlin, CONCEDING DEFEAT, in a new camera setup, #11, E-29 (Figure 6-22).

FIGURE 6-22

Shot E-29 from camera setup #11.

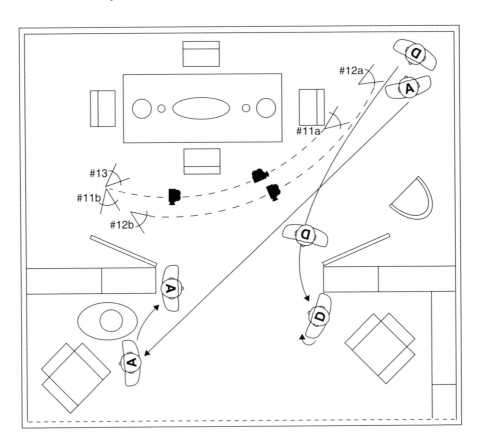

FIGURE 6-23

Floor plan for fifth dramatic block.

FIFTH DRAMATIC BLOCK

Figure 6-23 shows the floor plan for the fifth dramatic block. This new camera setup (#11, E-29) tracks Alicia's RETREAT and then pans with her into the living room and into a medium profile through the curtain of the French door (Figures 6-24 and 6-25).

FIGURE 6-24

Continuation of shot E-29, camera setup #11.

FIGURE 6-25

Final frame of shot E-29, camera setup #11.

FIGURE 6-26

Shot E-30, camera setup #12.

FIGURE 6-27

Continuation of shot E-30, camera setup #12.

Camera setup #12, E-30, tracks with Devlin from the patio and then pans with him as he enters the living room, as Alicia enters the right edge of the frame and looks out on the patio (Figures 6-26, 6-27, 6-28, and 6-29). (It is very likely that Hitchcock used the same set of dolly tracks for Devlin's move as he did for Alicia's and that it is not really a new setup.)

FIGURE 6-28

Shot E-31, from camera setup #13. Alicia's POV.

FIGURE 6-29

Shot E-32, continuation of camera setup #12.

Hitchcock makes good use of the French doors: first to frame Alicia's drinking (the curtain seems to imply shame) and then to indicate the distance between her and Devlin (each ends up at either side of the door frame, the farthest apart they could be in this geography). This is another example of *What does the shot tell you?*

PART TWO

MAKING YOUR FILM

If you've paid close attention to Part I you are now ready to begin making a film—conceptually—in your head—for that's where it all begins, and that is the basis of the methodology put forth in this book. We will now take what you have learned and apply it to a short screenplay that I have written especially for this purpose. There is a protagonist who wants something very much and an antagonist who wants very much to prevent him from getting it. We would like to engage an audience with this story, and to that end we will apply our detective work, staging, camera design, and preliminary work with actors.

One note of caution to you directors who might by nature want to move along quickly; make sure you have thoroughly digested Part I. You might need to look at the Patio scene from *Notorious* again. Go beneath the story's surface and appreciate the organizing of action by the dramatic blocks, the dramatic articulation by the narrative beats, and the function that the fulcrum serves. Do the same with the staging and camera. Understand the reason for every step the characters take either toward or away from the other, why Alicia sits, why she stands. Understand the job of each edited shot, why the camera is where it is, and why Hitchcock cuts at that moment. I know this takes time, but in the end it will serve you well as we begin to use the methodology offered in this book on your next film, *A Piece of Apple Pie*.

C H A P T E R   7

DETECTIVE WORK ON SCRIPTS

Every film begins with a screenplay; ideally, a good one. Still, even in very good screenplays the director's investigation might uncover flaws as the screenplay is broken up into its smallest parts, even if the director is also the writer. A more intense focus, a more powerful lens, must be brought to the text now. The essence of every dramatic moment should be discovered and related to a dramatic whole. If we think of the screenplay as a forest and the dramatic moments as trees, we ought to be able to immerse ourselves in the forest to see every tree in minute detail. At the same time, we should be constantly aware of each tree's specific place in the forest—its job in the film. The first step in this journey of discovery begins with reading the screenplay. This is also the first step in our previsualization methodology—to *see* our film before we shoot it.

READING YOUR SCREENPLAY

The film director Billy Wilder (*The Apartment*, 1960) commented on the subject of reading a screenplay: "It isn't necessarily helpful for a director to know how to write, but what is vitally important is that he know how to read." The stage director Harold Clurman, in *On Directing*, commented:

> The director reads the script. He reads it again and again and again. He need not read it in consecutive daily sessions. In fact, he would do well, if time permits, to set it aside for a while after each reading and check on what he remembers of it. He might even try to forget it. He should let it work on him before he works on it. First impressions—and he must regard the first two or three preliminary readings as first impressions—are often deceiving, that is conventional. To begin with, even experienced directors may see little more in a script than an intelligent theatergoer would. Like him, the director will be amused, laugh or cry, shudder or thrill. These reactions are not without value; they may even prove important. . . . But they do not suffice as guides to the directorial problem, which . . . is to translate the script's words into the language of the stage [film] where men and women of flesh and blood who move in three dimensions among real objects are to replace description.

To apply this book's methodology to an entire story of manageable length I have written a short screenplay titled *A Piece of Apple Pie*. Read the screenplay now as if it were going to be your next directing project.

A PIECE OF APPLE PIE SCREENPLAY

A Piece of Apple Pie
EXT. DINER - NIGHT
An Edward Hopper atmosphere.
MAIN TITLE AND CREDITS
INT. DINER - NIGHT
Close on last piece of apple pie being taken from a pie tin and placed
on a serving dish.
Wider as COUNTERMAN sets the pie on the counter along with a napkin and
fork. He looks toward the door as CUSTOMER enters.

                              CUSTOMER
        Good evening.

                              COUNTERMAN
        Hi.

Counterman looks at the wall clock: 11:55. Customer walks the length
of the counter, past the dish of apple pie, and sits at a table in the
empty restaurant, facing Counterman.

                              COUNTERMAN
        Need a menu?

                              CUSTOMER
                         (inspecting tabletop)
        No.

Customer stands and moves to the next table, sits, inspects it, finds
it unsatisfactory, gets up and moves to a third table. He runs his
hand over the surface. It seems to pass muster. He inspects the fork.
It'll do.

He looks up at Counterman.

                              CUSTOMER
        I'll have a piece of apple pie.

                              COUNTERMAN
        I'm out of apple pie.

                              CUSTOMER
        What's that on the counter?

                              COUNTERMAN
        I'm saving that piece.

                              CUSTOMER
        You're saving it?

                              COUNTERMAN
        There's a customer comes in around this time every
        night for apple pie - but I've got cherry, blueberry,
        lemon meringue, key lime -

                              CUSTOMER
I want the apple pie.

                              COUNTERMAN
I'm sorry. This customer would be very disappointed.

                              CUSTOMER
But you don't mind disappointing me.

                              COUNTERMAN
I'll tell you what. I'll give you a piece of any other pie you
want, on the house.

                              CUSTOMER
No.

                              COUNTERMAN
I'll make it a la mode.

                              CUSTOMER
Listen - if you don't give me *that* piece of pie right now, I'll
call the police.

                              COUNTERMAN
The customer is a cop.

                              CUSTOMER
I don't care if he's the King of Siam.

Customer gets up and approaches the counter. Standing in front of the
piece of apple pie, he takes out a gun.

                              COUNTERMAN
Hey, no guns allowed in here.

                              CUSTOMER
I want this pie!

                              COUNTERMAN
                          (looks toward door)
I can't.
                            (grabs pie)

                              CUSTOMER
Don't make me shoot!

                              COUNTERMAN
For a piece of pie?

                              CUSTOMER
I'll count to five. One . . . two -

                              COUNTERMAN
It's stupid.

                              CUSTOMER
        Getting shot when you don't have to is stupid.
        Four!

                              COUNTERMAN
        Okay! Okay! It's yours.

Counterman sets the pie back on the counter. Customer puts the gun away
and sits on the stool. He pushes the napkin and fork away.

                              CUSTOMER
        Could I have another fork and a fresh napkin,
        please?

Counterman places a new fork and napkin on the counter.

                              CUSTOMER
        Thank you.

                              COUNTERMAN
        Something to drink?

                              CUSTOMER
        I'm fine.

Counterman walks away from Customer. He leans on the end of the
counter, his head in his hands; a picture of utter defeat.
After a beat, he steals a glance at Customer who is wiping the new
fork vigorously – some might say compulsively. A ray of hope comes to
Counterman just as the fork is about to cut into the pie.

                              COUNTERMAN
        I never eat apple pie, myself.

Customer looks up at Counterman, quizzically.

                              COUNTERMAN
        I like it, but I just don't eat it.

                              CUSTOMER
        Why not?

                              COUNTERMAN
        Why? Well . . . because of that stuff they spray
        on them.

                              CUSTOMER
        What stuff?

                              COUNTERMAN
        Something that causes cancer.

                              CUSTOMER
        I know what you're trying to do. It's not going to
        work.

                         COUNTERMAN

Maybe I'm being too cautious. Nobody's gonna get
out of this world alive, anyway. Apple pie is as
good a way to go as any. Probably better than most.

                         CUSTOMER

Would you just shut up!

Counterman raises his hands in surrender. He begins busying himself with
a wiping rag.

The Customer stares at him.

                         CUSTOMER

  It doesn't make any sense.

Counterman says nothing.

                         CUSTOMER

You got this cop coming in here eating apple pie,
what - two, three times week?

                         COUNTERMAN

Sometimes five.

                         CUSTOMER

So why didn't you tell the cop about this spray?

                         COUNTERMAN

I did. But you know cops. They'll eat anything.
Sure you don't want a cup of coffee to wash that
down?

                         CUSTOMER

I don't drink coffee.

                         COUNTERMAN

Oh, no, why not?

                         CUSTOMER

I heard it wasn't good for you.

                         COUNTERMAN

If I had to stop serving everything that wasn't
good for you, I'd be out of business.

                         CUSTOMER

You have a responsibility to your customers.

                         COUNTERMAN

Hey, I'm not twisting anybody's arm.

Customer looks down at the piece of pie, hesitates, then places the fork
on the counter.

                         CUSTOMER
   What do I owe you?

                        COUNTERMAN
     Forget it, it's on me.

Customer lays two dollars on the counter and stands.

                        COUNTERMAN
      You sure you don't want to try the key lime?

Customer goes to the door, stops, and turns back to Counterman.

                         CUSTOMER
     Sorry about the gun.

                        COUNTERMAN
     Maybe you ought to get rid of it.

                         CUSTOMER
     I just bought it today. It's not even loaded.

                        COUNTERMAN
     No one knows that but you.

                         CUSTOMER
     I'm tired of being pushed around.

                        COUNTERMAN
     That's no excuse.

Customer hesitates a beat, then takes out the gun and tosses it to
Counterman.

                         CUSTOMER
       Give it to the cop.

Before Counterman can answer, Customer turns and exits.

Counterman looks at the clock: 12:00. He places the gun out of sight,
goes to the piece of apple pie, replaces the napkin and fork, turns to
the coffeepot and pours a cup of coffee.
   As Counterman turns to set the cup next to the apple pie, a FEMALE
COP sits down in front of it. It is obvious that she can take care of
herself.
   The Counterman smiles lovingly at the Female Cop. She picks up the
fork and smiles lovingly at the piece of apple pie.

EXT. DINER - NIGHT

It's quiet.

FADE OUT

WHOSE FILM IS IT?

In *A Piece of Apple Pie*, the Counterman is the protagonist. It is his film. He is the character in whom we place an emotional investment. He is the one we care most about. That is not to say that we are not interested in Customer, our antagonist. We hope that *all* our characters are interesting, even the ones we might not like.

CHARACTER

Our three characters in *A Piece of Apple Pie* are obviously not as complicated as the ones Tennessee Williams created, and which Kazan, along with the undeniable help of the actors, rendered so brilliantly in *A Streetcar Named Desire*. (Although writers' work is not dealt with extensively in this book, it in no way diminishes their contribution—certainly not in the case of Williams, one of the premier American dramatists of the twentieth century.) We have a much shorter train trip in *A Piece of Apple Pie*, not only in duration, but thematically. That does not mean that we skimp here on our character work—that we discriminate against them because they do not have the richness or the "immortality" of a Blanche, or a Stanley, or a Rick, or a Guido. As Constance Stanislavski (director of the Moscow Art Theater) said (admittedly in another context), "There are no small roles." As directors it is advisable for us to continually push to the outer parameters of all our dramatic categories. That does not mean that we bend them out of shape—that we attempt to turn Counterman into Hamlet. What it simply means is that *we attempt to render any story we are working on in the fullest, strongest way. That is our obligation.*

The key to the Counterman's character as a restaurateur is the tradition's cardinal rule: The customer is always right. However, this does not explain his adoration for his beloved. Why does he find *this* woman irresistible? It is located somewhere in his character, but the director does not necessarily have to delve into it unless the actor fails to do so. Each actor who plays the part will come up with different reasons for adoring the Female Cop. Reasons that work for him! It is enough that the director sees adoration in Counterman's behavior; the same for Female Cop's adoration of apple pie. As for the fact that "it is obvious that she can take care of herself," this can best be addressed in the small amount of time that she is on screen by the casting of an obvious physical type—one that "comes with the necessary baggage."

The Customer's character is more difficult to come up with, but if we look into his circumstance (often called backstory) we can find relevant clues.

CIRCUMSTANCE

What are the circumstances for the three characters in *A Piece of Apple Pie*? Let's start with the seemingly easiest one, Female Cop. She likes apple pie, right? Wrong! She *loves* apple pie! She *adores* apple pie! It is the *highlight of her day*. She eats it on an exacting schedule at this particular diner that she has come to expect will deliver precisely what she wants. *She has yet to be disappointed!*

Just think for a moment what would happen to the conflict in our story if Counterman felt he had an out from the very beginning—that he could satisfy Female Cop with a piece of key lime pie. To generalize this specific: *Never give your characters an easy way out!* Difficulty! Difficulty! More difficulty!

Counterman's circumstance seems obvious on first reading. He is in love with Female Cop and does not want to disappoint her, and he knows absolutely what would disappoint her. No apple pie would disappoint her. And then, who knows, she might never come back. But is there anything more than that to Counterman's circumstance *this* night? If there is, where can we find it?

A place where we often find *more* is in raising the stakes. What if Counterman had finally decided that tonight he was going to escalate the relationship—to metaphorically leap over the counter that separates customer from counterman and ask his love object for a date? Of course, it has taken him weeks—maybe months—to get his nerve up, so tonight he will allow nothing to get in his way! Counterman, then, is filled with expectation—one of the most powerful dramatic devices that we have in our storytelling arsenal.

Now, what about Customer's circumstance? I have found over the years that the tendency for most beginning directors is to not push relentlessly toward the most dramatic situation but instead to gravitate to the most obvious. For example, Customer comes in to eat a piece of apple pie, and when he is told he can't have it, he resorts to the threat of violence. Why? Because he is a bully. Or the other alternative is that he is simply crazy.

Is that the best we can imagine: someone who slinks into the diner in the throes of raging paranoia? How interesting can he be if he is that one-dimensional?

Suppose we imagine a man who is definitely not crazy, certainly not in the certifiable sense, but rather has been pushed around all his life—by his peers, by his wife, by his boss, maybe even by his kid. Like the comedian Rodney Dangerfield, Customer gets no respect, and he has finally gotten sick of it! And *today*, with the nudging of his psychiatrist, he has come to a momentous decision. He is not going to take it anymore! So he is actually in an expansive mood when he walks into the diner. He has come out on the town to celebrate the birth of a new man—the first day of the rest of his life. What about the gun? Well, one of the people who pushed him around recently—literally—was a mugger. He bought the gun just to be absolutely sure that *nothing* will spoil this evening. Through this invention of circumstance we have come up with a clear understanding of the Counterman's character, but how can we explain Customer's compulsive cleanliness regarding the fork? For this film the director needn't go any further into the genesis of that trait, although the actor who plays the part will have to *justify* it for himself.

SPINES FOR *A PIECE OF APPLE PIE*

Before we decide on the spine of the three characters, we must first decide on the spine of the screenplay—the main action of the film. There is no one answer. It is the director's interpretation of what the writer has written, but whatever the decision as to the main action of the film, it must be able to incorporate under its umbrella the spines of the characters. I have come up with the following spines:

- Film's spine: to live life to its fullest
- Counterman's spine: to win the heart of his love object (thereby fulfilling this area of his life)
- Customer's spine: to begin a new (and fuller) life
- Female Cop's spine: to continue this life (which would be less full without apple pie in it)

Aside from the unifying aspects of the screenplay's spine, it will, as pointed out by Clurman, help lead us to our style, tone, mood, atmosphere, and emphasis.

DYNAMIC RELATIONSHIPS

What are the relevant dynamic relationships for the characters in *Apple Pie*? For Counterman, Female Cop could be a "sex goddess." That would work for our story. So would "my happiness." I prefer the latter because it would impart a different tone to Counterman's psychology—one I believe is more interesting and more in keeping with the tone I would strive for as director of this piece. How does Female Cop see Counterman? How about "Mr. Reliable?" That does all the work we need from a dynamic relationship. I would keep it. But Counterman is not Mr. Reliable to Customer. What is he? If we pay heed to our circumstance, at the moment Customer comes through the door he should see Counterman as what? "Servant." Doesn't do the job at all. "Ally." Too general. How about "Celebrant?"

Webster's New Collegiate Dictionary defines celebrant as: one who celebrates; specifically, the priest officiating at the Eucharist. Do you think that's too much? I don't, but if you do, and you're directing it, choose another more to your liking. In much of this detective work, there is no such thing as right, but you should be relevant.

Celebrant cannot be used for the way Female Cop sees Counterman. It is too respectful. It makes him too important to her, thereby diminishing the job he must do—the distance he must go to achieve his goal.

Finally, what is Customer to Counterman? When Counterman is anticipating Female Cop and instead Customer enters, Customer is "disappointment." However, Counterman quickly overcomes this because he is a good restaurateur, and like any restaurateur worthy of the name, Counterman represses his personal feelings and assumes his public persona, in which he sees Customer as "always right"—even though in a few moments Counterman must go against that time-honored relationship, which has been handed down to him from generations of restaurateurs.

WANTS

Our protagonist, Counterman, wants to see Female Cop outside of the restaurant.

Customer, our antagonist, wants to begin living the life of a man who will not be pushed around—the life of a man who gets what he wants. He might not really want a piece of apple pie, and in fact he might not even be hungry.

Female Cop wants her fix of apple pie.

Even though wants are most likely contained in the circumstance, it is necessary to ferret them out and make them clear for *each* scene. (This entire film is basically one scene.) Even in this scene, both Counterman and Customer must change their initial wants. Customer must give up the idea of beginning his new life, on this night, in this diner, to not eat something that would be harmful to his life, even though it is a life that he can no longer stand. Counterman must save his life by giving up the key to his beloved's heart (the pie), but when the immediate danger is over (the gun), the original want is resurrected.

ACTIONS

We will assign actions to the character's movements and dialogue, keeping in mind that the overwhelming majority of actions are wedded to a character's immediate want.

Sometimes a character will say or do something that is not wedded to their immediate want and can be attributed to their innate character. An example of this is when Customer says, "I'm just tired of being pushed around." The action of this line has nothing to do with the scene want and everything to do with Customer's psychology.

ACTING BEATS

In *Apple Pie*, what is the acting beat for Counterman when he says to Customer, "I never eat apple pie, myself"? What verb would be most relevant? Is he "stating a fact"? It might very well be a fact. The problem in using "stating a fact" as our action verb is that it is not urgent. We need an action that contains the immediate intent. That narrows our choice considerably, especially if we remember the cardinal rule: the character's actions are wedded to her or his wants! Counterman's scene want, the want he began the scene with, was never completely extinguished—it just went underground when he was forced to change his original scene want to "save his life." Now that he does not have a gun pointed at him, his original scene want has been resurrected, and, miracle of miracles, the apple pie has not yet been desecrated. Instead, he sees the compulsive cleaning of the fork. "Is there an opening here?" he thinks. "Can I still save the day?" Counterman's cognitive functions race through the possible permutations, and he "tests" one of them, "I never eat apple pie myself." Hence, the action verb for that line of dialogue, "to test," is both relevant and urgent.

ACTIVITY

An example of an activity in *Apple Pie* occurs when Counterman "begins busying himself with a wiping rag." His action is "to back off."

TONE FOR *A PIECE OF APPLE PIE*

Obviously we are not dealing with a tragedy here, but it is also not a flat-out comedy. We hope that there will be some chuckles, but for the most part it is a safe drama. Safe for the characters, that is. We know from the beginning, or we should know, that no one will be killed or unduly traumatized during the film. It can probably best be described as a dramatic comedy. We will interpret the actions of our characters with this tone in mind, and it will be an important factor in selecting our cast and determining how we choose the music, the lighting, the camera moves (or lack thereof), and even the costumes.

Keep in mind that it is possible to impose an entirely different tone on this film. Another director, coming up with a darker film-spine (say, "to watch out for number one"), could imbue the film with a darker tone. This director would find different spines for the characters, which would change many of their actions significantly, and would affect the choice of cast and music, and it would most likely alter the lighting and camera design. I think I have chosen the spines, and hence the tone, best suited for this material, but not everyone has to agree.

BREAKING *A PIECE OF APPLE PIE* INTO ACTIONS

Mike Nichols, in talking about his work, described an analogy used by Lee Strasberg, the former director of the Actor's Studio. Strasberg said that directing a scene was like making a salad. You don't just take a head of lettuce, a tomato, and a cucumber, throw them into a bowl, and call it a salad. First, you must chop all the ingredients into pieces. In film, there are three salad makers at work, each dividing the ingredients into ever-smaller units. The writer divides the story into acts, sequences, and scenes. The director, if using the methodology laid out in this book, divides these units of text into dramatic blocks, then into narrative beats. The actor, in his performance, must break the text down into still smaller units—moment-by-moment units called acting (or performance) beats. Here's another way of looking at it.

WRITER	A			B			C
DIRECTOR	A1	A2	A3	B1	B2	B3	
ACTOR	a1 a2 a3	a1 a2 a3	a1 a2 a3	b1 b2 b3	b1 b2 b3	b1 b2 b3	

As you might imagine, the process is not at all as arithmetical as the chart suggests, but it does allow us to perhaps see more clearly where the narrative beats fit in our methodology. The director works within the parameters established by the writer (we are talking now about the point in the process where the director has agreed to the writer's latest revision) and the work of the actors. The director should be aware of all of the acting beats needed to "fill in the blanks" between the A1s and the A2s, but the director should allow the actors to unearth the acting beats (i.e., a1 a2 a3, and so on) on their own.

The director takes selected acting beats and frames them as a narrative beats (through staging and camera) if those beats denote a sufficient degree of dramatic escalation or change of direction to warrant the heightened articulation in her design.

DESIGNING A SCENE

The design of a scene (as well as the design of your entire film) depends on tone, style, specific narrative jobs, and placement in the film, but the key component of any design is the narrative beat—the director's beat. In addition, to use them in a design, we must first designate them. The catch is, we cannot begin to designate what beats we will articulate to the audience without first having some inkling—a rough sketch, if you will—of our design. Where does this first inkling come from? It comes from the process of visualization.

VISUALIZATION

From your first reading of the screenplay, certain images will appear to you. These might include a face, maybe the layout of the location, or a piece of blocking—even individual shots. In addition, as you become more visually experienced, a series of shots combined with staging will announce themselves. A large part of the methodology in this book will be aimed at encouraging and orchestrating this visualization—to both conceive images and "cut" them into edited shots, so that by the time you arrive on the set you have already made a rough cut of the film. On the first few readings of the screenplay you should not feel obligated to write down any of your images. Wait for them to appear again and again. *A good image will persist, and, if it does, pay attention to it.*

At this stage in the methodology, it is good to know the location in which you will shoot; but even if you do not, an approximate location can be imagined, and adjustments can be made to accommodate the actual location. Visualization at an early stage helps in choosing the actual location (or in constructing one) and is helpful in arranging furniture and similar items to accommodate the design that is in your head.

In all of my visualizations for *Apple Pie*, even the very first ones, I "saw" much of the film shot in *separation* (shots in which only one character is shown). This was because of the spatial separation in the staging, dictated by both the geography of the location and the character's actions.

IDENTIFYING THE FULCRUM AND DRAMATIC BLOCKS

I find it very helpful to first identify the fulcrum. It will anchor your design and will serve as a reference point for both your staging and camera. The fulcrum for *Apple Pie* occurs when Counterman "leans on the end of the counter, his head in his hands: a picture of utter defeat."

The next job is to identify your dramatic blocks. It will help enormously in organizing your narrative beats into coherent patterns of action and will indicate the possible need for new geographical paragraphs when you get to your staging and camera. In addition, knowing your dramatic blocks is immensely helpful when working with actors. In *Apple Pie,* there are four dramatic blocks:

- First dramatic block: begins on first beat inside of the diner and ends when "Customer gets up and approaches the counter."
- Second dramatic block: begins with reveal of the gun and ends when "Counterman walks away from Customer."

- Third dramatic block: begins with the fulcrum, "He leans on the end of the counter, his head in his hands: a picture of utter defeat." It ends when "Counterman looks at the clock: 12:00."
- Fourth dramatic block: begins immediately after the above "clock shot" and ends with the last frame inside the diner.

With this work accomplished, we can now proceed to identify our narrative beats. In the following breakdown of *Apple Pie* into narrative beats, some acting beats are included as examples and are presented in lowercase.

SUPPLYING NARRATIVE BEATS TO *A PIECE OF APPLE PIE*

```
EXT. Diner - Night
```

FIRST DRAMATIC BLOCK

```
Close on last piece of apple pie being taken        ENTRANCE OF PIE
from a pie tin and placed on a serving dish.
```

"Entrance of pie" is an example of a narrative beat that renders a plot point essential to the story. Likewise with "Entrance of Counterman" following.

```
Wider as COUNTERMAN                                 ENTRANCE OF COUNTERMAN
sets the pie on the counter along with a
napkin and fork.                                    TO ANTICIPATE

He turns towards the door as CUSTOMER               to check
walks in.
```

We must be careful here to see that "to anticipate" does not indicate "love object." The actor must withhold from the audience the true nature of the relationship with this cop or the film's ending would be spoiled. At the same time, he should not lie to the audience or to himself, but find a way to justify his behavior. The actor could choose to be cool—not wear his heart on his sleeve—knowing that this would only turn off the Female Cop.

```
CUSTOMER: Good evening.                             TO ANNOUNCE
```

Without being attuned to the requirements of drama—to the imperative to make more out of each moment—we might choose "to greet" for this beat. However, as we have discussed earlier, Customer is expansive, he is a new man, and he wants the whole world to know. And right now the whole world is Counterman.

```
COUNTERMAN: Hi.                                     to acknowledge
                                                    TO DAMPEN (anticipation)
```

Ordinarily Counterman's "Hi" would be a "greeting," but not this time. Remember, actions are wedded to wants and circumstance, and Customer, at this moment, is a "disappointment." It is important for the audience to realize this for them to participate in the story. However, this realization will not come from the acting beat "to acknowledge" but from the acting beat "to dampen (anticipation)," which is the essence of the moment—the narrative beat—and the psychology that must be manifested in the Counterman's behavior so that it can be conveyed to the audience.

```
Counterman looks at the wall clock: 11:55            TO CHECK
as Customer walks the length of the counter, past the   TO SELECT
dish of apple pie, and sits at a table in the empty
restaurant, facing Counterman.
```

My first choice here was "to locate," but that action doesn't give the actor enough to do while walking to his seat. If he is selecting the perfect spot to celebrate the beginning of the rest of his life, the actor will exhibit a different gait, perhaps, or he might be glancing this way and that so that something relating to his situation is *hinted at*, even though the audience will have no idea of its significance or that it has any significance at all.

The seeds of a character's behavior must be planted in the audience's mind before they mature into a tree, as in Henrik Ibsen's *The Doll House*. The seeds of Nora's behavior at the end of the play—her rebelling against her husband's oppression by slamming the door on their marriage—is planted in the first scene, when, against her husband's wishes, Nora nibbles on bonbons and lies about it to her husband. It seems quite innocent at the time, but that is all that is needed to indicate her *potential* for becoming her own person.

```
COUNTERMAN: Need a menu?                        TO INQUIRE
CUSTOMER: (inspecting tabletop)                 TO INSPECT
CUSTOMER: No.                                   to reply

Customer stands and moves to the next table, inspects   TO SEARCH
it, finds it unsatisfactory, gets up and moves to a
third table. He runs his hand over the surface. It
seems to pass muster.
```

On this search, Customer will still be inspecting, but I would choose not to "punch it up" until the next beat.

```
He inspects the fork.                               TO SCRUTINIZE
```

To scrutinize and to inspect are synonyms, but they do indicate shadings. If a character is performing a series of more or less the same actions, we should look for adjustments in the performance that lead toward escalation of the actions. For me, "to scrutinize" indicates more intensity, more concentration. It is as far as this particular action can go.

```
It'll do.                                           to accept
He looks up at Counterman.                          to include
```

Now that the inspection is over and Customer feels comfortable in the space, he wants to get on with his celebration, and he wants to "include" the whole world in it.

```
CUSTOMER: I'll have a piece of apple pie.        TO DECLARE
COUNTERMAN: I'm out of apple pie.                TO STATE (a fact)
CUSTOMER: What's that on the counter?            TO INQUIRE
COUNTERMAN: I'm saving that piece.               TO EXPLAIN
CUSTOMER: You're saving it?                       TO DOUBT
COUNTERMAN: There's a customer comes in around   TO ELABORATE
this time every night for apple pie -
but I've got cherry, blueberry, lemon meringue,  to suggest
key lime -
CUSTOMER: I want the apple pie.                   TO CONFIRM
COUNTERMAN: I'm sorry.                            TO APOLOGIZE
This customer would be very disappointed.        to explain
CUSTOMER: But you don't mind disappointing me.   TO ACCUSE
```

Remember, *all actions are wedded to a want*, and our characters do not give up their wants without a fight. Customer wants to celebrate. He does not expect to be deterred. After all, he is in the presence of a Celebrant, whose raison d'être is to serve him. Therefore, in the previous series of actions—in the verbal ping-pong that is going on—Customer is holding on for dear life to his want, and this will infuse *all* of his actions. At the same time, there is a growing reality that *conflicts* with Customer's expectation, and the struggle to hold on to his expectation while the reality of the situation begins to make itself manifest should be available to the audience in the actor's performance. If it is not, his action "to threaten" (which is coming up shortly) will arrive out of nowhere.

COUNTERMAN: I'll tell you what. I'll give you a piece of any other pie you want, on the house.	TO OFFER
CUSTOMER: No.	TO REFUSE
COUNTERMAN: I'll make it a la mode.	TO ENTICE
CUSTOMER: Listen - if you don't give me *that* piece of pie right now, I'll call the police.	TO WARN
COUNTERMAN: The Customer is a cop.	TO COUNTER
CUSTOMER: I don't care if he's the King of Siam.	TO DISMISS
Customer gets up and approaches the counter. Standing in front of the piece of apple pie, he takes out a gun.	TO THREATEN

"TO THREATEN" is an example of a narrative beat that is inherent in the explicit action described in the text. Still, when we add the camera, we can choose, if we wish, to articulate this beat further.

SECOND DRAMATIC BLOCK

COUNTERMAN: Hey, no guns allowed in here.	TO SCOLD

My first thought was "to protest" but I settled on "to scold" because it is incongruous, therefore comic.

CUSTOMER: I want this pie!	TO INSIST
Counterman looks toward door.	TO CHECK (for help)

"Looking toward the door" is another narrative beat that is dictated by the explicit actions of the text, but that can, if we wish, be punctuated further when we add the camera.

COUNTERMAN: I can't.	TO REFUSE
Counterman grabs pie.	TO PROTECT
CUSTOMER: Don't make me shoot!	TO WARN
COUNTERMAN: For a piece of pie?	TO QUESTION
CUSTOMER: I'll count to five.	to state (a fact)
One . . . two -	TO INTIMIDATE
COUNTERMAN: It's stupid.	TO PROTEST
CUSTOMER: Getting shot when you don't have to is stupid.	to disagree

Later, in the editing, we can make a final decision as to whether or not we will be on Customer for "to disagree," but in my visualization up to this point, I would put this line over Counterman, and so I do not regard it as an action that needs to be articulated.

Four!	TO CONVINCE

I am certain, however, that we should cut to the Customer for the above beat.

COUNTERMAN: Okay! Okay! It's yours.	TO SURRENDER
Counterman sets the pie back on the counter.	

Customer puts the gun away and sits at the counter.	TO CLAIM
He pushes the napkin and fork away.	to clear away (the past)
CUSTOMER: Could I have another fork and a fresh napkin, please?	TO OFFER (a truce)

"TO OFFER (a truce)" is a more pertinent and interesting interpretation of the previous action than a more obvious choice such as "to request," which is less so and is also redundant. The same goes for Counterman's response below.

Counterman places a new fork and napkin on the counter.	TO ACCEPT
CUSTOMER: Thank you.	TO FORGIVE

This is another interpretation of the action that goes beneath the surface of the dialogue. This is often referred to as the *subtext*.

COUNTERMAN: Something to drink?	to carry on (the tradition)

Counterman has lost this battle, but he has not lost his character or the tradition that he grew up in.

CUSTOMER: I'm fine.	TO PROCLAIM

This action is akin to Customer's first utterance: "Hi." The action then was "TO ANNOUNCE."

Counterman walks away from Customer. He leans on the end of the counter, his head in his hands: a picture of utter defeat.	TO GRIEVE

This is the fulcrum of our scene/film, the apparent defeat of Counterman's want. It is the nadir of the downward trajectory in his dramatic journey. Its full impact on Counterman must be made palpable to the audience, and a question should be raised in the audience's mind: "What will happen now?"

What we want to do is stop the action of our story here—to freeze the moment. If this story was being told orally, the narrator might choose this moment to relight his pipe. In blazing our trail through the forest we have come to an "apparent" end. I qualify *apparent* because the audience knows that the storyteller is not going to let the story fizzle out here—they have more faith than that. Or you can look at it another way: they *expect* more than that.

The question "What will happen next?" can only be answered with rising action, and that's what we find.

BEGINNING OF THIRD DRAMATIC BLOCK

After a beat, he (Counterman) steals a glance	TO MAKE SURE

Note: The term *beat* is used in screenplay texts to denote a unit of time and should not be confused with units of action.

```
at Customer who is wiping the new fork        TO MAKE CLEAN
vigorously - some might say compulsively.
A ray of hope comes to Counterman just        TO REALIZE
as the fork is about to cut into the pie.     (possibility)
COUNTERMAN: I never eat apple pie, myself.    TO TEST
Customer looks up at Counterman, quizzically. TO QUESTION
COUNTERMAN: I like it, but I just don't eat   TO CONFIRM
it.
CUSTOMER: Why not?                            TO CONFRONT
COUNTERMAN: Why?                              TO QUESTION (himself)
```

It is essential that we make it possible for the audience to participate in the unfolding of the story. One way of doing that is to make sure they are privy to the dilemma of our characters. For example, at this moment Counterman doesn't have a clue as to what he will say next.

```
COUNTERMAN: Well . . .                        to stall
because of that stuff they spray on them.     TO FIND (answer)
CUSTOMER: What stuff?                         TO CHALLENGE
COUNTERMAN: Something that causes cancer.     TO SPECIFY
CUSTOMER: I know what you're trying to do.    to refute
It's not going to work.                       TO DECLARE
COUNTERMAN: Maybe I'm being too cautious.     TO AGREE
Nobody's gonna get out of this world alive,
anyway. Apple pie is as good a way to go as any.
Probably better than most.
CUSTOMER: Would you just shut up!             TO ATTACK
Counterman raises his hands in surrender.     TO PLACATE
```

At the risk of being redundant, every action is an effect of a cause. The effect, "to placate," is due to the cause, "to attack."

```
He begins busying himself with a wiping rag.  to back off
The Customer stares at him.                    TO REGROUP
CUSTOMER: It doesn't make any sense.           TO PURSUE (truth)
Counterman says nothing.                       TO LULL


CUSTOMER: You got this cop coming in here      TO INSINUATE
eating apple pie, what - two, three times a week?
COUNTERMAN: Sometimes five.                    TO AFFIRM
CUSTOMER: So why didn't you tell the cop about TO ADMONISH
this spray?
COUNTERMAN: I did. But you know cops. They'll  TO DEFEND
eat anything.
Sure you don't want a cup of coffee to wash    to beguile
that down?
```

This last acting beat, "to beguile," will be heard over a shot of the Customer in my visualization. Hence, it would not be articulated and is not considered to be a narrative beat in my design at this point in the process.

```
CUSTOMER: I don't drink coffee.               TO NOTIFY
COUNTERMAN: Oh, no, why not?                   TO SHOW CONCERN
CUSTOMER: I heard it wasn't good for you.      TO EXPLAIN
COUNTERMAN: If I had to stop serving everything TO CONFIDE
that wasn't good for you, I'd be out of business.
```

```
CUSTOMER: You have a responsibility to your          TO REPRIMAND
customers.
COUNTERMAN: Hey, I'm not twisting anybody's arm.     TO JUSTIFY


Customer looks down at the piece of pie, hesitates,  to ponder
then places the fork on the counter.                 TO SURRENDER
CUSTOMER: What do I owe you?                          to admit (defeat)
```

I visualize this last group of three actions as being rendered in one shot. The narrative beat here, "to surrender," is articulated by the staging: placing the fork on the counter.

```
COUNTERMAN: Forget it, it's on me.                   TO CHEER UP
                                                     (Customer)
Customer lays two dollars on the counter and         TO REGAIN
stands.                                              (dignity)


COUNTERMAN: You sure you don't want to try           TO REACH OUT
the key lime?
Customer goes to the door,                           TO REJECT
stops, and turns back to Counterman.                 TO ADDRESS
CUSTOMER: Sorry about the gun.                        TO APOLOGIZE
COUNTERMAN: Maybe you ought to get rid of it.        TO ADVISE
CUSTOMER: I just bought it today. It's not           TO EXCUSE
even loaded.                                         (himself)
COUNTERMAN: No one knows that but you.               TO REJECT
                                                     (excuse)
CUSTOMER: I'm just tired of being pushed             TO COMPLAIN
around.
COUNTERMAN: That's no excuse.                         TO ADMONISH
The Customer hesitates a beat, then takes out        TO UNBURDEN
the gun and tosses it                               (himself)
to the Counterman.                                   TO CATCH
```

The last two narrative beats are examples of actions that require their own frame to render action palpably to the audience.

```
CUSTOMER: Give it to the cop.                        TO INSTRUCT
Customer turns and exits.                            TO VANISH
```

"To vanish" is an example of an action that requires its own frame to render a plot point that is important to understanding the story. The same is true of the following.

```
Counterman looks at the clock: 12:00.                TO CHECK
```

BEGINNING OF FOURTH DRAMATIC BLOCK

```
He places the gun out of sight,                     to conceal
goes to the piece of apple pie, replaces the        TO ANTICIPATE
napkin and fork, turns to the coffeepot and
pours a cup of coffee. As he turns to set it down
next to the apple pie,
a FEMALE COP sits in front of it. It is obvious     TO CLAIM
that she can take care of herself.
```

```
The Counterman smiles lovingly at the Female Cop.          TO WELCOME
She picks up the fork and smiles lovingly at the           TO CELEBRATE
piece of apple pie.
```

This last action verb resonates with Customer's initial want and therefore acknowledges the irony of the pie's ultimate demise.

DIRECTOR'S NOTEBOOK

You will want to keep an organized record of all of your work on the script, plus all of your "musings" on how you see the film, how you see the characters, the atmosphere, the "look."

Clurman writes:

> Whether or not directors set their thoughts down on paper, the general process goes on in their minds. It is this mental process I would stress rather than the "literary" activity. On the other hand, in *teaching* direction (wherever such a dubious course is hazarded) I suggest that the teachers insist on having the students state in writing all that they propose for themselves and their collaborators in the planning of a production. General notions or a nebulous inspiration may delude the student.

Your directing notebook will obviously include the work on narrative beats and also on staging and camera placement (consisting of floor plans, shot lists, and storyboards). This latter work will serve as a vehicle of communication to relevant crew members, for it is they who must execute your design.

We are now ready to proceed to our staging.

CHAPTER 8

STAGING AND CAMERA FOR
A PIECE OF APPLE PIE

STAGING

After we have drawn the floor plan of the diner (Figure 8-1), where do we start? In some scenes we might start at the beginning and work forward, and if we find that we are painting ourselves into a corner we can make adjustments. That's what our eraser is for. In general, you will find that for most dramatic scenes the fulcrum can be a fruitful place to begin choreographing your blocking. (Because *A Piece of Apple Pie* is also a complete film, some might call it the turning point, but because I consider the fulcrum to be a director's tool for articulation of this significant dramatic moment, I will refer to it as such.) However, for this scene, there is some other business to figure out beforehand.

The text tells us that "Counterman walks away from Customer." What it doesn't tell us is where Customer is, precisely, and we must know precisely. Before we figure out where

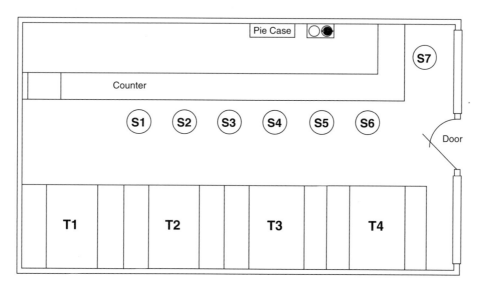

FIGURE 8-1

Floor plan for diner.

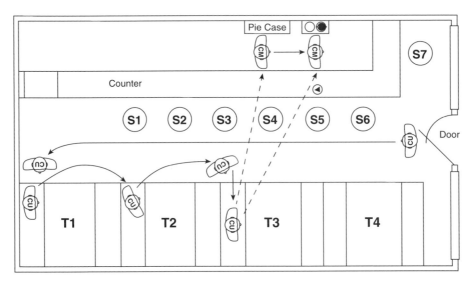

FIGURE 8-2

Finding pie's placement at the counter.

Counterman "walks to" when he "walks from," we should first determine in front of which stool the Counterman places the apple pie.

We have seven stools to choose from, but it becomes obvious fairly quickly that S1, 2, 3, 6, and 7 are not convenient to the pie case and coffee pot. Even if we move these two items (and sometimes we might choose to), my previsualization of the entire scene tells me that we should first try S4 or S5. The text tells us that Customer "walks the length of the counter, past the dish of apple pie, and sits at a table in the empty restaurant." Accordingly, S4 seems to be a likely choice because it allows time for Customer "to announce" himself, make his entrance into our film, and still gives him time to "take in" the apple pie on the counter. Before committing ourselves to S4, we should go through the rest of the scene and see if our selection holds up. Customer rejects two tables, so he would end up at table T3 if he initially chose the last table, T1, which makes psychological sense for his character and also gives us an opportunity to introduce the entire geography of the restaurant early on in the story. T3 is directly across from S4. Is that the spatial dynamics that will serve us best? Is there any reason why we shouldn't be satisfied with S4?

There is. If we put the pie in front of S4, the angle between the two men is less acute than if the pie were in front of S5 (Figure 8-2). In just a few moments, when Customer approaches the counter and sits, he will be head-on with Counterman, no matter which stool we choose. That being the case, it is better to begin with an angle between the two men that is appreciably different because changes in spatial angles can enunciate narrative beats, signifying to the audience that something has changed. S5 gives us an appreciable increase in the angle between the two men.

There is one more thing we should check before nailing down S5 as the spot at which the apple pie is placed. Will it accommodate Female Cop? We check the text: Counterman "turns to the coffee pot and pours a cup of coffee. As he turns to set it down next to the apple pie, a Female Cop sits in front of it." Perfect. S5 it is.

Now we are ready to decide on our fulcrum. Counterman is going to walk away "to grieve." We've already determined that it is necessary that we accentuate this moment. How can we contribute to this in our staging? How about changing the stage—using a part of the diner that has

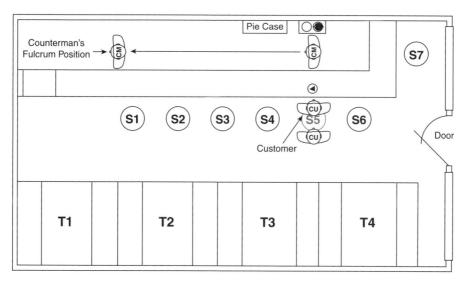

FIGURE 8-3

Finding a new stage for the fulcrum.

been introduced but not used up? Counterman would then walk to S1 (Figure 8-3). A new background comes into play, keeping the significance of the movement alive.

Another very important and often-used aspect of staging comes simultaneously into play here: *proximity*. When Customer stands in front of the piece of apple pie, takes out his gun, faces Counterman down, sits, requests a new napkin and fork—up through Counterman asking, "Something to drink?"—our adversaries are three to four feet apart. Sending Counterman to S1 decreases the proximity significantly (the distance between them increases). As mentioned earlier, change in spatial proximity is one of our key tools in making physical what is going on internally.

Notice that we have two narrative/dramatic categories (angle and proximity) working here simultaneously to establish our fulcrum—causing the moment to impinge quite palpably on the audience. Now all we have to do is to make sure we render with the camera the work we have done in our staging.

The remainder of our staging for this scene is relegated to rendering the action. Note that the text indicates that Counterman does not move from behind S1 until Customer exits. Do we agree with the screenwriter? Is there a reason why he would move? There is none that would not intrude on the exchange between the two men because any movement by Counterman toward Customer would be unnecessary and, therefore, dramatically wrong.

CAMERA

Obviously there is a difference between the specifics of designing a whole film and those of designing one scene, but our short film, which could be a dramatic scene in a larger film, is conveniently for our purposes a complete film, with a beginning, middle, and end. Continuing our Sistine Chapel metaphor, it will enable us to investigate dramatic/narrative concepts relating to a whole ceiling, while supplying us with an adequate variety of noses.

Before we begin adding the camera, I suggest that we make a list of the dramatic and narrative jobs that must be done. What I am stressing here by using the phrase *dramatic and narrative jobs* are actions, plot points, and all dramatic articulations that go beyond merely rendering the action. Some of these jobs are included in other categories, but a little redundancy is a small price to pay to ensure that we have everything we'll need to tell our story clearly and interestingly.

Jobs we have to do in *A Piece of Apple Pie*:

1. Pie's entrance into film
2. Counterman's entrance into film
3. Customer's entrance into film
4. Time on clock
5. Geography (layout of diner and fact that it is empty must be established early on)
6. Gun's entrance into film
7. Fulcrum
8. Light bulb (Counterman sees possibility)

Counterman sees possibility of what? Of still saving the pie! But what does he see with his eyes? What is the cause that establishes the effect of hope? He sees the vigorous cleaning of the fork. But how does he see it? A wide shot will not *signify* the essence of the moment. (My use of *signify* in relation to cinematic storytelling means simply the imparting of unambiguous information to the audience, whether it be behavioral, expository, plot, or atmospheric.) Counterman must see the wiping large in the frame—hands, napkin, and fork. An equation is then formed: along with Customer's past behavior, this new behavior will equal "possibility," or in general dramatic terms, "possibility" will signify the essence of the moment. Counterman and the audience should arrive at the answer to this equation at the same time. The audience will be more attuned to Counterman's dilemma—what will he do with this possibility?—if this information comes via Counterman's *strong* point of view. (A strong POV is one that calls the audience's attention to what a character is seeing and *implies a heightened significance.*)

9. Introduce Counterman's strong POV

After we decide to use a strong POV for the Counterman, we must first establish that he has one before we proceed too far into the film—certainly before we reach the moment of "seeing the possibility." He does look at the clock in a POV shot, and that helps, but it does not *signify*. We have to make it bigger, ratchet it up to prepare the audience for this more intense mode of Counterman's seeing: Customer's fork looming over the pie, visually compressed and isolated from the background, which is out of focus.

Can we introduce a strong POV earlier, one that will definitely signify? Yes, when Customer is inspecting the fork at the table, just before he looks up at Counterman. That way we kill two birds with one shot. We introduce strongly the POV of Counterman early on, with an image that will *resonate* when we see the POV of the second fork being wiped vigorously. At the same time we will have a close image size already in place when Customer "looks up at Counterman" in order "to include" him (narrative beat) and declares, "I'll have a piece of apple pie."

10. Customer relinquishes pie

This is a huge moment in the film. It must have a frame put around it so that its importance stands out. (Beginning directors often have trouble thinking in terms of "huge," especially for such an ordinary event, but there was nothing ordinary about it for Customer! If a director begins to think in these terms, the stories she tells will have a much better chance of being huge for an audience.)

11. Female Cop's entrance

How is Female Cop's entrance different from Counterman's and Customer's? Its function in the story is different. It is the punch line, if you will, and like any punch line, it must be set up so that when it appears, it stands alone, unencumbered. Counterman "pours a cup of coffee. As he turns to set it down next to the apple pie, a FEMALE COP sits in front of it." What could encumber this punch line—or any punch line, for that matter? Expository information could. It disrupts the moment, stealing much of its thunder. We want Female Cop to enter the frame so that she reveals herself fully, in all her glory. What possible expository material could get in the way? The frame could get in the way.

Every new shot contains an element of exposition. How do we solve this problem here? By using a *familiar image* (or in this instance, a *familiar frame*), in which we will replace one character in the frame with another. We will have Female Cop sit in the exact frame Customer did. But will that resonate with the audience after all the time and drama that has passed since Customer sat down at the counter? It will no doubt leave a trace, but it will not do the work that is required of it because it will not resonate *strongly*. Perhaps we could have Customer exit the same frame, but then we would be sacrificing the dynamics of the moment because, according to the spatial dynamics we have already set up in staging between Counterman and Customer, Counterman is at the other end of the counter. The camera will have no justification to be in the position to duplicate the familiar frame. Continuing our search through the screenplay, we discover an opportune moment to duplicate this familiar frame when Counterman replaces the napkin and fork after Customer leaves. Coming here, it will be appropriate to the essence of the moment, while it "forces" the audience to anticipate the empty frame being filled. Still, we have a problem. The frame is introduced too late in the scene to resonate fully. It seems to be an afterthought. We must then add another job to our list.

12. Introduce familiar frame early in the scene for Female Cop's entrance

Looking at the second paragraph on the first page of the screenplay, we have: "Counterman sets the pie on the counter along with a napkin and a fork." This is definitely where we should introduce the familiar frame, but the angle of this image points at Counterman, and that means that when Female Cop sits down, we would see her back. Now, in all my visualizations—including when I wrote the screenplay—I had always imagined Female Cop entering the shot from the front. Are there any drawbacks to the reverse angle; that is, seeing her back first? Actually, just the opposite is true. As is often the case, these glitches that we discover as we move along in our methodology can lead us to a solution that is superior to the original. In this case we will have a COP enter the film from the back (broadness of shoulders can indicate that this is a person who "can take care of HIMSELF"). Then in a reverse shot, we reveal FEMALE. Maybe we'll have her take her hat off and let her hair cascade down. So that we won't forget, we'll add it to our list of jobs.

13. Female Cop's reveal

One of the most dramatically effective entrances into a film is Guido's in *8½* (see Chapter 17). The reveal of Guido—the first time we see his face—is withheld from the audience for some time. That is an example of what I mean by "raising questions" in the audience's mind, thereby increasing their curiosity and their participation in the unfolding of the story. Coppola does it with Michael (Al Pacino) in *The Godfather* by showing him first entering the wedding reception from the rear. We know it is Michael because he is wearing an Army uniform. Only later is his face revealed.

We have two more questions to ask ourselves before we begin to put the camera to our floor plan. Is any narrative stylization necessary or desirable for this story? Do any of the characters need their own voice? In my visualization there is no point in complicating what is essentially a simple film with a recognizable style. (It could be argued that the accepted "generic" style—for want of a better word—is itself a style, just as Clurman considered "natural" acting a style.) Seeing no need for a subjective voice, we can say no to these two questions.

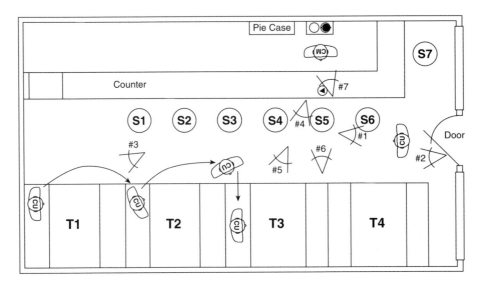

FIGURE 8-4

Camera setups imposed on floor plan for first dramatic block.

With no more questions for the moment (we should continue to be open to new discoveries and inspirations), the next step is to begin applying camera setups that render the staging as it is choreographed on the floor plan (Figure 8-4). We must keep in mind the 13 jobs we have identified, the narrative beats we must articulate, and the dramatic blocks and the fulcrum that we have uncovered. I suggest starting at the beginning of the scene/film.

As mentioned earlier, camera setups can contain one, or several, or many, edited shots. During the visualization process we imagine the edited shots. It is important to examine these edited shots carefully and take note of their orchestration, for without having an idea of how a scene will be edited, our "coverage" becomes at best generic, at worst a gamble.

CAMERA SETUPS FOR *A PIECE OF APPLE PIE*

Camera Setup #?: EXT. - LONG SHOT front of diner

Because the title shot and the end credit shot are basically the same and are not integral to what is happening in the diner (unless we can "read" who is inside), this shot (Figure 8-5) would most likely be taken after all interior shooting was completed.

BEGINNING OF FIRST DRAMATIC BLOCK

Camera Setup #?: CLOSE UP on APPLE PIE from pie tin to serving dish

Job #1: Pie's entrance into film. This is really the first shot of the film's action, and hence it should be visually strong. The strongest composition would be from an angle looking straight down on the pie (Figure 8-6). (Because this shot as described will take special measures [mounting camera over pie] and is purely mechanical with no acting required, it can be saved until last.)

The remainder of our camera setups will not follow exactly in the order in which they would be shot. They are arranged as closely as possible to the flow of the narrative and to show most clearly how the edited shots are embedded in the camera setups.

FIGURE 8-5 ——————————————————————————————————————

Front of diner for titles and end credits.

FIGURE 8-6 ——————————————————————————————————————

Pie's entrance into film.

Camera Setup #1: MEDIUM SHOT on CUSTOMER entering

Job #3: Customer's entrance into film. Customer enters the frame from the door and exits the frame camera right (Figure 8-7).

Camera Setup #2: LONG SHOT OF DINER as CUSTOMER goes to table

Job #5: Geography of diner. Customer walks to table T1 and sits, revealing that we are in a diner and that it is empty (Figure 8-8). The shot should be wide enough to include the area of the

FIGURE 8-7

Camera setup #1.

FIGURE 8-8

Camera setup #2.

counter (stool S1) where Counterman will go "to grieve" (see Figure 8-3). (When else would we have a chance to introduce this space so unobtrusively? This is an example of *expository material being embedded in action*.)

This shot also sets up the spatial dynamics for this dramatic block, so that when we go into separation, the audience will be sufficiently aware of where both men are in relation to each other. In other words, it precludes the need to resolve separation later.

Usually a camera setup will continue as long as it holds substantial cutting possibilities— meaning as long as it can continue to be relied upon to render individual segments of the action

FIGURE 8-9 ——

Camera setup #3.

commensurate with the overall design. Aside from this shot taking Customer to Table T1, I visualize it possibly being used to take Customer to T2 and T3, but I am quite sure that I will use it to take him to the Counter from table T3. I strongly suggest that you let the shot continue from Customer's entrance until "Standing in front of the piece of apple pie, he [Customer] takes out a gun." Then you can announce, "Cut!" The reason you keep it running between the sections that you have visualized as being in the edited film is to establish a rhythm and continuity for the actors for this entire dramatic block. (This is one of the great pedagogical advantages in shooting your first exercises on video.) Of course, if you are shooting film on a low budget and cannot afford this luxury, you'll cut sooner and get a "pick up" for the tail of the action when Customer goes to the counter.

Here is a very important point! The axis (explained in Chapter 1) between Counterman and Customer is established in this shot for this dramatic block. Customer will be looking camera right at Counterman, making it mandatory that Counterman look camera left in the reverse shot. Even if we cut at T1 before Customer looks up at Counterman, which most likely we will, the fact that Counterman is on the right side of the camera frame sets up the expectation that *if* Customer did look at Counterman, he would look camera right. Hence, in any subsequent shots using these spatial dynamics, we must pay heed to this expectation.

Camera Setup #3: MEDIUM CLOSE SHOT on CUSTOMER

This shot will begin with Customer moving into the frame and sitting at Table T1 (Figure 8-9) and will continue until he stands and exits the frame. (Elia Kazan admonished me once for turning the camera off before the character had exited the frame. I just didn't see how the exit from the frame would ever be used. His dictum was, "Always get an entrance and an exit to a frame." As for most dictums that are true most of the time, there are times when they might not be appropriate.)

We could have chosen here to track with Customer to the next table (or use the "master," setup #2), but a tracking shot would only continue the action rather then commenting on it. Instead, a cut on the Customer exiting the frame will serve as an exclamation point to his action and will then collide with a shot of Counterman "observing," camera setup #6 (Figure 8-13) or #7 (Figure 8-14).

FIGURE 8-10

Camera setup #4. Counterman's "ordinary" POV of Customer.

FIGURE 8-11

Camera setup #4. Continuation of Counterman's "ordinary" POV of Customer.

```
Camera Setup #4: MEDIUM LONG SHOT on CUSTOMER to MEDIUM CLOSE
```

This shot contains the spatial dynamics of the situation, in that it is not outside of the situation (as #2) but is between the two men (Figure 8-10). If a medium or close shot of Counterman precedes or follows this shot, it will "read" as a POV for Counterman. I call this an "ordinary" POV.

The shot will run from the Customer leaving T1 until he approaches the counter and takes out his gun (Figure 8-11).

FIGURE 8-12

Camera setup #5. Counterman's "strong" POV.

Camera Setup #5: COUNTERMAN'S "STRONG" POV

Job #9: Introduction of Counterman's strong POV. The camera should start rolling for this shot as Customer settles at T3, but the composition must be keyed to the fork being inspected. This is what we are going after here (Figure 8-12). This is not only what the Counterman sees but what is being *actively registered by his mind.* The shot will continue until Customer looks up at Counterman and announces, "I'll have a piece of apple pie."

All of our visualizations contain composition. How do you visualize the fork being inspected? Let's work backwards to the close image of Customer's face, declaring, "I'll have a piece of apple pie." That is where you will find your composition: the fork being held up in front of that face for inspection.

The use of a longer lens here, as suggested earlier, isolates the fork against Customer's face, and it does something even more important. It introduces this *mode of seeing* to the audience so that it will not seem "out of character" later on, when we will want to isolate from its background the fork being wiped vigorously, setting up Counterman's light bulb (the "possibility" that he might still save the day).

Camera Setup #6: MEDIUM SHOT on COUNTERMAN

Jobs #2 and #10: Counterman's entrance into film and introduction of familiar frame for Female Cop's entrance (Figure 8-13). We will write down at the end of the shot list that we will have to get two *inserts* of the clock (i.e., Job #4). (Just as *coverage* can be a dangerous word, so can *insert* because it can imply "afterthought" rather than an integrated element.) One thing to consider here is that the clock has the same angle and image size in both shots, so that the audience does not have to readjust its orientation for the second shot.

Camera Setup #7: CLOSE-UP on COUNTERMAN

Job #9: Required component of POV. For a POV to become assigned to a subject by the audience, it must come off a close-up (Figure 8-14) or medium close-up of the subject or end with either of them. The same is true of subjective shots.

FIGURE 8-13 ───

Camera setup #6.

FIGURE 8-14 ───

Camera setup #7.

This shot can be started when Customer sits at the first table, primarily to allow the actor to "get up to speed." In my visualization I do not see a close-up of Counterman until just before the last fork is being scrutinized, but I could be wrong! I won't be sure until my final edit. Camera set-ups are born from the director's visualization of an edited scene, but within reason I encourage you to give yourself alternative coverage by the use of generous overlapping of setups.

This shot will obviously be used for Counterman "to observe," but that narrative beat was not listed in the original detective work for this moment. Why was it overlooked? Because it is a *reaction* not written into the script! Reactions by actors, and the shots that render them, are often overlooked. However, if you employ the methodology suggested in this book, the "backup systems" will ensure that you get what you need. You simply reach back into the salad bowl, pull out a piece of cucumber, slice it in half, and then return both pieces to the bowl.

The connecting tissue between the first and second dramatic block is the moment when Customer, who has been sitting at Table T3, "stands and approaches the counter." As with most, but not all, connecting tissue, it acts as a bridge from one geographical area, or *stage*, to another.

My first choice is to render this action from camera setup #2 (see Figure 8-8), a familiar image. Because it is appreciably wider than the series of shots we have just ended, and because it is an angle that takes us outside of the spatial dynamics that exist between the two men, it will serve to act as a *release shot*—in this case, a brief release of the tension that has been building not only storywise but due to our sequence of separation shots. Now the separation is resolved once again (a key element in choosing this shot), and the audience is placed outside of the spatial dynamics, causing them to unconsciously relax a bit because the narrator has relaxed a bit. We should recognize this and pounce on it! *Just when we get the audience leaning in one direction, hit them with something from the other direction. Sometimes it's a freight train; sometimes it's a feather.*

What will we hit them with here? The entrance of the gun into our film, which is the beginning of the second dramatic block. We have the entrance of the gun covered from two camera setups: #2 (Figure 8-8) and #4 (Figure 8-11). Is there a third entrance hidden here? One that is stronger and more amusing? I believe there is: the entrance of the gun through Counterman's scolding, "Hey, no guns allowed in here," from camera setup #8 (Figure 8-16). Only then do we see it!

BEGINNING OF SECOND DRAMATIC BLOCK

This block should overlap in coverage with the first one; hence, it will start with Customer approaching Counter. It will run until "Counterman, defeated, walks away from Customer." The staging is relatively static in this block. There is no making physical of what is going on internally that we have to render through staging. When we get into static situations like this (people sitting around a table), unless we have an overriding style, we find ourselves resorting to classical coverage, and there is nothing wrong with that. In fact, it would be wrong not to because this section will rely solely on the changing of image size and angles to articulate the narrative beats, so we have to make certain that we have sufficient images to do the job. Figure 8-15 shows the classical coverage for this situation, except that the camera will *jump* the axis when Counterman grabs the pie, to protect it. The physical and dramatic action of grabbing the pie will generate sufficient energy to warrant such strong punctuation.

Camera Setup #8: MEDIUM CLOSE SHOT on COUNTERMAN

In this shot we will render Counterman "scolding," "refusing," and finally "protecting." He will lunge forward in the frame and grab the pie (Figure 8-16).

As Counterman starts backwards with the pie, we will jump the axis by cutting on the move to camera setup #10 (Figure 8-17).

Camera Setup #10: CLOSE SHOT on COUNTERMAN & PIE

On the cut from camera setup #8 (see Figure 8-16), Counterman will move backwards into the frame holding the apple pie, looking camera right (Figure 8-17) when a second ago he was looking camera left. For this to work, the shot must be "tight" on his head, but we also need to show the pie to convey "to protect." Aside from doing our dramatic jobs, the composition stresses the incongruity of the behavior, and hence the comedy.

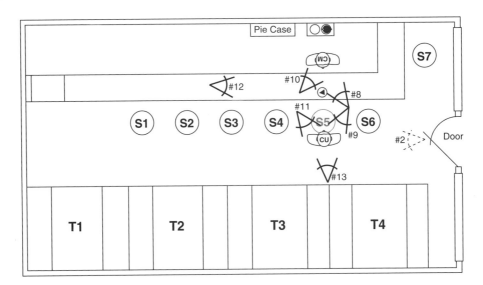

FIGURE 8-15

Camera setups imposed on floor plan for second dramatic block.

FIGURE 8-16

Camera setup #8. Counterman looking camera left.

```
Camera Setup #9 (Reverse of #8): MEDIUM CLOSE SHOT on CUSTOMER & GUN
```

   Job #6: Reveal of gun (Figure 8-18).

```
Camera Setup #11 (Reverse of #10): CLOSE SHOT on CUSTOMER & GUN
```

FIGURE 8-17

Camera setup #10. Jumping the axis.

FIGURE 8-18

Camera setup #9. Customer looks camera right.

I am relying on only camera setups #10 (Figure 8-19) and #11 (Figure 8-20) to elaborate the "face-off" between the two men. Others might see it differently. I did run through a visualization in which there was stronger elaboration: tighter and tighter images (finger on trigger, eyes, and so on). (Sergio Leone does it so well in *The Good, the Bad, and the Ugly* [1967, Italian-Spanish].) However, I feel that it would be a matter of overkill for this film. That's my sensibility. There is no reason you have to accept it if you direct this film. The point I want to emphasize is: *Recognize your dramatic moments and then go through all the possibilities for rendering those moments.*

FIGURE 8-19 ——

Continuation of camera setup #10. Counterman looks camera right.

FIGURE 8-20 ——

Camera setup #11. Customer looks camera left.

My choice in this case would be to rely more on the actors' performances, and hence just the two men in separation, cutting back and forth between them. Remember, we have yet to resolve the spatial separation since we've crossed the axis. We will have to do that, and when we do we will make sure that it also serves to articulate a narrative beat.

Camera Setup #12: MEDIUM TWO-SHOT

This shot (Figure 8-21) will resolve the separation of shots #10 and #11, and hence no part of it will appear in the edited version until after the axis is jumped. Still (in the best of circumstances),

FIGURE 8-21

Camera setup #12. Resolves separation.

we should begin the *take* as Customer approaches the counter and walks into the shot, camera right, and keep it running until Counterman walks out of the shot, camera left, "to grieve." When Counterman leaves the frame, it can be adjusted for the best composition on Customer. Give it a moment or so, and then announce, "Cut." Again, shooting this way gives us extra coverage that we most likely will not use, but it allows the actors to begin at, then keep going through, a complete block of action.

Note: When shooting actors within a composition that is subject to change, the tripod should not be locked in place, so that even slight adjustments to the framing can be made to accommodate the actor's movements.

Camera Setup #13: FAMILIAR FRAME TURNS INTO MEDIUM SHOT OVER CUSTOMER'S LEFT SHOULDER on COUNTERMAN, PANS WITH HIM

This camera setup (Figure 8-22) is exactly the same framing as camera setup #6, but a new number is given to reduce confusion.

The first job of this camera setup will be to show Customer taking command of the stool after Counterman surrenders the pie. Because its framing begins the same as camera setup #6 (Figure 8-13)—the familiar frame for entrance of Female Cop—it will serve to keep that frame alive. It can also serve to render some or all of the actions that Counterman performs after his surrender and before he walks away "to grieve" (Figure 8-23).

In panning with Counterman the shot will "lose" Customer. This will have the effect of isolating Counterman's grief.

The camera will come to a complete rest as, or slightly before, the Counterman reaches his new position, in a frame that now renders him in a medium shot (Figure 8-24).

Camera Setup #14: CLOSE-UP on COUNTERMAN (FULCRUM)

This shot overlaps with #13. Counterman will enter shot from camera right, "lean on the counter, his head in hands: a picture of utter defeat." *This is the fulcrum* (Figure 8-25). Because

FIGURE 8-22

Camera setup #13.

FIGURE 8-23

Beginning of pan in camera setup #13.

Counterman's grief is given its own frame, the audience is made more aware of it. It becomes more palpable to them, and the question is raised: What will happen next?

The audience knows the drama is not over. They expect Counterman will *do something* to save the pie. But what?

Note: A real possibility here is to slowly *push in* even closer on Counterman's "head in hands" to elaborate this moment—make it larger—and to set up Counterman's action, "to make certain," and his realization of the possibility that he can still save the day.

FIGURE 8-24 ——————————————————————————————————

Camera comes to rest in camera setup #13.

END OF SECOND DRAMATIC BLOCK

Camera setup #14 ends the second dramatic block by setting up the fulcrum. It also serves as con-necting tissue and carries us into the third dramatic block and the rising action of the protagonist that follows the fulcrum.

It is from camera setup #14, the fulcrum (Figure 8-25), that Counterman will steal a glance at Customer, and because it is a close-up, it will serve to generate the next edited shot, Counterman's strong POV of the vigorous wiping of the fork (Figure 8-26).

BEGINNING OF THIRD DRAMATIC BLOCK

Camera Setup #15: COUNTERMAN'S STRONG POV

This is the only shot involving an actor that might be referred to, for lack of a better word, as an *insert*. There is no performance required. The longer focal length introduced earlier will be used here to separate the fork, napkin, and hands from the background.

Camera Setup #16 & 16A: MEDIUM & MEDIUM CLOSE-UP on COUNTERMAN

Figure 8-27 shows the camera setups imposed on the floor plan for the third dramatic block. From setups #16 and 16A two image sizes of Counterman will be shot (Figures 8-28 and 8-29). Because there is change in proximity—more distance between Counterman and Customer—the medium shot will acknowledge that, but the medium close-up will allow for variation in articula-tion (for "punching up" narrative beats). These two shots, along with #18 (Figure 8-32), will be used to render Counterman from the fulcrum through catching the gun. From setups #17 and 17A two image sizes of Customer will be shot (Figures 8-30 and 8-31).

FIGURE 8-25 ——————————————————————————————

Camera setup #14. The fulcrum.

FIGURE 8-26 ——————————————————————————————

Camera setup #15.

Camera Setup #17 & 17A (Reverse of #16 & 16A): MEDIUM & MEDIUM CLOSE-UP
on CUSTOMER

Setup #17, with a focus change and perhaps a slight adjustment in lighting, will also render
Customer at the doorway for the exchange with Counterman concerning the gun (Figures 8-30
and 8-31).

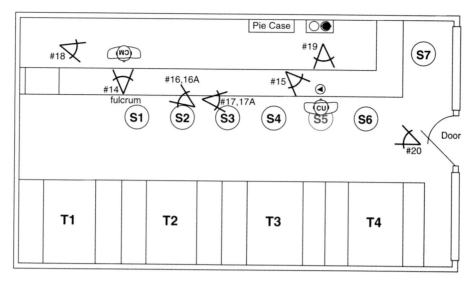

FIGURE 8-27

Camera setups imposed on floor plan for third dramatic block.

FIGURE 8-28

Camera setup #16.

Camera Setup #18: LONG SHOT OVER COUNTERMAN'S PROFILE

This shot resolves separation (Figure 8-32), and in my visualization of the edited scene I see it rendering Counterman's "busying himself with the wiping rag." It is an angle that underplays Counterman's action, making it more comedic, and at the same time we have Customer in the background, "pondering."

FIGURE 8-29 ————————————————————————————————————

Camera setup #16A.

FIGURE 8-30 ————————————————————————————————————

Camera setup #17.

As mentioned earlier in regard to coverage, in these static staging situations (and here we have many narrative beats to articulate) it is wise to begin this setup from the fulcrum and keep it going until Customer leaves the counter. It might come in very handy in the editing room. (When cutting between characters, it is not obligatory to use the same size image. You can use a medium shot for one character and a close shot for another, or you might go from an over the shoulder of one to a medium on the reverse. This disparity in image size helps to heighten the sense of space between characters.)

FIGURE 8-31

Camera setup #17A.

FIGURE 8-32

Camera setup #18.

Camera Setup #19: MEDIUM CLOSE-UP on CUSTOMER & PIE

Job #10: Customer relinquishes pie. In my visualization I cut to this shot when "Customer looks down at the piece of pie, hesitates, then places the fork on the counter."

In shooting this setup I would start from when Customer sits down at the counter in front of the pie (Figure 8-33).

FIGURE 8-33 ————————————————————————————————————

Camera setup #19.

FIGURE 8-34 ————————————————————————————————————

Camera setup #20.

Camera Setup #20: LONG SHOT on COUNTERMAN (same as Setup #2)

This is the farthest we have been from Counterman (Figure 8-34). Customer exits, leaving Counterman with a moment to deal with the consequences of what just happened. His victory has left a bittersweet taste. He did not hold up his tradition. Not all of this will be available to the audience intellectually at that moment, but as we see him standing there, at the far end of his empty restaurant, we will intuit much. We will understand, and it is the cut to the long shot that will help get

FIGURE 8-35

Continuation of camera setup #20.

FIGURE 8-36

Clock insert.

us there. Just as the grief didn't last forever, neither does this ambivalence. Counterman's old expectations come flooding back. He looks at the clock (Figure 8-35).

From this long shot, Counterman needs a large movement to signify looking at the clock. Going in closer merely to accomplish this would be an overemphasis, but if his action is large enough in the existing frame, the audience can read it. Because we can place a clock anywhere we want to, we will hang it on the back wall of the diner so that Counterman must turn away from the door to see the clock. Now that we know where to hang the clock, we will use the same image size and angle when we shoot the clock for the first insert (Figure 8-36). This will ensure that the

FIGURE 8-37

Camera setup #21. Renewing the familiar frame.

audience will not have to make an adjustment as to where the clock is to perceive immediately that it is now exactly 12:00.

Up until now we have dealt more with real time than film time. Oh, we might discover in the editing room that we might have to cut out a step or two before Customer gets to the first booth (this will depend on the size of the actual diner), but we have not used compression for dramatic purposes. Let's see what happens next if we continue this same narrative style.

Counterman would walk from stool S1 to S5 and replace the fork and knife. Do we really want to see him cover all that distance? What dramatic or narrative reason would there be for him doing so? None. So what can we do? Cut! To what? To the familiar frame that was set up for Female Cop's entrance! It was introduced in camera setup #6, when Counterman was anticipating her arrival by placing the pie and a fork and napkin in the frame. It was kept alive in setup #13, when Customer "claimed" the stool. Now, by simply cutting to this same frame, we jump the story forward. The predictable rhythm has been interrupted, and we stay ahead of the audience.

We cut from the clock to Counterman replacing the napkin and the fork (Figure 8-37). He then turns for the coffee. When his back is turned, Cop enters and sits (Figure 8-38).

What about the gun? Do we have to show Counterman concealing it? No. It is expository information that is dealt with when Counterman appears in the next frame without it. To ensure that the audience is satisfied with this information, we will see to it that Counterman "ponders over the gun" for a beat before he checks the clock.

BEGINNING OF FOURTH DRAMATIC BLOCK

Camera Setup #21: FAMILIAR FRAME FOR FEMALE COP'S ENTRANCE becomes an OVER THE SHOULDER on COUNTERMAN

Job #11: Renew the familiar frame for entrance of Female Cop. (This is the same frame as camera setups #6 and #13.) Counterman turns to get the coffee, and Female Cop enters and sits in the familiar frame (Figure 8-38).

FIGURE 8-38 ———————————————————————————

Continuation of camera setup #21. Cop enters familiar frame and sits.

FIGURE 8-39 ———————————————————————————

Camera setup #22. Reveal of punch line.

On a low-budget shoot, sets are not usually built (certainly not a complete diner). So, along with the clock alluded to earlier, the pie case and especially the coffeepot might not be in the ideal location, but with a little bit of ingenuity you can often make a real location work as well as if you had one built. The pot of coffee should be placed exactly where you want it—within the familiar frame—because if you have to pan to contain Counterman's actions, the familiar frame will no longer be the familiar frame.

As the action continues in this frame, Counterman turns and sees the Cop.

FIGURE 8-40 ――――――――――――――――――――――――――――――

Camera setup #23. Counterman could burst, he's so happy.

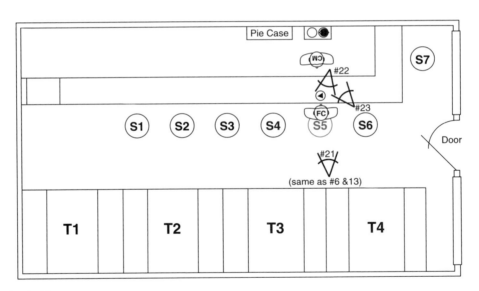

FIGURE 8-41 ――――――――――――――――――――――――――――――

Camera setups imposed on floor plan for fourth dramatic block.

```
Camera Setup #22: MEDIUM CLOSE SHOT on FEMALE COP & PIE
```

Job #13: Reveal of Female Cop (Figure 8-39).

When Counterman turns and sees the Cop, he is ecstatic (Figure 8-40). Figure 8-41 shows the camera setups imposed on the floor plan for the fourth dramatic block.

Camera Setup #23: CLOSE SHOT on COUNTERMAN

You must ask yourself here: Is this really the shot to end the film? I think it is, taking into account that we are going back to the "bookends" of the outside of the diner. The right music coming up at this point will most likely give us all the closure this story needs. That's what I feel in my present visualization, which should at some point before shooting include sound effects, line readings, and music. It should work for you fully before you ever get on the set. If it does not, don't count on finding how to fix it there, and do not rely on the editing room to rescue you. *In the best of all possible worlds, the editing process should be one of enhancement, not salvage.*

CONCLUSION

Directors who are on a tight budget might find the coverage for this scene to be too extravagant if they are shooting on film. The important consideration always is that the actors are given the time they need to get to an emotional place—to get up to speed psychologically—and the longer, overlapping takes offer the actor that opportunity. However, there is an unwritten rule that all successful directors obey: *We do what we have to do to get the film made with the resources that we have.* There is yet an even more important rule that should supersede that one. *We do nothing that is illegal or unethical, and we try as hard as we can to be kind.*

At the same time, directors must respect themselves and their work. There are times when they will, accidentally or out of necessity, ruffle feathers. It could be an actor or crewmember, and it is almost unavoidable with the tension that is generated during a shoot—due to the long hours, delays caused by weather, sudden loss of locations, clashes of personalities, and so on. What the director must try to do is keep her or his emotions under wraps. Do not lock horns; instead, try reason and logic. What if this approach does not work? My belief is that everyone in the cast or crew is there to serve the director's vision, so finally, the director must insist. How that manifests itself will depend on the director's character, the urgency of the circumstance, and of course the actions and reactions of those who are causing problems.

C H A P T E R   9

MARKING SHOOTING SCRIPT WITH CAMERA SETUPS

We want to make it easy to see schematically what coverage we have during the different sections of the script. It serves to double check the work we have done, and it will later serve as a guide for the director of photography, the assistant director, and the production manager, as well as the film editor in postproduction.

I have reduced the shooting script and placed it to one side of the page for economy, but all you have to do is place a blank page across from the text of your screenplay and make your marks on it.

The numbers above each shot refer back to the shot list numbers.

EXT. DINER - NIGHT

An Edward Hopper atmosphere.
MAIN TITLE AND CREDITS

INT. DINER - NIGHT
Close on last piece of apple pie being
taken from a pie tin and placed on a
serving dish.

Wider as COUNTERMAN sets the pie on the
counter along with a napkin and fork. He
looks toward the door as CUSTOMER enters.

                          CUSTOMER
Good evening.

                          COUNTERMAN
Hi.

Counterman looks at the wall clock: 11:55.
Customer walks the length of the counter,
past the dish of apple pie, and sits at
a table in the empty restaurant, facing
Counterman.

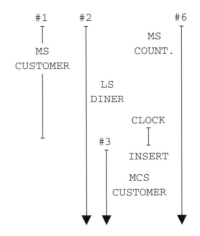

```
                                    COUNTERMAN      #2   #3              #6
Need a menu?                                        ▲    ▲               ▲
                                                   LS        MCS    MS
                                    CUSTOMER       DINER      CUST.  COUNT.
(inspecting tabletop)
No.

Customer stands up and moves to the                      │    #4
next table, inspects it, finds it                   │   #7        │
unsatisfactory, gets up and moves to a             │           #5
third table. He runs his hand over the             │   CV      │
surface. It seems to pass muster. He               │   COUNT.  STRONG
inspects the fork. It'll do. He looks up           │           POV
at Counterman.                                      │           │


                                    CUSTOMER        │           │
I'll have a piece of apple pie.                     │           │


                                    COUNTERMAN      │           │
I'm out of apple pie.                               │           │


                                    CUSTOMER        │           │
What's that on the counter?                         │           │


                                    COUNTERMAN      │
I'm saving that piece.                              │


                                    CUSTOMER
What do you mean, you're saving it?


                                    COUNTERMAN
There's a customer comes in around this
time every night for apple pie - but I've
got cherry, blueberry, lemon meringue, key
lime -


                                    CUSTOMER
I want the apple pie.


                                    COUNTERMAN
I'm sorry. This customer would be very
disappointed.


                                    CUSTOMER
But you don't mind disappointing me.


                                    COUNTERMAN
I'll tell you what. I'll give you a piece
of any other pie you want, on the house.


                                    CUSTOMER
No.                                                 ▼    ▼               ▼
```

COUNTERMAN
I'll make it a la mode.

                                    CUSTOMER
Listen – if you don't give me that piece
of pie right now, I'll call the police.

                                    COUNTERMAN
The Customer is a cop.

                                    CUSTOMER
I don't care if he's the King of Siam.

Customer gets up and approaches the
counter. Standing in front of the piece
of apple pie, he takes out a gun.

                                    COUNTERMAN
Hey, no guns allowed in here.

                                    CUSTOMER
I want this pie!

                                    COUNTERMAN
(looks toward door)
I can't.
(grabs pie)

                                    CUSTOMER
Don't make me shoot!

                                    COUNTERMAN
For a piece of pie?

                                    CUSTOMER
I'll count to ve. One . . . two –

                                    COUNTERMAN
It's stupid.

                                    CUSTOMER
Getting shot when you don't have to is
stupid.
Four!

                                    COUNTERMAN
Okay! Okay! It's yours.

Counterman sets the pie back on the
counter. Customer puts the gun away and
sits on the stool. He pushes the napkin
and fork away.

                                    CUSTOMER
Could I have another fork and a fresh
napkin, please?

Diagram annotations:
#2 LS DINER
#4 MCS CUST.
#6 MS COUNT.
#8 MS COUNT.
#9
#12
MC CUST. & GUN
#10 CS COUNT. & PIE
#11
CS CUST. & GUN
M2S
#12 M2S
#13
FAM. FRAME PANS

Counterman places a new fork and
napkin on the counter.

                   CUSTOMER
Thank you.

                 COUNTERMAN
Something to drink?

                   CUSTOMER
I'm fine.

Counterman walks away from Customer.

He leans on the end of the counter,
his head in his hands: a picture
of utter defeat. After a beat, he
steals a glance at Customer who is
wiping the new fork vigorously –
some might say compulsively.
A ray of hope comes to Counterman
just as the fork is about to cut
into the pie.

                 COUNTERMAN

I never eat apple pie, myself.

Customer looks up at Counterman,
quizzically.

                 COUNTERMAN
I like it, but I just don't eat it.

                   CUSTOMER
Why not?

                 COUNTERMAN
Why? Well . . . because of that
stuff they spray on them.

                   CUSTOMER
What stuff?

                 COUNTERMAN
Something that causes cancer.

                   CUSTOMER
I know what you're trying to do.
It's not going to work.

                 COUNTERMAN
Maybe I'm being too cautious.
Nobody's gonna get out of this world
alive, anyway. Apple pie is as good

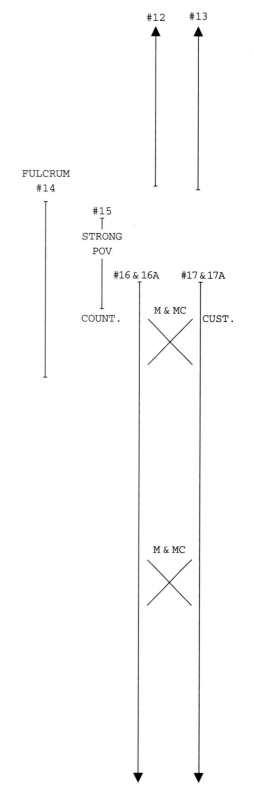

a way to go as any. Probably
better than most.

                              CUSTOMER
Would you just shut up!

Counterman raises his hands in surrender.
He begins busying himself with a wiping
rag.

The Customer stares at him.

                              CUSTOMER
It doesn't make any sense.

Counterman says nothing.

                              CUSTOMER
You got this cop coming in here eating
apple pie, what – two, three times a
week?

                              COUNTERMAN
Sometimes five.

                              CUSTOMER
So why didn't you tell the cop about this
spray?

                              COUNTERMAN
I did. But you know cops. They'll eat
anything. Sure you don't want a cup of
coffee to wash that down?

                              CUSTOMER
I don't drink coffee.

                              COUNTERMAN
Oh, no, why not?

                              CUSTOMER
I heard it wasn't good for you.

                              COUNTERMAN
If I had to stop serving everything
that wasn't good for you, I'd be out of
business.

                              CUSTOMER
You have a responsibility to your
customers.

                              COUNTERMAN
Hey, I'm not twisting anybody's arm.

Customer looks down at the piece of pie,
hesitates, then places the fork on the
counter.

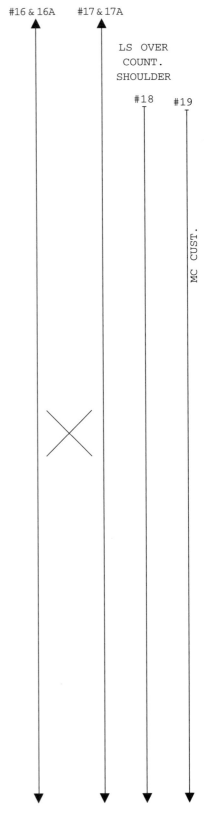

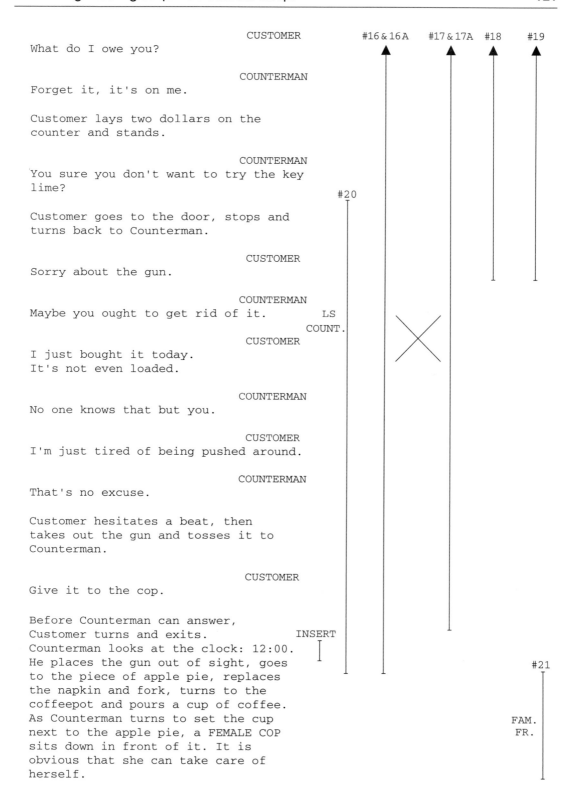

                                    CUSTOMER   #16 & 16A   #17 & 17A   #18   #19
What do I owe you?

                                    COUNTERMAN
Forget it, it's on me.

Customer lays two dollars on the
counter and stands.

                                    COUNTERMAN
You sure you don't want to try the key
lime?   #20

Customer goes to the door, stops and
turns back to Counterman.

                                    CUSTOMER
Sorry about the gun.

                                    COUNTERMAN
Maybe you ought to get rid of it.   LS
                                       COUNT.
                                    CUSTOMER
I just bought it today.
It's not even loaded.

                                    COUNTERMAN
No one knows that but you.

                                    CUSTOMER
I'm just tired of being pushed around.

                                    COUNTERMAN
That's no excuse.

Customer hesitates a beat, then
takes out the gun and tosses it to
Counterman.

                                    CUSTOMER
Give it to the cop.

Before Counterman can answer,
Customer turns and exits.   INSERT
Counterman looks at the clock: 12:00.
He places the gun out of sight, goes   #21
to the piece of apple pie, replaces
the napkin and fork, turns to the
coffeepot and pours a cup of coffee.
As Counterman turns to set the cup   FAM.
next to the apple pie, a FEMALE COP   FR.
sits down in front of it. It is
obvious that she can take care of
herself.

```
The Counterman smiles lovingly at        #22      #23
the Female Cop. She picks up the    REVEAL ⌐      ⌐ CU
fork and smiles lovingly at the       COP  |      | COUNT.
piece of apple Pie.                        ⌐      | SMILE
                                                  ⌐
```

```
EXT. DINER - NIGHT
It's quiet.
```

```
FADE OUT:
```

Now that we have got our detective work, staging, and camera completed, it is a good idea to *sit back and take it all in—as Michelangelo did. Get down off the scaffold and take a good look at the whole ceiling*, then climb back up if need be to take a good look at the nose that looks out of place, or perhaps, to our chagrin, to discover there is a nose missing.

If nothing jumps out at us, check these three areas: entrance of main characters, reveals, and elaboration. I've already decided not to overly elaborate the gun standoff a la Leone, but there is at least one moment that has begun to make its presence felt on me: when Customer "scrutinizes" the fork that he finally accepts. This beat should be prolonged by a cut to Counterman observing, and then in another cut to him when the fork is accepted. This elaborative *phrase* would be comprised of the following shots:

```
Customer picks up fork and begins to scrutinize.
CUT TO: Counterman observing.
CUT TO: Customer turning fork over.
CUT TO: Counterman weighing outcome.
CUT TO: Customer putting fork down on the table and looking up at
    Counterman (to include him), and declaring, "I'll have a piece of
    apple pie."
CUT TO: Counterman, blindsided by the order.
```

We must not forget to add another narrative beat to our list (to observe), and continue through the whole film in this manner, making our final "director's cut." Next we should make a final check on the overall camera design by looking at the schematic of the camera setups notated on the shooting script. This schematic offers a possibility of that design by telling us exactly what images are available and when. We should go through the entire screenplay now while asking the following questions: Does the camera render the staging clearly? Do the images available to us allow for a dramatic and aesthetic design for the whole piece while rendering the essence of every moment?

One aspect of our design that you should take note of is that our close-ups are saved, except for the above elaboration, for the showdown with the gun, when the two men are in the closest proximity to each other and tension is at its highest (second dramatic block). The third dramatic block, the longest, has the most coverage, giving us the most options, and the images acknowledge the space separating the two men, contrasting with the close proximity that existed in the prior dramatic block. There is no provision for a close-up on either man. Should there be? I feel that close-ups here would work against the overall design and would be a case of overuse of one of our most powerful dramatic weapons—but I should be aware of that lack.

Going over the possibilities inherent in the schematic of camera setups, I feel confident that the elaboration of beats can be articulated economically and powerfully with the shots we have. We save the last close-up for our last image inside the diner: Counterman beaming from ear to ear, so happy he could burst.

C H A P T E R   1 0

WORKING WITH ACTORS

Hitchcock said that if he were running a film school he would not let students near a camera for the first two years. In today's world, that film school would soon find itself bereft of students, for the camera serves as a validation that one is indeed pursuing a career in film. But too often, for too many new directors, the camera and its incumbent technology get in the way of what we will be touching on in this chapter: directing the actor. It might be instructive here to point out that there are fewer directors of photography who have made it as directors than there are actors who direct—many more actors: John Cassavetes, Robert Redford, Warren Beatty, Robert De Niro, Jodie Foster, Sean Penn, Mel Gibson, and Clint Eastwood to name but a few. Actors, aside from having experiential insights into the craft of acting, have also (those who have studied formally) been immersed in the "soup" of dramatic storytelling and have accepted (those who become successful directors) the dramatic imperatives.

Directing actors is the most experiential aspect of the craft of film directing. It is not something you can learn from watching film. It is not something that can be taught in a crash course. I can, and have, taught students the conceptual aspects of filmmaking in one semester, but never has it been demonstrated to me, or to the rest of the faculty at Columbia, that students can direct actors after 14 weeks—or even, for most, after two years. We are talking serious directing—which means getting performances that are not only believable but interesting.

Most actors who have studied formally have been told not to expect *any* help from the majority of film directors. That doesn't mean you can't surprise them, and in fact it is your obligation to your craft (and one hopes, your art) to learn this vital area—to learn to help in the creation of *life* from a page of text. There are some things that can help you in this process—things that can help you begin to work with actors in an intelligent, interactive way as you begin your on-the-job training while making films. For this is where the majority of film directors nowadays receive their training in directing actors.

You can help the process along, and make gigantic strides in your insight and confidence, by studying acting to find out what it is like. Secondly, to really learn how to work with actors—to sink your teeth into this rather delicate relationship—I strongly recommend that you direct theater. Choose a contemporary one-act play, something with no more than four actors, to begin with (two will suffice). It is also helpful to sit in on scene classes—classes where actors perform a scene that is then critiqued by a professional acting teacher. This is a very "safe" way to approach the process. After you are acclimated to the process you might choose to join in directing your own scenes for the class.

Years ago I studied acting, and I disliked it—just as you might if you study acting—but by forcing myself to act, I gained knowledge of the actor's craft that I could not get from books or from directing itself. I gained experiential knowledge that allowed me to understand, viscerally, the actor's fears and vulnerability. I also experienced something of the process to boot. I was asked to present a silent scene—just me, doing something meaningful. I chose a "goodbye" scene in which I would give my final farewell to a friend who had died.

On the day of my presentation I prepared a bed, placed a "body" (made from pillows) on it, placed a photograph of a bald model that I had cut out of a magazine (an actual friend had died, bald from chemotherapy) on top of the "head," and covered the pillows and the photograph with a blanket. I stepped outside the door of the studio, hoping to find the proper emotion in the hallway, but I felt nothing, only self-consciousness. I wanted to be anywhere but there. Inside, the 12 students and a very tough teacher were waiting. I opened the door and approached the bed. Nothing. I stopped in front of the bed with the stack of pillows covered by the blanket. Still nothing. Then I committed my action, "to say goodbye," by pulling up the blanket and looking. There was only the photograph of the bald model there. Yet, a surge of grief welled up from deep inside me—seemingly as powerful as when my friend had actually died; the tears began to well up and I had to fight to hold them back. The key to this "performance" was the circumstances I had set up, the dramatic relationship, my want, and my action. That's what led to the emotion. I didn't *act* it.

Actors work in various ways, and your job as director is to be attuned to what method they are using. No matter which school the actor comes from, making sure the actor is imbued with the circumstance of the situation, making sure the actor understands the dynamic relationships, making sure the actor knows what the character *wants* and what it is the character is *doing* to get it, is a solid foundation to begin building *any* scene. This becomes even more so when shooting a film because you will undoubtedly shoot out of chronological order, where it is possible for things that were once obvious to the actor to get lost or lessened in the hurly-burly of the shoot.

CASTING

Clurman writes that he advises students to "Choose a good script, cast good actors—and you'll be good directors!" He points out that "there is more than a little truth in the jest." Milos Forman has often stated, too modestly I believe, that casting for him is 80% of his job. Whatever the percentage of a director's work, casting is extremely important. How do we go about it?

I asked Kazan how he cast. He replied, "I take them out to Montauk for a few days." Although he had a beach house on the ocean there, I took Montauk to mean anywhere that he and an actor could hang out and Kazan could find out if this actor was right for the part. Kazan believed that for all but a handful of actors, the character had to be somewhere inside the actor. He told me the story of when he was casting for *East of Eden* (1955). The studio was pushing a young actor named James Dean, but Kazan was not impressed. When Kazan left the studio one day, Dean was outside, sitting on his motorcycle. He asked Kazan if he wanted a ride. Kazan accepted, even though he was afraid of motorcycles. Off they went with Kazan, ever the consummate director, using this time, this "Montauk," to pump Dean. By the time they pulled up in front of the studio a while later, Kazan knew he had found the right actor. He had steered the conversation into an investigation of Dean's relationship with his father and discovered it was very similar to the character Dean would portray in the film.

I once mentioned to Milos Forman that a certain actor in his latest film had done a remarkable job. Forman turned to me and said sotto voce, so-and-so (the actor) *is* so-and-so (the character). Both directors had made brilliant casting choices, but let us not fool ourselves. Their jobs did not stop there as far as the work with the actors, and neither will yours.

CHARACTER DESCRIPTIONS

One of the first places that our detective work pays off is in the casting process. Without this prior investigation, we would be at sea. Although films are told in the present, the characters come out of the past. Character *is* the past. It is everything that goes to make up who your characters are: family, social/economic background, and so on. Clues to character are imbedded in the screenplay, and they need to be dug out for you to be able to work intelligently with the actors.

Kazan asked me to help cast a film in Greece—a film that was never made—but the process for me was tremendously instructive. He and I sat down in his hotel room in Athens and went through the script. There were at least 50 significant characters, and he began "kicking around" his conception of who and what it was he was looking for. There is no set way to go about this. You can start with a physical type or a psychological profile—the spine of the character. It doesn't matter. As the director muses to herself or to another, an idea begins to emerge—a core of what the actor who plays this character should embody.

The trick to casting then is: Does the actor under consideration embody the core of the character? At the very least, the actor must be able to relate to and understand the core of the character. Many times, with a very good actor, that is more than sufficient. Physicality is easy, but we should not be tied to our initial visualization unless it is a plot point. We might envision a short man, when actually a tall actor changes our mind. The other categories are more difficult—more elusive. So let's go through a casting process, step by step. Everything the director does is easier, clearer, and more precise when it is taken step by step.

SELECTION OF SCENES

A former colleague of mine, a very fine actor who was nominated for an Academy Award, told me that for the life of him he could not cry as a character, and because of that, he never took a role where crying was a necessity. He mentioned a scene from Chekhov's *Three Sisters* in which the youngest sister had to be in a state of hysteria for the scene to work. This was not a choice for the actor; she absolutely had to get "there" somehow. Pity the director who finds out on the set that this very fine actor cannot deliver this critical moment. My colleague's advice to his directing students was to pick scenes for the casting sessions that would explore key areas of the character's behavior and mental state.

AUDITIONS

Preliminary auditions often consist of seeing the actor's work, either in the theater or on film. Here you get a chance to see the actor create and sustain a character through a whole film or play. This is extremely helpful, even if the character being portrayed is different from the one for which you are casting.

When actors are scheduled for formal auditions, they should be given *sides* (selected scenes) sufficiently ahead of time so that they can prepare. Cold readings are unfair to the actor and not profitable for the director.

Another actor friend of mine, who has earned her living for many years working in film and television, has often complained to me that she is usually given the sides at the last minute. She has the time to *justify* only a few of the elements in the text. Justification is a term used by some actors for work all actors must do. Let me give an example that most of you will be familiar with: Robert Shaw in *Jaws*. Shaw's character relates a gripping story of how his ship was torpedoed and sank and how he was afloat for a day in a sea that was filled with hundreds of man-eating sharks. He tells of the screams of the men as one after another was ripped apart by the sharks, turning the water red with blood. He tells specifically of "bumping" into his friend, "Herbie Robinson from Cleveland. A baseball player." He thought his friend was asleep in his life jacket, but when he reached out and touched him, his friend rolled over, revealing that he had been "bitten in half below the waist."

This entire story had to be justified by Shaw because it was not true. He had never been on a ship that had been torpedoed from under him and thrown into a sea of sharks, and he never knew a Herbie Robinson from Cleveland, or seen a man who had been bitten in half. But Shaw had to create all of this in his mind's eye. He had to create a clear image of a shark's "lifeless eyes, black eyes, like doll's eyes." Pictures or film would help the actor here. Or even better, a visit to an aquarium. As for Herbie Robinson, Shaw could have used a friend from high school. The point is that the actor must create a movie in his head that is *specific in every detail*. In this case, it must have included the sound of "high pitched screaming."

A word of warning: Auditions are not performances! Do not expect one. It is only the beginning of a process in which patience, faith, and trust are large components. Directors who are unsure of the rehearsal process want immediate results in the audition, and they often settle for actors who are proficient at getting to a superficial reality rather quickly. In cases like this, what you see in the audition is often all you get on film.

WHAT ARE YOU LOOKING FOR?

The following are casting considerations to keep in mind.

1. *Is the actor right for the part?* What you are really asking yourself in the first audition is, Do you see the character, even if it is a version of the character different than you had imagined? Some of these judgments are subjective and cannot be defended. Nevertheless, you must begin to listen to this side of yourself, and begin to have faith in it. If you see a talented actor at work but do not see the character you need portrayed, then if this is a significant film you are making (as opposed to an exercise where a proficient actor will be more than adequate), you must continue your search. At the same time, if you do have a "smell" of the character coming from the actor, it would behoove you to explore further. It is wise at this point to ask yourself this very important question: Is the actor interesting to watch? Does she surprise you, perhaps by playing against the most obvious reading of a line?

2. *The actor's attention to simple reality.* Two aspects that are key and are easily discernible are: Does the actor work moment by moment, and does the actor listen (to the other actor, even if it is a nonactor reading the lines in the initial audition)? Be on the lookout for anticipation. Because the actor has read the sides, the actor knows what's coming but must not convey that knowledge. If these basic items of the actor's craft are missing, the director faces an almost insurmountable task in helping to mold a consistently believable performance.

3. *Can you work with the actor?* Of course, if you have Al Pacino and he doesn't listen to you, most directors would settle for that, but even actors of Pacino's skill can benefit from good direction. The key here is not that the actor accepts as gospel everything you suggest but that he and you can communicate with each other—that an atmosphere of open and free exchange is possible. One way of finding out before it is too late is to begin directing in auditions. Make specific suggestions. Encourage the actor to go further in what they are only hinting at, or ask the actor to explore other actions. You do not have to prove that you are smart—only that you have a clear idea of what is required from this character and that you fully understand that you and the actor are *both* engaged in a process of attaining, changing, and (you hope) surpassing your expectations.

FIRST READ-THROUGH

The first read-though serves a few functions, not the least that of breaking the ice. The actors are introduced to the other actors and, even more importantly for the ultimate benefit of the film, they are introduced to the other characters—not the ones they have read on the page and supplied their own interpretation to, but the ones who have now taken on flesh and blood and are sitting across from them. Questions often arise during this stage. The meaning of a line is not clear. A relationship seems muddy. An action seems wrong. All of the questions that come up should be addressed before proceeding.

As a director, perhaps the most important question you can ask yourself during the first read-through is, Does the screenplay work or does it require rewriting? (In the last chapter of this book

I have included a list of questions that a director or a screenwriter should ask about any script. I suggest that this be done before the rehearsal process, but if it was not caught before, that is no reason not to take remedial action now.)

For the time being it is best not to correct the actors, except for asking them to speak so they can be heard. After all of their questions have been answered, you can correct a mispronounced word or any minor misunderstanding of the text, but do nothing to indicate that you are expecting a result. Now is a good time to make sure everyone understands their backstory—their circumstances. Some of this can be handled with the whole cast present—especially when dealing with historical facts, geography, climate, and so on—but personal biographies and their intimacies, and especially relationships, are best worked on individually.

DIRECTING DURING REHEARSALS

Acting is a process, but it is a process that works differently and at different speeds for different actors. Some actors work from the outside (the dialogue, relationships, costume, makeup, and so on) to the inside (so-called technical actors), while others start on the inside (use of selves) and work toward the outside (so-called method actors). The technical actor might give results sooner, but the character might lag behind. For method actors, the opposite would be more likely. It is important to give each actor the time they need *within the constraints of the rehearsal period*— another reason why casting is so crucial.

PUT AWAY YOUR DETECTIVE WORK

All of the work you have put in to understanding the text should now be locked away in a drawer, hidden from the actor. Much of it will not help them in its present form. Take an example from *Apple Pie*. Telling Counterman that the dynamic relationship between him and Female Cop is "my happiness" will probably not help him. It is nonspecific. Instead, you will make sure the actor understands just *how* the Female Cop makes him happy—something concrete, such as *her pure pleasure in eating the pie*. It is best if the *actor discovers this trait for himself*. The director can often help the actor in this discovery by asking questions that will lead to something that is right for the part and, very importantly, *something that works for the actor*.

The two active categories that you can, and should, talk about at the first rehearsal are circumstance and wants. Actors cannot begin their journey without being absolutely clear on both. By being clear on both, the actor will have a better chance of discovering actions that are akin to the ones you have imagined.

CREATING THE RIGHT ATMOSPHERE

It is important during this period that the director takes the pressure off the actor by creating an atmosphere that is conducive to exploration—that makes the actor feel secure and willing to take chances. An insecure actor will tend to play it safe—will tend not to take chances—and thus will never be as good as they could be. Equally important is for the director to convey that there is somebody home—that she has a strong sense of what "works" and what does not. *Actors will be more likely to go out on a limb in their exploration of the role if they feel confident that the director will catch them if they fall.*

Rehearsal is the time to try out the actor's ideas, and the detective work you have done will give you confidence in weighing the choices, because the ultimate choice must be the director's. By now we are probably beginning to understand that only the director can know what the entire ceiling should look like and whether it would help to make this or that nose larger. Be open to these new ideas and suggestions, and regard them carefully, but *beware of a "terrific idea" that solves a problem of the moment but might cause unwanted repercussions down the line.*

USING THE REHEARSAL TIME EFFICIENTLY

After the first rehearsal of a whole scene, it is more efficient and productive to break up further rehearsals into the scene's dramatic blocks. When the director is satisfied with the progress of all the separate dramatic blocks, it is advisable to run the entire scene again. Obviously, not all scenes need the same care and attention, and *it is smart to ladle out the rehearsal time you have to the areas most in need.*

WHAT DO YOU SEE?

The greatest help that a director can give to an actor is to see what they are doing or not doing. Stanislavsky said that on stage he "did not want to see a man acting like he was hungry, he wanted to see a hungry man." In other words, do you believe what the actor is doing? Do you believe that Counterman truly does want to be a good restaurateur and make the customer happy; that Customer is sorry for pulling out the gun; that Female Cop really does adore her pie? And on that last close-up of Counterman, do you believe that he absolutely adores Female Cop?

An actor might think they have justified something when they haven't. For example, in *Jaws*, Spielberg had to "see" the sharks that surrounded Shaw. If Shaw didn't "have" the sharks, if he hadn't justified them for himself, the story would not have had the ring of truth—but all the director would have had to tell the actor was, "I don't see the sharks." Shaw, or any actor, would have been very grateful for this information. When you can inform the actor what it is you are seeing or not seeing, you in effect become a mirror for that actor—the only mirror in the rehearsal or on the set. Because of this rather daunting responsibility, the director must be continuously *in the moment* while a scene is in rehearsal or shooting. At this point, all the detective work and preparation must be integrated into the director's being, forming an alive and pulsating presence within—a life in urgent need of birth.

SPEAK TO THE CHARACTER

Speak to the character, not the actor. Do not use abstract or intellectual terms—use the everyday vernacular of your character. "What do you think you would do if. . . ?" "How many times have you gone to bed with her?" Kazan had a very immediate and intimate method of working with actors both in rehearsal and on the set: he would aim straight for the actor's gut. He would take each actor aside after a scene had been run, or between shots on the set—maybe put his arm around them if he was "consoling" them, or perhaps place his hands on his hips if he was going to "prod" or "chastise" them. "Are you going to let her walk all over you like that? No? Then stand up to her, damn it! Let her know who the hell you are!" Then Kazan would go over to the other actor and talk to her character. "If this guy had any respect for you . . ." and so on, and so forth. Whichever character Kazan was talking to had the impression that the director was in cahoots with him. This method of talking directly to the character is especially effective when you're working on the set and do not have a lot of time, but it requires that you be a good psychologist and have a clear idea of what the dramatic moment requires.

IF IT'S BROKEN, FIX IT

Depending on the time constraints of the rehearsal period, it is best to correct actors—*especially in regard to their actions*—early in the rehearsal period. I realize this conflicts with the idea of a process, but you must get good at discerning when someone is going down the wrong road with little chance of finding the right way and when he is still engaged in profitable exploration. If you wait too long, your silence might convince the actor that he is on the right road, making it much more difficult for you to turn him around.

Make sure the actor understands the circumstances, the scene want, the dynamic relationships. Make sure you are giving *specific* directions using action verbs—"to accuse"—rather than state-of-mind verbs such as "to resent," "to fear," "to like."

A common mistake made by directors, even those with some experience, is to use adjectives: "Could you be a little more cheerful; could you be a little more sad, more angry, more grief stricken?" An actor cannot play these qualities. If you think that the character should be angrier, just what is it you might say to help accomplish that? What action verb would help? It would depend on the specifics of the moment, but you might ask the actor "to accuse," or "to intimidate," or "to confront." Ask the actor *to do* rather than *to be*.

Make sure you are using facts instead of attitudes. Instead of telling the actor that her husband "can't be trusted," remind her that "he slept with your best friend." Instead of "he's a good guy," you might say, "He buys groceries for the old lady across the hall."

Sometimes, all the detective work you have done will not mean beans to the actor—not in any way that will do him or her any good. It will be too abstract—too intellectual. It simply does not punch any buttons. If that's the case, then you will have to go to work on the viscera. Start with asking questions. *The Socratic method works as well in unearthing answers to questions an actor might have as it does for questions a philosopher might have.*

A tool that I have found to be extremely useful is to speak of my own connection to the material. You can do the same. Let the actor in on the fact that you were a nerd like this character, or that your father died before you could tell him you loved him, or that when you were a teenager you, too, had panic attacks. But do not make up stories unless you are an exceptional liar. For most of you, then, if you cannot relate to a feeling or situation on this level, don't.

Sometimes you just do not know the answer to an actor's question, or what is wrong with the scene, or how to fix it. If this happens, and it will happen to everyone at times, do not fake it. It's okay to say, "I don't know." Throw the ball in your actor's lap. Also, it is helpful at these times to go back to your detective work, or to take a long walk, or both. Let your actors do the same. The eureka factor should always be cultivated during the creative process.

IMPROVISATIONS

Improvisations can be helpful, or not, depending to a large degree on how they are set up. Parameters are necessary. An area that is fruitful for improvisations is the *"what" that happened before*. For example, two people have been married for 10 years when the film begins. It might be very helpful for the actors if they improvised a first date or even the wedding night. The *"what" that happened before* might also be a scene that takes place just before the scene you are working on but is not in the screenplay. In *Apple Pie*, the scene in the Customer's psychiatrist's office that day could be improvised, with the director playing the doctor.

It is most often foolhardy to improvise a scene as a take—while the camera is rolling—in lieu of having scripted lines. Actors, no matter how talented, cannot be expected to be instant screenwriters. There are a number of film scenes in existence in which very talented actors have improvised on film, and it shows. The English director Mike Leigh (*Secrets and Lies*, 1996; *Vera Drake*, 2004) works collaboratively with the actors on improvisations for months, but then he edits what they come up with *before* shooting. I observed John Cassavetes doing the same thing on *Husbands* (1970), with Peter Falk, Ben Gazzara, and himself improvising a scene that was then transcribed, edited, and rewritten. Improvisation handled in this manner can be extremely productive. As in any creative work, even one that is as collaborative as filmmaking, there must be one funnel that every ingredient that is poured into the film must pass through. And that funnel is the director.

CAN WE REHEARSE TOO MUCH?

Richard L. Bare, in *The Film Director*, says, "A perfect rehearsal is a wasted take." On the other hand, he says, "Insufficient rehearsals can lead to a wasted take." The answer to this dilemma?

Each director will have to feel this one out for herself, but you can count on most actors holding back until the camera begins to roll, and the director should do likewise, by saving some significant piece of advice or suggestion for the first take.

DIRECTING ACTORS ON THE SET

One of the reasons it is important that your camera and staging be worked out beforehand is that you can then give your actors the attention they need and deserve. If the director's main concern is with the camera, the actors can be made to feel like orphans. It is much wiser to make them feel that they are the center of attention—that the director needs them and is counting on them. By this time the actors should know that they can count on the director.

Much of the time, scenes are shot out of sequence. Obviously, the director must make sure that the actors know where they just came from (even if that scene has not been shot yet) and what they expect and want in the present scene.

If possible, physically and timewise, it is important to rehearse scenes in their entirety on the actual set. Let the actors get a feel for the complete arc of the scene in what, in many cases, is a new environment for them. Problematic areas can be rehearsed outside the context of the whole scene, but it is a good idea to keep the dramatic blocks intact.

The more psychological the scene, the more interior it is, the more the director has to work to change psychology into behavior that can be photographed. On the set, between takes, is the perfect time to fine-tune performances *for the camera*. In Jeff Young's interviews with Kazan in *Kazan, The Master Director Discusses His Films*, Kazan tells us how he would ensure that this behavior would be available for the camera.

> You make them go through the emotions in every take. You don't just do close-ups of a face sitting there. . . . There must be a thought. The best close-ups are pictorial records of a change from one attitude to another. They show a transition from one emotion to another. You see a man feeling or doing or about to do something. Instead, he changes his mind and starts to do something else. Or you see a man not notice something and suddenly he notices it. . . . In order to get that close-up and have it affect the other person in the scene, you have to take the time when you direct it to make the actor actually experience each of the moments. For example, you say to one actor, "Tell him to get out of here." You say to the other actor, "For a minute you want to do as he says. You look around to see where you can run, you look at him to see if he means it." Then to the first actor you say, "You know this guy is looking at you to see if you mean it. Just let him know that you do mean it. . . ." You describe what happens internally and you do it in a way that stretches the moments so you can photograph them. You can't photograph nothing.

Regardless of how much detective work we do on the kitchen table, and no matter how much we have rehearsed—and *preparation is the name of the game in filmmaking*—the experiential nature of the film set imposes a new reality. We are now working in a three-dimensional world that is in constant flux—one in which the director must remain alert, alive to each moment, beat by beat, at the same time being fully aware of each moment's job and position in the story, while at the same time attending to a thousand questions that have nothing to do with the moment.

The following is a list of things that will help the actors ease into the shooting process, help them stay oriented to where they are in the story, and keep them informed of what technical parameters they must pay heed to.

1. On the first day, shoot "easy" scenes: drive-ups and so on. As you get into the tougher scenes, shoot the most difficult parts and/or the shots that "you cannot live without" early in the day to make certain you do not run out of time or actors' energy.

2. Make sure the actors know their marks and the parameters of the frame they have to work in. (Marks are designated spots that the actor stops on, turns on, and the like.)

3. Remind actors precisely where they are in the story and where they just came from.

4. Be on the lookout for adherence to simple circumstance—cold, heat, being out of breath from running (even if the running was shot last week).

5. Continue to give direction to your actors in terms that relate to their characters' actions.

6. Make sure the actors keep going until the director announces, "Cut!" unless the camera operator or sound person calls "Cut!" for technical reasons. Wonderful surprises can sometimes happen when things do not go exactly as planned.

7. Do not ask for another take from an actor without giving them a new piece of specific direction. If a take is being done because the previous take was ruined by a technical problem, let the actor know that.

8. Position yourself as close to the camera lenses as possible so that you will see the scene from the same angle as the camera sees it.

9. When the camera is rolling, stay in the moment. Never take your eyes off of the action. Keep asking yourself, Do I believe him? Is she interesting? With experience, these questions will not have to be raised intellectually. They will come from your being.

10. Never ignore that thing in the pit of your stomach that is telling you that something is wrong. Figure out what it is. That *thing* is the most important friend a director has, so pay very close attention to it.

CHAPTER 11

MANAGERIAL RESPONSIBILITIES OF THE DIRECTOR

Milos Forman told his directing class at Columbia that the director had to inhabit two chairs: one for the artistic/creative side, the other for the managerial/logistical side. The trick to being a good director, he said, is to develop an ass big enough to sit in both chairs at the same time.

The elements of preproduction and production that must occupy the director from the second chair begin months before shooting. As from the creative chair, the director's motto from the managerial chair is "preparation." For if the locations have not been cleared, and the transportation has not been arranged, and the hundreds of details to be dealt with and anticipated—thousands on a feature film—have not been handled satisfactorily, they can intrude on, even destroy, the work the director has done up until now.

DELEGATING AUTHORITY WHILE ACCEPTING RESPONSIBILITY

Many of us have trouble delegating responsibility. We want to do everything ourselves because no one can do it as well as we can. Even if that were true, we do not have enough hands, nor are there enough hours in the day, to handle all the countless tasks that must be taken care of. We must therefore choose those who help us with great care. When we have chosen, we must trust them to do their jobs.

The flip side of not being able to delegate responsibility is to not accept responsibility for the actions of those we have chosen. Yes, we must trust them to do their jobs. But simultaneously, we cannot close our eyes to signs that the job is not being done satisfactorily. For most of us, it is a lot easier to hire someone than to fire them, but sometimes letting someone go is absolutely the right thing to do *for the sake of the production.* It is my contention, and I believe one that will stand you in good stead, that the director must take responsibility for the *entire* production—screenplay, acting, production design, camera, sound. This responsibility extends to the managerial/logistical aspects, such as adherence to the schedule and set discipline.

THE PRODUCER

The producer's job is to do everything possible to help the director achieve his artistic goal. She is a key figure in giving the director the support and encouragement every director needs to cope with the pressure of filmmaking. That's the ideal goal, but there are many kinds of director/producer relationships, and most start with who brings the project and the money to the table.

If it is the producer, then we have the hired gun relationship. The director's choice is limited here: Do I like the project and will the producer give me the creative freedom I need to fulfill my vision? Obviously this is a judgment call, depending on just where the director is in the firmament of the film industry. Do not sell yourself short. At the same time, do not be perverse. Because of the amount of money involved in making films, compromises most likely will have to be made. A director must make films.

A very fine student of mine with his first feature-length original screenplay, after three or four years of struggling to raise the money, was offered 60 thousand dollars by an independent producer to direct it. Almost simultaneously, a major studio offered to produce the film with a five-million-dollar budget, but this studio was known for interfering with a director's vision. My student chose to ensure his control, and he made the film with the much lower amount. I'm happy to say, the story has a happy ending. The film was an artistic and financial success and paved the way for the director's next film, made with a much larger budget, but this time, with the control he wanted.

At the entry level, surely at the student level, directors fund most films, and they seek out a producer who has the necessary skills and temperament—and hopefully who shares the director's vision. (People skills are necessary in this area, and I have observed that the great directors I have had the privilege to know were wonderfully adept at interacting with those they depended on. There was respect, expressed gratitude, a willingness to listen to others, and an ability to bond—to establish a camaraderie, a sense that we are all in this together.)

The producer needs to have people skills as well—in fact, it is one of the key requirements—but she should also have some nuts and bolts knowledge and experience in overseeing a production. She is responsible for managing the budget; negotiating contracts including the Screen Actors Guild (SAG); managing crew; and arranging insurance for equipment (and on substantial budgets, negative insurance). On small productions, the producer might organize casting sessions (in the absence of a casting director), scout and secure locations, handle petty cash, and in consultation with the director and director of photography (DP), formulate schedules.

One of the greatest assets that a producer must have is the ability to anticipate what could go wrong at any stage of the production. The idea that if something *can* go wrong, it *will* go wrong is always lurking around the corner of any film set. A cool head and an ability to think on one's feet are essential assets for any producer.

THE ASSISTANT DIRECTOR

In reading *Something Like an Autobiography* by the great Japanese film director Akira Kurosawa (*Rashomon*, 1959, Japanese), I was struck by the attention and praise he lavished on his assistant director (AD), a man who served him in that capacity for many years. Even on a small film, the assistant director is of paramount importance to the director. Thus, the director must choose with great care the person who occupies this position.

On smaller productions, such as the ones my students undertake at Columbia, the roles of producer and AD differ from the roles filled by these key personnel on larger, professional shoots. In the student film or low-budget area, their duties are often more extensive and onerous because they might be forced to make do without important help such as location managers, transport coordinators, payroll, and a number of assistants and second assistants.

In preproduction, the AD coordinates with the director and the DP to schedule the shots that are to be required at each location, and to schedule, with the director's input, the most efficient order in which to complete the shots.

During production, the key role of the AD is to ensure the smooth running of the set; to ensure that all personnel are informed of the schedule and given "call times"; and if need be, to organize transportation for both cast and crew. The AD coordinates with all the various departments (camera, grip, electric, sound, wardrobe, hair/makeup, props, *and cast*) to ensure that everyone is aware of the schedule. Equally important is to inform all departments if there is a change in the schedule.

The AD is responsible for on-set discipline and is vitally important in affecting the on-set atmosphere. He will call for quiet before each shot, and at the end of each shot he will announce the next camera setup.

A REALISTIC SHOOTING SCHEDULE

The length of a shoot is usually dependent on the budget. How many days can you afford to keep the cast and crew together and pay for the rental of equipment and vehicles? This restraint almost always conflicts with the amount of time the director would like to have. Therefore, the preparation that we have gone through in this book will stand the director in good stead. The actors will have been prepared, the staging and camera will have been worked out. And yes, it will not go exactly as planned. Adjustments might have to be made in the staging, the actors might require more takes than expected, technical problems with equipment might occur, and Mother Nature might not be kind with the weather.

So how do directors ensure that they will have enough time? There is no such insurance, but it is possible to draw up an informed and realistic schedule by taking into account the number of locations and the number of camera setups at each location. Other factors to consider are the technical difficulties of scenes (dolly shots that require rehearsal), precision lighting, shooting in a public area that you do not have complete control of, and the emotional weight of the scene. Give the actors more time for the "big" scenes—the scenes that require time for emotional preparation or intricate staging.

Like anything in life, the more you direct, the better you get at it, and the more you can judge how much time you will need to fulfill your vision.

WORKING WITH THE CREW

It is a good idea in the training of a director that they become conversant with the different craft disciplines. It is not necessary that the director become proficient in these disciplines, although that certainly does not hurt. It is more important that the director has a clear visualization of what he wants and the ability to convey that to others. Much of what the director wants from the various craft disciplines will be conveyed by the AD. The same clarity that is essential in directing actors is needed in directing a crew. The director must state clearly the dramatic or atmospheric function of the color of a room, of the props, costumes, hairstyles, and makeup. Then it is important for the director to let the craft people do their jobs and to count on them doing those jobs well. However, as stated earlier, the director must assume responsibility for the final decision. *Everything that goes into making a film should pass through the prism of the director's vision.*

WORKING WITH THE DIRECTOR OF PHOTOGRAPHY

The most professionally intimate relationship on the set, aside from director/actor, is director/director of photography. After all, it is the DP who controls the key to the final images that are projected on the screen. In film, only the DP will really know what those final images will look like, so trust must be implicit in the relationship. Although the DP's first responsibility is lighting, the director will invariably rely on him for concurrence on framing (a good eye to bounce off of is a welcome friend to any director) and choice of lenses.

There are more than a few directors who relinquish the narrative responsibility of the camera to the DP. This is not a good idea in most cases because the director is then assigning a second voice to the film—a voice that may or may not be in sync with the director's. Of course, if the director has no voice. . . . No, do not even think like that. *The director's job description requires him to be the undisputed narrative voice.* You should try to work only with DPs who respect that concept.

Choosing a DP has some of the qualities of casting actors. The director must look at the DP's previous work and find in it the images, atmosphere, and texture that the director envisions for the current project. If it is not found, it is proper to run lighting tests. Most DPs will welcome this, and here they might pleasantly surprise the director by delivering images that are beyond the director's expectations, and maybe they are quite different. Only with the director's *clear* enunciation of tone, atmosphere, and texture can the DP supply and augment the director's vision. Just like any intimate relationship in our daily lives, the one between DP and director requires communication.

CHAPTER 12

POSTPRODUCTION

A great sense of accomplishment mixed with a good dose of physical and mental exhaustion usually occasions the "wrapping" of a film. At this time, for the good of the film, the director should go away to rest, relax, and cleanse the artistic palate. The film is by no means finished, and much psychic energy is yet to be expended.

EDITING

A dear friend of mine and former colleague at Columbia, the late Ralph Rosenblum, one of the great film editors, author of *When the Shooting Stops, the Cutting Begins: A Film Editor's Story*, had a jaundiced view of directors and believed that he and all good editors existed to salvage the film—to cover up errors of omission, to fabricate meaning when there was none—in short, to save the director's skin. Ralph, like many editors (and producers), believed that the director's job was to work with the actors and create life but that life was then to be rendered in "coverage," said coverage to be the palette with which the editor paints his story. I do not subscribe to this and have been teaching my students to design their films, to previsualize, to make their films in their head *before* shooting. If this is done, the editing takes care of itself. Well, not quite.

What you are looking for in choosing an editor is, again, someone who will defer to your vision, *but* someone who has a strong narrative and dramatic sense—again, a strong presence for the director to bounce off of. Many directors hand their film over to an editor for a first assembly or even more. This is probably not a good idea if you do not know the editor very well. Even then I caution against it. The initial task of choosing a "take" of a performance is a crucial decision and should not be made by someone else. The director has worked too hard to lose the film in the editing process.

Many independent filmmakers nowadays, and especially those who have been trained in film school, have already edited their early exercises and short films, so editing is not foreign to their conception of directorial responsibility. However, on many big-budget productions, scenes are cut by an editor while the shooting is still going on. *The beginning filmmaker*, however, has too much still to learn about cinematic storytelling to forgo this experience. The feedback necessary to grow in one's craft—what works and what does not, what is the relationship between the director's visualization before shooting and what appears on the screen—is never more available for study than in the uncut camera takes.

DIRECTOR'S ASSEMBLY

During the director's much-needed vacation, the editor or assistant editor will log all the material, keeping careful records of where all the various takes are. The takes can then be assembled in the chronological order of the screenplay. Returning refreshed and eager to see how everything cuts together, the director can now sit down and look at all the footage in order, selecting performance takes and making a shot list for an *assembly* that approximates, as much as possible, the director's original visualization. (An assembly consists of various shots that are not yet intercut but have been "cleaned up"—slates removed.) I encourage this step-by-step approach to shaping the edited film. It might seem to be time consuming, but I have discovered just the opposite. Beginning to cut too early can lead to wrong choices because we have not immersed ourselves enough in the material and allowed the material to speak to us. This makes it more likely that we will have to rummage through the outtakes more often than necessary—a time-consuming process.

FIRST ROUGH CUT

Edited shots are now extracted from the camera takes and intercut with other shots, using the director's final visualization before shooting. This is one of the most exciting times in the filmmaking process: seeing performances that make us laugh or feel sad; the power of the narrative beats as they are rendered by the cutting; the narrative thrust of the story unfolding on the screen. However, it can also be one of the most frustrating times. We begin to see our mistakes: performance beats that we did not get because we did not insist on them; errors of omission in our shot selection because we just weren't "smart" enough to realize the need for a certain angle; or a missing shot because we ran out of time or lost the light. *Our original visualization is almost never fully realized on the screen.* However, if we have followed the methodology laid out in this book, the chances of having an error of omission should be reduced to a minimum.

It is in the area of performance that the beginning director will most likely find disappointment. Do not blame it on the actors. It is the director's fault. So what can be done about performances in the editing room? A lot. Yes, our story will change somewhat, depending on how much we have to "cut around a performance," but hopefully the essence will remain, and the story will not suffer too much.

Another problem is that we might find flaws in the screenplay. The story doesn't work. It is not clear. Or, the worst, it is not interesting. This calls for resolve on the director's part. Sometimes it is necessary once again to take some time off—clean the artistic palette once more and attack anew. What we hope to discover is that there is some latitude in the way we tell our story, and it is now up to the director, along with the editor, to discover solutions.

Does this mean that my insistence on cutting the film in our heads before shooting is a waste of time? Quite the contrary. It means that the director needs more seasoning—must go through the complete cycle from script to screen a few more times—so that on the next film the work on the page and in the head will be informed by the present experience. This is a key point. We do not get many chances to make films, so all the possible learning should be squeezed from every one of our fledgling efforts.

If we are true artists, we will never be satisfied with our work. Forman once said to his class that a craftsman always knows whether or not his work is good—an artist never does. Kazan, when asked why some of his films weren't artistically satisfying as his best work, answered, "Ah, but that's the beauty of it."

FINE CUT

After we have gotten the larger aspects of the story to work, it is time to fine-tune the film. Ninety percent of this will involve shortening. Shots will be too long or unnecessary. Perhaps on the third run-through—or seventh—of the entire film, we come to the realization that a scene can be eliminated because it is redundant. But it makes us laugh! Or it contains one of our more pithy lines. Still, there is only one question to ask: *Does it serve the overall story?* Yes, it works on its own, but does it load the film down with an extra minute or two that you will pay the price for later on? Remember, *duration is a dramatic category*, and it can be a plus or a minus, depending on the moment. William Faulkner, one of America's undisputed great novelists, who also had a hand in more than a few screenplays, said this about deleting material that he was fond of because it intruded on the story as a whole: "Sometimes you have to kill the little darlings."

During this phase, performances should be scrutinized carefully. Is the character believable? Interesting? If you are not quite satisfied—something is bothering you—it is a good time to go back to the outtakes. Take another look at takes or portions of takes that were neglected. More than once I have been pleasantly surprised to find something that works better, even if for just one beat. *Be tough because the audience will be tougher.*

MUSIC AND SOUND

I strongly recommend getting an experienced sound editor to "build" the sound tracks and prepare for the sound mix. As with lighting and the DP, the sound editor has technical knowledge and experience that the director most likely does not have. Like the DP, he can be counted on to offer wonderful creative suggestions. Still, it is the director who has the last word in the *orchestration* of sound because it is a conceptual category. When and where to have ambient sound, and what kind, is crucial in creating dramatic tension or creating the proper atmosphere. It is wise to incorporate sound in the early stages of your conceptualization. Skip Lievsay—a sound designer who has worked with Spike Lee, Tim Burton, and the Coen brothers—told my colleague, the director Bette Gordon: "If you want interesting sound, shoot for it." Sometimes that means simply leaving room for it.

Of course music can help enormously to create atmosphere and tension. There are films that are carried by the sound track, but don't count on it. Music is a complement, not a supplement, to the story. It is also very subjective. Most directors will have some idea of the *type* of music they want for their film, and this is a good place to start. If an original score is being composed, the director's sense of what dramatic job the music should do, what atmosphere it must help to create, or what theme it should embody can be communicated to the composer. As in choosing the other collaborators, an important consideration for the director is whether or not the composer will listen to your ideas. It is guaranteed that they will have ideas of their own—hopefully wonderfully exciting ideas. Be open. You do not just hand the music over, but at the same time, as with all your collaborations, you should supply a clear input along with a good deal of faith.

Listen to the music against the picture. Look at it again and again. If it doesn't work, if that thing in your stomach tells you something is not quite right, pay attention to it, and communicate that to the composer.

Music is all around us in today's world. It is playing on my computer as I type this. That doesn't mean I can use it for a film that has commercial pretensions. Rights must be secured, and sometimes that requires the payment of a fee. If a piece of music is important to you, attempt to secure the rights. A student of mine who wrote and directed a wonderful 20-minute film wanted the rights to a Ravi Shankar/George Harrison piece. She had used it for her "scratch track," and when it came time for the final mix, she could not think of making a substitution. It was too perfect. As we might expect, the music company turned her down. Being persistent, as all directors must be, she e-mailed Shankar, telling him the nature of her film, and in three days he e-mailed back his permission and got Harrison and the music company to agree. Do not count on this happening a lot, but at the same time it doesn't hurt to try. All directors should take the following dictum to heart: *Positivity begets positivity; negativity begets negativity.*

LOCKING PICTURE, OR, HOW DO YOU KNOW WHEN IT'S OVER?

We are faced with a paradox at the end of the editing process. We want to get it over with, but we cannot let it go. The first attitude might cause us to skip crucial steps in the editing "end game."

The second might cause us to go around in circles, never really solving the film's problems. We will continue to cut a frame here and there, add shots, and recut scenes, never giving up trying to make it perfect. Well, it will never be *perfect*. Anyway, *perfection is not an aesthetic category.*

Perhaps the biggest mistake made by my students during editing is that they do not look at the completed film (before mixing the sound track and locking the picture) enough times. These times should be spaced so that you will be able to go away from the film for at least a long weekend. (One of the reasons why directors might not have time to look at a film again and again is that they have not worked it into their schedules. This time pressure can harm a film and is another reason a director must develop an ass big enough for the second chair.) These repeated viewings are much more important to the novice film director, who usually has more difficulty "seeing" the fruits of their art with some objectivity—which, of course, is not entirely available to even the mature artist in any field. Forget about the art for the moment and concentrate on only the craft. Is that shot too long, is that line of dialogue necessary, is that narrative beat clear? To you!

AN AUDIENCE AND A BIG SCREEN

The first audience should consist of a few film-savvy people—people who can respond with some objectivity to the film. Your family and friends might not be the most help here. These screenings can be done on the editing table or monitor. Ask specific questions. Do they understand the story—the characters' motivations? What bothers them? After a number of these small screenings, it is time to show the film to a larger audience (10 or 12 is a manageable number) on a large screen. Here you will be able to judge by the "feel" in the room as the film is projected. The pacing might seem slower to you than on the monitor. Take note of this phenomenon. It is real.

When the screening is over, listen carefully to the comments. If they are not specific, related to what can be fixed, it is not relevant. It's nice if everyone adores your film, but they might not. Even if they do, there is probably work still to be done: things you can fix through cutting or sound and music manipulation. This is also the time when we realize irrevocably—we can fool ourselves no longer—that the scene we were unsure about is worse than we thought, or the crucial close-up that is missing is destructive to the story. This is the time when extraordinary courage is called for. The unthinkable might have to be considered—a reshoot. (Hopefully the necessity of a reshoot is detected much earlier in the process, but if not, this is your last chance. I myself have gone back for reshoots, as have many famous directors. I have seen my students make that decision and turn a film that doesn't quite work into a "calling card" for their careers.)

Getting it as right as it can be is probably the singular most important attribute, after clarity, that a director can possess. This often takes a good dose of tenacity—a trait Kazan once told me was as important, if not more important, than talent.

PART THREE

ORGANIZING ACTION IN AN
ACTION SCENE

Everyone will recognize an action scene, even though there are many kinds from different genres. What they have in common is that they all consist of *overt physical action*. The difficulty for the character or characters in the scene is always a physical threat—whether a hurricane, an enemy with a weapon, or a monster—that can only be overcome by physical action. Films that have a preponderance of such scenes are known as action films, but action scenes also exist in dramas and comedies. The danger can come upon our hero unexpectedly, or she can choose to become embroiled in it for a host of reasons: to rescue someone, to apprehend someone, or to save her own skin. But in all cases, the resolution of the scene's conflict will come through physical action.

It is probably obvious to the reader that these scenes need special attention from the director. It might also be obvious that directors rarely get to practice rendering action scenes outside of the actual filming of one, and when making the film they do not often get a chance to rehearse these scenes that might consist of many extras, extensive damage, stunts, and special effects. Most likely the first action scene you will shoot will be for keeps, making the previsualization extremely important. The question becomes, How best to prepare?

First, it is crucial that the director familiarize herself with how master directors have rendered such scenes, whether it is from *The Seven Samurai* (Akira Kurosawa, 1954, Japan), *The French Connection* (William Friedkin, 1971), *Crouching Tiger, Hidden Dragon* (Ang Lee, 2000, China) *Gladiator* and *Black Hawk Down* (Ridley Scott, 2000 and 2001), *Master and Commander* (Peter Weir, 2003), *Flags of Our Fathers* (Clint Eastwood, 2006), *The Host* (Junho Bung, 2006, Korea), or *The Bourne Ultimatum* (Paul Greengrass, 2007). The list of "reference films" is endless, but the films you will choose to study will depend on their relevancy to the scene you are preparing. It's not that you will duplicate what others have done, but by studying masterfully rendered action scenes closely, it is possible to infer what the director's process might have been.

Some action scenes suffer because the director has "chopped up" the action into confusing pieces without sufficiently resolving the various separations between characters and/or objects, such as a loose gun. If we don't know who is nearest to the gun, the good guy or the bad guy, or we are entirely confused as to the geography in a chase scene, we lose a large part of the scene's power. When viewing these scenes, even from master directors, use your critical faculty to judge whether the scene supplies you with the necessary information to *fully appreciate* what is going on.

In the next chapter we will explore general principles that can be applied to any action scene, and we will use these principles to prepare a staging and camera design for an action scene from *Over Easy*, an unproduced feature screenplay written by the author. I chose this scene because the action is almost entirely concentrated on our protagonist or reactions to him, so we must deal with continuous action (as opposed to parallel action as in a battle scene where there are many significant actions going on at the same time that have to be accounted for to present a complete picture). By learning how to plan for continuous action, we can more easily manage scenes in which we have the freedom *and the obligation to the story* to leave our protagonist.

As in *A Piece of Apple Pie*, we will continue, before shooting, to imagine how we are going to edit the camera setups together. Our primary concern here will be to keep the audience abreast of the continuous action at the same time using the juxtaposition of camera angles, image size, and/ or movement to impart *dramatic impact*, only secondarily to articulate psychology, because the interior life of the characters can usually be "read" by their overt action. This butting together of images can be likened to our narrative beats, but the other two elements of a dramatic scene that have been introduced in this book—the fulcrum and dramatic blocks—are less relevant to action scenes because the unfolding of the overt action might not and *need not* be "constrained" by these categories. However, the pattern of beginning, middle, and end should be paid attention to in our orchestration, somewhat akin to a symphonic movement: quiet beginning in which the danger is introduced; rising action in response to the danger reaching a crescendo; dispatch of danger leading to a release of tension.

C H A P T E R   1 3

STAGING AND CAMERA FOR *OVER EASY* ACTION SCENE

Synopsis: GEORGE, mid-thirties, returning to his hometown after a 10-year absence, has just visited his comatose father in the hospital where he runs into TOM, a friend from high school who is driving a volunteer ambulance. Tom offers George a ride home.

EXT. COUNTRY ROAD - DAY

Bumper-to-bumper traffic crawling along. The ambulance stuck in the middle of it all, its lights flashing to no avail.

>   TOM
>   Lotta jerks moved out here
>   since you left. Come Labor
>   Day it quiets down some, but
>   it never gets like it was when
>   we were kids. Hell, I don't
>   know half the people in town
>   anymore. They're crowding out
>   the locals with the prices they're
>   paying for houses - Hell, if it
>   wasn't for my father leaving
>   me his place, I'd probably be homeless.

George looks intently through the passenger side window.

>   GEORGE
>   There's something wrong.

>   TOM
>   You're telling me - they're
>   crowding the locals out with
>   the prices they're paying -

>   GEORGE
>   (emphatically)
>   The bulldozer!

A BULLDOZER CRASHES into a BARN and SMASHES out the other side.

INT./EXT. AMBULANCE - CONTINUOUS

                          TOM
                      (noticing)
            Something very wrong.

The bulldozer is now headed for an EXPENSIVE NEW HOUSE.

                          GEORGE
                      (turning to Tom)
            Don't you think we ought to
            do something?

                          TOM
            There's an access road up ahead.

Tom punches the SIREN, pulls into the ONCOMING LANE and ACCELERATES.

An IMPATIENT PORSCHE pulls out behind the ambulance using it to run
interference.

MAYHEM as the ambulance drives in the ONCOMING LANE, forcing cars off
the road.

                          GEORGE
            Let me out!

                          TOM
            Don't worry, I've been to school for this.

                          GEORGE
            Maybe I can head it off on foot!

                          TOM
            Good thinking.

The ambulance cuts back sharply into the RIGHT LANE.

The Impatient Porsche, its protection lost, is faced with a HEAD-ON
COLLISION with an oncoming car. It chooses to run through a FRUIT STAND.

The ambulance SKIDS to a stop on the RIGHT SHOULDER as George jumps out
and starts running across the FIELD.

EXT. DRIVEWAY/EXPENSIVE NEW HOUSE - DAY

A LAWYER, in red-framed glasses, polo shirt, and Bermuda shorts, is
washing his JAGUAR. He turns to see:

LAWYER'S POV
The bulldozer bearing down on him and George chasing after it.

LAWYER
Do something!

GEORGE
If anyone's in that house you
better get them out!

George jumps onto the bulldozer, finds the unconscious OPERATOR slumped forward inside the open cab and tries to wrest the controls from him.

LAWYER
Stop that thing or I'll sue
you for every penny you've got!

The Lawyer jumps away from the Jaguar as the bulldozer scoops up the car and pushes it through the wall of the house.

INT. LIVING ROOM - CONTINUOUS

Large - richly appointed.

The LAWYER'S WIFE SCREAMS from a BALCONY above, as chairs, tables, couches - everything - is CRUSHED beneath the tracks of the bulldozer.

Then, in absolute horror,

LAWYER'S WIFE
NO, NO, NO!

as the bulldozer heads for a LARGE PAINTING of two glamorous comic book characters kissing and PUSHES IT THROUGH THE REAR WALL.

EXT. BACKYARD - CONTINUOUS

The bulldozer exits the back of the house, as a 10-wheeler dump truck, air brakes HISSING, SKIDS to a stop only yards away.

CATHERINE BRADFORD, 30s, beautiful, jumps out of the truck wearing jeans, T-shirt, and work boots.

CATHERINE
Daddy!

George manages to push the Operator's body away from the controls and stop the machine.

CATHERINE'S FATHER falls to the ground, dead.

Catherine runs to her father, kneels down beside him and pounds on his large chest.

CATHERINE
Daddy! Daddy, don't leave me!

                              LAWYER
                         (running up)

          Look what he's done to my house,
          my car! Look at it! Who's going
          to pay for all this? Priceless
          art and antiques were destroyed
          by this idiot! They can never be
          replaced! I'm going to see -

                             CATHERINE
          You bastard!

Catherine springs up and socks the Lawyer in the face then begins
kicking and punching him unmercifully.

                              LAWYER
          Stop it, you maniac!

George hesitates for a moment then decides he must intervene. He jumps
down from the bulldozer and pulls Catherine from the Lawyer. She
struggles in his arms to get free.

                              LAWYER
          I'll have you in jail for
          the rest of your life!

                             CATHERINE
          Let go of me!

                              GEORGE
          Not until you calm down!

Catherine manages to free an arm and hit George in the face. George
grabs the arm and pulls Catherine tight to him, forcing all resistance
from her. She starts to cry. George continues to hold her. She accepts
his consoling embrace.

We hear the ambulance SIREN approaching.

DEVELOPMENT OF SCREENPLAY

The generative image for this film (a valuable dramatic concept introduced to me by my colleague
at Columbia, Professor Lewis Cole) began with the image of a bulldozer going through a barn
with an unconscious operator at the controls. That image persisted for a few years, but a single
image does not a story make. Then it dawned on me that the bulldozer operator might be dead,
and that led, by some circuitous path in my subconscious, to a memory.

   I grew up across the street from a funeral parlor, and when I was a boy my family and
I would often sit on the front porch in nice weather and watch the proceedings across the street.
These memories ultimately led me to a metaphor that was tremendously helpful in writing the
screenplay. No matter where we actually live, we all live our lives across the street from a funeral
parlor. Now I was finally on my way to developing a story that allowed me to make use of the
bulldozer crashing through a barn, but to prevent it from seeming gratuitous, I needed something

else. That something else was Catherine, and this scene would be her entrance into the film. I also needed to make the scene *bigger* to dramatize another aspect of George's character, but as importantly, *to set up the possibility and further likelihood of other exaggerated scenes containing both humor and pathos in the face of death!* Hence the Lawyer, the Jaguar, the house, and the painting.

DIRECTOR'S PREPARATION FOR DIRECTING AN ACTION SCENE

This action scene, along with the previous scenes in the first act, establish the parameters for the tone of the film: a dramatic comedy, not an action film, so this scene we are going to work on does not have to, nor should it attempt to, fully emulate one. Yet it should be exciting, and the audience should be amused by the fate of the Porsche Driver and the Lawyer's car, house, and painting, and they should be moved by Catherine's grief. Without bending the film's genre out of shape, our job is to design an action scene that delivers the suspense, the humor, and the pathos that the screenplay calls for.

WHERE TO BEGIN?

I had an image of the location in my mind when I wrote the screenplay—that was necessary to describe the action—and all of you came up with your own image when you read it: the road jammed with cars, the bulldozer smashing through the barn then heading for the house, and so on. Most of your imaginings would be somewhat akin to mine. It would have to be to contain the action described on the page. That's where I recommend we begin.

If I could have drawn my image, it would be what is called a *concept sketch*, an important tool for scouting and/or building the set. This concept sketch in my head was vague, and when it came to figuring out the staging, it was not specific enough. I had to first come up with an approximate bird's-eye view (exterior floor plan) that would accommodate all the action, but to do that I had to first answer some questions (the same types of questions we asked when designing *A Piece of Apple Pie*). Where was the ambulance situated on the road? Where was it in relation to the barn? Where was the barn in relation to the house? Where should the ambulance stop? From what direction should the 10-wheeler truck approach the house? Where is the fruit stand in relation to all this? I made many iterations of the bird's eye, constantly making adjustments to first accommodate and then enhance the action.

Some of you might ask, Is this really part of the director's job? I think it is. Of course someone else can work out a first iteration—the director has every right to delegate jobs—but when it comes to locking down the staging, it should be the director's call.

Figure 13-1, drawn by my storyboard artist, Alex Reyes, includes not only the geography of the location and the architecture but some of the major action. It grew out of the description in the screenplay plus the bird's-eye view that was taken from my final iteration (that was not exactly final), which is why Alex worked in pencil until everything was finalized.

As always, for whatever type of scene we are designing, it is important to keep in mind the jobs that must be done within the scene. I've imbedded the jobs that must be done in this scene in the instructions for the storyboard artist. Also, the scene's job within the film must be kept in mind, and these too are imbedded in the instructions for the action that the storyboard artist is asked to render.

Now that you've seen a depiction of the location, I encourage you to come up with your own camera design for the entire scene, to imagine how you might render the action described in the screenplay. (You will have to imagine the interior of the house and the backyard.)

An important consideration in the design is the scene's *rhythm*. In the beginning it unfolds slowly, but when George and Tom decide to take action, the pace quickens considerably, reaches

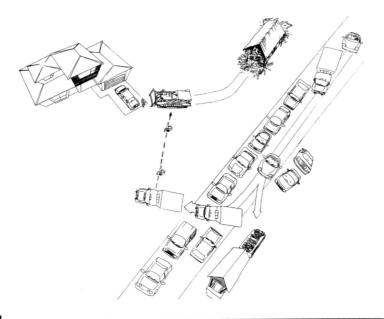

FIGURE 13-1

Concept sketch.

a crescendo, then at the very end of the scene the pace slows down and comes to a halt: George holding Catherine in his arms. It is a moment that needs to be extended—made larger. Because it is the end of the first act, we need to frame a question for the audience: What will happen *to* and *between* George and Catherine? We are able to orchestrate the rhythm with our camera movement and shot length to do that, and we will keep this in mind as we proceed.

OVER EASY ACTION SCENE/STAGING AND CAMERA ANGLES FOR STORYBOARD ARTIST

Note: The concept sketch has been broken down into six discrete *bird's eyes* for clarity of presentation of each stage of action, and camera setups with extensive movement have been rendered in more than one frame. All of the bird's-eye views were finalized *after* adjustments were made to earlier iterations to best accommodate the staging *and* camera. The bird's-eye view with the camera setups imposed on it for stage #1 is shown in Figure 13-2.

```
EXT. COUNTRY ROAD - DAY

Bumper-to-bumper traffic crawling along. The camera discovers the
ambulance stuck in the middle of it all, its lights flashing to no
avail.
```

Much of what was presented in the chapters on dramatic scenes will apply to action scenes. The first imperative is to tell the story clearly, to give the audience a clear understanding of the circumstances. Second, we must try to convey this information to the audience in the most dramatic and exciting way—to attempt to make all of the action vivid and to make our protagonist's difficulty palpable to the audience. Our aim is to strike them in the viscera. We don't want the

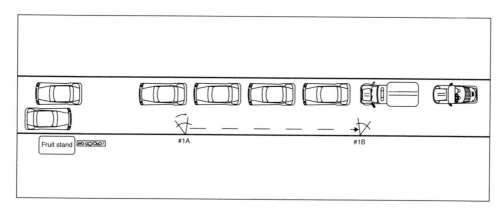

FIGURE 13-2 ──

Bird's-eye view with camera setups imposed on it for stage #1.

audience to sit back and watch without being engaged emotionally. Third, as has been mentioned, the camera design must pay heed to the overall tone of the film, in this case a dramatic comedy.

The first decision we have to make is what do we want to show in the first frame of the first shot, keeping in mind that this is a *transition* from the previous scene where George and Tom (the ambulance driver) were sitting inside the ambulance talking about old times. The question is, Do we reveal the new circumstance all at once—the ambulance mired in traffic—or do we reveal it slowly, first showing the line of traffic, then the ambulance stuck in it? I chose the *slow* reveal, a cinematic device used over and over and yet remaining a staple of cinematic language. It raises a question. Where are we and what is going on? With this in mind, we must first choose the initial position for camera setup #1. The left shoulder of the road is the logical choice, and the choice of the slow reveal requires that the camera moves (Figure 13-2).

The instructions to the storyboard artist follow in italics. (Unless otherwise indicated, the camera is always at eye level.)

CAMERA SETUP #1

WIDE TRACKING/PANNING shot FROM LEFT SHOULDER OF ROAD, past bumper-to-bumper traffic CRAWLING along (Figure 13-3). The shot SLOWLY TRACKS IN and STOPS on the ambulance stuck in the middle of it all, its lights flashing to no avail (Figure 13-4).
I've placed the dialogue off-screen to *carry* the camera move. We know who is talking because of the previous scene.

TOM (O.S.)
Lotta jerks moved out here
since you left. Come Labor
Day it quiets down some, but
it never gets like it was when
we were kids. I don't know half
the people in town anymore.
They're crowding out the locals
with the prices they're paying
for houses - Hell, if it wasn't
for my father leaving me his
place, I'd probably be homeless.

FIGURE 13-3

Camera setup #1A, beginning position.

FIGURE 13-4

Camera setup #1B, end position.

George looks intently through the passenger side window.

The first cut in the scene is to George "looking intently," articulating to the audience that "something is up," raising a question for them. The questions for the director are: Does the camera stay outside of the ambulance for this shot? What is the image size? From what angle? The first

FIGURE 13-5

Camera setup #2.

consideration is that there is no *need* to go into the ambulance at this moment, and the *strongest* cut, the one with the most impact, would be from the wide shot of the ambulance's driver's side to a close shot of George on the passenger side. The change in spatial dynamics coupled with the change in image size supplies a dramatic impact *absent of the content of the image*. Of course, because it is a close shot of George, we can read his psychology and understand immediately that his attention is elsewhere. As to the camera angle, do we want George to look camera left or camera right? Camera right would mean that the bulldozer is up ahead while camera left can indicate that it is abreast of the ambulance. The latter would set up a stronger image of the bulldozer smashing into the barn (Figure 13-8).

CAMERA SETUP #2

MEDIUM-CLOSE on George looking intently through the passenger side window, CAMERA LEFT (Figure 13-5).

                        GEORGE
                There's something wrong.

The sight line instruction establishes an axis between George and the bulldozer, and it must now be obeyed when Tom looks out the window.

The bird's-eye view with the camera setups imposed on it for stage #2 is contained in Figure 13-6.

CAMERA SETUP #3

TWO-SHOT through the front windshield of ambulance (Figure 13-7). *George is still concentrated on the bulldozer, while Tom doesn't have a clue as to what is going on. Nor does the audience.* (It is helpful for the storyboard artist to be kept abreast of what is going on in the shot if it is not explicit in the screenplay. In this case it is not.)

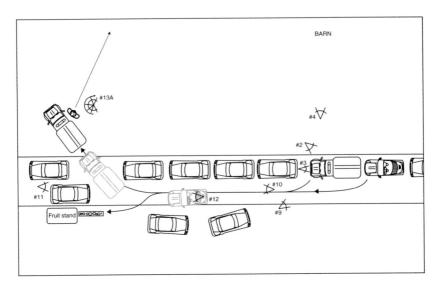

FIGURE 13-6 ————————————————————

Bird's-eye view with camera setups imposed on it for stage #2.

FIGURE 13-7 ————————————————————

Camera setup #3.

TOM
You're telling me - they're
crowding the locals out with
the prices they're paying -

GEORGE
(emphatically)
The bulldozer!

FIGURE 13-8

Camera setup #4.

What this two-shot does, and this is suggested by the screenplay, is to hold off on the reveal of the bulldozer. This delay makes the audience curious as to what is concerning George, and because they must wait for the answer, it has more dramatic impact when it is delivered.

CAMERA SETUP #4

WIDE ANGLE of the bulldozer CRASHING into a barn (Figure 13-8), *containing the spatial dynamics of the ambulance as shown in the bird's-eye views for stages #2 and #3* (Figure 13-6 and Figure 13-20).

The camera contains the spatial dynamics of the ambulance, and we assign it as both George's and Tom's POV.

INT./EXT. AMBULANCE - CONTINUOUS

There is no floor plan for the interior of the ambulance.

TOM
(noticing)
Something very wrong.

CAMERA SETUP #5

MEDIUM-CLOSE from passenger seat of Tom craning to see outside, CAMERA LEFT (Figure 13-9).

The camera goes inside the ambulance for the first time in this scene, differentiating between the *before and after* of Tom's awareness, and sets up the next shot of the bulldozer smashing out through the back of the barn.

FIGURE 13-9

Camera setup #5.

CAMERA SETUP #6

The bulldozer SMASHES out the other side of the barn and is now headed
for an EXPENSIVE NEW HOUSE.

There are many places one could place the camera to render the bulldozer smashing through
the back of the barn, but if we want to make a dramatic impact on the audience *we must do
more then simply convey the information.* We must try to evoke SMASHING in the audience's
viscera. Stop and think for a moment of the possibilities for camera placement. How about if we
placed the camera *on* the bulldozer? There would be more *immediacy* to the image, more sense of
the machine's *destructive force,* while establishing the ability of the objective camera to "go for a
ride," which, in my last previsual iteration, is used four more times. (This back and forth previsualization offers the director the chance to *see* a more organic design, an integration of stylistic elements, *where none existed before starting the process.*)

There is another dramatic opportunity in play here. The screenplay says the bulldozer "is now
headed for an Expensive New House," but suppose we hold off that reveal for a beat? It would be
best if SMASHING (through the back of the barn) does not "step on" the REVEAL (of the expensive house). Let us have the bulldozer clear the barn with open farmland ahead, *then* the veer to
the right revealing, more dramatically, the "new target" (the house). Also, to announce to the audience that this is indeed the *actual* view from the bulldozer, we would place its blade at the bottom
of the frame. The next step is to convey that information clearly to the storyboard artist.

*WIDE-ANGLE (MOVING) from bulldozer, top of bulldozer blade at bottom of the frame,
as it SMASHES through the back of the barn revealing OPEN FARMLAND ahead, then VEERS
RIGHT to REVEAL an EXPENSIVE NEW HOUSE* (Figure 13-10) *and bird's-eye view for stage
#3* (Figure 13-20).

George turns to Tom.

　　　　　　　　　　　　　　　GEORGE
　　　　　　　　Don't you think we ought to
　　　　　　　　do something?

FIGURE 13–10

Camera setup #6.

FIGURE 13-11

Camera setup #7.

 My choice here would be a close-up of George to articulate his sense of urgency, and it would be from the interior of the ambulance, an urgency that would be diminished if we returned to the exterior.

CAMERA SETUP #7

CLOSE-UP on George from interior of ambulance (Figure 13-11).

TOM
There's an access road up ahead.

FIGURE 13-12

Camera setup #8.

Tom punches the SIREN.

    Tom's dialogue, "to inform," could be delivered off-screen over George's shot, but by cutting to Tom for his line, it articulates the moment, making sure we understand that he has a plan, while at the same time placing the camera in the right place to render Tom punching the siren. Why show that? Because another important concept is at play: announce the beginning of a dramatic event, in this case, the race to save the house. When Tom punches the siren, we will cut outside for its first blast.

CAMERA SETUP #8

MEDIUM on Tom from passenger seat (Figure 13-12), *same angle as shot #5.*
    The shot PANS from Tom's face to his hand moving to the dashboard and turning on the siren.
    Why should we use the same angle as camera setup #5? Simply because it is already in position to render Tom's dialogue and his turning on the siren. (Unless you have a justifiable reason for moving the camera, I suggest you keep it where it is.)

The ambulance pulls into the ONCOMING LANE and ACCELERATES. An IMPATIENT PORSCHE pulls out behind the ambulance, using it to run interference.

    A wide-angle lens, placed low, increases the sense of speed of an oncoming vehicle.

CAMERA SETUP #9

WIDE LOW-ANGLE in front of the ambulance, from LEFT SHOULDER of road. Ambulance pulls into the ONCOMING LANE and ACCELERATES. An IMPATIENT PORSCHE pulls out behind the ambulance, using it to run interference (Figure 13-13), *bird's-eye view for stage #2* (Figure 13-6).

MAYHEM, as the ambulance drives in the ONCOMING LANE, forcing cars off the road.

FIGURE 13-13

Camera setup #9.

To make the mayhem most palpable for the audience, I would place camera setup #10 inside the cab of the ambulance. Nowhere else would the audience feel as powerfully the immediacy of the near head-on collisions. The radical change from the low angle of camera setup #9 to this eye-level moving camera pointing in the opposite direction is *in and of itself* energizing. This setup is also the second image of the stylistic element that has previously been introduced, and it is one that we will continue to build on: that of "taking the camera for a ride."

SHOT #10

MEDIUM WIDE-ANGLE (MOVING) through the ambulance windshield, showing TWO CARS from oncoming lane being forced off the road (Figure 13-14), *bird's-eye view for stage #2* (Figure 13-6).

> GEORGE
> Let me out!

> TOM
> Don't worry, I've been to school for this.

> GEORGE
> Maybe I can head it off on foot!

> TOM
> Good thinking.

The ambulance cuts back sharply into the RIGHT LANE.

This dialogue could be rendered from inside the ambulance or through its windshield, but those two shots would have a redundant quality to it, and more importantly, it would not *acknowledge* the unfolding escalation of action. Plus, we need to resolve separation at this point—to "glue" together the ambulance and Porsche in relationship to the other cars. We could

FIGURE 13-14

Camera setup #10.

accomplish both jobs by putting the dialogue over an exterior shot, but where would we place the camera? The camera setup that would render both of these jobs strongly *and* economically would be above the traffic from the middle of the road. If we placed it just ahead of the spot where the ambulance will cut back into the right lane, we will have accomplished two more important jobs: the ambulance pulling off the road *and* a clear reveal of the Porsche left without its protection. Looking ahead (as we must), a fifth job is accomplished by the sustained length of this overhead shot. It sets up, by way of contrast, the rhythmic change and juxtaposition of shorter edited images envisioned for camera setups #12 and #13, which follow immediately.

Note: Is there a rhyme or reason to when you use one shot to accomplish more than one job? It is easy to discern a reason *after the fact*, but we are attempting to previsualize *before shooting*, the simple fact being that if you have not rendered the action in a strong way on the set, there will be a price to pay in the editing room. Is there a hard and fast rule to follow? No, there are too many extenuating circumstances, but the film's tone and the director's vision are paramount.

CAMERA SETUP #11

HIGH WIDE-ANGLE from in front of the ambulance racing down the LEFT LANE, covering the preceding dialogue (Figure 13-15), bird's-eye view for stage #2 (Figure 13-6). The ambulance cuts sharply back into the RIGHT LANE. It should be the only hole in the bumper-to-bumper traffic, leaving the Impatient Porsche totally exposed.

The Impatient Porsche is faced with a HEAD-ON COLLISION with an oncoming car. It chooses to run through a FRUIT STAND.

You will not be surprised about my choice of placement for camera setup #12: through the windshield of the Porsche. It is the third use of this stylistic element—the camera going along for a ride—rendering viscerally the impending head-on collision with another car as well as the actual collision with the fruit stand. In the editing we will have two choices: to keep the entire shot running from beginning to end (Figures 13-16 and 13-17) or intercut the ambulance skidding to a stop

FIGURE 13-15

Camera setup #11.

FIGURE 13-16

Camera setup #12, beginning position.

(Figure 13-18), camera setup #13A on the bird's eye for stage #2 (Figure 13-6). Visualize this possibility for a moment and see if you agree.

CUT TO: The Porsche narrowly averting a head-on collision, now heading for the fruit stand.
CUT TO: PANNING with the ambulance skidding to a stop on the right side of the road.
CUT TO: The Porsche colliding with the fruit stand.

FIGURE 13-17

Camera setup #12, end position.

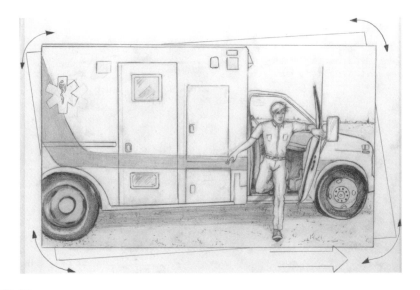

FIGURE 13-18

Camera setup #13a.

Each one of the separate edited shots is made stronger by virtue of its juxtaposition to one another, along with the change in rhythm due to shortened lengths.

CAMERA SETUP #12

The Impatient Porsche, its protection lost, is faced with a HEAD-ON COLLISION with an ONCOMING CAR (Figure 13-16), bird's-eye view for stage #2 (Figure 13-6). It chooses to

FIGURE 13-19 ——————————————————————————————————

Camera setup #13, position (B).

RUN THROUGH A FRUIT STAND (Figure 13-17). *Oncoming car and fruit stand FRAMED THROUGH THE PORSCHE WINDSHIELD.*

CAMERA SETUP #13

The ambulance SKIDS to a stop on the RIGHT SHOULDER as George jumps out and starts running across the FIELD.

   With the idea of heightening the action, I have envisioned a medium-wide STEADICAM PAN WITH THE AMBULANCE as it turns sharply from the road and skids to a stop, then as George leaps from the ambulance and begins running toward the bulldozer, the STEADICAM PANS WITH GEORGE AND RUNS BEHIND HIM. Why this choice rather than a smooth tracking shot? Because the jostling of the steadicam frame will impart more of a sense of urgency to George's exertion. Why from behind? Because from this angle we simultaneously orient the audience spatially to what's up ahead—the bulldozer, the Lawyer, the Jaguar, and the house—before we begin taking the scene apart in separation. Why are we rendering *all* of this action with one take if we are planning to cut after the ambulance skids to a stop? Because the Porsche's collision with the fruit stand is only a "hiccup" in the introduction of this new stylistic element, which the audience will "feel," even in the short rapid pan of the ambulance skidding to a stop.
   MEDIUM-WIDE STEADICAM PANS LEFT TO RIGHT with Ambulance skidding to a stop and George jumping out (Figure 13-18), *bird's-eye view for stage 2* (Figure 13-6).
   As George runs to head off the bulldozer, the STEADICAM PANS LEFT TO RIGHT with him (Figure 13-19), *with the house, bulldozer, Lawyer, and Jaguar in the background, then RUNS BEHIND HIM, camera position 13B on bird's-eye for stage #3* (Figure 13-20).

EXT. DRIVEWAY/EXPENSIVE NEW HOUSE

A LAWYER, in red-framed glasses, polo shirt, and Bermuda shorts is washing his new JAGUAR. He turns to see:

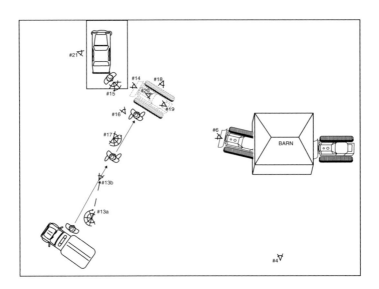

FIGURE 13-20

Bird's eye for stage #3.

```
LAWYER'S POV
The bulldozer bearing down on him and George chasing after it.
```

First *we see* a picture of utter satisfaction, announcing to us, "ain't life grand." Our job is to inject some menace into this idyllic picture. My strongest visualization is the camera back on the bulldozer (first used in Figure 13-10), moving inexorably toward the Lawyer and his car. The bulldozer blade at the bottom of the frame for a second time has the resonating effect of a familiar frame, *even if now that frame contains an entirely new image.*

```
CAMERA SETUP #14
```

WIDE-ANGLE (MOVING) from bulldozer; its blade in lower foreground of frame, Lawyer and Jaguar in background (20 feet or so) (Figure 13-21). *Indicate Lawyer turning toward bulldozer.*
     He turns to see:
     I don't recommend assigning POVs to secondary characters unless it is clearly *appropriate to the moment*, which is the case here. Indeed, what other image would generate such power? Does the Lawyer see both the bulldozer and George at the same time? No. First one, then the other. For the Lawyer, the bulldozer is the problem, while George is the solution. How do we connect them?
     Camera design should be organic, growing out of what came before, but as mentioned more than once in this book, we can rarely ever see the whole picture as we are proceeding in our design shot by shot. Still, one piece of advice will hold you in good stead: *Explore first the stylistic elements that you have already introduced.* Here it would be the pan, *even though when it was initially introduced, the objective narrator generated it.* It would connect the bulldozer and George. It wouldn't be a casual camera movement but an *energizing* swish-pan (Figures 13-22 and 13-23).

```
CAMERA SETUP #15
```

LAWYER'S POV: MEDIUM on bulldozer (Figure 13-22), *SWISH-PAN RIGHT to discover George running toward the bulldozer, MOVING FROM RIGHT TO LEFT IN THE FRAME*

FIGURE 13-21

Camera setup #14.

FIGURE 13-22

Camera setup #15, starting position before swish-pan.

(Figure 13-23), *bird's-eye view for stage #3* (Figure 13-20). (The storyboard artist must always check the position of the camera setup on the bird's eye before drawing the storyboard.)

　　Earlier in this book, I pointed out that POVs usually should be preceded or followed by a close or medium shot of the character so that the audience can assign that POV to the character. However, here there is no question as to who the audience will assign the POV to because it contains the spatial dynamics of the Lawyer, the only possible choice, as well as the immediacy of the moment.

The Lawyer yells to George.

LAWYER
　　　　　Do something!

FIGURE 13-23

Camera setup #15, position at end of swish-pan.

We'll keep the Lawyer's dialogue on-camera. There is no need for anything special here. In fact, if we attempted to heighten this moment by, say, a fast zoom into the Lawyer, it would seem forced *because it would be unnecessary*. A shot wide enough to show the Lawyer *and* the Jaguar, and containing the spatial dynamics of George, would be my choice. (I recommend that the camera usually be placed *inside the dramatic dynamics of a scene*, in this instance George and the Lawyer. This, of course, is not always applicable because sometimes a camera outside of the dynamics of a scene is more suitable. An example would be a *release shot* to announce the end of a dramatic block or the end of a scene.)

Camera Setup #16

MEDIUM on Lawyer and Jaguar LOOKING CAMERA LEFT, containing the spatial dynamics of George.
     Camera setup #16 (Figure 13-24) establishes an axis between the Lawyer and George that must now be obeyed. Because the Lawyer is looking camera left, George must now look at him camera right.

Off of Lawyer's look:

> GEORGE
> If anyone's in that house you
> better get them out!

George jumps onto the bulldozer.

This camera setup is from the objective camera (no longer the Lawyer's POV), and because it is juxtaposed against a static frame of the Lawyer, I would choose to render George with a static frame instead going back to the steadicam, which by now has run its course. George would be running *toward* the camera (right to left in the frame), and as he passes the camera, it would pan with him right to left, the pan ending with George leaping on the bulldozer.
     I then visualized what the next shot would be *after* George leaps on the bulldozer: George entering the bulldozer cab *from the opposite side*. Again, a change in angle that *in and of itself*

FIGURE 13-24

Camera setup #16.

is energizing. To make this next cut smoother, it would be best if at the end of this shot (camera setup #17) George *and the camera* were at the same height as the bulldozer's cab, so I added a *crane up* with George to the cab level, allowing a *match cut* in the action.

We haven't mentioned *film-time* in this scene, but we should constantly be aware of it, especially in an action scene. When we cut from the shot of the Lawyer (camera setup #16) to George, we cannot have him continue running for more than a few steps because it is now imperative that *something else must happen*, such as George reaching the bulldozer. Here is a good place to "shorten" the distance between George and the bulldozer so that as soon as we pan with him to the bulldozer it is *right there* for him to leap aboard. We don't shorten the distance so much that the audience is aware of it, but we do shorten it enough so that when we end the pan to the bulldozer its closeness is a momentary surprise, giving impetus to the moment. As I pointed out earlier, this flexibility in film-time is one of the major tools directors have to work with.

An important point that you might have noticed is that because of the Lawyer's POV of George (Figure 13-23), which reoriented George's position vis-à-vis the bulldozer, we are now able to place the objective camera on the opposite side of George, changing his original axis (and screen direction) vis-à-vis the Lawyer and the bulldozer. In camera setup #13A (see Figure 13-20 bird's eye for stage #3), George approaches the camera left to right (Figure 13-18). In placing camera setup #17 across the original axis, George is now approaching the camera right to left (Figure 13-25). Another way to look at it is that the camera is shooting George's right profile as it pans with him in camera setup #13A, and it is shooting his left profile as it pans with him in camera setup #17. This would have disoriented the audience without the intervention of the Lawyer's POV, which reorients George and the bulldozer, and instead of creating confusion, this jump in screen direction energizes the moment.

CAMERA SETUP #17

MEDIUM-CLOSE SHOT of George approaching. He TURNS CAMERA RIGHT toward Lawyer (Figure 13-25). *The shot continues as GEORGE PASSES THE CAMERA, which PANS RIGHT TO LEFT AND CRANES UP with him as he leaps aboard the bulldozer* (Figure 13-26), *bird's eye for stage #3* (Figure 13-20).

FIGURE 13-25

Camera setup #17, first position.

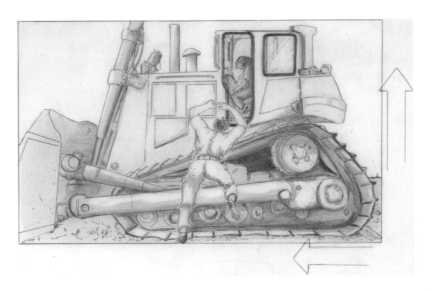

FIGURE 13-26

Continuation of camera setup #17, position after pan.

```
George finds the unconscious OPERATOR slumped forward inside the open
cab and tries to wrest the controls from him.
```

George will reach the cab in the previous shot (in the crane up) and enter it in this shot. The cut will be on the continuation of action, but it will also be from a wide shot to a much tighter shot on the opposite side of the bulldozer. Aside from making for an energizing juxtaposition of images, the right side of the bulldozer will be introduced—the side on which the remainder of the action takes place. (I knew this to be the case because of my previsualization.) This is an ancillary

FIGURE 13-27

Camera setup #18.

benefit because the main concerns here were the continuity of action and the Operator's entrance into the film, even though we have seen him from a distance. Here he is in the foreground, dominating the frame.

CAMERA SETUP #18

MEDIUM TWO-SHOT of George and Operator from OPPOSITE SIDE of cab (Figure 13-27).
The Lawyer yells to George.

                              LAWYER
              Stop that thing or I'll sue
              you for every penny you've got!

The Lawyer jumps out of the way of the bulldozer.

We can do this by having the preceding action take place from George's POV through the window of the bulldozer's cab, establishing direct eye contact between the two just before the Lawyer scurries away. The windshield wiper blades in the foreground will establish it as George's POV even before we cut to a close-up of George with the blades prominent in the frame. The main consideration for George's POV, however, is that it makes palpable, as no other shot can, that George is *aboard*. If we follow this POV with his close-up, we will be able to *read* George's psychology as he heads inexorably toward the house. (We've not taken any pains to get inside George's head since he began running, nor have we needed to, but now we must reintroduce his *psychological presence*, first because we want to see his reaction [a good enough reason in itself], but also because being in George's head is important for the full appreciation of the end of the scene. This close-up of him keeps alive the narrator's [camera's] ability to do that.)

CAMERA SETUP #19

George's MOVING POV from bulldozer through front window of cab; the Lawyer jumps out of the way of the bulldozer, CAMERA RIGHT (Figure 13-28), *bird's eye view for stage #3* (Figure 13-20).

FIGURE 13-28 ───

Camera setup #19, George's MOVING POV.

FIGURE 13-29 ───

Camera setup #20.

Having the Lawyer jump left to right sets up the logistics that give us the ability to have him reappear at the rear of the house, running toward Catherine and her father, right to left (Figure 13-43). Without having to think about it, we understand immediately the path he took *around* the house.

CAMERA SETUP #20

CLOSE-UP of George through windshield of bulldozer (Figure 13-29), *bird's-eye view for stage #3* (Figure 13-20).

FIGURE 13-30

Camera setup #21.

The bulldozer SCOOPS UP the Jaguar ...

Where would you place the camera? Continue thinking about getting the most impact. For me it would be a low angle with the Jaguar in the foreground. Again, the radical change in camera angles in and of itself supplies dramatic energy absent of the content of the action.

CAMERA SETUP #21

LOW ANGLE from behind the Jaguar (Figure 13-30), *bird's-eye view for stage #3* (Figure 13-20).

... and pushes it (the Jaguar) through the wall of the house.

   We could cut to the camera mounted on the bulldozer and go through the wall of the house with that shot, and we will, but in the edited version I'd like to try to hold off this inevitable moment by first cutting inside the house where everything is tranquil.
   Note: There are no floor plans for the interior of the house because the angles for each shot seem to be quite clear.

INT. LIVING ROOM - CONTINUOUS

Large - richly appointed.

   I've previously mentioned that it is desirable to strongly convey the inexorable movement of the bulldozer, but here I am suggesting the opposite: first seeing "richly appointed" by placing the camera *inside*, facing the interior wall, and holding this shot for a couple of beats to create suspense while we wait, then wait for another beat, *then* the Jaguar comes crashing through the wall into the room.

CAMERA SETUP #22

WIDE on the INTERIOR wall as the Jaguar is pushed through it (Figure 13-31).

FIGURE 13-31

Camera setup #22.

FIGURE 13-32

Camera setup #23.

We still have our camera mounted on the bulldozer, and now I would cut to this, elaborating the crashing through the wall by combining the two shots. In some films this moment could be further extended with slow motion, but it would be wrong for this film.

CAMERA SETUP #23

WIDE on the OPPOSITE wall as the bulldozer enters the house (Figure 13-32).

The LAWYER'S WIFE SCREAMS from a BALCONY above...

A wide angle looking up at the Wife on the balcony establishes where she is in the room and her spatial relationship to the bulldozer. There is no need to do more.

FIGURE 13-33

Camera setup #24.

CAMERA SETUP #24

WIDE ANGLE from below looking up at Wife standing on a balcony (Figure 13-33).

```
...as chairs, tables, couches - everything - are CRUSHED beneath the
tracks of the bulldozer.
```

The best place to see this destruction is from a high angle, and appropriately enough it comes immediately after the Wife's low angle, giving us a strong change in perspective. Because of this high angle, the audience will assign this as the Wife's POV *and* her emotional involvement in the destruction.

CAMERA SETUP #25

HIGH WIDE ANGLE from balcony OF DESTRUCTION BELOW containing spatial dynamics of Wife (Figure 13-34).

```
      Then, in absolute horror,

                        LAWYER'S WIFE
            NO, NO, NO!
```

We will definitely cut back to the Wife for this dialogue, and to articulate the escalation of her "horror," the image size will be considerably tighter. You might have noticed that we have not resolved separation between the Wife and living room, nor the bulldozer, nor the painting. Does it matter, and if it doesn't, why? It is not necessary because the high angle that we assign to the Wife as her POV will orient the audience satisfactorily.

CAMERA SETUP #26

MEDIUM LOW ANGLE of Lawyer's Wife, with balcony ledge in foreground (Figure 13-35).

```
The bulldozer heads for a LARGE PAINTING of two glamorous comic book
characters kissing and PUSHES IT THROUGH THE REAR WALL.
```

FIGURE 13-34 ——————————————————————————————————

Camera setup #25.

FIGURE 13-35 ——————————————————————————————————

Camera setup #26.

As with any push we have to see the pusher, and here it is more than a momentary push, it is a *driving force* that has some duration. The best place to show this destructive power is once again from our camera on the bulldozer, the blade in the lower part of the frame.

CAMERA SETUP #27

MEDIUM WIDE ANGLE (MOVING) of painting with top of bulldozer blade in foreground (Figure 13-36).

FIGURE 13-36

Camera setup #27.

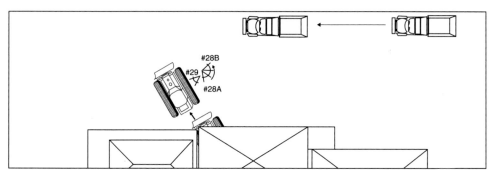

FIGURE 13-37

Bird's eye for stage #4, rear of house.

EXT. REAR OF HOUSE - DAY

Bird's eye for rear of house, Figure 13-37.

The bulldozer exits the back of the house as a 10-wheeler dump truck, air brakes HISSING, SKIDS to a stop only yards away. CATHERINE BRADFORD, 30s, beautiful, jumps out of the truck wearing jeans, T-shirt, and work boots.

CATHERINE

Daddy!

The destruction has run its course. It has hit its apex with the painting. *Now the audience is expecting something else to happen*. We do not want them to get ahead of us, so the *next thing*

FIGURE 13-38

Camera setup #28, beginning position before swish-pan.

should be something *unexpected* (Catherine's entrance). We *must* show the bulldozer coming through the rear wall of the house, but as soon as the maximum force is expended, we should move to introduce Catherine. My choice would be to use one more swish-pan. It is both energizing and does the job of resolving the separation.

The image of the bulldozer exiting the house should be strong, as should Catherine's entrance. To satisfy the needs of both images, you have two variables to work with: the focal length of your lens and the distance of the truck from the house. I would start with placing the truck in its end position—getting a strong frame for it—then pan the camera (or director's viewfinder) back to the house to see what kind of a frame you have for the exiting of the bulldozer. With a few back and forths you'll get the right balance of image size for both the beginning and end of the pan.

CAMERA SETUP #28

LOW WIDE ANGLE on bulldozer exiting the rear of the house (Figure 13-38), *then SWISH-PAN LEFT, to LOW WIDE ANGLE on truck MOVING INTO FRAME, STOPPING, and CATHERINE JUMPING OUT, LOOKING CAMERA RIGHT* (Figure 13-39).

George manages to push the Operator's body away from the controls and turn the key off, stopping the machine.

We will not show what causes the machine to stop. We toyed with the idea, but it "got in the way." When we cut to the shot of the body falling from the machine, everyone will assign their own cause. *Do not let mechanical details get in the way of the drama unless absolutely essential for the story,* and then try to do it elegantly, although sometimes it is not possible. In that event we can take solace that *perfection is not an aesthetic category.*

CAMERA SHOT #29

MEDIUM ON GEORGE from RIGHT SIDE OF CAB PUSHING OPERATOR OUT OF FRAME (Figure 13-40), *same frame as* Figure 13-27.

FIGURE 13-39

Camera setup #28, end position after swish-pan.

FIGURE 13-40

Camera setup #29.

The bird's eye for stage #5 is illustrated in Figure 13-41.

CATHERINE'S FATHER falls to the ground, dead. Catherine runs to him.

How many shots must we use to show the father falling and Catherine running to him? It could be as many as three: angle on father falling; reverse angle of Catherine seeing it; reverse angle of Catherine running to her father, resolving the separation between them. Does this elaboration get us anywhere dramatically? No, in fact just the opposite; we would be bending the moment

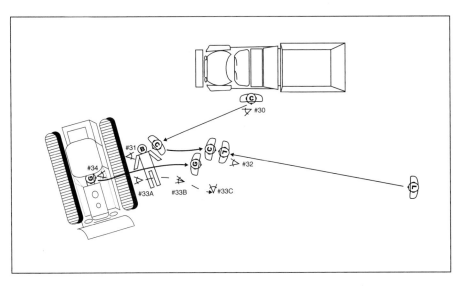

FIGURE 13-41 ——

Bird's eye for stage #5.

out of shape, articulating Catherine's reaction when we can already imagine what it would be, and giving undue attention to a character we have yet to "meet." I would elect for one shot: the father falling from the bulldozer as it comes to a stop. It would contain Catherine's spatial dynamics (we know she is at the truck and we know where the truck is vis-à-vis the bulldozer) then have Catherine enter the frame running to her father.

CAMERA SETUP #30

WIDE ANGLE OF MR. BRADFORD FALLING FROM THE BULLDOZER, containing Catherine's spatial dynamics (Figure 13-42). CATHERINE ENTERS THE SHOT running.

Catherine kneels down beside her father and pounds on his large chest.

                              CATHERINE
                Daddy! Daddy, don't leave me!

                              LAWYER
                         (running up)
                Look what he's done to my house,
                my car! Look at it! Who's going
                to pay for all this? Priceless
                art and antiques were destroyed
                by this idiot! They can never be
                replaced! I'm going to see -

A reverse shot at ground level wide enough to capture not only the foreground of Catherine and her father but also the Lawyer running up and standing over them. I would continue to hold off a close-up of Catherine that would articulate her grief unnecessarily.

FIGURE 13-42

Camera setup #30.

FIGURE 13-43

Camera setup #31.

CAMERA SETUP #31

MEDIUM-WIDE GROUND LEVEL, Catherine and her father in foreground, Lawyer running up, then standing over them in background (Figure 13-43).

Catherine springs up...

                                CATHERINE
```
        You bastard!
```

```
...and socks the Lawyer in the face.
```

In editing together the beginning of this shot and the end of the previous shot, we have an overlapping of action. During shooting Catherine would sock the lawyer in camera setup #31, then again in setup #32. For maximum force, this match-cut would occur just before Catherine's blow strikes the lawyer. This reverse angle along with the height change will further energize the moment.

CAMERA SETUP #32

REVERSE ANGLE, EYE LEVEL (Figure 13-44).

Let's step back for a moment before we decide how we will continue to the end of this scene, which is also the end of the first act. Remember the rhythmic pattern that is inherent in the written scene: starts slow, speeds up, slows down. To follow the dramatic and emotional trajectory that the camera must illicit in these final moments of the first act, let us first read the screenplay's description of action from here to the final frame so that we can get a sense of its flow.

```
Catherine begins kicking and punching the Lawyer unmercifully.
```

                                 LAWYER
```
        Stop it, you maniac!
```

```
George watches for a moment then decides he must intervene. He jumps
down from the bulldozer and pulls Catherine from the Lawyer. She
struggles in his arms to get free.
```

                                 LAWYER
```
        I'll have you in jail for
        the rest of your life!
```

FIGURE 13-44

Camera setup #32.

                                    CATHERINE
                        Let go of me!

                                    GEORGE
                        Not until you calm down!

Catherine manages to free an arm and hit George in the face. George
grabs the arm and pulls Catherine tight to him, forcing all resistance
from her. She starts to cry. George continues to hold her. She accepts
his consoling embrace.

We hear the ambulance SIREN approaching.

The first question we should ask ourselves is, What must we convey to the audience? The
answer is in two parts: Catherine's psychological change from anger to grief—to make it palpable
to the audience—while at the same time making it clear that this is the beginning of a romantic
relationship. As I pointed out earlier, it is important to leave the audience with a moment to frame
a question at the end of this first act, even if unconsciously.

We know what we have to do; let's figure out how to do it. Again, we'll start with some
questions. Do we want to elaborate the fight between Catherine and the Lawyer? It would serve no
purpose. However, when George looks down from the bulldozer (Figure 13-45) we are obligated
to show what he sees—Catherine beating on the Lawyer (Figure 13-46)—but we need not make
more out of it. Do we need to show George intervening, pulling Catherine from the Lawyer and
subduing her? We do. We must shoot the action described in the screenplay (Figures 13-47, 13-48,
13-49). We could accomplish all that with one wide shot, couldn't we? Or we could cover the
scene with multiangles that when cut together would fully convey the action of the story. However,
just rendering the action is not enough, nor is hyping it with multiangles. To fulfill our obligation
to this story, we must create an emotional vortex that pulls the audience into the lives of these two
people, and as we know, the camera can help do that (Figures 13-50, 13-51, 13-52).

We'll need some help from our staging to get rid of the Lawyer as soon as possible, leaving
George and Catherine alone. (The Lawyer obviously cannot disappear from the scene, but he can

FIGURE 13-45

Camera setup #33A, beginning position.

FIGURE 13-46

Camera setup #34, George's POV.

FIGURE 13-47

Continuation of camera setup #33, positon (B).

disappear from the frame, and that's enough.) We will elaborate both Catherine's journey from anger to grief while at the same time cementing the beginning of a love story. To accomplish this I will assign the job to our steadicam operator. This shot (camera setup #33, bird's eye for stages #5 and #6), will be interrupted in the editing by George's POV (camera setup #34) but will then continue uninterrupted to the end of the scene. The camera's movement will not only render the action of the scene—the first order of business—but it will extend the emotional moment, making

FIGURE 13-48 ————————————————————————————————

Continuation of camera setup #33, position (C).

FIGURE 13-49 ————————————————————————————————

Continuation of camera setup #33, position (D).

it larger. If we hold the last frame for a few beats (Figure 13-52), the audience will have time to form a question concerning the nature of the story they are about to see.

The storyboards for the remainder of the scene and the accompanying bird's eye for stage #6 follow.

CAMERA SETUP #33

MEDIUM ON GEORGE hesitating (Figure 13-45).

FIGURE 13-50

Continuation of camera setup #33, position (E).

FIGURE 13-51

Continuation of camera setup #33, position (F).

CAMERA SETUP #34

GEORGE'S POV: HIGH ANGLE LOOKING DOWN FROM BULLDOZER as Catherine continues to pummel the Lawyer (Figure 13-46).
MEDIUM ON GEORGE JUMPING DOWN from the bulldozer, CAMERA RIGHT (Figure 13-47), *continuation of camera setup #33B.*

FIGURE 13-52 ──────────────────────────────────────

Continuation of camera setup #33, end position (G).

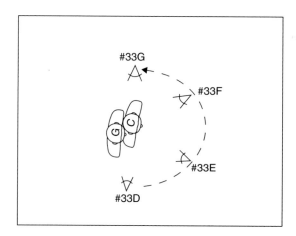

FIGURE 13-53 ──────────────────────────────────────

Bird's eye view for stage #6.

George reaches Catherine (Figure 13-48) *and pulls her away from the Lawyer.*
George pulls Catherine into their own TWO SHOT (Figure 13-49) *as the STEADICAM BEGINS TO CIRCLE their struggle* (Figure 13-50), *MOVING AROUND THEM 180 DEGREES for the embrace that ends the scene* (Figures 13-51 and 13-52), *bird's eye for stage #6* (Figure 13-53).

At one point in the screenplay I had the Lawyer's Wife arriving in the scene on-camera, but it unnecessarily complicated the main job here—getting George and Catherine alone in an extended moment. Yet it would be a good idea to let the audience know that the Wife was not hurt and to answer the question, What is the Lawyer doing? (We don't want to leave unanswered any questions that the audience might have.) I would have the Wife arrive *off-camera*, and both of them would be heard off-screen vociferously accusing and threatening both Catherine and George—in stark contrast to what we are seeing on screen. And then:

```
We hear the ambulance SIREN approaching.
```

Hopefully you will be able to take away from this analysis a methodology to approach the directing of *any* action scene, even those with a cast of thousands. It consists mainly of asking questions, *but the answers can only come from your familiarity with cinematic possibilities*, and these we find in films by master directors. I named a handful in the introduction, but there are thousands more. It's not that we slavishly follow anyone else, but as in all art forms, we progress from what has come before.

P A R T F O U R

ORGANIZING ACTION IN A NARRATIVE SCENE

There are film scenes that do not fit into the dramatic paradigm, nor are they dominated by physical action, yet in most films these are the scenes that comprise the majority of screen time and carry the burden of telling most of the story. I have labeled them *narrative scenes.* They supply exposition, circumstance, character delineation, relationships (both static and dramatic)—in short, *most,* and in some cases, *all,* of the information that is crucial to a story. Some of these scenes might contain conflict and some might contain overt action, while others might contain a good deal of suspense.

If narrative scenes make up most of a film, why wait until now to introduce them? It is because their structures are so much more elusive, less easy to define, coming as they do in such a great variety. *(It is their variety that is one of the great strengths of cinema; their elusiveness is what beguiles us, and it is often in narrative scenes that the full power of cinema is unleashed.)* However, due to this "looser" construct, it is easier for the beginning director to become "lost" when directing these scenes, and I have discovered that students who first became familiar with the *grounding* found in the structure of a dramatic scene and in the inherent physical tension in an action scene (both leading to the creation of a palpable conflict) are better able to apply these lessons to scenes where dramatic tension is more diffuse or is absent altogether.

Here are two examples that I hope will help clarify the distinction I am making between dramatic and narrative scenes. We have two card games. In the first, men are playing high-stakes poker. The necessary exposition—circumstance, dynamic relationships—has been given earlier. *Whose scene it is* and the *want* are clear at the outset, as is *the discernable conflict* that leads to *rising tension.* The consequence of losing is great!

We can already imagine what the *fulcrum* will be: the point in the game when our hero decides *whether or not* to bet the farm. This is an example of a dramatic scene that fits nicely into the paradigm put forth in this book, and if we use the organizing power supplied by this paradigm to render the action on the screen, we ought to be able to maximize the drama that's inherent on the page.

In the second example, a group of women friends are playing bridge. Here the card game is an activity for the women to share time with one another, but *it functions in the screenplay as a vehicle to introduce characters* (their social and dynamic relationships), deliver circumstance (such as social class), foreshadow the future (that the pecking order of the group will change), or a host of other pertinent expository material (this one's rich, this one's not, this one has kids, this one doesn't). There is no *significant* conflict in this scene! Then, *what supplies the tension* to keep us interested for two or three minutes, maybe longer? It depends a great deal on where it is situated in the film.

In the first act, an audience can be engaged for 10 minutes or more with *the unfolding* of ordinary life—character and circumstance, dynamic relationships, lifestyle, and so on—then *the point of attack* (inciting incident) occurs that changes that life, leading to a question of why we are watching the film. It is in these first-act narrative scenes that a film's *distinct visual style* is often introduced. *A distinct visual style, on its own, can create dramatic tension!*

After the first act, a narrative scene obtains its dramatic tension from being *contextualized by a larger conflict that is contained within a sequence of which the narrative scene is an element.* Thus it is important to understand the scene's job in the sequence.

To render these scenes you will once again rely on your friends, the narrative beats (the director's beats), cinematic syntax (*the order in which the audience receives its information*), and *film time* (using *elaboration* and *compression* to make moments larger or smaller). Staging in narrative scenes is often relegated to rendering the scene's action—for example, "Debbie goes to the window," "Bob looks under the bed"—but that does not rule out its availability for making physical that which is internal in the characters (as in a dramatic scene), nor does it rule out any of the other six functions of staging that are discussed in Chapter 4, most significantly *picturization— helping to generate a dramatic frame that can create suspense or portend danger.*

To explore the rendering of a narrative scene, we will analyze a scene from *Wanda*, written and directed by Barbara Loden and starring Ms. Loden and Michael Higgins. I photographed and edited the film. It was the winner of the International Critics Prize, Venice Film Festival, 1970, and when released on DVD in 2006, *The New York Times* film critic Dave Kehr called it a "masterpiece" and "is evidence of a great career that never was." Barbara Loden died in 1980.

CHAPTER 14

STAGING AND CAMERA FOR *WANDA* NARRATIVE SCENE

Aside from the fact that this scene is an example of one that *obtains its dramatic tension from being contextualized within a sequence*, there are two ancillary reasons for my choosing it. First, it offers the chance to demonstrate the use of a *controlled* handheld camera and how it can supply a visual style that supports the tone of certain types of stories by supplying a fluidity of camera movement. Second, this is the type of production many of you will embark on for your first feature: low budget, small crew (*Wanda* had four crew members including Barbara and me), extensive use of nonprofessional actors, and very importantly for this production, community involvement. Today, with the advent of the digital camera, this type of scaled-down production has become available to almost anyone, making it possible to produce industry standard films of high artistic quality.

A synopsis of *Wanda* to this point: Wanda (Barbara Loden) has recently left her husband and two children and hooked up with Mr. Dennis (Michael Higgins), a small-time crook who is going to rob a bank and needs Wanda's help. In the narrative scene we will explore, Wanda and Mr. Dennis take the bank president, Mr. Anderson, hostage. (The scene is number 20 on the DVD and is entitled "The Andersons." It is three minutes in length and comes toward the end of the second act. I recommend viewing the scene on screen before delving into the analysis. The film is available on Amazon and Netflix.)

WHAT IS THE SCENE'S JOB?

This scene immediately follows a dramatic scene in which Mr. Dennis convinces a reluctant Wanda that she must follow through with their plan. "I can't, I can't," she says. "You *can* do this," he tells her. "Maybe you never did anything before, but you're gonna to do this." Wanda reluctantly acquiesces, but when Mr. Dennis takes out his gun, Wanda is overcome with a violent wave of anxiety, causing her to vomit. We leave the scene with Wanda seeming to be totally incapable of fulfilling her crucial role in the robbery.

The job of this narrative scene is to offer a "platform" for Wanda to act in a manner that neither she, nor Mr. Dennis, nor we, believe possible. It offers Wanda an opportunity to save the day—at least temporarily. It is the first scene of the final sequence of the second act; an act that culminates with Mr. Dennis being shot dead by the police, leaving Wanda as a wanted felon. But of course the audience doesn't know that yet.

WHOSE SCENE IS IT?

Whose head does the audience have to be in to fully appreciate the scene? In scenes in which the psychology is made available to the audience through the overt action of the characters, this question is not relevant, and that is true of this scene. However, it is important to keep in mind that in the larger framework of the story, the scene is much more than the unfolding of plot. *It is the high point in Wanda's character arc*, and the full import of this moment must be conveyed to the audience.

JOBS TO DO IN THE SCENE

The jobs to do in the scene are as follows:

1. Introduce geography of location.
2. Entrance of Wanda and Mr. Dennis.
3. Reveal of gun.
4. Entrance of Mrs. Anderson.
5. Entrance of Anderson Daughters.
6. Entrance of ropes (to tie hostages). The entrances into the film of Mr. Anderson, the gun, bomb, and Wanda's pregnancy (a pillow) have all occurred in previous scenes.
7. Reveal of the bomb.
8. Elaborate the placement of the bomb.
9. Start and finish tying the hostages' hands.
10. Make sure Wanda's "heroics" are conveyed strongly!

Some of these jobs might seem to be trivial, such as "entrance of ropes" and "start and finish tying the hostages' hands." Yet it is these small jobs of ordinary narrative that can undercut our scene if left undone, raising questions in the audience's mind and leaving them dissatisfied. Protect yourself and take the time to make a list of jobs for the scene, and then pay attention to it when designing your scene and again when you are filming.

CHOOSING A LOCATION

We looked for a house by a lake because there had originally been a reconnoitering scene in a rowboat that was left in the cutting room. Even without that scene, the lake serves a marvelous function, as you will soon see, and the layout of the cottage—its doors, windows, and even the couch—were each placed in an ideal spot for the scene to unfold. Another bit of luck was that the entire "Anderson" family came with the house.

STAGING

All staging is dictated by the action of the scene, because both Wanda's and Mr. Dennis's current emotional states are clear to the audience from the previous scene, and the actions committed in this scene are clearly wedded to the characters' scene wants and to the job at hand. The most significant piece of staging is the physical struggle that occurs between Mr. Anderson and Mr. Dennis and the challenge this presents to Wanda. It had to fall far short of turning into a knock-down, drag-out battle that would have bent the tone of the film out of shape, but it had to present Wanda with a sufficient challenge to render her subsequent actions "heroic." Lastly, the staging is responsible for the familiarization of the audience with the geography of the location and grows out of the scene's action. As the action broadens spatially, the audience is introduced to additional "pieces" of the geography, keeping them apprised of the spatial dynamics between the characters on a *need to know* basis, allowing them to make a "whole" of the location before the scene ends.

CAMERA STYLE IN *WANDA*

I had spent years shooting cinema verité documentaries with a handheld camera and mostly available light, and this is the style that was adopted for *Wanda*. The idea was not to emphasize the handholding but to use it in lieu of dollies and a jib arm (an extension mounted on the dolly to increase the camera's range of motion), with as little "wobbly-scope" as physically possible. (*Wanda* was shot before the steadicam was invented.) Approximately 90% of the film was handheld and the remainder was on sticks (tripod).

The camera's ability to be fluid—to move with the action in sustained takes—imparts a more naturalistic tone to the film (due to the *relative absence of articulation* through the use of multiple angles) because we were aware of the fragile nature of the story and that any attempt to "oversell" a dramatic moment would go against the grain of the story's "realism." We felt that in this case, *less was more*. In keeping with this "muted" approach, there is a minimum of close-ups. (It's interesting to note that Barbara Loden and I talked to her husband, Elia Kazan, about this style and he concurred—he, a master of dramatization, of creating tremendous conflict on the stage and screen.)

Note: To render the full range of the camera's motion on the page, some of the shots have been broken up into a series of stills, while others have been scanned off of the film to simulate the camera's fluidity of movement.

I've broken up the staging on the interior floor plan of the Anderson house into three parts, commensurate with the beginning, middle, and end of the scene. However, the first shot of this scene is an exterior (Figure 14-1).

EXT. ANDERSON LAKE HOUSE - DAY

TWO ANDERSON DAUGHTERS are swimming in the lake then begin to exit.

In the previous scene, we see Wanda in a cheap hotel bathroom vomiting from anxiety, seemingly unable to go forward with the plan. Mr. Dennis stands by helplessly, doubting if this woman whom he barely knows has the fortitude to perform her crucial role in the bank robbery. Without resolving this situation, there is a zoom into two girls swimming and laughing in a lake (Figure 14-1).

FIGURE 14-1

Transition. E1 from camera setup #1.

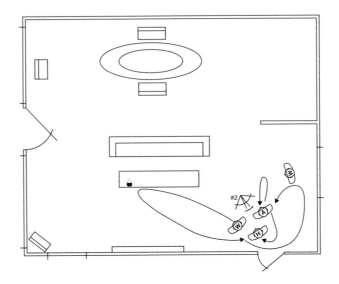

FIGURE 14-2 ————————————————————————————————

Floor plan #1 for staging and camera.

That shot is held for 15 seconds during which one of them begins to climb out. This transition is a surprise leap forward in the story, supplying both narrative energy and mystery. Because the girls (the two Anderson Daughters) begin to leave the water, it will very shortly supply suspense. (This camera setup was one of two in this scene in which the camera was placed on a tripod.)

Transitions between scenes are opportunities for the director (and also the screenwriter) to inject surprise, energizing narrative jumps, contrast (interior/exterior, light/dark, fast/slow, loud/soft), or mystery—in this case, where are we? This transition also does an additional job: It helps in the transition from a seemingly helpless Wanda to one who springs into action and saves the day. If there had been a butt-cut—if the vomiting at the hotel had been placed directly up against the entrance into the Anderson house—Wanda's heroic actions would not have been so readily accepted by the audience, especially in light of where we left her in the previous scene. *Her psychology needed time to transition off camera.*

                                                                                    CUT TO:

INT. LIVING ROOM/ANDERSON LAKE HOUSE - CONTINUOUS

Mr. Anderson shows Wanda and Mr. Dennis into the house.

The staging for the entrance of Wanda and Mr. Dennis into the Anderson house and the ensuing struggle (Figure 14-2) was simply choreographed, and spatial parameters were established for the actors. The camera's job was to follow the significant action (Figure 14-3).

                              MR. ANDERSON
The telephone is over here.

                              MR. DENNIS
                         (pulling out gun)
Mr. Anderson!

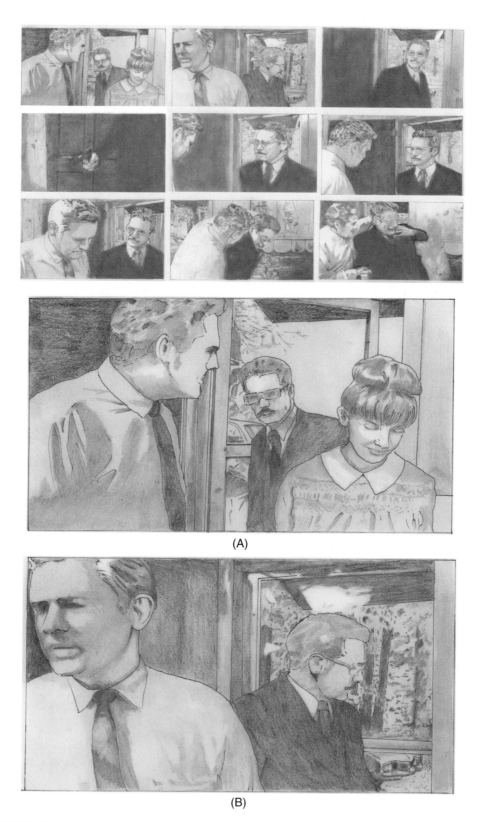

(A)

(B)

FIGURE 14-3

E-2 from camera setup #2.

(C)

(D)

(E)

FIGURE 14-3

(*Continued*)

(F)

(G)

(H)

FIGURE 14-3

(*Continued*)

(I)

FIGURE 14-3

(*Continued*)

                              MR. ANDERSON
What is this?

                              MR. DENNIS
Get over there.

                              MR. ANDERSON
What's going on?

                              MR. DENNIS
Get over there!

As the two men begin to move further into the Living Room, Mr. Dennis
looks to set down the bomb. This momentary distraction gives Mr. Anderson
an opening; he grabs Mr. Dennis, knocking the gun and the bomb (which is
never seen but is assumed) to the floor.

   Up until now this sequence has proceeded at a rather unhurried pace, but now the pace
must pick up. There is no knocking at the door or invitation to enter the house. The scene starts
abruptly with just enough exposition to satisfy the audience ("The phone is over here."), then
without any warning Mr. Dennis's plan immediately goes awry. This is an example of surprise
rather then suspense, which I believe is more effective *in this case* because Wanda and Mr. Dennis's
surprise mirrors ours.

                                                              CUT TO:

EXT. ANDERSON LAKE HOUSE - CONTINUOUS

The Two Anderson Daughters make their way toward the house (Figure 14-4).

FIGURE 14-4 ──

Shot E-3 from camera setup #1, continued.

Cutting to this parallel action just as Mr. Dennis loses his gun and is in the grasp of Mr. Anderson creates suspense and forces a question: What will happen now?

An adjustment was made in the focal length of the zoom lens to render this shot. (The entire film was shot with a zoom lens, but that effect was used sparingly. However, the capability for changing the focal length *during a shot* was used more extensively in lieu of a dolly in or out.)

CUT TO:

INT. LIVING ROOM/ANDERSON LAKE HOUSE - CONTINUOUS

Mr. Dennis loses his glasses in the struggle and is held in a bear hug by Mr. Anderson, while Wanda attempts to free Mr. Dennis (Figure 14-5). Her actions are futile until she picks up the gun from the floor.

WANDA
Turn him loose! Turn him loose!
(picks up gun from floor)
You turn him loose...!
(sticks gun in Mr. Anderson's ribs)
Stop it...! Stop it...! Stop it!

Wanda's heroics are unexpected, yet from somewhere deep inside her all the hurt and feeling of unworthiness that she has lived with her entire life are transformed into a fierceness that will not be denied, and when exhibited they *seem totally appropriate to her character in this moment.*

Given the nature of the film's style, there was no *framing* of Wanda's decision to intervene by a pan or cut to her. To repeat: It would have broken with the narrative style that precludes a heavy use of narrative beats to heighten the drama.

The floor plan with staging and camera for the middle of this scene can be found in Figure 14-6.

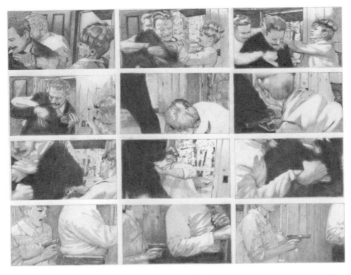

(A)

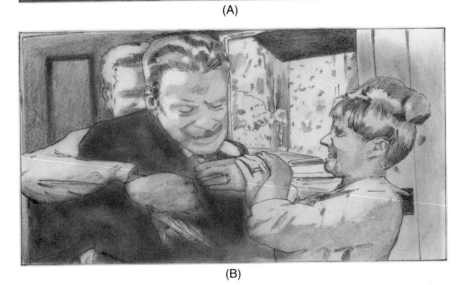

(B)

FIGURE 14-5

E-4 from camera setup #2, continued.

(C)

(D)

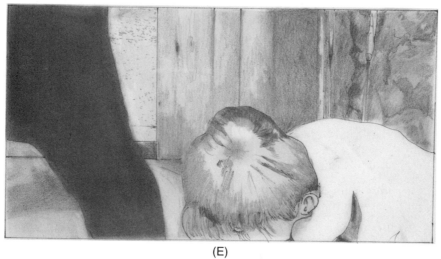

(E)

FIGURE 14-5

(*Continued*)

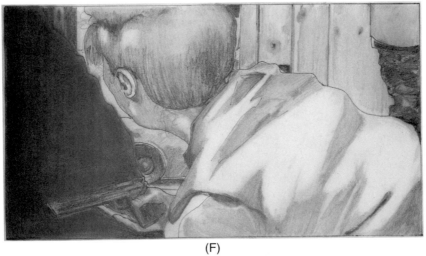

(F)

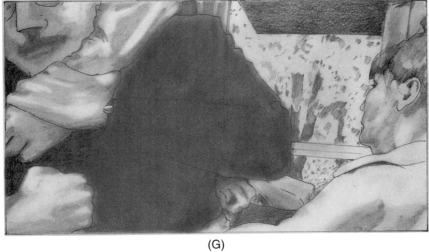

(G)

(H)

FIGURE 14-5 _____

(*Continued*)

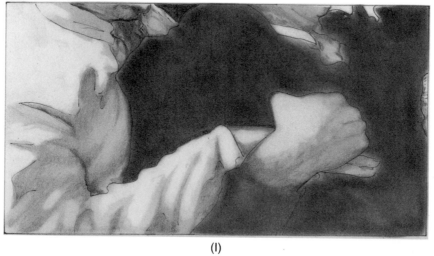

(I)

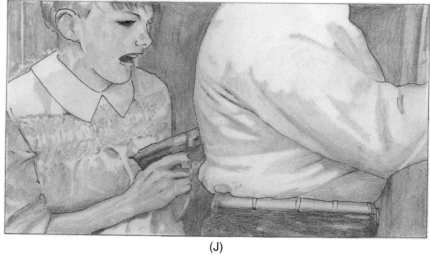

(J)

(K)

FIGURE 14-5 ——————————————————————————

(*Continued*)

(L)

FIGURE 14-5

(*Continued*)

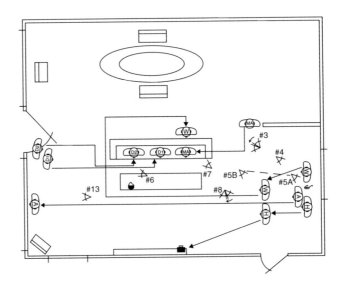

FIGURE 14-6

Floor plan #2 for staging and camera.

```
MRS. ANDERSON enters (Figure 14-7).
Wanda notices Mrs. Anderson (Figure 14-8).

                        WANDA
            Get over there on that couch!
            Get over there!
```

Wanda has taken control, bringing order to the situation, and this is reflected in the static framing of the single on her. Camera setup #3, which covered the entrance of Mrs. Anderson (E-5) into the film, is also used to take her to the couch (E-7).

FIGURE 14-7

E-5 from camera setup #3.

FIGURE 14-8

E-6 from camera setup #4.

Mrs. Anderson moves to the couch (Figure 14-9).

There is no spatial resolution between Mrs. Anderson and Wanda (shots E-5, -6, -7), but because of their sight lines *and* the quick action/reaction of both women, we do not ask to be further oriented. E-7 cuts before Mrs. Anderson sits down, keeping the momentum of the scene moving forward.

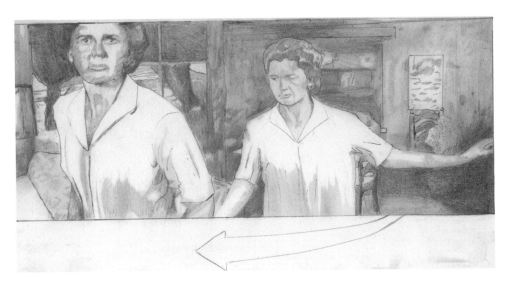

FIGURE 14-9

E-7 from camera setup #3, continued.

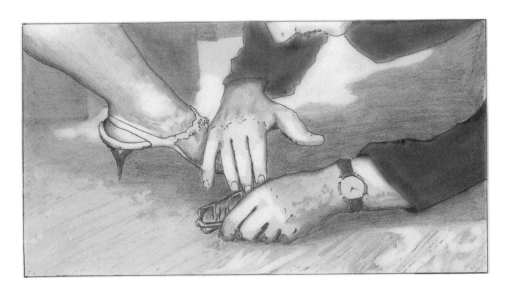

FIGURE 14-10

E-8 from camera setup #5.

Mr. Dennis searches the floor for his eyeglasses, and Wanda points them out to him with her foot (Figure 14-10). Mr. Dennis puts on his eyeglasses and takes the gun from Wanda (Figure 14-11), stands and shoves Mr. Anderson forward (Figure 14-12).

                    MR. DENNIS
          (shoving Mr. Anderson forward)
          You, get over there!

FIGURE 14-11

E-8 from camera setup #5.

FIGURE 14-12

E-8 from camera setup #5.

E-8 is part of the sustained camera setup #5. The edited shot begins with a downward-angling close-up of Wanda's foot guiding the eyeglasses to Mr. Dennis, it moves up with Mr. Dennis and widens as he puts on his eyeglasses and takes the gun from Wanda, then it raises to eye level as Mr. Dennis stands and shoves Mr. Anderson forward. It is a good example of the fluidity of the handheld camera. Figures 14-10, 14-11, and 14-12 are all part of E-8 but are presented here as discrete images to emphasize how *each behaves as a separate shot in its power to articulate the essence*

FIGURE 14-13

E-9 from camera setup #6.

of a moment. As a brief review of our film grammar, edited shot E-8 is a compound cinematic sentence composed of three clauses: Wanda helps a *lost* Mr. Dennis locate his glasses; he puts them on and takes the gun; he stands and pushes Mr. Anderson forward. We see the process whereby Mr. Dennis goes from being *lost* to being *in command*, and we attribute this turnaround to Wanda.

The Two Anderson Daughters enter from outside (Figure 14-13).

MR. DENNIS (O.S.)
You girls sit down!

The Daughters burst into the room laughing, but they stop immediately upon seeing the situation. Their consequent move to the couch is done with alacrity because prolonging their entrance would serve only to slow down the progress of the scene.

The entrances of the Anderson Daughters and Mrs. Anderson were done without either area of the living room being introduced beforehand. Mr. Anderson's position in the room since Mr. Dennis pushed him has yet to be resolved, nor have Wanda's and Mr. Dennis's positions been resolved vis-à-vis the other characters. Why isn't the audience confused? One reason is the alacrity in which the scene unfolds. (This fragmentation of the scene is readily noticeable in the still frames we see in this book, but on screen our film is unfolding in time.) Another, more crucial reason is that the eye lines between characters establish a connection that satisfies us until the spatial resolution ultimately takes place. A minor reason is that the wood paneling in the room unites everything. If one wall had been brick or painted white, a sense of disconnectedness would have been more pronounced.

I made a big point of resolving separation when designing *A Piece of Apple Pie*, but in that film the unfolding of action was slower, and the lack of a palpable connectedness between characters would have intruded on the story. When the pace slows down in this scene, there is spatial resolution of all the characters except for Mr. Anderson, whose whereabouts are *assumed* as he is standing in front of the picture window—the same one that was in the frame when the Two Daughters came through the door. It is not until the last shot of the film that Mr. Anderson's separation is resolved, and that is done with a pan. Suppose this resolution never happened? Would

FIGURE 14-14

E-10 from camera setup #5, continued.

there be any consequences to pay? I believe that the audience would have felt cheated somehow, although they would not be able to put their finger on it.

What, then, is the rule about resolving separation? My advice is to do it *unless it interferes with the moment*. It's a judgment call, or more exactly, an artistic call. As with all the rules and principles laid down in this book, we must feel free to break them when necessary, but only in the service of a larger purpose. Remember, the world we create on screen must have cohesiveness—it must stick together or the audience will become confused—but on the other hand, to tell our story we must break that world into pieces. Both are necessary.

You will notice that Mr. Dennis's voice was placed underneath shot E-9 because the point has been made that there is no reason to "drag out" the Daughters' entrance and also because we want the next two-shot of Mr. Dennis and Wanda not to be undercut by that line of dialogue.

```
Now a willing accomplice, Wanda stands beside Mr. Dennis for the first
time in the film. They are a couple (Figure 14-14).
```

Previous to this moment in the film, Wanda always walked behind Mr. Dennis, sometimes running to keep up with him, never his equal; but now, standing beside him, we see them as a couple for the first time. The shot *announces* this change in the *dynamic relationship*. It doesn't shout it out, but it's there. Like much of how an audience is affected by a film, the audience *feels* the change. To reinforce this new dynamic relationship, the shot is repeated (Figure 14-16).

```
The Two Daughters sit down next to their mother on the couch (Figure
14-15).
```

A new camera setup (#7) was necessary to render a strong image of the daughters joining their mother on the couch, but at the same time, because it is new, it imparts a dramatic thrust to the moment. Note that Mrs. Anderson dominates the frame because of her position in the foreground.

FIGURE 14-15

Shot E-11 from camera setup #7.

FIGURE 14-16

Shot E-12 from camera setup #5 continued. Two-shot of Wanda and Mr. Dennis.

```
                    MR. DENNIS
                 (to Wanda)
        Get over there and don't waste time.
        Hurry, tie them up.
                 (Wanda exits the frame.)


                    MR. DENNIS
                 (to Mr. Anderson)
        Turn your head around.
```

FIGURE 14-17

Shot E-12 continued from camera setup #5 continued. Mr. Dennis walks into a single after Wanda exits.

The two edited shots (E-10 and E-12) that are used to cover the preceding action are from that old workhorse, camera setup #5, which began on the close-up of Wanda's foot and the eyeglasses, and it moves up to single on Mr. Dennis as he shoves Mr. Anderson forward. In these two edited shots, the camera widens to a two-shot of Wanda and Mr. Dennis, and it ends on a single of Mr. Dennis ordering Mr. Anderson to turn around (Figure 14-17).

Michael Higgins, who played Mr. Dennis, commented that this method of shooting was very "freeing" to him because it allowed him to continue without the stops and starts of a more "multi-angle coverage." Obviously, this style is not suited for all films. (With the advent of digital shooting, many directors are now using two camera setups. This necessarily results in a compromise on some setups, but if used judiciously it can give the actors the freedom that Michael Higgins felt, and at the same time it can offer additional editing possibilities.)

Mr. Dennis has yet to acknowledge Wanda's crucial contribution. In the preceding "instructions" to her, he seems to have reverted to form. This holding off of praise serves to make it much more significant to Wanda, *and to the audience,* when later it comes unexpectedly and at a time when it can be given its own space.

```
Mr. Anderson obeys Mr. Dennis's order to turn around (Figure 14-18).
```

Camera setup #13 was the final setup. The reason that we saved it for last is that it is disconnected from the rest of the action. Nevertheless, Mr. Anderson stood with his hands above his head for every take even though he was not in the shots. This was important for his family, especially his wife, who related to him throughout the scene. Had they been trained actors, it would still have been advisable that the husband be there.

Note: I was once on the set of a John Wayne movie when he delivered lines in a close-up. After one take Wayne barked out, "Get Kirk out here," and a few moments later, Kirk Douglas appeared on the other side of the camera to accept John Wayne's lines. Back to our scene:

```
Mrs. Anderson and her daughters anxiously monitor the situation (Figure
14-19) as Mr. Dennis goes into action (Figure 14-20).
```

FIGURE 14-18

Shot E-13 from camera setup #13.

FIGURE 14-19

Shot E-14 from camera setup #7, continued.

The fear and apprehension that is felt by the Anderson family is an important dramatic component of the scene and is kept alive throughout.

In the rest of the scene, the blocking remains static except for small adjustments by Mr. Dennis. This action is rendered on floor plan #3 with five camera setups (Figure 14-21).

As Wanda begins to tie up the three women, Mr. Dennis presents the bomb enclosed in a briefcase.

FIGURE 14-20

Shot E-15 from camera setup #8.

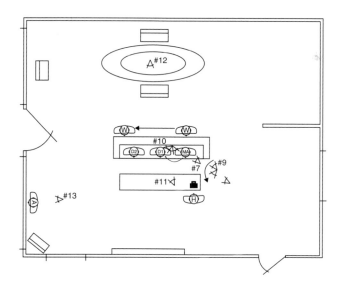

FIGURE 14-21

Floor plan #3.

                              MR. DENNIS (O.S)
See this, huh? That's a real live bomb . . .

This shot (E-16, Figure 14-22) serves as the entrance of the rope into the film, and it keeps Wanda "alive." It shows the beginning of her job (securing the hostages), and as the shot "cranes" downward, it "ties" Wanda to the three women, and the three women to the bomb and Mr. Dennis. In the next shot (Figure 14-23), Mr. Anderson is connected to the bomb and his wife by his sight lines, tying all five characters together for the remainder of the scene.

FIGURE 14-22 ————————————————————————————————

E-16 from camera setup #9.

FIGURE 14-23 ————————————————————————————————

E-17 from camera setup #13, continued.

In a previous scene, the bomb had made its entrance into the film in a wide shot as it was being assembled. This close shot is a much "stronger" reveal, especially in context of the action.

E-16 begins an orchestration of seven shots, E-17 through E-23. Their juxtaposition against one another *combines* to articulate the palpable tension of the hostages along with the elaboration of planting the bomb—one of our scene jobs. We are able to elaborate the planting of the bomb with multiangles without calling undue attention to the break with the overall narrative style because it is entirely *appropriate to the moment*.

FIGURE 14-24 ——

E-18 from camera setup #10.

Note: My teaching style is to give names to general concepts, which might not have been previously identified as such, so that we can *use them*. This is the case of "appropriate to the moment," a concept that is open to such a wide interpretation that it can be rendered meaningless. It seems to open up the door to arbitrary changes in tone and style—a sort of "anything goes." Perhaps if I explain the genesis of this concept, it would help clear things up. Early in my tenure at Columbia a student directed a short exercise in which an evil ventriloquist, in a fit of anger, hung his dummy from the ceiling. As the dummy slowly twisted back and forth, the director cut to the *dummy's POV*, which was moving back and forth across the room, creating an atmosphere of menace as it watched the ventriloquist. It was such a powerful choice, one that was totally accepted by the audience, even though there was no preparation for this *subjective voice*. I wondered if there was a general rule that could be applied to this breaking of style. I then recalled a scene from Fellini's *8½* in which the camera goes suddenly into fast motion, mimicking a farcical moment from the silent movie era—breaking the stylistic tone of the film—*and it was brilliant*. Again, in the third act, Fellini introduces a completely new style, changing to a highly kinetic camera at a press conference, again tonally brilliant and totally appropriate to the scene. Since then I have been aware of many examples of this concept working, but there are also many more in which changes in tone or style are arbitrary and not appropriate.

Mr. Anderson looks on helplessly (Figure 14-23).

Mr. Dennis addresses Mr. Anderson while concentrating on the family before him (Figure 14-24).

MR. DENNIS
Anderson . . . you cooperate with us and
we'll be back in time to disarm it.

Mrs. Anderson and her Two Daughters, their hands being tied behind their backs, keep their eyes glued on Mr. Dennis and the bomb (Figure 14-25), camera setup #7 on stage #2 floor plan (Figure 14-6).

FIGURE 14-25 ──

E-19 from camera setup #7, resulting from the use of a longer focal length from the initial setup position.

The *reactions* of the three women to Mr. Dennis presenting the bomb and giving instructions were shot first, while both Loden and Higgins went through their actions *as if they were on
camera.* Because the "Andersons" were not actors, we thought that their first reactions to this
simulated situation (which had a surprising reality) would be more "real" the first time, and all
three did a very credible job.

```
Mr. Dennis begins to gently move the bomb forward and place it on the
lap of one of the daughters (Figure 14-26).

                            MR. DENNIS
                 Hold it in your lap. . . Okay. . . ?
                 Don't move. . . !

Mrs. Anderson looks to her husband (Figure 14-27), but he can only look
on helplessly at the bomb sitting on his daughter's lap (Figure 14-28).
```

Again a slight extension of the focal length on the zoom lens was used as the scene "heated"
up, and the shot pans to Mrs. Anderson as she looks up at her husband.

```
Mr. Dennis sets the bomb's trigger and closes the briefcase (Figure
14-29).

                            MR. DENNIS
                 I set the trigger . . . It's set for
                 the proper time . . . You hear that . . .
                 huh. . . ?
```

Mr. Dennis is extremely deliberate at making his point, allowing time for his warnings to sink
in, and the medium-close shot of him with the profile of Mrs. Anderson in the foreground of the
frame creates an atmosphere of intimacy filled with menace.

FIGURE 14-26

E-20 from camera setup #10, continued.

FIGURE 14-27

E-21 from camera setup #7, pan to Mrs. Anderson using longer focal length.

E-23 (Figure 14-29) is one of five edited shots that have come from camera setup #10 (E-18, -23, -26, -32, -29). This setup, along with the other workhorse, camera setup #5, make up the majority of screen time for this scene and together supply the *through-line* of action. All of the remaining action in the scene is a *reaction* to this "through-line." In a sense these two camera set-ups can be regarded as *master shots,* but unlike the classical master shot that is wide and encompasses a larger area of action, these two setups are *focused* on the main action at hand.

Wanda finishes tying up the women (Figure 14-30).

FIGURE 14-28 ——

E-22 from camera setup #13, continued.

FIGURE 14-29 ——

E-23 from camera setup #10, continued.

This wide shot is a release of tension, signaling that the end of the scene is upon us, and it accomplishes the job of showing Wanda finishing up her work. Again, it is understated. It was the second camera setup to be placed on a tripod.

MR.DENNIS
                    Be careful.

Close angle on the bomb sitting on Daughter's lap (Figure 14-31).

FIGURE 14-30

E-24 from camera setup #12.

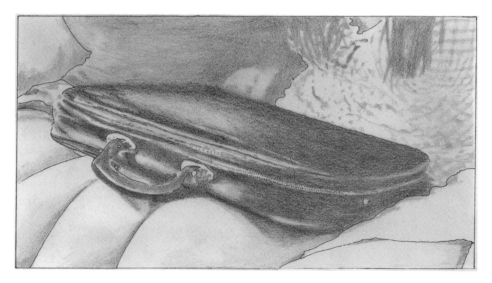

FIGURE 14-31

E-25 from camera setup #11.

The entire process of "planting" the bomb is spelled out in detail because it is necessary to convince the audience that the Anderson family will not be a factor in foiling the bank robbery. This would set up a false tension, conceivably appropriate in a different story, but here it would introduce a red herring that goes against the tone of this film. If Wanda and Mr. Dennis are going to fail in robbing the bank, it will be for other reasons, and the audience must not be misled by a false insertion of suspense. At this point in the film, the audience does not *expect* a happy ending, although they might *hope* for one.

FIGURE 14-32 ————————————————————————————————————

E-26 from camera setup #10, continued.

Mr. Dennis stands, picks up Mr. Anderson's jacket, and tosses it to him (Figure 14-32).

> MR. DENNIS
> Anderson . . . you're taking me to
> work with you . . . Come on, put that
> coat on.

In keeping with the style of a fluid camera, E-26 begins with a medium-close of Mr. Dennis kneeling, it rises with him as he picks up Mr. Anderson's jacket, and it pans and widens as he tosses it to Mr. Anderson, ending in a medium-wide of him catching it. This shot resolves Mr. Anderson spatially for the first time by *connecting him* to Mr. Dennis.

CUT TO:

EXT. ANDERSON HOUSE – MOMENTS LATER

The dramatic payoff, or *aftermath*, of the previous scene occurs in this brief scene outside the Anderson house in which Wanda runs to the Anderson station wagon to get the keys for the get-away car from Mr. Dennis, who has neglected to give them to her.

The camera cuts to inside the station wagon; Mr. Dennis's profile in the foreground of Wanda's medium close-up in the passenger side window—an ideal framing for what comes next—comes unexpectedly both to Wanda and to us. In handing over the keys to Wanda, Mr. Dennis tells her, "You did good. You're really something, you know that?" Wanda doesn't say a word. Her smile says it all (Figure 14-33). No one had ever told her that she was "really something." This genuine admiration expressed by Mr. Dennis is the high point of the film, and we suspect, the high point of Wanda's life. In a short time Wanda will lose her way to the bank, and Mr. Dennis, the only person in the world who ever thought she "was really something" will be shot dead by the police.

It should be clear that the preceding scene is different in structure than *A Piece of Apple Pie* or the dramatic Patio scene in *Notorious*. Those two dramatic scenes contain an escalating progression of action/reaction articulated by narrative beats that are orchestrated by dramatic blocks.

FIGURE 14-33

Aftermath of hostage-taking scene.

In both of those scenes, a character whose scene it is has a clear *want* that is *opposed* by another character, reaching a climax with the fulcrum where the character whose scene it is succeeds or fails in obtaining their want. The hostage-taking scene from Wanda is more descriptive than dramatic, more of a process of unfolding than of sustained conflict. Narrative beats are still needed to articulate the essence of each moment, but dramatic blocks and the question raised by the fulcrum are not available for organizing the action in the scene; hence, they are not available for creating tension. The tension in the scene comes from being contextualized within the sequence, which contains the dramatic question, Will the bank robbery be successful? Taking the hostage is one element in the process of robbing the bank. *Making this process interesting is the director's job.*

As you proceed with the in-depth analysis of the three films presented in Part Five, Chapters 15, 16, and 17, ask yourself, From where does each scene receive its dramatic tension? In other words, why is it interesting? Is the dramatic question contained *in* the scene itself or does it come from being contextualized from *outside*? You will now begin to take notice that there are much *looser constructions* that can engage an audience. Ask yourself, *Why do these scenes engage us?* and *What does the director's craft and imagination bring to the scene*?

In gaining more and more insight into the director's job, we should not forget that a good film begins with a good screenplay. In Chapter 19 I will suggest how you might go about acquiring a screenplay using what you have learned about directing.

LEARNING THE CRAFT THROUGH FILM ANALYSIS

One of the quickest ways to learn the conceptual side of the film director's craft is by close reading of films made by master directors. By close reading I mean not only watching a film many times but asking different questions with each successive viewing. What you are looking for is the armature—the craft—that supports the film. You begin to unearth this by watching a particular scene until you grasp how it is put together—how the camera and staging and work with actors have all been orchestrated into a harmonious whole. You watch for the dramatic power of transitions between scenes, for entrances of characters, for reveals, for the cinematic cohesiveness of a sequence, the personality of the narrator: in short, everything that was discussed in Parts One through Four.

On your first viewing of a film, sit back and enjoy it. On the second, look for the dramatic structure and the narrator's voice. Particular sequences and scenes will have caught your attention. Pick one. Watch it again. Why is it effective? Is it the staging? Is it the camera? Or is it a combination of both? Draw a floor plan of the location. Figure out the camera setups. Look for the articulation of narrative beats. By diligently working through the films mentioned in this book and particularly those featured in Part Five, you will go a long way toward being able to use these dramatic elements as tools in your own films. It is my hope that readers will also apply this investigative technique to their favorite films, to unearth for themselves the cinematic craft imbedded in the rendering of the story. Then the entire world of cinema can be your classroom.

The three films that we will analyze in depth in Part Five have been chosen because they offer clear examples of the dramatic categories that have been introduced in Parts One through Four. All of the films, although vastly different in content and style, are based on the three-act dramatic structure. Before we proceed, let us take a brief look at this structure. It is the first step in the organization of action, and therefore it is something the director must pay heed to. All three of the films have a chronological ordering of acts. (This is not always the case.) In the first act we will find ordinary life interrupted by a point of attack, which leads to a dilemma for the protagonist. This structure helps the audience form a question at the end of the first act: Why are they watching the film? What do they expect might happen? Even better: What do they hope or fear will happen?

The second act begins with rising action by the protagonist. This action is aimed at extricating the protagonist from the dilemma. Of course, in a well-told story there are significant obstacles that the protagonist must surmount or be defeated by. In all three of the films there is a first culmination of action by the protagonist in the middle of the second act, then the final culmination at the end of the act, exhausting the protagonist's action vis-à-vis the question raised at the end of the first act.

The third act consists of the consequence of the protagonist's action and usually has a false ending or twist before the final resolution. (Does all this seem too programmatic for you? Well, it is not the only story structure available to us. See Terrence Malick's *The Thin Red Line* [1999], which is discussed in Chapter 18.)

This organization of action in each act is further divided by the writer into sequences and scenes. Then the director continues to divide the action into ever-smaller units—dramatic blocks and narrative beats—while guiding the actor to the smallest unit of action, the performance beat.

On the first viewing of the films explored here, allow yourself to become caught up in the story—to become immersed in the emotional life of the characters. This requires turning off your analytical mode. There is plenty of time for that during the second, third, fourth, or fifth viewing—with some films, countless viewings—that it takes to truly understand a master's control of the director's craft.

C H A P T E R   1 5

ALFRED HITCHCOCK'S
NOTORIOUS

OVERVIEW OF STYLE AND DESIGN

Alfred Hitchcock's *Notorious*, used for examples of various principles and techniques in previous chapters, bears further analysis in regard to the overall design of a complete film.

CAMERA AS ACTIVE NARRATOR

Hitchcock's design calls for an active narrator: a camera that can move away from the "ordinary" to draw our attention to the essence of the moment—to what is vital to the audience's appreciation of the story. This is often the case in films that have crucial plot points that absolutely must be comprehended by the audience.

Hitchcock introduces the camera (narrator) that can go off on its own—needing no motivation other than the fact that it knows what is important—in the first shot of the film. He announces to the audience that it will be guided through the story by this moving camera—that when something is important to know, it will be pointed out. We will discover that this guidance is not necessary most of the time, and in fact this aspect of the active narrator is used sparingly by Hitchcock. (In this film, as in all Hitchcock films except *Rope*, he relies to a great extent on the *juxtaposition of images* through cutting to articulate escalation of or changes in actions, or to signify a plot point.)

SUBJECTIVE CAMERA

In this film, Hitchcock assigns a subjective voice to Alicia (Ingrid Bergman). The question is, why? It is my guess that it stems from his visualization of the design for the final scene of the second act. In it, Alicia is drugged into a hallucinatory state, and because we have access to her subjective voice, we are allowed to *participate* in her direct perception, making her helplessness palpable. *Orchestrated* with the active narrator, Alicia's voice gives this climactic scene a psychological richness and dramatic complexity that it wouldn't have had otherwise.

TRANSITIONS

You will notice that many of the transitions between scenes involve fades and dissolves, due mainly to the cinematic conventions common to films made in the 1940s. They enabled the audience, not as cinematically sophisticated as today's audience, to follow the time jumps and movement from one location to another.

ENTRANCES

The entrance of the protagonist, Alicia, into this film is adequate ("adequate" is not meant to be pejorative), but the entrance of the antagonist, Devlin, is weak; it is not dramatic and not cinematic. (I have the feeling with Hitchcock that expository information bored him, and he paid scant attention to making it interesting. His penchant for uninspired establishing shots, of which we will see a good many in this film, is a case in point.)

ART DIRECTION AND PRODUCTION DESIGN

This film appears to be less "real" than the others we will analyze, due in part to the use of painted backdrops and rear projection. Today, the sophistication of these elements and the prevalence of shooting on location bring a reality to films that we do not question.

WHAT ARE WE WATCHING FOR IN THIS FILM?

We will concentrate on Hitchcock's clear articulation of narrative beats, superb staging, use of the camera as an active narrator, and the assigning of a subjective voice to the protagonist. We will discover how Hitchcock, a master of suspense, goes about creating it.

FIRST ACT

TITLES and OPENING CREDITS, along with the date and place, appear over a painting of the Miami skyline. The key ingredient here is the romantic music playing underneath, indicating that we are about to see a love story. However, just before the music and titles fade out, the music turns menacing. What does that tell us? It's more of a hint at this point. Yes, we are promised a love story, but it will take place against a backdrop of considerable danger.

INT. COURTHOUSE CORRIDOR: The film starts on a close-up of a press photographer's camera and moves to discover a courtroom that contains the source of everyone's curiosity. Although this camera movement draws little attention to itself, it announces subtly to the audience that this narrator has the ability to physically seek out significant story points.

INT. COURTROOM: A Curious Man's POV, rendered in a long shot, captures the courtroom proceedings. Because we are distant from the action, we are forced to pay close attention to what is being said—expository information that we need to appreciate the story. Because it serves no narrative purpose for us to know anything more about those present, we see them from the back only. (Hitchcock uses the Curious Man as a device to get us into the courtroom, then uses him to announce, "She's coming!" alerting the waiting press *and us*.)

COURTHOUSE CORRIDOR: Alicia Huberman (Ingrid Bergman) enters the film, and the camera tracks with her as she makes her way through the phalanx of newsmen. The camera allows her to exit this frame, and then it veers off to discover two Mystery Men. In this one shot we can see two different aspects of the narrator. First, as it tracks with Alicia, it is "merely" rendering Alicia's action. Then in the move to the two men, it provides *significance*, telling us that these two men represent an important plot point.

EXT. ALICIA'S HOUSE: Hitchcock appears momentarily in every one of his films, and in this film he chose this establishing shot to do so. He did what he could to make the shot more interesting by having the trunk of the palm tree in the foreground. (Hitchcock appears again in the second act.)

INT. ALICIA'S LIVING ROOM: The party in progress is rendered with a single shot from behind a man who remains in silhouette throughout and is referred to as Handsome (Cary Grant/Devlin). Although Alicia is always the focus of the shot, and the camera moves to the right and left to capture her movements, it never entirely loses Handsome in the foreground, making us curious about who he is. Just before the scene fades out, the shot moves in close on the back of Handsome, fades out, then fades back up to another shot on him in profile. This widens into a two-shot with Alicia. A love song plays on the phonograph.

From the two-shot Hitchcock goes into over-the-shoulders of both characters, a classical rendering of countless scenes where two characters are facing each other. It is our first chance to really take in both characters and to see the beginnings of the chemistry between them. Notice that the cutting back and forth is *always* on a narrative beat (a change or escalation of action).

When this dramatic block is over, Alicia stands (the connecting tissue to the next dramatic block). This block is rendered in one take that follows the action of the two characters toward the door. One very important observation here is that as Alicia moves toward the door, the staging allows the camera to separate her from Devlin while she finishes the last of her alcoholic drink. This focusing of our attention on this act causes it to impinge more fully on us, nailing down the fact that Alicia takes her drinking seriously. When she finishes the drink, Devlin reenters the frame.

EXT. ALICIA'S HOUSE: This scene is one take. Here Hitchcock gives Devlin's action of tying a scarf around Alicia's waist its own stage. It is an intimate act, one that supplies the promise of love, and Alicia's recalling of it will end Act One. The scarf will be reintroduced late in Act Two. Therefore, the audience must remember it and everything it implies, and changing the stage here helps supply the necessary significance for that to happen.

EXT./INT. CAR: The important element for us here is the introduction of Alicia's subjective voice. It is a good scene to point out the difference between an ordinary POV and a subjective voice. Off the close-up of the hair blowing in Alicia's face, we see the road ahead through the windshield, causing us to assign it as her POV. Then, when we see the same shot of the road with her hair blowing across the frame in the foreground (the camera is shooting through the hair), we understand instantly that this is *Alicia's direct perception*. No one else is seeing the world like this: not Devlin, not the narrator. Because it is only the first time we have experienced her direct perception, it does not firmly establish to the audience that Alicia has a subjective voice. It is too incidental. It must be followed by a much more powerful, unequivocal example of Alicia's direct perception, and Hitchcock gives us such an unequivocal example in the very next scene.

- The separate shot of the policeman getting off his motorcycle and approaching the car sets up a question mark. What will happen now? Setting up question marks for the audience is an important part of the director's job, allowing the audience to participate more fully in the unfolding of the drama.
- Devlin's professional identity is contained in his wallet, and the nature of that identity is revealed through the policeman's behavior after viewing the contents of that wallet. Therefore, Hitchcock draws our attention to the wallet, giving it a significance and setting up a curiosity in us: What is so important about that wallet? (At the beginning of a film an audience will have faith that the narrator will not draw its attention to insignificant details. If the narrator violates this trust, the audience will begin to lose interest in the story.) Hitchcock gives an entrance to the wallet by having Devlin reach into his jacket for it. The camera move taking it to the policeman draws our attention to it. Again a question is framed: What is in the wallet? We are participating in the unfolding of the story. When the policeman hands the wallet back to Devlin, the shot stops on Alicia, who is pondering what just took place. Her thinking is rendered by the camera and is made accessible to us—an example of *psychology changed into behavior that can be photographed*.

INT. ALICIA'S BEDROOM/LIVING ROOM: The first thing that Hitchcock nails down here is the aftermath of the night before. Alicia has a major hangover. Then, from an objective close-up of her looking camera right, Hitchcock cuts to Devlin and the doorway off-kilter. We assign this subjective view of the world to Alicia. The shot continues with Devlin moving toward Alicia, turning him completely upside down. That image firmly establishes Alicia's direct perception, and because it has impinged on us so strongly, Hitchcock does not have to worry that we will soon forget it. (We will see how he keeps her subjective voice alive so that it is ready for the climactic scene at the end of Act Two.) Intercut with Alicia's subjective voice and immediately following it are close-ups of Alicia rendered by the objective narrator.

- When Devlin walks from the bedroom to the living room, this is the connecting tissue to a new dramatic block. Notice how it announces quite strongly that something new is going to happen. Our interest is piqued.
- This new dramatic block is rendered in separation, cutting from one character to another to articulate narrative beats. Some narrative beats are changes in, or escalation of, actions, while others are significant plot points that the audience must take notice of to appreciate the story fully.
- We have to watch Hitchcock carefully or we are likely to miss the subtleties of craft that are always present in his work. As Devlin moves from the phonograph, which is playing a secretly recorded conversation between Alicia and her father, the camera cuts to a moving shot toward the empty doorway of Alicia's bedroom. Is this Devlin's subjective POV? We don't know yet. More importantly, *because* we do not see Alicia, we wonder what she thinks of the conversation on the phonograph (another question mark raised by Hitchcock). Then Alicia moves into the doorway, and we discover that she is obviously affected by what she is hearing. (Many times in film we have to get a character from one psychological place to another, but we need to do it in a much shorter time than it would take in real life. By holding off the reveal of Alicia, we, the audience, supply part of the work of getting her to a new psychological place by formulating a question. Her reveal gives us the answer.)

Still, it would have seemed too easy for Alicia to agree so readily to Devlin's request that she become a spy. Yes, we have just seen the seeds for that possibility, but we would not accept her agreeing too readily. The staging (Alicia moving away from Devlin) makes physical that rejection. Hitchcock realizes that he has to help Alicia's transition. He uses her movement as connecting tissue to another dramatic block in which the seed of Devlin's request is given room to flower. What does Devlin do? He backs off. How is that conveyed to the audience? He sits and listens to her. He lets the words coming from the phonograph work on her even as she resists them. Then comes the intrusion of the ship captain. His alternative invitation forces Alicia to confront the reality of her life: more frivolity and squandering of her life, or some kind of atonement for her father's treason. Now when she says yes to Devlin's proposition, we accept it. Her journey to this decision seems convincing.

- Notice Devlin's move from the doorway to the chair. It is without motivation. It is mechanical. How could it have been fixed? If Hitchcock had recognized the problem during shooting he could have asked Grant for the "backing off" beat *before* the move to the chair. This would have supplied the motivation for the move.
- At the end of this scene, romantic music comes up, and Alicia recognizes the scarf around her waist, thus ending the first act with two clear and very different dilemmas for our protagonist. The first is her involvement in the spying business, which serves as a battleground for the second: her romantic attraction to Devlin.

SECOND ACT

EXT. MOUNTAINS/PLANE: A second act usually begins with the rising action of the protagonist attempting to extricate herself from her dilemma(s). (In this case, Alicia must redeem herself through sacrifice for her country and win the love of Devlin. The latter is the goal the audience has already invested their emotions in. If Alicia were to do a good job as a spy but not connect with Devlin, we would be sorely disappointed. That is why this is a love story.) This rising action is conveyed first in the aerial shot of a new landscape and then with the shot of the plane moving into an uncertain future.

INT. PLANE: The camera singles out Alicia sitting next to an empty seat that we assume is Devlin's. When she turns her head to look for him, the camera cuts to what she is looking at. Note that the angle Hitchcock cuts to is *outside* the spatial dynamics of Alicia. Still, for a moment, it is her POV. (A remarkable elasticity is possible in whether or not the audience assigns a shot as a POV, and Hitchcock takes advantage of this. Later we will see him have a joke or two on us because of this elasticity.) This two-shot is the introduction of Devlin's boss, Paul Prescott. Hitchcock stays with this take, tracking back with it in a single as Devlin returns to Alicia and sits next to her in another two-shot.

This sustained take, which serves as connecting tissue to the next dramatic block, also has another function. It serves as a contrast to the articulation through separation that occurs in this dramatic block. (This is something we see a lot of in Hitchcock films: long takes preceding a dramatic block that relies on cutting. Without this contrast the cutting has less power. This is especially true when he is setting up a scene that will be heavily elaborated through multiple angles. We will see this clearly demonstrated in the "love scene" that precedes the classically elaborated staircase scene at the end of this film.)

- Take note of the narrative beat that initiates the first shot in this separation. It comes off of the two-shot that is rendered when Devlin returns to his seat and says, "He had news of your father."
- What narrative beat is articulated when Hitchcock cuts to Devlin *even though he does not have a line of dialogue*? It is not just to show that he is listening to Alicia. Look at it again. What Hitchcock is *framing* for us here is Devlin's growing attachment to Alicia. It is crucial in preparing us for the evolution of Devlin's dynamic relationship with Alicia.

EXT. CAFÉ: Note the camera setups in this scene: a two-shot, then over-the-shoulder, and a close-up of each character. These are edited together to articulate the narrative beats that lead to a growing sense of intimacy *even though Devlin resists it*. Also notice the Waiter's intrusion into the scene after Devlin's "Then what?" It is staged to occur at precisely the moment when it will supply needed dramatic punctuation.

EXT. COUNTRYSIDE: This new stage and the romantic music creates the atmosphere for us to more readily accept the first kiss. Devlin's car is introduced.

EXT. PRESCOTT'S OFFICE: This is an establishing shot. (Later we will see an example of Hitchcock cutting from one scene to the next without this device. The resulting momentary confusion we will feel because we do not know exactly where we are will supply a welcome narrative jolt.)

INT. BOARDROOM/PRESCOTT'S OFFICE: This is a purely expository scene rendered in two shots. The "pop out" to the second shot, which violates the 30-degree rule, is jarring.

EXT. RIO BEACHFRONT: In the second shot, Devlin's car drives up to the front of Alicia's apartment building.

INT. LIVING ROOM/PATIO, ALICIA'S NEW APARTMENT: Hitchcock wastes no time in setting up the geography of this room and its spatial relationship to the patio. This first shot, panning from the door to the patio, will be repeated in a little while, but it will carry a totally different emotional component.

- The camera is placed high for the first shot on the patio. The reason? To give us a good look at the curved shoreline below and its geographical relation to the two lovebirds on the patio. Because the narrator's reason is obvious, we assign no psychological or dramatic significance to it. Later we will see high shots that, because of the context in which they occur, *will* carry an emotional or dramatic component.
- As soon as we can absorb the information of the previous shot, Hitchcock cuts to eye level for the hugging and kissing that ensues. Why eye level? Obviously, this is the best place to see what's going on. In the staging of this shot, Alicia is on the right side of the frame and Devlin is

on the left. In the next scene in this location, this staging will be repeated for a scene that contains much different emotional and dramatic components, except then Alicia and Devlin will be on the *opposite* side of the frame from where they are now.

- In this second shot on the patio, the camera pushes in from a medium-close two-shot to a close two-shot. It stays in this framing without a cut for two-and-one-half minutes. It tracks with the two lovebirds from the patio, to the phone in the living room, to the door from which they entered. You can bet that Hitchcock covered this with no other shots. For him this design fully conveys the essence of the moment—romantic intimacy. (At the end of the second act, this same intimate framing combined with tracking will be repeated. This repetition will supply a resonance to that scene that it would not have if rendered differently. The fact that the audience might not be *consciously* aware of this "mirroring" does not matter.)

EXT. PRESCOTT'S OFFICE: Devlin drives up and exits his car with a bottle of champagne.

INT. PRESCOTT'S OFFICE: This is a good example of that old adage, "True love never runs smooth." This scene collides with the one just preceding it, and Devlin is blindsided. The pan (active narrator) from the bottle of champagne to Devlin's disturbed demeanor makes this collision clear. We *feel* his dismay because we are inside of his head. (This is Devlin's scene.) We stay inside his head for the entire scene because of the judicious use of staging and cutting. For example, there is an intercutting between Prescott and Devlin on Prescott's line, "Because Sebastian knows her." Then again, "He was once in love with her." Devlin stops dead in his tracks, and we are made fully aware of this dagger to his heart.

- Because of its established ability to seek out what is important, the camera can leave Devlin as he exits the room and discover the champagne bottle that he has left behind, indicating to us the level of Devlin's consternation with what has transpired.
- The scene is shot entirely in separation except for a three-shot that "ties" everyone together and a two-shot of Devlin and the Third Man that is set up by the staging. Why did Hitchcock feel it necessary to have Devlin and this minor character in the same shot? Precisely because he is a minor character. A cut to him in separation would have given him too much weight, but not so in a two-shot that calls no special attention to him. *(This is an example of separation being resolved through staging.)*

ALICIA'S LIVING ROOM/KITCHEN/PATIO: This elegantly rendered scene has been extensively covered in Chapters 3, 4, and 6. It might be beneficial for you to review these chapters in the context of the entire film up to now.

EXT./INT. CAR: Aside from the expository information rendered clearly and economically, the scene establishes the new dynamic relationship between Alicia and Devlin.

EXT. RIDING PATH: The first shot immediately announces where we are geographically, and the next four shots establish Alicia and Devlin in spatial relationship to Alex Sebastian and his companion. Again, the information is unambiguous. We know exactly where everyone is. Then in a series of 10 shots, Hitchcock *elaborates* Devlin and Alicia coming abreast of Sebastian. A question is framed: "Will Sebastian recognize Alicia?" The answer is withheld for the duration of these 10 shots, thereby creating tension. Let's look at the sentence structure of this "paragraph" of elaboration.

Alicia and Devlin make their move.
Alicia and Devlin get into position.
Alicia looks at Sebastian.
Sebastian (glances at the two riders abreast of him but) does not notice Alicia.
Alicia and Devlin continue to ride abreast of Sebastian.
Alicia attempts to get Sebastian's attention (by staring at him).
Sebastian "feels" someone looking at him and turns his head toward Alicia.

Alicia's hat blocks Sebastian's view of her face.
Sebastian gives up (trying to view the mysterious lady).
Devlin and Alicia realize their plan has failed.

- The fourth shot in this series is Alex Sebastian's *entrance* into the film. It will take the remainder of the scene to *reveal* something significant about his character.
- The fifth shot in this series resolves the separation that has occurred and is about to occur again. It tells the audience *exactly* where everyone is so that when the scene is fragmented, the audience will be spatially oriented.

The question that has been raised is answered in the 10th shot. Sebastian does not recognize Alicia. The plan has failed, but another question is immediately raised: What will Devlin do now?

Devlin thinks of a plan.
Devlin executes his plan.
Alicia's horse is spooked (and gallops away).
Devlin reins in his horse (signaling to Sebastian that he will not be the one to save the damsel in distress).
Sebastian sees his opportunity (to meet the mystery lady) and initiates pursuit.
Sebastian pursues Alicia.
Devlin (and Sebastian's companion) watch.
Sebastian "saves" Alicia.
Devlin watches his plan unfold.
Sebastian and Alicia greet each other.
Devlin realizes that his plan (of handing Alicia over to another man) has worked.

- To appreciate this scene we must be in Devlin's head. Hence, six of the above shots are of Devlin. Because of the context in which each appears, they allow us to enter his thought process, elucidating for us his attitude toward Alicia's involvement with Sebastian.

INT. BAR: This is a scene of aftermath, locking down Devlin's attitude toward what transpired on the bridle path. Devlin contemplates his handing over Alicia to another man, and he is not happy about it.

INT. HOTEL BAR: Hitchcock establishes the geography in the first shot, and it is no accident that it conveys a much different atmosphere than the bar Devlin was sitting in.

- Sebastian sits at a 90-degree angle to Alicia, a more intimate position than the across-the-table seating of Devlin and Alicia at the outdoor café.
- Notice again the convenient appearance of the waiter just when a dramatic punctuation is warranted, ending one dramatic block and thrusting us into another.
- We assign the POV of Prescott to *both* Alicia and Alex.
- Ask yourself, Why does Hitchcock change his camera angles when he does? Or why does he change the image size? Why does he go from over-the-shoulder to a close-up? You will always find that it is because he is articulating what is happening in the scene through narrative beats. He is framing the story for us. Remember, *if it doesn't happen for the audience, it doesn't happen!*
- Notice the second use of the frontal two-shot. It not only resolves separation, but it does so while punctuating the end of a dramatic block and serving as a *release* from the tension that has been created so that a new tension can begin (talk of Devlin).
- It is important to realize the distance that the two characters have traveled in this scene and why we buy it. The two haven't seen each other in years, then they see each other only briefly a few days ago. Yet at the end of the scene there is the promise of intimacy between them. True, Alicia is "working him," yet Alex Sebastian's "courtship" in this scene is progressive—step-by-step—and *all* of the steps are *available* to us not only through the dialogue and performance but then

framed by the director through the narrative beats. Hitchcock is restricted here to articulating with only the camera because staging, except for the initial seating position, is not an option (as it was in the patio scene).

INT. HOTEL ROOM: Staging *is* an option here and Hitchcock relies on it almost exclusively, rendering the scene in one take, except for Alicia's entrance and exit. Spatial positioning sets up Devlin's "snub" of Alicia's request for help with her necklace then serves to remind us again what has come between them (i.e., Prescott and all he stands for).

The extended take in this scene contrasts with the extensive cutting that took place in the prior scene, supplying a welcome modulation to the narrator's voice.

EXT. SEBASTIAN'S MANSION: The movement of the camera up and over the car, revealing the front door, is a reverse of the camera movement that occurs at the end of the film. Introducing not only the geography but also the camera movement gives the end shot a power it would not have had otherwise.

INT. SEBASTIAN'S MANSION—FOYER/PARLOR, MAIN HALL: We assign the moving shots of the interior to Alicia because they *come off of her look* and because *she is moving*, but do we assign them as her subjective voice or merely her POV? It doesn't matter. What these two shots do is remind us, subliminally, that Alicia does have a subjective voice. Hitchcock uses this to trick us. When Madame Sebastian comes toward Alicia, we think for a moment that she is looking directly into the camera (that this is Alicia's direct perception), but at the last instant, Madame Sebastian looks camera right, rendering her approach through the objective view of the narrator. Even though it does serve to keep Alicia's subjective voice alive for us, I can't help thinking that Hitchcock smiled when he thought of the momentary confusion he would engender in us.

- The door is opened by a "butler" (Joseph), his introduction as a significant character.
- The staircase is introduced in all its glory. It is the most dramatically important location in the film and will be used and reused, gaining power in its familiarity. Also, as this sequence unfolds, Hitchcock continues to take pains to spatially connect the various rooms of the mansion with one another so that we will feel *comfortable* there later on.
- Madame Sebastian is introduced. It is quite a theatrical entrance, befitting the major role she will play.

INT. STUDY/DINING ROOM: There are five more people to be introduced here, and Hitchcock does it with alacrity, yet giving each character his due. Eric is introduced first, Doctor Anderson last, giving them greater importance than their colleagues. (The same goes for information in a pan or a paragraph of dialogue. The last position is the strongest, the first position is the next strongest.)

- Alicia repeats Doctor Anderson's name to guarantee that he will "stick out."
- Hitchcock fragments the scene in the study, as he does in the dining room, but in between the entire assemblage of characters is rendered in a wide shot, resolving the separation between everyone for the first and last time. It is enough, however, to keep us satisfied as to who is present.
- Dinner is announced off-screen. Then in the first shot in the dining room, we see a waiter off to the left side of the frame, drawing no attention to himself, *but we read him*. We are satisfied that this large house does have help, but we also know that none of them will have a plot function.
- The dining room is revealed to us in pieces. Just exactly where the sideboard containing the wine bottles is in relation to Alicia is not made clear to us until after the "commotion" regarding the wine bottles has occurred—not until Sebastian moves past the sideboard. Even though it is received as ancillary information, we "read it." If its position in the room had not been spatially resolved to our satisfaction, if it had remained floating in space, we would have been

left with a nagging, unanswered question (even if we were not aware of it). It would have inter-
fered with Alicia's subsequent subjective view of the wine bottles—the push in—that tells us she
finds them significant.

Much of the information the audience receives in film is in the background of the frame, so
the director must be aware of this background to *count on it* to deliver expository information
or atmosphere that is essential to telling the story or to make sure that information that would
intrude negatively on the story is not included.

I once had an undergraduate student who shot a silent scene between two characters in an
apartment. At one point, the camera, in panning, revealed a third character sitting at a desk. The
scene continued, paying no attention to this third character. When I asked the student who the
third character was, he said dismissively, "Oh, it's his apartment."

INT. DOORS OUTSIDE OF DINING ROOM: In this film the narrator has the ability to
leave Alicia and go with Devlin. It also has the ability to leave both of them to follow an important
plot development, such as Emile awaiting his fate. This ability was established (in the screenplay)
early in the second act when Prescott met with his colleagues in the boardroom. In Fellini's *8½*
(Chapter 17) we will see a narrator that *never* visits a scene that does not contain the protagonist.

INT. DINING ROOM: Why start with an overhead shot of the men at the table? What does
it imply, if anything? Because all our shots are read in context, we assign the one Hitchcock wants
us to: a time jump has occurred, and we realize it immediately. Second, the narrator shows us all
the players in the room at the head of the scene, so it is then free to break up the scene. The fourth
shot, which is an extended take that renders the bulk of the scene, imparts an aesthetic and dramatic symmetry. It begins with Emile entering and ends with him leaving with Eric. It is Emile's
exit from the film. We know we will never see him again. (It is a good idea to provide an exit from
the film for our characters, certainly for our principals.)

EXT. RACETRACK: Hitchcock introduces the racetrack with a shot that could not be inter-
preted to be anything else. We never see the track again, directly, but Hitchcock finds a way within
the body of the scene to keep the public space alive without spoiling the intimacy of the scene.

● It is important that directors know at all times where they are in the story. In this scene, the
relationship between Alicia and Devlin reaches its nadir. An apparently insurmountable obstacle
is introduced: Alicia informs Devlin that she has slept with Alex Sebastian. This hits Devlin like
a ton of bricks. He *shuts off* any sympathetic feelings he might have continued to harbor for
Alicia. *They are farther apart now than they have ever been.* This is a point that occurs in every
good love story, and Hitchcock makes sure this fact impinges on the audience *viscerally*. He
does it with the skillful juxtaposition of three shots.

Hitchcock sets up this moment with a prolonged two-shot of Alicia and Devlin "talking shop"
at the rail.

                          DEVLIN
Anything else?

                          ALICIA
Nothing important. Just a minor item that you may want for the record.

                          DEVLIN
What is it?

                          ALICIA
You can add Sebastian's name to my list of playmates.

                              (last word overlaps the cut)

CUT TO DEVLIN!

                                             DEVLIN
Pretty fast work.

CUT TO ALICIA!

                                             ALICIA
That's what you wanted, wasn't it?

CUT TO PROFILE OF DEVLIN!

                                             DEVLIN
Skip it!

   It's as if a steel grate has been pulled down between the two of them, *and we feel it!*

- The binoculars serve two dramatic purposes. The reflection in them keeps the public arena alive without breaking up the intimacy, and they hide the depth of Alicia's feelings until she takes them from her eyes and we see a tear. This delayed reveal has more impact because it was preceded by our curiosity as to what she is feeling.
- When Devlin leaves Sebastian and Alicia at the rail, they assume the same position that she and Devlin had just been in, *but* it is rendered in a way that supplies a slightly different stage— just enough difference, however, to keep the narrative thrust going. What does Hitchcock do? Instead of shooting the separation on each character head-on as he has just done, he moves the camera a bit on each character to give a slight change in angle.

   INT. PRESCOTT'S OFFICE: A deceptively simple scene—more skillfully crafted than might be apparent on first reading. Its emotional center is the deep feelings that still exist between Devlin and Alicia—feelings that cannot be expressed to each other. Even though there are four other people in the room, Hitchcock has them all but disappear for us. It becomes a scene between the two estranged lovers.

- As we've seen before, Hitchcock arranges all the participants in this meeting into one strong grouping that can be read quickly in one shot. Devlin's position at the window, his back to the others, speaks volumes about his deep feelings for Alicia, *even before he turns to defend her honor.* (A good example of "What does the shot tell you?") Secondarily, but very importantly, because we are secure where Devlin is spatially vis-à-vis everyone else, Hitchcock can cut to him in separation for the remainder of the scene. Devlin's separation from Alicia is not resolved until the last shot.
- The door is not "tied" to the geography of the room until Alicia enters and the shot takes her from the door to her chair. This resolving of spatial separation between Alicia and the door is important in making the final shot effective: Devlin exiting behind Alicia. This is an example of where the expository information (the door's location) would have intruded on the emotional essence of the moment (Alicia's distress).
- There is movement in the room by Prescott and others, but it is not dramatically important, so Hitchcock doesn't bother to clarify who is moving where. The people who matter—Devlin and Alicia—are anchored: him by the window, her in a chair. Consequently, when Devlin does make his move to the door, it is a much more powerful indictment of Alicia's choice. Also, an

important, and I'm sure calculated, result of the movement by Prescott and his operatives is that it clears the frame around Alicia so that she is left alone in the frame after Devlin's exit.

- Notice how Hitchcock uses Prescott in this scene to supply "editorial commentary" on the proceedings, not by what he says, but by what he is *thinking*.

INT. MADAME SEBASTIAN'S BEDROOM: A one-take scene with one camera move that renders strongly Sebastian's move to the door, signifying his defiance. This is a good, strong use of foreground/background.

- Madame Sebastian's *strength* in the frame is significant. It suggests her power. It hints that although she has lost this battle, she is still someone to be reckoned with.

EXT. SEBASTIAN'S MANSION: The drive-up is a familiar image. Alicia and Alex exiting the chauffeur-driven car is a wonderfully economical expository device. We understand that the two have been on a trip. We might not be sure that they have just returned from their honeymoon, but it *prepares* us for the fact that they have gone somewhere that we have not been privy to. (When the audience is to be given information that might be difficult to believe—or, as in this case, that they might feel cheated by not having been told—we can discharge these feelings by preparing the audience for what we are about to tell them.)

INT. SEBASTIAN'S MANSION: Following an unprepared Joseph to the door gives the audience time to reflect on where Alicia and Alex could have gone. The chauffeur, carrying in luggage (an example of important background information), helps in supplying a vestige of the trip, allowing us to come to a satisfying conclusion as to their whereabouts—satisfying because we have participated in unraveling the puzzle.

- Why the cut to Joseph turning on the lights? Because it articulates the fact that this is not a "very bright homecoming."

INT. MASTER BEDROOM/MANSION: The initial framing of the first shot shouts out, MOVING IN! The mobile narrator that has been set up in the first shot of the film follows the overt action of the scene. The staging—Eric shadowing Alicia's every move—makes us aware of the difficulties her "snooping" will encounter.

- The final framing in the scene, the only close-up of Alicia, allows Hitchcock to render for us Alicia's thought process and serves as a "springboard" into the next scene, which will answer the question that was raised: Will Alicia be successful in obtaining the keys? (The more questions the audience asks, the more they will be participating in the unfolding of the story, and the more they will be engaged by it.)

INT. STUDY/MANSION: Again, all participants are rendered in one grouping. This time Doctor Anderson occupies center stage. This is important to "keep him alive" for us because he will play a more significant role in the unfolding of the plot than he has so far.

INT. FOYER/STAIRCASE: Why is it necessary for the camera to follow Alicia and Alex from the door of the study to the staircase? The reason is that it strongly establishes the proximity of these two areas of the main hall and resolves their separation—an important consideration in setting up the final dramatic scene inside the mansion.

UPSTAIRS HALLWAY/MASTER BEDROOM: The upstairs hallway is introduced and will also be used in the final scene.

INT. MONTGAGE OF DOORS/MANSION: This is an efficient way to compress action that is not interesting. Its main purpose is to set up the plot point that the only key Alicia does not have is the one key that will unlock the secret she is after.

EXT. PARK BENCH: In the cut from the wide shot to the close-two, Hitchcock again violates the 30-degree rule, but here it is not jarring because of Devlin's overlapping movement between the two shots. The same thing occurs when cutting back out to the wide shot, but this time Alicia is the one that moves.

EXT. MANSION—NIGHT: This establishing shot serves mainly to indicate a passage of time.

INT. MASTER BEDROOM: Alicia must work fast. From the shot of her standing in the doorway, the camera moves in rapidly to the key ring lying on the dresser. Because we assign this camera movement to Alicia's subjective perception, we assume it is her making this move, but it is not! Hitchcock has fooled us, and we realize this when he cuts back to a long shot of Alicia still standing at the doorway, still having to traverse this "mine field." She is still so far from her goal. A twinge of anxiety overcomes us because we do not want her to be found out by Alex, who could come out from the open bathroom door at any moment.

- Alex's shadow on the open bathroom door keeps alive the imminent danger for Alicia, providing a good deal of suspense. This is used three times. Hitchcock adds to the suspense by elaborating (elongating)—taking eight shots to cover the action of Alicia's "theft."
- Just when we hoped that Alicia would escape through the doorway undetected, Sebastian exits the bathroom, moving toward Alicia. The camera moves in close on his hands reaching out to clasp both of Alicia's two clenched fists, one of which contains the key. The narrator's deliberate movement into Sebastian's hands, followed by a second shot that moves emphatically in on Sebastian opening the first of Alicia's clenched fists (both examples of the active narrator), heightens the suspense another notch by allowing us to fully appreciate Alicia's dilemma.
- If you know that you need very tight close-ups on a small object—in this instance, the key—it is important to set up this stylistic imagery beforehand. If it comes out of the blue during a dramatic moment, it will seem jarring. Yes, we will get it, but not elegantly. When was this imagery introduced in this film? When Alicia first visits the wine cellar door. Here the close-up comes naturally out of the action of the scene and does not intrude on a dramatic moment. Then to make sure this imagery stays with us, Hitchcock cuts to a close-up of the door lock (off of Alicia's look) to end the sequence. (In a film such as *Tokyo Story*, discussed in Chapter 18, you can see how jarring it would be to go to a tight close-up on anything, let alone a key, because of the different aesthetic that has been set in motion by Ozu.)

MAIN HALL/ADJACENT ROOMS/WINE CELLAR/GARDEN/MASTER BEDROOM: The fade up on the overhead view of the main hall marks the beginning of a 14-minute suspense sequence that begins at the party and ends with Sebastian discovering the broken wine bottle. It contains many plot points that the audience must understand to appreciate the jeopardy that Alicia is in. Understanding her increasing jeopardy creates suspense.

- After the party is announced in the first shot, notice how little attention is paid to it, although it is always present, serving as background to the main action.
- The geographical relationship of the adjacent rooms off of the main hall is fuzzy to us, but we don't mind because the main hall and staircase establish a familiar space to which we constantly return. Hitchcock does help us to stay oriented by tracking with Alicia and Devlin when they leave the main hall and go to the bar, tying the two areas together. Another aspect of geography that is not resolved is Alex's POVs. The "glue" that ties his look to what he is seeing—Alicia and Devlin—is merely the butting together of the two shots. This occurs in the main hall as well as when he catches Alicia and Devlin kissing. Although it is often desirable and sometimes necessary to resolve spatial differences, it is absolutely not necessary to do so all the time. Is there a rule? No, not an absolute one. We have to become sensitive to when the audience might become spatially disoriented. We have much more freedom in a narrative sequence such as this one than

we do in, say, a dramatic scene such as the one on the patio, where continuous spatial resolution is necessary to the understanding of the psychology of the scene.

- Hitchcock inserts himself a second time in this film. He can be found downing a glass of champagne at the bar.
- The overhead shot that says "the party is over" is the same shot that earlier announced the party.
- Hitchcock makes sure we clearly understand the essence of every moment, beginning with the first shot, which moves from the chandelier to the wine cellar key in Alicia's hand. (Notice how the first shot says "party" at the same time it is directing our attention to the essence of the moment.) The crucial actions and plot points in this sequence are all made visually (although some are supported by dialogue). It is advisable that you watch this sequence without sound to fully realize how much crucial information is given to us clearly and unambiguously with the camera. The actions and plot points that are supplied visually are:

The transfer of the key to Devlin.

Alex watching Alicia like a hawk.

The champagne ice chest full, half full, then with only three bottles left.

The tray loaded with champagne glasses (indicating that it is going fast).

The 1940 label on the row of wineglasses.

The two shots show the wine bottle moving incrementally closer to the edge of the shelf, then falling on the third shot. (If Hitchcock had shown only the last shot of the wine falling, he would have been creating merely a surprise, which would have been over in a second. For suspense you must have duration—something that the audience can participate in as it unfolds. Hence the first two shots of the bottle being moved, allowing us to anticipate the fall.)

The sand and broken bottle on the floor.

Alex noticing the wine cellar key missing from his key ring (while with Joseph).

The key ring with the missing key being placed on the dressing table.

Alicia asleep.

Time passing. (The use of the grandfather clock is "clunky," but it gets the job done.)

The missing key has been replaced.

Alex noticing that wine has been spilt in the sink.

Alex discovering the disparity in dates on wine bottles, then discovering that sand has been removed, then discovering that the cork has been tampered with.

Alex discovering sand and the broken wine bottle with the correct date under the bottom shelf of the wine rack (ending the sequence).

MAIN HALL/STAIRCASE: The short dissolve from the tight close-up on the label of the broken wine bottle to the wide overhead shot of Alex entering the main hall is an example of the use of *visual contrast in transition*.

- This scene is rendered in one beautifully designed shot that does three things: It renders the action of Alex coming from his discovery in the wine cellar. It also helps us to get inside of Alex's head. *Because of the context* in which the high angle appears, it feels as if it were "pressing down" on Alex, *exposing* his anxiety and utter dismay, making it *palpable* for the audience even before we read it in his face at the top of the stairs. It keeps the staircase supremely alive.

MADAME SEBASTIAN'S BEDROOM: The strongest lesson here is the metamorphosis of Madame Sebastian from an old woman sleeping into a powerful, evil force. This is done with the staging and the use of a prop—the cigarette.

- As in so many other scenes, Hitchcock immediately gives us our bearings—where we are and whom we are with. By having Alex and his mother in the same shot at the head of the scene, he is free to go into extended separation. The separation is resolved only after Alex establishes a new spatial position.
- The high close-up of Alex continues the "pressing down" framing that was introduced in the previous scene. Again, it imparts this psychological interpretation only because of the dramatic context in which it appears.
- A handy piece of staging is to have a character turning his or her back to another. Alex does it here because he is resisting what his mother is saying. It supplies the *necessity* for Madame Sebastian to come around Sebastian to make her point more forcibly.

GARDEN: The previous scene ended with Madame Sebastian's words, "She could become ill and remain ill for a time, until. . . ." Hitchcock wastes no time in showing us this plan in effect, and he does it with the ability of the active narrator to build an equation for us. It is all done with a tracking shot that takes us from Alex suggesting that Alicia drink her coffee, to the coffee cup that Alicia picks up and drinks from, to Madame Sebastian acting as if she does not know what is going on. The *result* of these three factors is given to us on the cut to the close-up of Alicia in the next scene in Prescott's office.

PRESCOTT'S OFFICE: This is a rare transition to another location unimpeded by a dissolve or fade, and you can see its power. We don't know where we are, and it doesn't matter for this first moment. What matters is that we understand that Alicia is being drugged. Only then do we discover that we are in Prescott's office.

- Notice the first cut from the two-shot on the couch into separation. What narrative beat does it articulate?

MANSION GROUNDS: The purpose of the close-up of the coffee cup should be clear. But why is Doctor Anderson there? Because we haven't seen him for a while, and because his presence will play a significant plot point in the final scene of the second act, Hitchcock places him in the scene to keep him alive.

PARK BENCH: We've been here before, but this time the camera is not angled head-on. The camera is angled off to the left. Why? What does it do? It imparts a sense of narrative thrust. By changing the shot, Hitchcock subliminally indicates that the dynamics of the scene have changed, and they have, significantly. Alicia and Devlin are about to lose each other, and both are aware of it.

- We remember the scarf, even before Alicia mentions it, because of the care Hitchcock gave to its entrance into the film, and then his making sure its image remained imprinted on us when Alicia suddenly remembers she has it tied around her waist at the end of the first act.

STUDY: The reason that Hitchcock gave Alicia a subjective voice becomes apparent in this scene. He wanted it to serve as a measure for the audience of Alicia's utter helplessness. An audio element is added to it, making Alicia's hallucinatory state totally accessible to us because we perceive it directly. The active narrator is used here also, guiding us to what is important in the scene: to where the danger lies. Hitchcock orchestrates these two stylistic elements to make a scene that is much richer, more suspenseful, than if they were not available.

- As the scene begins with Sebastian, his mother, and Alfred talking of travel plans, the camera chooses not to stay with the conversation, but instead it elects to take off on its own (to draw undue attention to Alicia's coffee cup), hence raising the level of suspense considerably. The three shots of the coffee cup—large in the foreground with Alicia in the background—are another aspect of the active narrator. In these shots it is the unmistakable clarity of the composition, and its repetition, that formulates for the audience the true nature of the drama inherent in the moment.

- Hitchcock uses three fast tracking shots in a row to dramatically reveal to us Alicia's coming to understand that she has been drugged. The first two tracking shots—on Sebastian and then on Madame Sebastian—are Alicia's subjective voice. The third, the track in on Alicia standing, is the active narrator's voice. This is a wonderful three-shot equation that tells us clearly, and *powerfully*, the essence of the moment.

MAIN HALL/STAIRCASE/MASTER BEDROOM: Alicia collapses in a familiar image. Hitchcock then follows Alicia being carried to her bed, mirroring the exact route she will take for her escape with Devlin. Also, realize how skillfully Hitchcock familiarized us with the geography beforehand—not only the main hall and staircase, but also the upper hallway and the master bedroom.

- This is the end of the second act. Alicia has exhausted her action in regard to both of her dilemmas: her love for Devlin and her dangerous occupation.

THIRD ACT

The third act in a classically organized drama deals with the consequences of the protagonist's actions. (It is very rare for the protagonist to be comatose and unable to act in the third act, but it in no way harms this drama. Although it is Alicia's story, Devlin has been woven so elegantly into it that his driving the action of the third act does not have a negative impact on the dramatic resolution.)

BENCH/MASTER BEDROOM/BENCH: These three scenes serve to indicate passage of time.

PRESCOTT'S HOTEL ROOM: This is an example of the *master shot design* for a scene. In this case, the "master" is used as a bookend—opening and closing the scene—that is "magnified" (a term coined by Steffan Sharff in *The Elements of Cinema*) by the two shots that render Devlin and Prescott in separation.

EXTERIOR MANSION: This is a familiar image that will be repeated at the end of the film.

MAIN HALL AND STARCASE: At the door Hitchcock chooses to exit the two-shot by pushing (tracking) into Devlin in separation, drawing us into his thinking.

STUDY: This is Sebastian's scene. Notice how Hitchcock allows us to get inside of his head.

MAIN HALL AND STAIRCASE: We are familiar with all of the geography.

MASTER BEDROOM: Devlin's approach to the bed from Alicia's POV resonates with his approach to her in bed in the hangover scene in Act One. When Devlin gets to the bed, the remainder of this love scene, running three-and-one-half minutes, is rendered in three very close shots that emulate the love scene that took place in Alicia's apartment when she and Devlin moved from the patio, to the phone, to the door in the same intimate staging and framing.

- The three long takes here not only serve to render the scene in the most powerful way, but they also establish a rhythmic contrast to the next scene with its intense use of multiple angles.

SECOND FLOOR HALLWAY/STAIRCASE/MAIN HALL: This is a classic example of dramatic elaboration using multiple angles: 59 shots in just a little over two minutes. Hitchcock uses the four-shot (all four characters in one frame) to glue together the separation. The Germans at the foot of the stairs do not have to be spatially resolved with the four on the staircase because we are very familiar with the geography, and we connect the two spaces from our past visual experience here.

EXT. MANSION: The tracking move over the car roof and down to the driver side window and the shot of Sebastian walking back toward the mansion are familiar images that allow us to fully appreciate the dramatic and emotional elements in the scene without being distracted by expository geographical material.

SUMMARY

It is obvious that this is a film that was completely visualized before shooting began. It is crystal clear at all times, as to both plot development and the emotional life of the characters. Hitchcock's use of staging to make physical what is going on internally with a character, his dramatic economy (never doing more than he has to), rhythmic changes in sentence structure, use of the active narrator, and precise articulation of narrative beats all contribute to a masterful telling of this story.

Hitchcock was not known as an actor's director, but he cast wonderful actors, determined the narrative beats, and then articulated them through a skillful combination of staging and camera. He once told François Truffaut, "When a film has been properly staged, it isn't necessary to rely on the player's virtuosity or personality for tension and dramatic effect." Because this attitude limits the power of the emotional journey on which a director can take an audience, it is not one that I would recommend.

C H A P T E R   1 6

PETER WEIR'S *THE TRUMAN SHOW*

OVERVIEW OF STYLE AND DESIGN

OBJECTIVE NARRATOR

Weir's objective narrator does not actively interpret for us as overtly as Hitchcock does in *Notorious*, yet the story and plot points in *The Truman Show* are more numerous and complicated. How, then, does Weir allow us to participate in all the twists and turns of the story at the same time he allows us full access to the psychological life of the characters, especially the protagonist? It is due partly to the construction of the screenplay, which juxtaposes actions in such a way that cause and effect are immediately available to us through the narrative device of *parallel action*. However, the screenplay does something else: as in *Notorious*, the objective narrator has help from another voice in telling the story. This time the help is not supplied by the subjective voice of a character but by an *antagonist's voice* that is embedded in the circumstance of the screenplay. (Hitchcock's decision to give Alicia a subjective voice was a directorial decision. He could have told the story without it but not as powerfully.)

Although Weir does not take us is such a firm headlock as Hitchcock does with his active narrator, Weir's objective narrator is every bit as effective in telling *this* story. The strong articulation of narrative beats through staging and camera and the artful modulation of the objective narrator's voice—at times speaking quietly and softly, other times rapidly and with greater volume—maximizes the audience's emotional involvement. An example of the latter happens in the opening sequence of the light fixture falling from the sky. Its flight and impact is elaborated for us by the narrator in three shots, making the fact of its fall more significant, and of course more dramatic. (A modulation in the voice of the narrator is a significant tool of the master storyteller and one that directors in the twenty-first century should have in their toolboxes, but we also see in Yasujiro Ozu's *Tokyo Story* [1953, Japanese; Chapter 18] that strong stories can be told without it.)

ANTAGONIST'S VOICE

In this story, "five thousand cameras" are watching Truman. They are everywhere, and one of the first jobs Weir has to accomplish is to inform us of that. Some of the antagonist's cameras are indicated by an irising around the edges and are easily identified. Others are not identified so easily. Weir cleverly relies on this ambiguousness, this "fuzziness" as to which image belongs to the antagonist and which to the objective narrator, to increase the antagonist's arsenal by having the objective narrator, at times, serve as the antagonist's voice. This is because even with five thousand cameras available for the antagonist's voice, Weir knew that voice would be severely restricted if he slavishly adhered to the division of labor implied here: that every shot was either solely the objective narrator's or solely the antagonist's POV. What we discover is that Weir begins to assign *both* functions to certain shots, and we accept it—another example of the fluidity of POV.

In the very first shot, the antagonist (Christof) speaks directly to us through what we assume is the objective narrator, but in fact it is his own camera that he is speaking to. For a moment *we are his television audience*, although we do not know it at the time. Already the hard line between the objective and antagonist's camera is muddied, and the seed of Weir's freedom to combine their narrative jobs has been planted.

ENTRANCES

There is nothing special here, but note that every significant character is introduced within their own frame the first time we see them, unless they are characters who go through the film in tandem with another (the twins who profess interest in buying insurance from Truman, the waitresses in the bar, and the two old ladies on the couch).

ART DIRECTION AND PRODUCTION DESIGN

Truman's world is fake, yet the images we see of that world are real. Yes, we readily accept them as part of a movie set, but it is a *real* movie set. We feel that life exists outside of the frame, even if that life is fabricated. (Life outside the frame did not exist in *Notorious*.)

Christof's world—his studio—is an extension of his job, but more importantly of his personality. It adds significantly to his aura, making the power he arrays against Truman palpable to us.

WHAT ARE WE WATCHING FOR IN THIS FILM?

We will be watching for the clarity of all the plot points in what is a complicated story with many characters. We will pay attention to how we get this expository information within the *uninterrupted flow of narrative thrust*. The key ingredient for us to be aware of is the strong emotions that Weir succeeds in generating in the audience. It is very difficult to resist Truman's innocence, goodness, humanity, and ultimate dilemma. Yes, the vehicle for this possibility was embedded in the screenplay, but Weir rendered it fully. He created compelling *life*, the most difficult job of a director. Without it, the rest doesn't matter.

Of course, Weir relied on Jim Carrey's beautifully modulated performance to "carry" this story. Truman is the emotional center of this film. Yes, Weir cast well (in all the roles), but it would be wrong to assume that Weir did not have a hand in orchestrating this performance, in ensuring that it was not only believable but also interesting. We should not take for granted the fact that the camera was always in the right place to render Carrey's performance fully and powerfully.

FIRST ACT

TITLE SEQUENCE: As mentioned earlier, the first shot is Christof's entrance into the film through the voice that he controls—the antagonist's narrator—but we are not aware of that yet. When Truman enters the film in the second shot, we understand that he is being photographed by a television camera because of the visible lines across the screen in close-up. But who do we think is photographing the wife and friend? We quickly assign this to the television show (the antagonist's POV) *because of the context in which they appear.*

EXTERIOR OF TRUMAN'S HOUSE AND NEIGHBORHOOD: Although Truman enters the film in the bathroom, he is not *revealed* to us until the first shot of him exiting his house. Here we discover his public persona; we understand that he has a white-collar job and that he lives in a middle-class neighborhood—a lot of information we do not even know we are getting. (This layering of narrative information—building crucial narrative information into the frame—is a key job of all directors. Of course, Weir relied on his costume designer, set designer, production designer, casting director, director of photography, and so on to create this world. Even if we shoot on location—when we do not build our universe from scratch—it is important to realize the importance of background, which is a scene's "wallpaper" that the director relies on so heavily to impart important information or to create atmosphere in cinematic storytelling.)

- When Truman exits his house, it is quite clear in the very first shot that he is being watched by the antagonist's camera. This is made clear by the irising around the edges of the frame and then the fast track-in on Truman (mimicking a zoom). The cuts to the neighbors and the encounter with the dog are a clever mixture of antagonist's camera and objective narrator without a clearly discernible reason for either one at this point. Why is it clever? Because it introduces the amalgam of the two narrative voices Weir will use to tell the remainder of the story.

- It is clearly the objective narrator talking to us when the stage light falls from the sky—an instructive piece of expository information. In addition, the narrator "raises his voice" here through the use of elaboration, dramatically injecting alarm and danger. The elaboration consists of four shots of the light falling (generated by the objective narrator), a reaction shot of Truman (antagonist's camera), a shot of the light crashing into the street (objective camera), another reaction shot of Truman (antagonist's camera), and a final close shot of the damaged light lying still in the street (objective camera). Because of this design Weir now has complete freedom to "cheat" in his use of the antagonist's camera whenever it serves his purpose. (There is no need to cheat on what the objective narrator can see: it is omnipotent—it can see everything—as exemplified by the light falling.)

- Weir must begin to introduce us to Truman's environment, and he does so quite gracefully by revealing it to us as part of the action of a scene. (Truman goes to inspect the fallen light in a long shot that reveals the street he lives on.) We do not feel as if the story has stopped just so we can be told where we are.

- INSIDE OF THE CAR: We are introduced to a more insidious form of the antagonist's voice, one I'll call the "spy cam" because of the voyeuristic quality that the angle and pronounced irising gives to it.

- INSIDE OF THE NEWSPAPER STAND: We are introduced to another of the antagonist's fixed cameras. We assign it as such *even though* there is no irising present. We assign it because of the distortion caused by the extra-wide-angle lens. This lens is next used when shooting TRUMAN AND THE TWINS on the street, which along with the high angle in which it is placed signals us that this is the antagonist's voice. But notice the eye-level shot of Truman. It is not from the extra-wide-angle lens. It can only be the objective narrator. We accept this stylistic mixing because Weir has taken pains to set it up. In fact, most of us don't even notice it.

TRUMAN'S OFFICE: A lot of work is done in this scene aside from showing us where Truman works: We learn that he is being watched by his coworkers and that he is obsessed with an image of a girl.

- Observe the "tunnel" framing of the first shot. The files and the stack of books in the foreground supply a claustrophobic atmosphere. We know immediately that this is not a happy workplace. In subsequent shots from the angle in front of Truman's desk, you will not find this foreground material. It was arranged specifically for this shot and does not exist after this shot.

- When one of Truman's coworkers moves behind the glass partition to spy on Truman, the objective narrator mimics the coworker's visual movement *over* the glass divider, making the intrusion on Truman's space more palpable to us. We feel the violation. (In actuality Weir is giving this coworker a subjective voice for one shot. It works because it comes out of the momentum established by the shot preceding it; it is *appropriate to the moment* and therefore does not have to be introduced earlier or used again.)

- Two high shots of Truman hunching over his desk with the edge of the glass partition in the frame are the objective narrator's shots that *contain the dynamics of the intruder*, keeping the threat of spying eminently alive.
- This scene consists of three dramatic blocks: the phone call, the search through the magazine, and the job assignment. Each block has a clear beginning. In the first, Truman looks to see if anyone is watching him. In the second, Truman reaches under a contract to reveal a fashion magazine. In the third, Truman swings around to face his desk.
- The six shots of Truman from below the desk are from the *omniscient* objective narrator. It can be anywhere. Its framing says "secretive." Its repetition makes "secretive" vivid to us.
- This shot from under the desk with its frame-within-a-frame is the second shot of a visual motif that began the first time we saw Truman in the bathroom mirror, and this motif continues throughout the film. The frame-within-a-frame evokes a sense of being boxed-in, constricted, a lack of freedom, which of course is the essence of Truman's life.
- The second coworker who is overhearing Truman's conversation is tied to him spatially with just a hint of partition on the right side of the frame. We do not know exactly where he is, but we *assume* that we do, and that is enough.
- The extra-wide angle that was introduced with the twins is kept alive when shooting the coworker who delivers the new assignment.

PIER: Truman's psychology—his fear of the water—is made perfectly clear to us by his struggle to overcome it. It is rendered in the staging, and thus the narrator (camera) does not need to interpret for us what is going on. Like much of Truman's psychology, it is understandable from a distance, and hence there is no need for a close-up to access Truman's head.

- Although we would have understood Truman's psychological struggle even if it had been rendered in one shot, Weir uses multiple angles to elaborate it, making it palpable to us by making it "larger."

TRUMAN'S BACK YARD: A high, wide shot of early evening does not have the expository feeling of the establishing shots we saw in *Notorious*. This is because it serves to punctuate Truman's defeat in the last scene. It says, in context of what just occurred, "The adventure is over."

- Truman's wife enters the body of the film on her bicycle, and we understand immediately that she is playing the role of a nurse. But more importantly, her psychology is revealed through the product endorsement. We understand that she has unquestionably accepted her role in the fiction surrounding Truman.
- Although we understand the product endorsement is being photographed by the antagonist's camera, none of the antagonist's camera's peculiarities are evident. It could just as well be the objective narrator, and it actually is. At this point Weir relies on us to switch back and forth, and we readily comply. For Weir to have intruded on the scene with the irising effect would have been redundant.
- Weir builds on our acceptance of the dual function of the objective narrator to reveal Truman's friend in the first shot of the next scene. He, too, is revealed as an actor who readily accepts all of the conditions of his job.
- We are still in the first sequence of the film, and Weir knows where the sequence will end and what he must do to prepare the audience for that end: Truman's reliving the moment when he lost his father at sea. The urgency that is necessary for Truman's psyche to generate this memory *must be available to the audience*. We must accept it. It cannot feel arbitrary. So, aside from telling the story moment by moment—making sure we understand the circumstance, the plot points, the dynamic relationship of the characters to Truman—Weir makes Truman's "yearning for more" constantly available to us, and the terrible memory of losing his father comes out of that.

UNFINISHED HIGHWAY: This scene is rendered with a combination of the objective narrator and the antagonist's narrator (the irising is much less visible because it is nighttime, but it is sufficient for us to "feel" its presence).

- Weir gets maximum power out of the "highway to nowhere" by saving its reveal until the end of the scene.
- Notice the *change in stage* (Truman leans against the pickup) for Truman's rhapsody on Fiji.
- The use of the golf ball to represent the earth is a good example of how a prop can be used to enhance a scene. (It seems as if the idea was in the screenplay, but often ideas like that can come from an actor.)
- It takes three seconds or less from Truman saying, "Bonus time is just around the corner" until we see him driving the golf ball. Could anyone walk to the tee, put down the ball, and swing their club in that amount of time? Yet we accept it. This is a small but important example of how film-time is used constantly to cut out the boring parts.

BEACH: This scene points out, perhaps more than any other so far, the fluidity of the actual source of the narrative voice in this film. When Truman is looking out to sea, we assign the shot to the objective narrator. When we see a sailboat in the sea and a flash of lightning, and then we hear the little boy's voice, we assign all of these to Truman's imagination. The cause and effect is too strong for us to come up with any other conclusion. Yet, as Truman imagines that terrible night when he lost his father, the *images are those of the antagonist's narrator.* Why is that? Because Weir is doing two things at once here. First and foremost, he is allowing us to partake directly in Truman's psychology, *even though the images come from the antagonist's narrator.* At this moment we are barely aware of the irising of the images, announcing unequivocally that they are from the antagonist's camera. Notice I said barely. We are aware *on some level.* A narrative layering is going on here. Although we partake directly in Truman's psychology (the first and immediately most important layer), we are also aware that this dream is being manufactured by the antagonist with archival footage and being broadcast to an audience. Weir has it both ways and is thereby able to present us with a much richer story.

UNFINISHED ROOM IN TRUMAN'S HOUSE: Because of the "muddying" of the distinction between the antagonist's and the objective narrator's voices that has taken place, we accept the cut to the "audience," assuming that they have just experienced precisely what we did.

SECURITY GUARDS: Our first shot of an audience. We will always return to these two men in exactly the same framing. That is also true for the rest of the audience *except for the bar.* If the shots of the audience changed each time we returned to them, we would be looking for a significance *beyond the editorial commentary* that they supply. Changing the frame would intrude on their dramatic job. Why is this not true for the bar? Because the waitresses move (it is a function of their job), giving Weir license to move with them.

MAIN SREET: When Truman leaves the newspaper stand, *we know something significant is going to happen.* How do we know that? Because the narrative has set everything in motion for that something to happen: A promise has been made to us, and we *expect* the storyteller to deliver on that promise. Of course, he does.

- The significant action that occurs next is the *point of attack* for the first act. (The point of attack intrudes on the "ordinary life" of our protagonist, causing a dilemma that must be solved before that person's life can go back to "normal.") The point of attack in this film is the reappearance of Truman's father. It occurs right after Truman leaves the newspaper stand.
- The father's entrance, then reveal, is the most powerful of any of the characters. His dramatic function in the story requires it, and Weir makes sure that the emotional thunderbolt that strikes Truman here is not lost on the audience.

- Weir uses 21 shots in 70 seconds not only to render the action but to dramatize it—to make us *feel* its effect on Truman. It is a very complicated action scene and took much planning and coordination among many assistant directors, actors, extras, stunt people, and so on to render what is a symphony of action with its own clear beginning (setup), middle (event), and end (aftermath). Weir's narrative beats in this scene not only render the *unfolding* of the action clearly and dramatically but even more importantly articulate powerfully the essence of the scene, its emotional core: Truman's ferocious want to be reunited with his father.
- Observe here the workings of film-time. The events portrayed could not have happened in 70 seconds, yet we accept it all as "real time."
- To understand the director's work here, both in the staging and camera, let's assign a sentence to each of the 21 shots. The first sentence (Truman noticing his father) is a compound sentence, so the shot is longer in length, as is the last shot of this sequence. The sentences in the body of the sequence are simple, declarative, and shorter—tumbling out one after another in a rapid flow of action that builds to a crescendo, and then this tension is released with the return of a longer sentence.

What happens in every shot is *clear to everyone in the audience.* What is probably not nearly as clear is how specific Weir was in constructing the action in each frame *to prevent the ordinary from overwhelming the essence of the moment.* To that end, we will concentrate on the essence of the images (their unequivocal "message" to the audience) the sine qua non of this book: *If it doesn't happen to the audience, it doesn't happen.*

1. Truman walks to work, passing a bum who seems to be waiting for him and whose presence is felt by Truman. (The bum's placement in the frame as well as the "hole" opened up in the pedestrian traffic guarantees that our attention is drawn to him.)
2. Truman searches his memory for a connection to this man.
3. The bum announces himself (by removing his hat), and Truman recognizes him (off camera we hear him say, "Dad?").
4. Two undercover agents hear this alarming news and immediately rush to intervene!
5. The father reaches out to Truman as the two agents come upon them.
6. The father is *wrenched* from Truman!
7. Truman is stunned!
8. The father is helpless to resist.
9. Obstacles to Truman's pursuit are quickly mobilized. (This high shot of the runners is a very effective choice by Weir. It immediately gives us a significant plot point while setting up the first obstacle that Truman must overcome to reach his father.)
10. The "wall" of runners is impenetrable!
11. Truman struggles (against the runners)!
12. Truman breaks free (of the runners) only to be faced with another obstacle (the newspaper-carrying pedestrian)!
13. Truman "runs through" the newspaper-carrying pedestrian (the newspaper serves as a measure of the violence of the collision) only to collide with a bicycle. (The bus at the end of this shot is not consciously read by us, but its *presence* is felt enough to set up the next shot.)
14. Father is being pushed onto a bus (with Truman in close pursuit)!
15. The door is closed in Truman's face! (He protests to no avail as the bus pulls away.)
16. Truman will not be denied! (He is running alongside the bus.)
17. Truman cannot keep up with the bus.
18. The bus "escapes" from Truman.
19. Truman continues his pursuit until all hope is gone. (This shot/sentence—"Truman runs into a taxi, recovers, then looks for the bus"—is longer than the shots/sentences preceding it, signaling with the rhythm change that Truman has lost his battle.)

20. The bus has vanished. (In a shot that we assign as Truman's POV, we see no trace of the bus.)
21. Truman tries to make sense out of what just happened.
    - This is the end of the first act. We understand clearly why we are watching the film because an unambiguous question has been raised: Will Truman discover that his world is artificial, that his relationships are lies, that he is the star of a television show? What's more, *we have accessed the story emotionally.* We *hope* that Truman will succeed, yet we *fear* that he will not. Weir has gotten us emotionally invested.

SECOND ACT

Truman goes into action to resolve his dilemma. As he meets obstacles, which supply the conflict, the action will escalate.

TRUMAN'S MOTHER'S APARTMENT: The last scene ended with a big question mark: What is Truman going to *do* now? The cut to the next scene answers the question: seek advice. We don't know from whom at first, but we are curious. We wonder who this woman is. We are participating in the unfolding of the story. This is a very effective way to jump ahead in the narrative, letting the expository work (Who is this woman?) hang for a bit, whetting the audience's curiosity. The dialogue soon informs us of the woman's identity. (This is Truman's mother's entrance into the film.)

- Weir renders this scene in two over-the-shoulder shots (the one on Truman is the antagonist's camera) and one wide shot, relying on the cutting between the two for the articulation of narrative beats until the fulcrum of the scene, *where the staging takes over the articulation.* Truman fights his mother's "talking his father away," and his sudden movement out of the chair makes physical his certainty that it was his father he saw. A big question is raised: Will he get help in solving this dilemma from his mother? When Truman returns to his chair, we understand that he will not. The staging enables us to feel his defeat more strongly. Of course, it is in Carrey's performance, but Weir's framing of that performance has succeeded in making it impinge on us more powerfully.
- Not only does the wide shot, which is used twice, render the action of the staging when Truman leaves his chair, but the same shot is used to articulate the last narrative beat of the scene, which is: Truman does not buy his mother's explanation. This is a crucial plot point that supplies the narrative thrust into the next scene. (Truman's psychology at this moment is available to us not only in Carrey's interior life but because it permeates his body language.)

TRUMAN'S CELLAR: The first shot (combination lock being opened) tells us what the scene will be about ("unlocking"), and we soon discover that Truman is searching for clues from his past to unlock the present mystery. There are two main narrative jobs for this scene, and a host of smaller jobs, and Weir is aware of each one of them. The first big job (aside from keeping alive the narrative thrust, which is always a constant) is to *unite* Truman's quest for his father *and* his quest for his dream girl into *one overarching want for the audience*—which is for Truman to break free of the soap opera he is trapped in and be able to lead an authentic life. The second big job is to set up the imperative for us to *accept* Truman's conjuring up of his entire past with Lauren *at this time.* This backstory is crucial for us to fully appreciate Truman's sense of loss, but it is also crucial that it not feel "shoehorned" in—that it is merely expository information. The past must be generated by the urgency of the present moment.

- There are many smaller narrative jobs that are imbedded in the immediate action of this scene, and Weir skillfully weaves them into the scene's visual design:

Reveal of the "past" contained in the "treasure chest."
Reveal of the photos of the Young Truman with the Young Dad.

The "intruder" (wife) into Truman's "sanctuary."

Setting up of the geography of the cellar and the introduction of the cot (which plays an important
    role later in Truman's escape).

Reveal of the map.

Reveal of the sweater. (Remember the scarf in *Notorious*.)

Keep antagonist's narrator alive without intruding on the scene. Weir does this with a tracking
    shot (simulated zoom) into the wife, who looks directly at the camera when delivering her
    lawnmower commercial.

BAR: Introduction of two new audience members (the waitresses), who, like the security
guards, supply both expository and psychological editorial commentary.

FLASHBACK: Again Weir muddies the identity of the narrator. When the cut is made to the
bar and the flashback dissolves on, we understand that this backstory is being generated from
archival footage by the antagonist narrator. Yet at the same time we accept the backstory as
Truman's memory, which is being generated, in the moment, by his psyche (objective narrator getting us inside his head). We accept both of these explanations simultaneously, all because of Weir's
dexterous manipulation of narrative viewpoints from the very beginning of the film.

● Think for a moment about the romantic distance traveled by Truman in such a short time. He has
    gone from his first seeing Lauren (smitten), to the dance (flirting), to the library (courtship), to the
    beach (first date), in which they both *commit to each other for life*. Why do we accept this? In real
    life it might take a month, three months, a year—certainly more than the five minutes total that
    they spend together. We accept it because *none of the narrative beats in the evolving relationship
    have been left out*. Weir takes ample time to fully develop each of these beats so that we *partici-
    pate in their unfolding*, making Truman's psychology both accessible and palpable to us.

COLLEGE CAMPUS: This scene is nicely staged to keep the essence of the scene paramount
(smitten) while keeping very much alive the ordinary (manipulated and controlled) universe.

DANCE FLOOR: The same here as for the previous scene, but the rhythm changes to up-
tempo staging (the vigorous dancing) driven by the music. This staging is coupled with the articulation of narrative beats through short sentences that build a "paragraph." Notice once more how
clear and unambiguous each sentence is:

> Truman is having a good time.
> Dream girl (Lauren) is there. (We find out before Truman does. [*When* the audience gets its
> information is always an important narrative consideration.] We now *anticipate* Truman's
> reaction.)
> Truman spots dream girl.
> She spots him.
> He can't take his eyes off her.
> She can't take her eyes off him.

A longer shot (in length) of Truman dancing without looking at dream girl sets up anxiety
on our part. Because of this rhythm change, we *expect* that the next time he looks for her something will have changed, and we *fear* it will be for the worst. This longer shot/sentence ends with
an independent clause: "Truman looks for dream girl." Then the rhythm becomes staccato again.
Three short shots/sentences of dream girl being taken from the floor are intercut with short shots
of Truman's reaction to this. (This is another example of elaboration through multiple angles—the
stretching of the dramatic moment by breaking the action up into short sentences, thereby making
that moment more compelling.)

- All of the looks between Truman and dream girl contain the spatial dynamics *between* them. Therefore, we assign these looks as each character's POV. (Usually the closer the camera is to the axis between two characters, the more "connectedness," and hence the more tension, is created between the two characters.)
- The camera shoots from a "neutral" angle (outside the spatial dynamics of the characters) before dream girl appears and after she disappears.

LIBRARY: The transition here is momentarily confusing. We don't know where we are or what we are seeing, but then the obstruction (book) is removed and we understand that we are in a library. Aside from being an efficient way to announce where we are, the obstruction of our view at the head of the shot *bridges two different psychological states*. At the dance Truman was very concerned. Here, the concern has been dissipated. If these two varying states collided with each other directly, Truman's concern would have seemed less important. As it is, the momentary confusion allows us to adjust to Truman's altered psychology.

- There are four dramatic blocks in this scene, and each has its own stage. The first block is with Truman, Meryl (his wife to be), and Marlon. When they leave, the second block begins, and the stage changes (a new geographical paragraph). Weir uses elaboration here to increase tension, but this time not through multiangularity. This time he uses the *duration of the shot* to stretch the moment: Truman notices the bracelet, looks around to see if anyone is watching him, ponders what to do next, decides to act, stands to get a look but finds that his view is obstructed by the bookshelf, moves around the partition, and sees her. This stretching of the moment creates tension, forcing the audience to frame a question: What will happen when she sees him?
- A second question is framed by the fulcrum of the scene, which occurs when Truman asks Lauren to go out for pizza, "Friday, Saturday, Sunday, Monday, Tuesday, Wednesday. . . ?" Lauren does not answer verbally, but she begins to write on a pad. Because her response is not immediately available to us, we have time once again to participate in the unfolding of the story, to frame a question: Will Lauren agree to see him?
- The high angle on Lauren in the second dramatic block reflects the spatial dynamics between her and Truman, but it does something else. It sets up a contrast to the eye-level angle for the third dramatic block *(an example of how a new camera angle can create a new stage)*.
- The third dramatic block begins when Truman squats down. This change in staging in and of itself *announces* a forward movement in the narrative. Truman asks Lauren if she has a boyfriend. This change from the casual to the intimate is underscored not only by the closer proximity of Truman to Lauren but by the new eye-level angle on her—in effect, the new stage.
- The extreme close-up of Lauren's eyes mirrors the collage of eyes that Truman had collected and that will be revealed to us later on in this sequence. Knowing this, Weir made sure that Carrey stared directly into those eyes, imprinting their image on Truman *and us*.
- The fourth dramatic block shows Truman and Lauren making their way out of the library. We haven't "felt" the presence of the antagonist's camera in this scene, but in the single shot that comprises this dramatic block the pronounced irising of the frame returns, calling our attention to the fact that Truman's movement is being noticed. This irising is also evident in the exterior shot of Truman and Lauren running to the beach.

BEACH: The increased "presence" of the antagonist's narrator that is felt in the shots taking Truman and Lauren here contextualizes this scene, adding tension by increasing the possibility of intervention. Without this increased threat of intervention, the arrival of the "father" would have been a surprise. (As mentioned earlier, suspense has duration, whereas surprise does not. Which one you will choose to use depends on the circumstances of the story at that moment. For example, at the dance, the tension in the scene was the "flirting." Foreshadowing the intervention of the men in black, who force Lauren off of the dance floor, would have "stepped" on the flirting beat. Also, because the intervention is unexpected, it is all the more powerful *at that point in the story.*)

- The full moon and the beach create an atmosphere for romance to happen.
- The black SUV makes a dramatic entrance coming over the dunes (which were introduced earlier by Truman and Lauren first climbing, then running down them). It approaches in three shots—each tighter, each more menacing. The fourth shot of the SUV is an over-the-shoulder, spatially resolving the vehicle with Truman and Lauren before her "father" gets out. This allows Weir to shoot the remainder of the scene in separation, with closer shots of the characters, never having to go wider to orient the audience as to where everyone is vis-à-vis the vehicle. (Often the beginning director gets lost in the vastness of an open space. The absence of parameters, such as walls, can lead to weak spatial compositions because the characters seem to float in limbo. Weir solves that problem immediately by establishing the SUV as the physical anchor for the entire scene.)

TRUMAN'S CELLAR: This is the "bookend" for the end of the flashback that started with the reveal of the sweater in the trunk, setting up Truman's completing the collage.

LAUREN WATCHING: This shot ends the sequence of "remembrance" that started at the beginning of Act Two in Truman's mother's house.

INT. TRUMAN'S CAR: This scene begins the second sequence of Act Two, which lasts for 16 minutes, ending with an editorial comment in the bar. The third sequence of Act Two follows immediately. It, too, begins in Truman's car and lasts for 16 minutes, ending Act Two (Lauren watching Truman on television after the hearty congratulations in the control booth).

- It is essential for a director to be aware of what the job is of each sequence—to realize the distance a character must travel in that sequence, and to understand the job of every scene in the sequence. Before we get into the details of these two sequences, watch these 32 minutes unfold uninterrupted. Observe the psychology, the overt action, and the plot unfolding in a cause and effect relationship—*each moment causing the next*—building into a powerful emotional climax (Truman's embrace of his father).
- Stop the film after the cut to Lauren watching television. Take a moment purely as an audience member and recognize the emotion that has been generated in you. Emotional access to a story is what most audiences want from a film, and it is important for a director to recognize this obligation.
- How does Weir cause the story to impinge on us so strongly? He does two things at once. He keeps us fully aware of what is going on *inside* of Truman moment by moment while simultaneously keeping us fully aware of what is going on *outside* of him. Weir is doing more than simply supplying us the facts of the story; he is *orchestrating* them so that they will have maximum emotional effect on us in much the same way that Christof is orchestrating his story for the television audience.
- When you have watched these two sequences straight through, go back to the beginning of the first sequence, TRUMAN DRIVING TO WORK, and we'll see how each scene is put together.

INT. TRUMAN'S CAR: This is the beginning of a five-minute minisequence with almost no dialogue (it is not technically a scene because it contains more than one location). The action is rendered by both objective and antagonist narrators. Truman's psychology in the preceding scene is carried over so that the trouble with the car radio is enough to generate the large reaction in him (kicking the dashboard). We understand his frustration. Let's watch now for how the changes in Truman's psychology are made available to us not only through Carrey's performance but through the use of narrative beats to articulate and punctuate that performance. Narrative beats are also used to frame the forces impinging on Truman. Again, we are simultaneously inside and outside of Truman.

- Weir uses two narrative beats to tell us how the world around Truman is controlled. From the interior of the car we hear a high-pitched frequency. Weir then cuts to a shot of four pedestrians grabbing for their ear sets. Immediately we understand the connection—cause and effect is crystal clear. Weir then cuts to a high, wide shot of the street where many more pedestrians, stopped in their tracks, recover, and resume their routine. (It is important to realize that the wide shot could not have done all of the work on its own because the information it contains would take too much time to read without the four-shot "setting it up." The information in the four-shot can be read immediately.)
- Weir uses narrative beats to articulate Truman's thinking process after he parks his car. Through the window we see Truman look down at the dashboard. Cut to a close-up of the radio. Cut back to the shot through the windshield. This simple juxtaposition of images makes it clear that Truman "smells a rat."
- NEWSPAPER: This is a strong transition that ties together two of the elements that have disturbed Truman (the car radio and the appearance of his father) while at the same time *jumping* the narrative ahead energetically. We receive a mild "jolt" when the cut is made from the newspaper to Truman on the street reading the headlines.
- While watching Truman in the revolving door we understand that he is formulating a plan, and we have time to ask ourselves, "What is he going to do now?" When he exits back onto the street, his continuing cogitation—trying to figure out what is going on—is totally available to us. When he sits down at the outside table, a very clear equation is set up that we *participate* in solving:

TRUMAN LOOKS FOR ANSWERS in the world around him
+ He sees nothing out of the ordinary (couple having breakfast)
+ Truman continues his search
+ He sees nothing out of the ordinary (two men having coffee)
+ Truman persists in his search
+ Suspicious behavior (man looking at him, then checking his watch)
= THINGS ARE NOT WHAT THEY SEEM!

This realization prompts Truman to stop traffic and then run unpredictably, "testing" how the world will respond to this behavior. *We understand every step of Truman's internal process*, partly because of Carrey's performance and partly because Weir has framed and articulated that performance for us using staging and camera to articulate the essence of each moment.

- When Truman decides to make a statement by holding up the traffic, Weir makes his action "big" by elaborating the moment with five shots, one of them being the overhead, which is a strong example of "What does the shot tell you?" It proclaims loudly, "Truman is rebelling!"

LOBBY OF OFFICE BUILDING: This deceptively simple scene is very well designed to seamlessly accommodate the expository material while continuing the action of the story. It is composed of 16 shots, two of them coming from the "master" of the scene (the high-angle wide-shot of the lobby that takes Truman toward the elevator, and then it is used to render his being shoved out of the door). Weir likely ran the entire scene in this camera setup—from Truman's entrance through his ejection—and it was probably the first camera setup of the scene. Going through a scene from head to tail before it is broken up into smaller units of action establishes an overall rhythm that permeates the rest of the shots in the scene, making for an organic flow of action.

- To heighten tension, Weir alerts us to the fact that there is "something funny" about the elevator *before* Truman realizes it.
- Weir articulates the action of the scene with short sentences and then chooses a longer sentence (a tracking shot) to render Truman being pushed toward the door. The action of this longer

sentence is interrupted by the cut to the high angle of Truman being ejected out the door. This "interruption" articulates the violation done to Truman. Weir then makes another nice choice by cutting from the high shot inside of the lobby to the low angle of the two security guards outside. In context, this low shot imparts a "feeling" to us of an implacable obstacle to Truman's continuing this struggle, and it signals the end of this scene.

STREET: Notice again how well we understand what is going on with Truman. He doesn't know quite what to do next. He looks for a solution and finds it in the market across the street. He runs toward it.

MARKET: Weir continues the motif of the frame-within-a-frame with the shot through the candy dispenser.

BEACH: This is a huge jump in time. It was morning, now it is sunset. Where did the time go? *We never ask that question* because Weir discharges it on the transition with a strong shot that shouts out, "The sun is setting." We are thrown off balance for a moment. Then we discover Truman and Marlon on the beach. If these shots had been reversed, the jump in time would have been jarring.

- The question we should ask is, Why the sunset? Couldn't this scene have happened in daylight? Of course it could have, but the *atmosphere* of sunset at the beach pervades the scene, giving it a resonance it would not have had otherwise.

TRUMAN'S LIVING ROOM: The cut to the baby photo is a strong transition. We don't know where we are for a moment. We have to play catch up, and we take pleasure in doing just that—in participating in the unfolding of the story.

- Another aspect of the unfolding process is manifested in the slow reveal of everyone present: first Truman, then his mother, then his wife.
- Notice the *planting* of the magnifying glass that is later used in the payoff of this scene.
- The frame-within-a-frame motif is used again.
- When Truman returns his attention to the photo album, *it is not accidental* that he raises the magnifying glass into the frame, keeping it alive for the ensuing payoff. (This expository information barely registers in our consciousness—but its trace remains.)

KITCHEN: There is no hint here of the antagonist's narrator in this scene, but it returns with a vengeance in the next scenes (PORCH/HOSPITAL).

TRAVEL AGENCY: Weir uses a slow reveal here (a pan from the travel poster to Truman carrying his suitcase and wearing his traveling costume) to enable us to fill in the narrative holes—to make the narrative jump from the hospital to here. Again, we are actively participating in the story, and we enjoy our ability to figure things out.

- Weir's low angle of Truman sitting in the chair "punches up" the suitcase while at the same time enabling him to render an important plot point (the poster on the wall of the airplane being jolted by lightning). If Weir had to "work" to get the poster, it would have seemed heavy-handed.
- Weir uses three shots to render Truman at the desk. The first is a medium over-the-agent's-shoulder. You might look at this shot as a "baseline." Changing it will connote a change in, or escalation of, action.
- The second shot on Truman brings back the motif of the frame-within-a-frame and is tighter. It is used for only one line of dialogue, but it is a line that needs to have a strong impact on us: "I want to leave today."
- When Truman is told that leaving today is not possible, he is undeterred. He will find other means to leave. This escalation of action begins a new dramatic block in which Truman is rendered with an entirely new shot, closer and in separation.

- The travel agent is rendered at the desk with the same medium-close shot except for the close-up that punctuates her line: "It's the busy season." The subtext of this line is "It's impossible to leave," and the change in image size punctuates that, making sure we *feel* the "brick wall" that Truman has run up against. The change in image size makes it palpable. *Mere comprehension is not enough for us to fully enjoy a story.*

BUS STATION: This pleasing composition contains a hint of the visual motif while answering the question raised in the last scene: What is Truman going to do now? The answer comes immediately. He is going to take a bus. (Whether to give answers to audience questions immediately or to make them wait is an important consideration that a director must weigh each time a question is raised.)

BUS: Truman has three distinct psychological states on the bus. At first he is upbeat and expectant, then concerned, then disheartened. Watch how his psychology unfolds and is made available to you.

- The last state, disheartened, is held off from us. We actually imagine it before we see it in Truman. Weir accomplishes this by going away from Truman (while the bus is being emptied) during which we begin to frame a question: "How is Truman taking this setback?" When we see him still sitting in his seat, it only confirms what we had already felt. Weir holds this last shot for more than five seconds. Why? Because Truman's psychology here must serve as a springboard to the next "leap" in Truman's action, and his next leap is huge.
- Because Truman's next action is so large, Weir needs to set it up by *preparing us for it*. First he cuts to the bar for editorial commentary, then to the neighbor, then to his wife. All of them are wondering, like us, What is going on with Truman?

INT./EXT. TRUMAN'S CAR: The first dramatic block is rendered in separation: Truman, his wife, and the action in the rearview mirror. Then, the quick cuts of tight images of the door locks snapping shut, DECLARING AN END TO THIS NONSENSE.

- The exterior shot of the rear of the car dramatically *announces* the beginning of a new dramatic block. We might call it "nothing's going to stop him now!" Weir uses a mix of exterior and interior shots to render this dramatic block. Its last exterior (Truman's car exiting an empty street) collides with the first shot of the next block, which we could call "the end of the road."

THE BRIDGE: Weir sets up the problem facing Truman with a high-shot of the car stopped at the foot of the bridge. He then cuts to Truman's frightened eyes in the rearview mirror, then to a two-shot from behind Truman and his wife. These three shots clearly define the situation, and the action within the frame of this third shot sets up the solution (Truman grabbing his wife's hand). The fourth shot (tight on Truman's hand pressing his wife's hand to the wheel) begins an elaboration that does not end until they have made it across the bridge. Weir makes the journey across the bridge exciting, using multiple angles to punctuate the narrative beats, going inside and outside of the car (including the right front tire responding erratically).

- Weir introduces a new two-shot of the passengers in the car. It is from the front, through a grille. Because we have never seen it before, this new shot imparts a dramatically heightened perspective to the scene. It serves this specific function and is never used again.
- The long shot of the car exiting the bridge could signal the end to this dramatic block, but it does not. Weir keeps the "running the gauntlet" (a more inclusive title for this block when we understand the complete job it must do) alive by cutting immediately to the forest fire sign, continuing the obstacles to Truman's escape. When the car clears the smoke, it is on the open road—headed for freedom.

- The fourth dramatic block is ushered in by still another new shot in the car that is again a two-shot of Truman and his wife, but it no longer has the grille in the foreground. Weir has been saving this shot for just this moment: for Truman to savor the taste of his newfound freedom, and more importantly, to make sure that *we* partake of it fully. (If the grille had been in the foreground of the shot, because of its implication of confinement, it would have intruded on the freedom beat.)
- Take a moment to reflect on the emotional roller coaster ride that Truman has been on in the last few minutes, just from the bridge to here: from fright, to euphoria, to pleasant anticipation. We have understood all of these changes not only because Truman's psychology has been changed into behavior but also because Weir has framed that behavior for us with his camera.

ROADBLOCK: This is the last scene in this sequence and is the first culmination of action in the second act. Truman attempts to escape on foot and is surrounded by men in contamination suits. Weir imparts an eerie tone to the latter part of the capture by rendering it mostly through the eyes of the antagonist's cameras. Not only is the action rendered fully, but we simultaneously feel the presence of the larger force that Truman is attempting to escape from.

- Did you notice a subjective voice of Truman when he is surrounded? Look again. There are four shots that are *direct perceptions* of Truman. Weir did not bother to set up this voice (as Hitchcock did so carefully with Alicia in *Notorious*), yet we accept it. Why? We accept it because it is *appropriate to the urgency of the moment*. This appropriateness carries with it a license to break the narrative style, even this late in the film. (To give Truman a subjective voice without this dramatic imperative, say, in the market, would have seemed gratuitous.)
- The staging of this scene should not be overlooked. The chase and the capture had to be precisely choreographed, and Weir had to convey his vision to many craft people. We've talked about the clarity that is needed when talking to actors. That same clarity is needed in communicating with a crew.

TRUMAN'S HOUSE: Weir withholds Truman's condition from us, raising our curiosity. Following Truman's wife with a tracking shot from the front door, the camera pans to reveal Truman, devastated. We read this instantly because of his body language.

- The tracking shot also reveals a new area of the kitchen: the dining area. Truman's wife takes a position in front of an island counter that we have not noticed before. Weir makes us feel comfortable in this new geography by connecting the two areas with a shot from behind the wife.
- The placement of Truman's wife also gives her a nice stage for the cocoa commercial.
- Once again we should realize the distance this scene goes in a very short time. Yet none of the psychology that drives the action is missing. Every escalation and change in psychology is registered, not only in Carrey's performance but through the staging (which helps to physicalize what is going on internally in Truman and his wife) and through the camera, which articulates the narrative (director's) beats. (Mentioning narrative beats articulated through camera implies the editing that juxtaposes those camera images against one another.)
- The scene consists of four dramatic blocks. (Technically the living room is another scene, but the director must view it as a part of the whole.)

1. The first dramatic block is at the door with the policeman. It's short. Its main purpose is to supply narrative catch-up: the "what" that happened between the scenes.
2. The connecting tissue to the second dramatic block occurs when the wife turns and picks up the cocoa. When she turns to face Truman, a new block begins with the camera movement into her and the product. Her behavior infuriates Truman, and he gets up and approaches her. She feels threatened and picks up a sharp implement to protect herself. Their "dance" is rendered with

an antagonist's camera concealed in the wife's necklace (we assume). But what about the camera that is apparently concealed on Truman? He has no buttons or necklace or pin, and it has never been established that he has such a camera placed on his person. Yet, this break in logic does not get in the way of us being engaged in the scene. We don't think about it (unless we look at the film more than once, and maybe more than twice). This speaks again to the fluidity of the narrative style and how it can be broached if there is the appropriate energy in the scene.

3. The shot changes to an overhead that we consciously assign to the narrator, but then it changes. The overhead view is now rendered on a monitor. Why? What does this do? It establishes more strongly the presence of the antagonist. *The monitor implies that someone is looking at it.* In the next scene, on the uncompleted highway, the antagonist materializes physically. The monitor is a harbinger of that. The fulcrum of the scene occurs when the wife cries out, "Do something!" Truman's actions have forced this call for help. It brings Truman closer to his objective: to decipher what is going on. Momentarily all action stops, and we have time to frame a big question: "Will Truman now understand what is going on?"

4. The connecting tissue to the fourth dramatic block occurs when the camera cuts back to eye level and the wife tries to escape through the living room and out the front door. The fourth block begins with the knock on that door.

- Weir draws out Marlon's entrance, stretching the moment to create tension.
- Truman's arc in this scene begins in despair. He fights to gain insight. He is defeated. At the end of the scene, he is back where he started. As was mentioned earlier, *every* psychological step of this journey is available to us.
- Weir chose to have a darkened stage for the fourth block because it supplies a sense of menace at the beginning of the block and then serves to darken Truman's despair at the end of it.

UNFINISHED HIGHWAY: Setting this scene in a familiar location allows it to unfold without being impeded by expository information. We are comfortable here for this quiet scene. We know exactly where we are from the first frame, and the staging—the two friends sitting at the end of the highway—says "heart-to-heart talk." Another piece of important information is included in this first shot: The crane is reintroduced. Its "crane-cam" will be used before long. This shot does one more job: It resolves separation at the onset so that Weir can then go into extended separation.

- By concentrating our attention on Marlon's sensitive evocation of friendship, Weir draws us in so deeply to his psychology that we begin to wonder about its sincerity. This questioning of Marlon's true nature prepares us to accept the cut to the CONTROL BOOTH. Again Weir uses a slow reveal. We don't know where we are or who we are looking at when the cut is made from a close-up of Marlon to a close-up of a woman we have never seen before. Yet we have been prepared to accept just such an explanation, and so we do not find it to be jarring. As the camera pans from the strange woman (Christof's assistant), past the director, then on to Christof himself, we are in no way surprised to see him. (If Christof had not made his entrance in the film's first shot we would have found his entrance here jarring.)
- The reintroduction to Christof is made smoother by a sound bridge continuing "Marlon's" dialogue.
- The monitor that we first saw in the kitchen scene is now gracefully revealed in the control booth.
- The scene continues in parallel action, intercutting the bridge with the control booth.

One of the aims for us in watching this particular film was to become aware of the strong emotions that Weir generates in the audience. This is his objective. If he fails to do this, the film fails. *Emotion is the single most powerful ingredient in a film.* Directors should not shy away from creating it and doing their utmost to make sure that it impinges strongly on the audience, and Weir doesn't. In this scene (bridge/control booth), the elements that generate *our* emotions are *orchestrated*.

What are the elements in this orchestration?

> Truman's character. His goodness, his trust in his friend Marlon, his longing for his father. Because of who he is, we want Truman to find happiness. It saddens us to see him sad.
> The music is a key element in evoking our emotions, and Weir underlines this by having Christof "conduct" the music for the father/son reunion to maximize the emotional impact on *his* audience.
> Atmosphere. The father comes out of the fog. The two of them are isolated. There is no one else in the world for the two of them. Yet the whole world watches.
> Audience. The waitresses in the bar, the two old ladies on the couch, and the Japanese family are plot points, but they also serve as emotional commentators. Their emotions augment ours, making ours stronger.

- Weir and his screenwriter, Andrew Niccol, are very clever here. They allow us to participate fully in Truman's joy at the reunion with his father. "I never stopped believing," he says. When he hugs his father tightly and says "Dad," Truman's happiness is our happiness. However, if the story is going to continue—if Truman is going to find an authentic life, one not built on lies—then *we* must be brought back to this reality. As soon as the maximum emotion is "wrung" from the scene, Weir cuts to the celebration in the control booth. We are reminded that Truman's life is about manipulation for the purpose of maximum ratings, and we are brought back on the story track (end of Act Two). To remind us now of what it is we should be rooting for—Truman's Liberation—Weir cuts to the one person in the film who embodies that dream: Lauren.

THIRD ACT

At the end of the second act, we saw Truman hug his father. We believed that he accepted this actor as his father—that his emotional reaction was authentic. We assumed that although he had been suspicious of what was going on around him he was now "brought back into the fold." Yet the next time we see Truman, in the bathroom mirror, his character seems to have new insight. He seems to understand that someone is watching him. This conviction on his part, which will soon be reflected in Truman's action, happened off camera. We did not see it, yet we do not feel cheated. We make that narrative leap in Truman's psychology. Why are we willing to do this? Because we don't realize that we have. This is due to the insertion of the *backstory* that acts as a buffer between the two differing psychological states. We are distracted for a bit. Then when Truman appears on camera *seemingly* a new man, we go with it.

- It is important for directors to realize the "holes" in their stories so that they can either fill them or obfuscate them, which is what Weir and Niccol do. (This is by no means a criticism of the screenplay. What counts in the end of any story is that it engages an audience from beginning to end. If a scene or sequence had been included where we saw Truman discover something suspicious about his father that then enabled him to make that psychological transition, it would have been more logical but would have intruded negatively on the *total effect* of this story.)

BACKSTORY AND INTERVIEW WITH CHRISTOF: Coming at the beginning of the third act, this is actually first act material. Chronological placement alone does not determine the dramatic function of a scene or sequence. If the backstory had been placed at the beginning of the film, it would have taken away much of the mystery; it would have intruded on the unfolding of the story; it would have slowed down the narrative thrust. We are ready for it here, and it does a lot of valuable work:

> It supplies important expository material.
>
> The interview serves as a vehicle to gain insight into Christof's character. By responding to the host and then to Sylvia (Lauren), we have an opportunity to see the character of Christof *revealed through action*. Weir undoubtedly was completely aware of this function of the interview, and he and Ed Harris collaborate to create, in a very short time, a fully developed human being. We understand every aspect of his psychology that is *relevant to the drama and emotional life of this story*. (The production design of the control room magnifies Christof's character. It makes palpable his total control of Truman's universe. Also note the costume designer's choice of a beret for Christof—how effective it is in allowing us to be constantly aware of his artistic pretensions.)
>
> It broadens the audience base so that it can be used to orchestrate a greater emotional response.
>
> It covers up the hole in the story.

- A totally new camera style has been introduced for the backstory: the visuals *illustrate* the content of the dialogue. This is often the case in documentaries, which is just what the backstory is.
- It is important for the story that Christof takes center stage as the antagonist. Yes, he has underlings, and yes, there are network bosses, but for the story's drama to be maximized it must boil down to the two men going head to head: the protagonist and antagonist, Truman versus Christof. One of Weir's jobs, one that he was obviously aware of, was the necessity that Christof emerge as a palpable obstacle to Truman's happiness. Of course, much of it was in the screenplay, but look at the staging in that regard from here on in: be aware of our access to Christof's cognitive functions at work; recognize Weir's mastery in revealing to us Christof's psychology moment by moment, just as he has done with Truman. Christof is no one-dimensional character.
- Christof's encounter with Sylvia (Lauren) gives us great insight into the heart and soul of Christof. He is imbued with a gravity that speaks to the way he views himself: as the center of a universe—Godlike. This character could have been played with other choices, but the choices made by Ed Harris and Weir make for a very formidable, complicated (and thus *interesting*) character.

TRUMAN SLEEPING: This is the calm before the storm. It brings the forward action of the story to a halt momentarily. It allows us to frame the question, How will Truman free himself from this formidable opponent? It is not a question of "Will he?" but "How will he?" How do we know he will succeed? Because the story has promised us he would. The promise was unspoken, but nevertheless, great pains were taken to assure us of that fact. It is a pact that has been made between the storyteller and the audience. If the storyteller violates compacts such as this, the audience will not forgive him. Hence, it is always a good idea for the director to be consciously aware of what it is the audience has been promised. (*You can have a story with an unhappy ending, but whatever the ending, it's best if it is inevitable—but not predictable. It should emerge from everything that has come before it.*)

- The most intimate moment in the film occurs when Christof approaches and gently strokes the giant image of the sleeping Truman. It speaks volumes about Christof's complicated relationship with his creation. This one image is so powerful and so evocative that it easily could have been the main reason such a huge screen was created for this set. Because Christof will lose his creation at the end of this act, it is extremely important that we feel his closeness to Truman now. For every "apart" there must first be a "together."

TRUMAN'S NEW DAY: Out of the quiet of the night, a new Truman prepares for a new day in a familiar image: Truman looking into the bathroom mirror. It is the beginning of a host of familiar images or plays on familiar images, but something is different from when we first saw these images, and it is Truman. He is onto something.

- When Truman leaves the house, we have a familiar image along with a familiar phrase: "In case I don't see ya, good afternoon, good evening, and good night!" This is the second time we have heard this, and to make sure it resonates with us, it is repeated by the Japanese family. This pattern of three repetitions sets up the *payoff*: the last lines of the film.
- Note how the pace picks up as we approach the end of the film with the narrative jumping from one location to another.
- From the moment Truman leaves the house until the very end of the film, it is possible to turn the sound off and still understand the actions of the characters, which in turn allows us to understand the plot points of the story. This is due to the strong staging, compositions, and juxtaposition of unambiguous images. Cause and effect is evident. It is worth your time and energy to view this final section of the film without sound.
- Weir renders the action (overt physical action as well as cognitive action) fully and clearly, but it is important to note that not every moment gets the same treatment. Overt physical action, such as the entrance of Vivian, the new love interest (OFFICE), is elaborated—made larger. It is rendered in 10 shots. This serves to punctuate the ongoing attempt to manipulate Truman's life.

CONTROL ROOM: Notice how Weir draws our attention to the fact that something is bothering Christof when he finds out from the director that Truman is sleeping in the basement. Christof walk away from the director. We see him come to a stop in the background. His body language tells us that he is "chewing" on something. That is confirmed when Christof turns sharply and rapidly approaches the director with instructions. *Staging and camera* isolate Christof just before he makes the decision to "Cue the sun." Later, when Truman is nowhere to be found, Christof, in a close-up, turns from us. The shot is now of the back of his head, and because of the context we again know that he is thinking, "Where could he be?" When he turns, we are not at all surprised that he asks for the "sea-cam." What all three of these examples succeed in doing is *raising our anticipation*, forcing us to ask questions. "What will Christof do next?" becomes *palpable* to us, allowing us to *participate* in the further unfolding of the story.

- The television audience's job as expositors is over. Now all of their editorial commentary supplies solely emotional reactions, *mirroring our own*. (An "audience" can be used in many instances to heighten the tension of a scene or supply emotional resonance. Take, for example, a scene where characters are playing poker. As long as the game is for low stakes, the "audience" around the table does not pay attention. Then the stakes begin to rise. The audience begins to pay attention. Card players drop out, leaving only two men. A large pile of chips is pushed to the center of the table by one of the card players. Now the audience becomes larger, more attentive. The second card player "calls" by placing the deed of his farm on top of the pile of chips. The audience waits with bated breath. Even in much less dramatic scenes, the idea of editorial commentary is important in creating dramatic tension. In Hitchcock's *Vertigo*, Jimmy Stewart demonstrates his ability to overcome his fear of heights by climbing a kitchen stool. In the elaboration through multiple angles that renders his movement up each step, one of the components is a female friend, watching with anxiety, *heightening* our own.)

TRUMAN AT SEA: From here until the end the film, the action is rendered in parallel action, principally intercutting Christof and Truman, but also interspersing the audience and Lauren for emotional commentary.

- It is worth noting here the use of a clever screenwriting device that occurs when Truman is discovered in the sailboat. Someone says, "Isn't he terrified of the water?" Having a character in the film raise this question discharges that question *for us,* allowing us to accept Truman's behavior. (Any question that the film audience might have must be answered, or it will interfere with their participation and appreciation of the story. In Michael Cimino's *The Deer Hunter* [1978], three childhood friends from the same hometown meet by chance half a world away in Vietnam. This meeting is crucial to the advancement of this story, but this convenient coincidence could raise the question of disbelief in the audience's mind. Cimino discharges the question before it is ever raised by having one of the characters ask, "Can you believe this?" We never get a chance to ask the question ourselves, and the convenient coincidence passes. It is not possible to tell a dramatic story without coincidences. Directors should attune themselves to them and make sure that the screenwriter has found a way to discharge any questions stemming from them.)

- Weir introduces a familiar image early on in this sequence: the jutting bow of the sailboat. It is used to connote first a sense a freedom, then a sense of danger, then again freedom. However, the main reason for this image is expository—to set up the fact that there is this pointed protrusion on the front of the sailboat. Familiarizing us with this information leaves us free to fully participate in the bow's puncturing of the fake horizon.

THE STORM: This is a wonderfully orchestrated sequence. Like any effective dramatic scene, it can be broken up into separate dramatic blocks and a fulcrum. The first dramatic block begins before the storm and starts with Truman sailing undeterred. The second begins with the heavy weather, which Truman conquers, setting up the fulcrum: "You'll have to kill me!" This raises a question: "Will Christof answer that challenge?" The third dramatic block is the intense storm, which does kill Truman, *but only temporarily!* The fourth dramatic block begins when Truman begins to show signs of life.

- A slow reveal, rendered in one shot, tells us that Truman is alive. We participate in his resurrection.
- The storm was heavily elaborated—stretched. Now that it is over, Weir uses compression for Truman's recovery. Notice especially the cut to the main sail being raised. It jumps the action of the story, cutting out boring and undramatic action.
- In the three familiar images of the bow of the boat, it has always been jutting toward the right side of the frame. In the wide shot just before the boat perforates the set, the bow is pointing to the left side. This "jumping" to the other side of the boat sets up a different dynamic, even though we are not consciously aware of it. It adds to the heightened expectation that the shot frames: "What now?" Then the powerful answer is given as the boat crashes into the limits of Truman's universe.

AFTER THE SAILBOAT CRASHES: Weir frames Truman's surprise with a cut to a close-up after the crash, sets up the spatial geography in a wide shot, and then goes back to Truman to watch his reaction. Then, in a one-minute take, Weir "merely" observes Carrey's powerful performance—Truman confronting his discovery. Weir does isolate Truman's hand against the painted scenery, but he does not attempt to articulate through cutting Truman's beating against the wall or his slumping down under the full enormity of his realization. Weir does not move the camera to show us Truman's face, knowing that withholding it is the strongest choice because *we imagine* what he is going through. Then when we do see Truman's face, filled with a deep sadness for the lie that was his life, it has much more power.

- Observe the transition to Truman's final psychological state. Note in Carrey's performance the graduated psychological movement from deep sadness to optimism for the future.
- In the control booth, Christof talks to Truman's image on a laptop. Why not talk to one of the many monitors or to the giant screen? Because Weir wanted this interchange to be intimate. Christof sits in a chair, holding Truman (the laptop) in his lap, speaking to him like a father.

- The shot of the heavens that frames Christof's Godlike voice is a nice payoff of the sky that was introduced early in the film by Weir and kept alive throughout. The sky has been a part of the universe of this story. (The sky was not a part of the *Notorious* universe.)
- The door in the set is a payoff on the visual motif with which Weir surrounded Truman—the closed frame that restricted his freedom. Now Weir gives Truman the opportunity to escape these restrictions, to break free from them, and it is all represented by the door in the universe.
- Kazan told me that he believed that the end of a film should be pure emotion. It is like a wave set in motion by all the events preceding it, surging forward, pulling the audience along with it. This is what Weir believes too. Again, *orchestration* is the operative word: image upon image, like note upon note in music, builds a surging wall of elation in the television audience *and in us*, the film audience. It is very difficult to resist. We applaud the storyteller for making us feel deeply.
- What elements does Weir use to increase the emotional impact of the ending? First of all, he sets up very clearly the final obstacle for Truman: the doorway to his freedom. Christof says, "You're afraid; that's why you can't leave." Weir immediately cuts to Truman standing before the door. Before Truman gets up enough nerve for his final "In case I don't see ya . . . ," Weir stretches Truman's decision using 16 shots, intercutting Christof and Truman (whose back is turned toward us). When Christof exclaims, "Say something, Goddammit, you're on television!" Weir begins the second to last movement in this orchestration with shots of the television audience, including Lauren. Everyone is holding their breath. Then Truman turns, and Carrey delivers his final lines with bravado and a gracious bow that sets up the final movement—an elaborative phrase—one of pure exhilaration, again *mirroring and heightening our own*. This exhilaration begins with Lauren and ends with the two old ladies on the couch.
- The last plot point ties up the last loose end to the story: transmission is permanently terminated.
- The final scene of the film with the security guards is known as a coda. It is not absolutely necessary dramatically, but it supplies a tone for the audience's entrance back into their own world (and in this case, an ironic comment).

SUMMARY

My main reason for picking this film was not only for the total control of the director's craft that Peter Weir demonstrates but even more for the emotional journey its main character undergoes and for the emotional journey the film engenders in most audiences.

Jim Carrey's superb performance drives the story. It is not only eminently believable but truly interesting. It is interesting because it is both *modulated* and *pushed*. By modulated, I mean that his behavior varies according to his psychology. By pushed, I mean that Truman's emotions run very deep. They are not puny. When he is happy, he is very happy, sometimes extremely happy. When he is sad, he is capable of despair. (I once asked my acting teacher, Paul Mann, "How are actors different from ordinary people?" He replied, "They are the same, only more.")

CHAPTER 17

FEDERICO FELLINI'S *8½*

A MASTERPIECE?

When I show *8½* in my lectures at Columbia, most of my students respond to it in probably the way Fellini hoped an audience would: amused by the foibles and weaknesses of an artist attempting to give birth in a world that is quite unsympathetic to his dilemma. (Fellini regarded this film as a comedy and had taped a sign above the eyepiece of the camera: "This is a comedy.")

Film students are naturally interested in gaining some insight into this specific dilemma, in which they hope someday to be embroiled themselves. This dilemma—will Guido make a movie?—is only the *McGuffin* (a term coined by Hitchcock, which stands for any object or device that exists solely for initiating the plot). Guido's problem with finding a story for his movie is the vehicle for Fellini to explore the second, the deeper, and the main dilemma of the protagonist: Will he find a way to lead an authentic life? A life without a lie? This is a dilemma that all of us face—it is universal—and thus it raises this film into the category of art. It speaks to all of us.

Of course, as in any form of art (film or painting, music or dance), the theme must be rendered in a powerful voice that can resonate within the soul of each member of the audience. This is a tall order. It is rarely achieved. However, for years now, *8½* has been regarded by many as a true work of art—a masterpiece. Is it possible to discern what some of the ingredients are that make it so? Is it possible to find something in this work that you can bring to your own work? Absolutely. Although whatever you learn from it will not guarantee that you will produce a work of art, it will certainly help you to tell more interesting and powerful stories that will engage audiences—a huge and noble accomplishment in itself.

THE DIRECTOR AS AUTEUR

In this book I have encouraged you to assume responsibility in all the areas that are often thought of as encompassing distinct craft disciplines, and now I would like to encourage you to at least entertain the idea of also inventing the stories you tell. Just as in editing, production design, lighting, music, or producing—where you most likely will rely on others to help you achieve *your* vision—you might, as Fellini did, collaborate with screenwriters who can offer their skill and insight into fashioning your story into an evocative blueprint for your rendering onto the screen. Or, as many directors today do, you might choose to write the screenplay yourself.

Where will your stories come from? The most original source would be you. Look here first. Dig down below the surface of your public persona where your fear, sorrow, joy, aspiration, and hope exist. Your story is unique. It has never been told before. In fact, you are still writing it.

In *What Is Art*, Leo Tolstoy said:

Art is that human activity which consists in one man's consciously conveying to others, by certain external signs, the feelings he has experienced, and in others being infected by those feelings and also experiencing them.

For Fellini, much of what he has conveyed to others was experienced through dreams. A devotee of the psychologist Carl Jung, Fellini was acutely attuned to the workings of the very rich substratum of the unconscious that is made available to us through dreams. He recorded these dreams, thought about them consciously, and used them as the elemental driving force of his narratives. *8½* is a clear manifestation of this process.

DRAMATIC CONSTRUCTION

As was mentioned, there is both an external and an internal conflict that besets the main character of this film. In the first—Will Guido make his film?—the tensions between the protagonist and the antagonist(s) (producer, screenwriter, crew, actors, wife, mistress) are dramaturgically similar to those in *Notorious* and *The Truman Show*, in that they are *external*. However, in the internal conflict there is a vast difference because the protagonist and antagonist of this conflict are contained in the same character, and it is this internal conflict that is the main conflict of the film; it is where the most important action of the film takes place. Because it is internal, the most important action of this film takes place inside the hero's head; *it is generated by his psyche*.

OVERVIEW OF STYLE AND DESIGN

OBJECTIVE NARRATOR

The objective narrators of *Notorious* and *The Truman Show* each had specific attributes, but neither had a *discernible personality*. The narrator of this film does. It is curious, has a sense of humor, and is at times playful; at other times it is exuberant, expansive, life affirming. Sometimes the exigencies of the story require that it become serious, even solemn. All in all, a total personality emerges—one that most likely resembles Fellini himself.

SUBJECTIVE VOICE

Guido, the main character, is given a subjective POV by Fellini, but he uses it rarely. Why is this, when the crucial action of the film takes place inside of the protagonist's head? That is precisely why. To have a subjective voice within a subjective mode of reality would be redundant. (Alicia's subjective voice in *Notorious* always manifested itself in reality.)

However, in the first scene of this film, Fellini does assign a subjective POV to Guido, then "plays" with it, and us, in the scene of the exterior of the spa, preparing us for the shifting narrative perspective to come.

TRANSITIONS

Fellini understood, as well as any director who ever lived, the power of transitions, and in this film we will see many wonderful examples. We will also have a chance to see what is perhaps the greatest transition in the history of cinema to date. Because of the different modes of reality in this film—dreams, memories, fantasies, active imagination—the transition between any two modes takes on added significance. We will see how deliberate Fellini is in "signaling" the onset of a new mode of reality during Acts One and Two. In Act Three, the "walls" between what is real and what is not become blurred. This lack of clear transitions between the different modes of reality is used by Fellini to go beyond the logic of linear narrative to reach a more powerful resolution to the story.

ENTRANCES

All of the main characters have strong, even dramatic, entrances into this film. Many of these entrances are followed closely by a *reveal* of a significant aspect of the character. The reveal of Guido's face does not occur until three minutes after his entrance into the film.

ART DIRECTION AND PRODUCTION DESIGN

Fellini's imagination was filled with images from his dream life, and these images appear throughout the film. To a large extent they dictate the choice and design of much that we see in the film. Yes, each location serves its story function—a spa is a spa, a hotel room is a hotel room—and each supplies the necessary story requirements, but many of the locations do *more*. They serve as metaphors, imparting a richness, a resonance, a meaning that goes beyond their logical function in the story.

WHAT ARE WE WATCHING FOR IN THIS FILM?

- We will see a lot of craft at work here. Fellini once said that making a film for him was as scientific as launching a rocket, and we will pay close attention to how that craft is rendered. More importantly, we will be watching and marveling at how that craft has been wedded to a profound and fertile imagination, and imagination is what defines the artist.
- One aspect of the craft we will be concentrating on is the mise-en-scène. (This term is used to describe what goes on *within the frame*, in contrast to building a scene through cutting from one camera angle to another. It could be argued that this was present in both *Notorious* and *The Truman Show*, but not to the extent or with the artistry that we see here.) Fellini was a master at maximizing the atmosphere created by his locations, staging the actors, then rendering it all with an elegantly fluid camera in extended takes.
- It can be said, without being at all derogatory, that *Notorious* and *The Truman Show* contained no poetry. *8½* does. It also has narrative thrust and conflict, and the stakes are high—all the ingredients of drama. What sets this film apart from most films, including the other two mentioned, is the imaginative rendering of many scenes in a highly lyrical, poetic film language. Action sometimes takes a back seat; cause and effect are not always important to our understanding; the essence of a moment might resonate within us at a point below our conscious mind. This integration of the poetic with the dramatic, more than anything else, is what sets Fellini apart from most directors. (There are directors whose films are very poetic, but the dramaturgy—the engine that drives the story—is not sufficient to engage most audiences.)
- Much of the poetry occurs in the *other modes of reality* that pervade this film. What we will be looking for here is how each one of these different modes is generated out of the urgency of the present reality. (That urgency comes because Guido's dilemma *never* leaves him—or Fellini.) Also, we will be analyzing the narrative thrust of the dreams—how each has a beginning, middle, and end, and how Fellini makes use of narrative beats, dramatic blocks, and fulcrums to convey to us this sense of forward movement.
- Fellini's collaboration with the composer Nino Rota is one of the keys to the power of this film, and we should listen to the film at least once *just for the music*. I also suggest that you watch the last sequence of the film without any sound.

DETECTIVE WORK

The sections that follows explore various aspects of *8½* in regard to "detective work."

CHARACTER

Alicia in *Notorious* and Truman in *The Truman Show* were fairly uncomplicated characters. Alicia wanted a man and Truman wanted a girl. This is a bit reductionist but true. No dimensions of character were revealed *that were not absolutely essential to the demands of the story*, and that is how it should be! Remember what was said earlier. A film story is like a train trip, and the character gets on the train with just enough baggage *for this trip*. However, *8½* is a longer trip than the two previous films. It winds its way through the labyrinth of the protagonist's (Guido's) psyche. The interior conflict that is raging inside his head insists that Guido be more psychologically complicated than Alicia or Truman.

SPINES

The following are the spines I have identified for this film.

- Film's spine: to seek an authentic life
- Guido's spine: to live a life without a lie
- Guido's wife: to have a marriage that is not a lie
- Carla: to be loved (by Guido and her husband)
- Mezzabota: to deny an authentic life (by seeking escape in an inauthentic relationship)
- Gloria: to seek salvation in abstractions
- Screenwriter: to seek meaning in art
- Cardinal: to seek union with God through the church (the only authentic path)
- Woman in White: to seek the true, the good, the beautiful

Because the spines of the major characters are all subsumed under the umbrella of the film's spine, the film achieves the thematic unity that is a basic requirement of art.

FIRST ACT

DREAM

At the beginning of a film, mystery is a welcome dimension. The audience is forced to come out of their own lives by being pulled into another. This is what Fellini offers in the very first shot of this film. Within the first three shots he also offers us an equation that allows us to participate in the unfolding of this mystery:

> Driving in silence, a man wearing a hat slows his car to a stop.
> He is in a massive traffic jam.
> He sees a man staring (accusingly?) at him from another car and a woman dozing; then with a cloth he wipes the dashboard and the windshield, while people indifferent to his situation sit trapped in other cars. Smoke begins to fill his car, and the man begins to gasp for breath and pound on the window in an attempt to break free.

- Already, in the first three shots, Fellini has established a surreal universe and introduced a very fluid objective narrator. In every shot there is camera movement, and in the third shot—a compound sentence—the movement is extensive. Because the second pan in this shot is unmotivated by any action (in the first pan the man with the hat looks outside the driver's-side window, motivating the camera movement), it establishes that the objective narrator has an inherent curiosity. This curiosity and fluid camera movement continue until the man finally escapes.

- The man's hat serves to identify him from the back of the head when we have no other "marker." The cape supplies a strong indication of the man's aesthetic (artistic) sensibility. Both help to create a powerful image when the man escapes into the air—like a bird—free. It is an image that pervades the remainder of the film, and it is just the first installment of Fellini's rich imagination.

- During the flight the man's subjective voice is introduced. We might not assign the first two subjective shots as such—the sun through the clouds, the steel scaffolding—but we certainly do assign the shot looking down at the rope tied to his foot. (It was said that a subjective voice, as well as a POV, should be preceded or followed by a medium-close or close-up so that we can assign it to a character, but here is a case where that is not necessary because the source of the image is completely unambiguous. Who else would be looking down at his shoe from this height?)

- When the cut is made to ground level—the man on a horse and the man pulling the rope—we are *outside* of the dream, logically, but Fellini does not let logic intrude on the moment. He is well aware of how much license he has in dealing with narrative perspective, as were Hitchcock and Weir in earlier examples. If there is any hard, fast rule to violating narrative perspective to tell our story in a more powerful way, it is this: *Is it appropriate to the essence or urgency of the moment?*

REALITY

GUIDO'S HOTEL ROOM: The first shot of an arm grasping at air announces the end of the dream and returns the dreamer to reality. It is usually a requisite when going from one mode of reality to another that you announce it, or announce your exit from the former reality. In this film Fellini is very clear in keeping us informed as to when we have returned or when we are entering another mode of reality, *until it no longer serves his purpose.*

- Notice the entrance into the film of the two doctors and the nurse. No *undue* attention is paid to them, and we know immediately that they will not play an important role in this story. Contrast this to the entrance of the screenwriter—the close-up, the little turn before he sits. It is apparent that this man is significant to this story. What about his costume? The bathrobe. What does it tell us? It speaks a great deal to his aesthetic sense while telling us that he is a close confidant of the man in bed. Look at the screenwriter's body language. We know for sure that he has plenty of problems with the screenplay.

- Photo of American actress: the camera move into the photo alerts us to the fact that we will be seeing more of her (and we do in the next scene). We "read" the pile of other photos on the bed in the background because of their arrangement in the shot—an example of *important information within a frame that we receive tangentially.* The background says, This is a man who is surrounded by his work.

- The man, Guido, remains covered throughout the scene; we see his hands, his leg. When he stands, his face is in shadow. Fellini extends this mystery even longer by having Guido get up from his bed and walk slowly to a door, yet because of the shadows we still cannot see his face, and we are becoming very curious!

- The long shot that takes Guido from his bed to the bathroom door further establishes the geography of the bedroom and locks down the spatial relationship between the two beds, preparing us for the scene in Act Two with Guido's wife.

BATHROOM, GUIDO'S HOTEL: Here Fellini breaks the rhythm of Guido's leisurely pace in the bedroom, and on the cut to the bathroom he pushes quickly into the mirror, dispensing with the walk from the door to the mirror, thereby dramatically "punching up" the still-shadowed face of Guido a moment before the dramatic full reveal when the light comes on. His face speaks volumes. It was Fellini's choice to use a reluctant fluorescent light because he had two jobs to do here. For the first job he uses a close-up in which the harsh shadows cast on Guido's face mirror his inner state. We understand immediately that we are looking into a ravaged soul. This image, because it is our first image of Guido, will stay with us. Then having given us this insight, Fellini cuts to a long shot of Guido in the middle of the bathroom. It is a dramatic contrast not only in image size but also in the contrast from dark to light—from one psychological state to another.

Fellini uses this new stage to begin a new dramatic block for job number two, in which the man with the ravaged soul is transformed into a man with a somewhat amused view of his situation. How do we know he is amused? How else could we interpret his graduated lowering of himself in front of the mirror? (I want to make sure that we understand the huge narrative job that these two short dramatic blocks have accomplished.) The story Fellini wanted to tell could not be told if Guido was *only* the ravaged face in the mirror; after all, Fellini wanted a comedy. At the same time, the story would not have the significance—the gravitas—it requires if we hadn't been privy to this dark side of Guido's soul. The juxtaposition of the two dramatic blocks allows Fellini to have it both ways, with the help of a few tools from the director's toolbox: a change in image size, a change in lighting, *business* with the bathrobe that helps in the transition from one psychological place to another, and the buzzing sound that prompts the final stages of the transformation—the "shrinking" in front of the mirror. This shrinking (trying to disappear?) occurs throughout the film.

EXT. SPA AND GROUNDS: Although the first part of this scene is purely expository, it is rendered delightfully and purely cinematically. The music that started in the bathroom continues on the cut, and a panning, wide shot is "interrupted" by a close-up in the foreground, a pattern that is repeated throughout this scene and punctuates the end of this first dramatic block. The camera is rarely still—moving up, down, sideways. Characters enter from all four sides of the frame. We enjoy the playful nature of the objective narrator—so playful, in fact, that we can understand why characters (lady clients) smile at him, wave, blow him kisses, turn away in embarrassment. He must be a *very* charming narrator; yet he gets his work done. He informs us not only what kind of people frequent this spa but the nature of the "cure." The mineral water is introduced, which then becomes ubiquitous through the judicious integration of it within the action of the frame. It *prepares* us for the lines of clients waiting for this water and the women serving it from behind the bar.

- We should recognize the dramatic *and* narrative power of the close-shot of the old hand on the cane—how the change in music infuses that image with even more power as the shot moves to another old man shielding himself from the hot sun with a newspaper, then continues to the women serving mineral water behind the bar. This one shot is one segment of the intricate dance that Fellini has choreographed throughout this scene between the characters and the camera—one of his trademarks. (Notice that the old man with the cane is moving from left to right while the man with the newspaper enters the frame going right to left. This opposition of movement supplies a surge of narrative energy, just like one that occurs when a foreground character "jumps back" into a wide-shot.)
- Fellini saves the reveal of the full grandeur of the spa's geography until the end of this dramatic block. Coming here it is dramatic. Suppose he had started with that long shot explaining everything. There would have no unfolding of the space—no narrative journey for us to participate in.
- Immediately after the full reveal of the location, the camera drops down to reveal a woman in a large hat in the foreground, signaling the end of the first dramatic block. The music comes to an end. We understand that this part of the story is over, and we now expect that *something new* is going to happen. (I refer to this first grouping of action as a dramatic block even though what is being organized is narrative information. It is precisely because of this organization *of*

like information that a dramatic tension is created. We *feel* the narrative thrust of the story and *anticipate* what is to come.)

- A new musical theme begins over the women serving mineral water at the bar, acknowledging what we already knew. Exactly what is it that we know? We know for sure that Guido will be arriving very soon. Fellini, understanding the imperative that he has set up, does not disappoint us. (If he had waited another shot before revealing Guido, our anticipation would have begun to slacken.)
- The pulling down of the sunglasses is used to announce a new mode of reality. The stopping of the music confirms it. I call this new mode of reality *active imagination*. You might call it a fantasy. However, the former is a Jungian term, one that Fellini was familiar with and I'm sure engaged in, and fantasy implies something more frivolous. Guido is not being frivolous here. He is working. We know already that he has major problems with the screenplay for his new film and that this Woman in White is a well-known actress.

INTERCUTTING OF ACTIVE IMAGINATION AND REALITY

- Here we are both inside and outside of Guido's head.
- Woman in White: It is very important that a director understand what dramatic function every character performs. Remember the train trip? Well, no passenger is allowed on the train who does not *deserve* to be there. What is the dramatic function of this character? It is not the same as her spine, which we said was to seek the true, the good, and the beautiful. What we are looking for here is the Woman in White's dynamic relationship to Guido. This not for the audience to know at this point—perhaps they will not ever come to that conscious conclusion—but it is of paramount importance that the director knows. The Woman in White is Guido's *possible solution* to the problems of the film. (I don't know if Fellini thought of her that way. I'm sure he didn't think of her in the same terms, maybe not even consciously. However, as I said in the introduction, the methodology espoused in this book should be paid attention to *on some level*, even if that level is below the level of consciousness.)
- Guido taps his nose, introducing a Pinocchio motif. (An actor often invents a mannerism such as this, and it is up to the director to be on the lookout for what works and what does not. Fellini obviously agreed here because it is repeated, and later on Guido actually wears a Pinocchio nose. The idea, whoever thought of it, most likely came from a line in the second act in which Guido is addressed as Pinocchio.)
- A voice calls Guido back to reality, and he replaces his sunglasses, giving a "bookend" to this other mode of reality.

REALITY

- The long shot of Guido with the high walls behind him keeps the geography of the spa alive and sets up a dramatic reveal of the screenwriter in the foreground—another character who enters through the bottom of the frame.
- The next cut to the screenwriter (Daumier) compresses Guido's approach (film-time). This scene is then rendered in two extended takes with marvelous staging. Daumier is given a stage all to himself at the onset; then when he moves to the bench we discover Guido already seated—a nice surprise. We had imagined that Daumier was talking directly to Guido but realize now that he had his back to him—an obvious mark of disrespect. It also shows how full of himself Daumier is. Notice how his arm and body "traps" the distraught Guido.
- Thematically, Daumier is Guido's alter ego—the rational, intellectual side—but that doesn't help supply the dynamic juice between the two. For that the director must come up with a dynamic relationship. Guido might see Daumier as a "thorn in his side." Daumier might see Guido as a "hopeless case," or at the very least, "misguided."

- The actual point of attack for this film occurred before the film started (hence the nightmare), but this scene with Daumier acts as a *surrogate point of attack*. It restates Guido's dilemma in the strongest terms, closing off all hope he might have had that the screenplay was somehow serviceable.
- Notice also how the world of the spa continues to be very much alive in the background of the frame.
- Fellini's style, and hence that of the objective narrator, is to articulate narrative beats through staging—with a minimum of cutting. We see that exemplified here. The only cut in this dramatic block is to Daumier, "framing" his handing of his notes to Guido, while at the same time getting the camera in position for the transition to the new dramatic block with Mezzabota. (If the handing of the notes to Guido were not emphasized—if it occurred in the two-shot that precedes the cut—then what Guido takes from his pocket at the train station would not have been as immediately available to us.)
- Notice the performance beat where Guido's attention is caught by something outside of the frame. What is it? we ask ourselves. Then he stands and shouts a name. With wonderful economy, Guido takes three steps, revealing an entirely new stage for the scene with Mezzabota.
- Mezzabota: Yes, he is an old friend of Guido's, but what dramatic function does he have? Like other characters in this film, he does nothing to advance the plot. So why is he here? To serve as a thematic alternative to the life Guido has chosen. Mezzabota's continued presence makes us aware that Guido did not choose to divorce his wife for someone young enough to be his daughter. It reminds us that Guido is not so easily satisfied. He wants more yet can commit to no one. His relationships are a lie: not only his romantic relationships but also those with his producer, star actress, and so on.
- Mezzabota enters the film as a "cripple" and is then revealed to be quite robust, even youthful. His casual dress—white straw hat, white sweater, and tan slacks—is in direct contrast to Guido's "mature" dark suit and tie.
- Gloria: Again Fellini prolongs her reveal. Then what do we see when she lifts her hat? Immediately we notice her altered eyebrows, fake eyelashes, and white lips. Next we realize that her expressions are not sincere; they too are fake—inauthentic. That is what Gloria thematically represents—the direct opposite of the Woman in White. This had to be understood not only by the director but by the makeup artist. As was pointed out earlier, all of this information is contained in the text and must be dug out through detective work.
- The last shot of the scene is a cut to Guido. Why? The cut to him obviates his isolation from the other three characters. He is "stewing"—working on his film. What this shot does is *propel* the narrative into the next scene, where Guido continues stewing. (Guido is the perfect example of a character whose *want to extricate himself from his dilemma* never relinquishes its hold on him. That is why most of us will find him to be compelling.)
- Author's Digression: I say that most of us will find Guido to be compelling, but some might be offended by his behavior, especially his attitude toward women. Personally, I do not think that is reason enough to reject the craft that is in this film and the learning experience that this master craftsman/artist offers us. Sometimes the flip side of this occurs. Badly made films with little craft gain wide popularity among young filmmakers *because of their sensibility*. I suggest that for a student of directing it is often profitable to separate content from craft.

TRAIN STATION: This is another evocative location and a wonderful use made of the possibility it offers. Look at the composition of the first shot. You could freeze it and hang it on the wall. We have already noticed, and we will continue to see, beautifully composed wide shots that gain much of their dramatic, narrative, and thematic power from the location. Because Fellini uses so many wide- to medium-shots, his close-ups take on added power. (So many of today's films are shot by directors who have learned much of their visual vocabulary from television, which of course features close-ups. However, television screens are becoming much larger, which might lead to a more balanced visual element in shows that are made for television.)

- There is another strong entrance, entertaining us while doing a ton of expository work. Carla's sashay alone is worth a thousand words of character description.
- The three close-ups of Guido after the train comes in not only show his anticipation, then his resignation, but also serve another very important purpose. They allow Fellini to compress the train's stay in the station into seconds (film-time). Then he uses the foreground/background for Carla's entrance. (Entrances of main characters almost never share a frame with another character, but it works fine here because of the dynamic composition.)
- Carla: She does have a dramatic function: adding another complication to Guido's life. However, her function is even broader. She serves as a presence of *all of Guido's women outside of his marriage*, but she is specific—in the here and now, an ever-present temptation as well as a source of guilt. A relevant dynamic relationship for Guido toward Carla would be "my weakness."

CARLA'S HOTEL DINING ROOM: The hotel is second class, just like Carla's position in Guido's life.

- The scene starts with one extended take, but if your attention were not called to it you might imagine it as several or more shots because of the varying compositions. It starts off with an over-the-shoulder of Guido, goes to a two-shot of Carla and Guido, then a single over Carla's shoulder, which turns into a three-shot over Guido's shoulder, which turns into a two-shot over his shoulder, then ends as a single of Carla from the rear sashaying into the restaurant. A terrific piece of staging. Note the alacrity with which the action unfolds.
- Carla and Guido, seated at the table, are rendered in separation. Why? Because Fellini is acknowledging to us that there is a clear separation between Carla's agenda and Guido's. She wants to talk about her husband while he wants to get her into bed, so his mind is elsewhere, and the shooting in separation conveys that to us palpably. The last shot in the sequence, the long two-shot, crystallizes Guido's attitude in one image.

CARLA'S HOTEL BEDROOM: The long two-shot from the previous scene sets up the cut to the close-up silhouette that begins this scene. It is a "cut to the chase," a strong jump in the narrative that begins with a mystery that we become engaged in solving.

- The silhouette of the back of Carla's head wrapped in a "turban" is the first distinct image in the extended take that begins this scene. Through staging and camera movement, this first image changes into several more distinct images, and because they are *held*, they have *almost* the same effect as separate shots. An over-the-shoulder of Carla revealing her frontal image in a judiciously placed mirror, to another over-the-shoulder of Carla revealing Guido in bed (to our surprise this image is from a second judiciously placed mirror), to a profile two-shot, to a single on Guido lying down. Watch this entire shot again. It is inventive, unconventional, surprising, and most of all, engaging. Imagine for a moment if this scene had been shot "conventionally." (Renderings like this speak volumes concerning the wisdom of directors who view every section of their film with an open mind, and they debunk the idea of "coverage," at least when it comes to creating art. Does anyone think that Fellini *covered* this section with other shots?)
- The remainder of the scene is rendered in separate takes. This has much less to do with the geography than it does with Fellini's desire to stretch this moment so that we can fully understand *how important this aspect of Carla is to Guido*. What do we see when the camera cuts to him? We see a totally committed man—totally in the present moment—with a totally different attitude toward Carla than what we saw in the previous scene just seconds ago. It might seem

like a contradiction to say that the separation in the dining room showed that he was disconnected from Carla, and now separation is used to show that he is connected to her. However, the thing to always remember is this: *meaning depends on the context in which shots occur.* Context is our interpreter.

- Author's Note: I was able to use the analogy of shots with sentences up until now. It worked for *Apple Pie*, *Notorious*, and *The Truman Show*. It would even work for the dream sequence that began *8½*, but it will not do justice to the dream sequence that is coming up. Perhaps an analogy will help clarify what I am getting at. When scientists explain light, they need two totally different, mutually exclusive categories: particles and waves. It takes both to explain how light behaves. For certain films, or sections of films, sentence structure—with its emphasis on subject, object, and verb—is much too logical an analogy to convey the deeper meaning of an image. Yet that in no way frees the artist from the need to be clear to an audience *on some level* because if something occurs in your film that is not in some way relevant to the total appreciation of the story, then it does not belong. Can I give you a surefire methodology for ensuring that your intuitions will be relevant to the story and accessible to an audience? No. It is a place that you will have to get to on your own.

CARLA'S HOTEL ROOM/LATER: The dissolve to Guido asleep in bed and Carla reading is visually weak, but it keeps the story moving by setting up very quickly the aftermath of the previous scene, clearing the way for the next thing to happen. Sometimes that is the wisest choice. However, in combination with the next two shots, Fellini orchestrates a powerful and graceful transition from the world of reality to the dream world. The first shot, Guido sleeping, is grounded in reality. The second shot, the overhead, bridges reality and the dream. In the third shot, reality has disappeared and we have fully entered the dream. This movement in three steps—reality, bridge, dream—is conveyed not only by what is happening in the frame but by the acute change in angles from one shot to the next. In the first shot, the camera is angled at Guido and Carla in bed (away from the left wall of the room); then from the ceiling the shot angles down at the bed *and* the left wall; then it is at ground level again, shooting *only* the left wall.

DREAM

- It is a dream of guilt. Characters appear whom we have not seen before and whom Guido has either disappointed or betrayed: father, mother, producer, Conocchia (a gray-haired man in white hat and short-sleeved shirt).
- We have seen the cape that Father puts on Guido before, but underneath he is wearing his Catholic school uniform, which we will see next worn by the Young Guido.
- This is another evocative location of which Fellini makes maximum use. What does the final shot of this dream tell you?

REALITY

HOTEL CORRIDOR: The geometrics of the last shot of the dream (converging parallel lines) are duplicated in the first shot in the hallway, making for a satisfying aesthetic resonance. However, the dissonance between the two shots is what supplies the narrative thrust, the biggest difference being that Guido is moving with alacrity toward a moving camera where a moment ago he was frozen in space by a static camera.

- The two shots of Guido waiting—long and then close—pay extraordinary attention to this action. What is its effect on us? It causes us to anticipate what will happen next. When the elevator does arrive in a separate shot, the lighted glass door with shadows behind focuses our anticipation more specifically. We ask ourselves, Who is in the elevator?

ELEVATOR: The entrance of the Cardinal and his entourage. What do we learn from this scene? That Guido regards his Eminence with great deference. We are aware of something else, something that has already been set in motion. Guido lives in a society in which religion plays a pervasive role. The nuns and priests are symbols of that.

HOTEL LOBBY: I suggested earlier that one of the questions directors should ask themselves before directing any scene is, What job does it have to do in the story? What is the job of this scene in the hotel lobby? It is devoted almost exclusively to locking down the external conflict of the film. Will Guido make his film? This is the McGuffin. The more interesting internal conflict (and its concomitant question) has not yet been *clearly* stated, and one of Fellini's jobs in the remainder of the first act is to begin to introduce this conflict.

- To keep the job of a scene or sequence clear for a director, it is useful to put a label on it as part of the detective work. This title can also suggest a tone. This scene might be called "Bombarded from All Sides." Guido is attacked as soon as he exits from the elevator, and in Fellini's elegant staging—in which Guido's escape attempts are constantly being thwarted—his frame (that signifies his personal space) is constantly violated. With beautifully choreographed, extended takes, Fellini makes Guido's plight palpable to us and makes it amusing.
- Fellini uses 18 shots for this scene. Let's see what each shot accomplishes:
  1. This wide shot of the lobby identifies immediately where we are and that it is continuous in time from the previous scene. The camera moves to cover the action of a hotel clerk (wearing tails), then Guido's assistant, Cesarino (wearing a white straw hat and black turtleneck), steps into the foreground of the frame and pulls the camera into Guido.

     Guido's hiding behind his coat and going into his "shrinking" walk allows us to enter into his dilemma without being bored by it. (Suppose Guido's response was always somber, depressive? *Even if the circumstances justify it*, we would soon tire of his problem. Yes, it would still be true, but it would not be as interesting. In wanting to engage an audience, it is perfectly okay at times to *entertain* them, even in works of art.)

     As the shot continues, Claudia's agent (balding with glasses) *invades* Guido's frame. Guido gets rid of the agent only to be *seized* by Conocchia (man in white hat and shirt who we assume has a position of importance, perhaps as assistant director. It is not important to the story that we know exactly what his position is).

     Guido *extricates* himself from this *distraction* and makes his way to an *obligation*, the Actress's agent, pays his respects, and then makes his *pilgrimage* to an *albatross*, the Actress herself. (The choice of inflated action verbs and exaggerated nouns for dynamic relationships pushes a director to create scenes that are larger than life and, in the present context, comic.)
  2. On the cut to the Actress, the camera pushes in on her slightly, mimicking Guido's movement toward her. The new shot gives added importance to this new character, and we understand that she is significant. The Actress stands to inquire about her screen test. This movement makes her *pestering* more aggressive, while at the same time economically setting up Daumier for his inclusion in the conversation.
  3. The close-up of the Actress articulates the attention she is *expecting* from Guido.
  4. The cut back to the three-shot sets the stage for a *barrage* on Guido. First the American journalist appears, who is shunted aside by Agostini, whose position is usurped by Claudia's agent, and who loses Guido's attention to a mystery lady (large-brimmed hat). This is her entrance into the film.
  5. The close-up of the mystery lady signifies her importance in the film. (Her job in the film is thematic, representing the untouchable, the unknowable aspect of womanhood.)
  6. When the shot returns to Guido, he is still observing the mystery lady, still talking to Claudia's agent, but Fellini's camera has crossed to the other side of Guido, imparting a sense of dramatic escalation. Sure enough, the camera widens slightly, announcing that Cesarino is

hovering. Guido uses him as an excuse to escape from the agent, only to be *cut off* by the American journalist and his Italian wife, whose pushy presence is rendered in a close-up that ends this shot.

7. The cut to the next shot articulates the relentlessness of the concerted attack on Guido and sets the stage for the entrance of the prospective "fathers."

8. Guido's close-up articulates his inability to make a decision.

9. The shot over Guido's shoulder extends his indecisiveness, but more importantly it places the camera angle away from the staircase, so that Guido can turn into the shot and finally discover the person he seems to have been looking for throughout this entire scene.

10. In the high, wide shot Guido pays extreme homage to this mystery personage, piquing our interest and setting the stage for an entrance.

11. This is a nice contrast in angles—high to low—for the entrance of the producer and his entourage coming down the stairs.

12. The reverse angle points up the shapeliness of a woman who we immediately assume is the producer's girlfriend, while compressing the time it takes to descend the stairs.

13. The close-up of the producer from over Guido's shoulder locks down his importance in the film and sets up the next shot—the close-up of the girlfriend—needed for the comic exchange between them.

14. The close-up of the producer rendering his attitude to the pool question from the girlfriend is as full an explanation of their relationship as this story requires. (Notice that the second person in the producer's entourage gracefully fades away.)

15. The three-shot resolves separation between the producer, the girlfriend, and Guido, but more importantly storywise it punches up the producer's gift of the wristwatch to Guido. Between it and Guido's bowing, the nature of their relationship is quickly established. Each one needs the other.

16. The close-up of the girlfriend for the line, "It's self-winding," is for comic effect.

17. The two-shot of Guido and the producer extends their symbiotic relationship, but more importantly it serves to frame the producer's statement, "Well, I hope your ideas are clear by now."

18. Whether they are or not is a large question mark that hangs in the air over the high, wide shot of everyone exiting the lobby.

● This scene feels like it could be the end of Act One because Guido's external dilemma is so clearly defined, but in addition to the introduction of Guido's internal conflict, there is still one more crucial element of the story that must be developed further before the rising action of the second act can begin. It is the *urgency* for the deeper journey that Guido must make into his psyche. It has not yet been established as his only salvation. Yes, we realize he has a problem, but it does not yet seem insurmountable. The fire must become hotter; the screws have to be turned tighter to force Guido to seek a solution to his dilemma *inside* of himself. Just as importantly, the last sequence in this first act must *prepare us* to accept that urgency along with the primacy of this interior universe, which we will inhabit, along with Guido, for all of the significant action for the remainder of the film.

"CABARET" SCENE: The close-up of the female singer supplies an energizing transition from the wide-shot of the hotel lobby. We don't know where we are, but the next shots begin to supply the answer. Because Fellini has revealed the space earlier, we are oriented very quickly and feel comfortable here. From out of the general populace, Gloria and Mezzabota appear. His unabashed happiness is in direct contrast to the cut to Guido, alone, wearing the Pinocchio nose. *Notice how the scene unfolds.* We continue receiving *new* information about who is present and what the dynamics are between characters, saving the reveal of Carla, a "safe" distance from Guido, for last. The large space between them is a reminder of the propriety that Guido, the husband, maintains in the social sphere. Of course it is a lie, and he knows it—hence his donning the "Pinocchio" nose.

- Fellini maintains a leisurely pace, letting us get into the rhythm of the participants, but he understands this cannot go on too long. So he escalates the action by jumping the narrative ahead, using Nino Rota's music to propel us into the middle of a passionate outburst of frustration by the actress, Claudia. The music continues, driving the producer's question, "Didn't our director explain your role to you?" This little peak of dramatic tension dissipates, but it has changed the dynamics of the scene and its rhythm enough so that Fellini can become "quiet" again for Guido's talk with Mezzabota. (A dramatic musical phrase was also used to energize the cut to the beginning of this scene—the close-up of the female singer—and will be used again shortly.)
- The magician is illuminated by a spotlight, the beginning of a visual motif that will have its payoff in the last shot of the film.
- Realizing that he will need the blackboard for the end of the scene, Fellini weaves it into the background of several shots, quietly announcing its existence to us. (This preparing the audience for something that is important to a scene, but not necessarily endemic to it, is the same job that Weir was aware of in *The Truman Show* when he introduced the magnifying glass to us, and kept it alive, *before* it was needed.)
- Gloria's fright is a put-on—inauthentic—keeping her thematic persona alive.
- The phrase "Asa Nisi Masa" is the key that unlocks Guido's unconscious. (In can be translated as *anima*, a Jungian term meaning soul or spirit.) For Guido it is a magical phrase from his childhood, and he goes back there to try to find a solution to his lack of inspiration *through magic*.
- Maurice (in top hat and tails) asks the question, "What does it mean?" marking the end of Act One. All the major characters have been introduced. (Although Guido's wife has not materialized in *reality*, we have seen her briefly, but memorably, in his dream. Saraghina, his first sexual memory, has been hinted at in the theme music that was played under the role-playing scene in Carla's hotel room, where Guido painted Carla to look more like Saraghina.) The dilemma for the external conflict (making the film) has been firmly established, as has Guido's penchant for looking into himself for answers. It is here that the seeds have been planted for the emergence of the film's main conflict—Guido's need to live a life without a lie—*but this has not yet been developed to the point where we realize it*. In fact, that question will not be fully articulated until the end of Act Two, although we will certainly be able to "smell" it before then.

SECOND ACT

MEMORY

KITCHEN/GUIDO'S CHILDHOOD FARMHOUSE: There is no visual announcement that we are moving to a new mode of reality—memory—but we are not at all confused. The forceful action by Guido's Young Mother that begins in the first frame of the new scene immediately orients us to a new place; then the lullaby, and the image of a Young Guido, orients us to past time.

- Aside from rendering this scene in the present (in film language the past and future are always in the present tense), Fellini has another job to do: to familiarize us with the geography of the location so that later in the film we can fully participate in the unfolding of one of Guido's fantasies (Harem fantasy) without expository geographical information intruding. Why doesn't that information intrude here? First, because it is made organic to the action of the scene. Second, in narrative scenes such as this, the exposition of space is not at all intrusive. It is part of the *unfolding* of our story. (Does this mean that every dramatic scene must be preceded by a scene that introduces us to the space? Obviously this interpretation would be much too restrictive, if not impossible. The general rule is that *if* we visit a space before a dramatic scene, it is *advisable* in most cases to familiarize the audience as to its geography.)

What is the job of this scene? There are two main jobs. The first is to introduce the warm, lov-
ing, playful relationship between Young Guido and his mother. The second is to introduce
the theme of the "beleaguered wife," as represented by the grandmother. Later, in Guido's
fantasy, which mirrors to a great extent this present scene, Guido's own wife will play the
beleaguered wife's role, *but she will accept it.*

- In many films, other modes of reality are often depicted in a noticeably different style, but Fellini
does not change his style because he does not want to make a clear distinction between them
and reality.
- Guido is carried up the stairs in his mother's arms in a frame that will be repeated in the Harem
fantasy.

BEDROOM/GUIDO'S CHILDHOOD FARMHOUSE: On the cut from the staircase to the
bedroom, the shot pushes into the bed. It is a strong transition from the previous shot, thrusting
the narrative forward and calling our attention to the "lump" in the covers. (Fellini has used this
quick push-in when cutting from Guido's hotel room to the bathroom mirror that reveals his face.
He will use this emphatic movement to bridge locations several more times in this film.)

- Notice that Guido's mother wears a black top, whereas Auntie Olga has a white one. This is
important in distinguishing one from another. More to the point, it is relevant to our under-
standing that Guido receives nurturing love from more than one woman.
- An elegant transition is made from "lights on" to "lights out." It is efficient and atmospheric.
- Closing the double doors by the grandmother sets the stage for magic to happen.
- The fire in the hearth that closes this memory sequence is an image of warmth—a metaphor for
the love that Guido remembers receiving in this house—and it is an image that will be repeated.
(Logic would dictate that every image that we saw in Guido's memory would have to be generated by his psyche, but many times the images were outside his purview. He was not present for
much of what we saw. Yet we assigned everything to Guido's psyche—another testament to the
fluidity of narrative perspective.)
- The transition out of the memory to present reality is made through a dissolve to an indistinct
location, which is then revealed by the short track to the concierge.

REALITY

HOTEL LOBBY—NIGHT: Guido's enters the scene by entering a moving frame that has already
anticipated his move—a clear example of the objective narrator's omniscience. It already knows
the story it is telling. It is not improvising. In this scene we again marvel at the elegant simplicity
in which it unfolds. Its jobs are to keep the pressure on Guido, to bring his aimlessness, his "lost-
soulness" to the fore. The shot of him standing alone in the vastness of the lobby says that clearly.

- Fellini takes Guido to the seating area in one extended shot that starts with Guido in the middle
of the lobby and ends with a close-up of the Actress. During this shot, Fellini's superb choreographing of staging and camera movement to render changes in image size, as well as fore-
ground/background composition, is again on display.
- We are surprised to discover that Guido has made an unexpected shift in his position on the set-
tee when the cut is made from the Actress to him. (Usually I caution that no physical movement
within a scene should happen off camera, but here is one that works nicely. It surprises but does
not confuse.)
- The next dramatic block of this scene is rendered in separation with seven shots to better articulate the tension between the Actress and Guido. The eighth shot of this separation reveals that
the Actress's agent is present, and in the next shot he is "tied" to the scene with a two-shot of

him and Guido. It punctuates the end of this dramatic block, and when Guido turns his attention elsewhere, his head movement serves as a segue to the next dramatic block.

- This short dramatic block begins with the close-up of Gloria and her come-on to Guido. It keeps Gloria's inauthenticity alive and also serves to break up the Actress's harangue. When Fellini cuts from Gloria and Mezzabota at the piano to go back to the seating area, he employs a new camera angle—one that re-resolves the separation between the two spaces while *anticipating* the approach of the hotel clerk with news of Guido's phone call.
- The push-in to the phone being held by the hotel clerk is another example of the effectiveness of this transitional device.
- The camera follows the hotel clerk as he walks off to allow Guido a private conversation. His action imparts significance to the phone call.
- In the next shot, Fellini has Guido with his back to the camera. This staging creates a sense of dramatic escalation when Guido turns to face the camera. As the scene progresses, the camera moves in for a tight close-up of Guido, giving us full access to his internal struggles to say something that is not a lie.
- The camera move to the lobby clock combined with the cut to the camera moving through the opening door to the production office jumps the narrative ahead and is another example of Fellini's artful transitions.

PRODUCTION OFFICE: *Quickly* we get a sense of a production in progress. Then a comic entrance into the scene for Cesarino. Then comic reveals of first one "niece," then another. Comic punctuation at the end of the scene. The light tone in this scene contrasts with the much heavier tone of the next scene.

HOTEL CORRIDOR: In the production office, the camera was fluid. Here it is restrained, in keeping with the tone.

- The over-the-shoulder of Guido resolves the initial separation between him and Conocchia, orienting the audience spatially before the separation is reintroduced.
- The staging makes dramatic use of the geometry of the space, and the shot compositions enhance that geometry.

INTERCUTTING OF REALITY AND ACTIVE IMAGINATION

GUIDO'S HOTEL ROOM AND BATHROOM: Again no announcement of another mode of reality: active imagination. We accept the appearance of the Woman in White *as a logical consequence* of the evening, as the scene continues, alternating between the two worlds.

- Again and again Fellini surprises us with his narrative shorthand. From the push-in to a tight close-up of the Woman in White, we understand that Guido has fallen asleep. From the buzzing sound of the telephone we understand that he is being awakened.

REALITY

CARLA'S HOTEL ROOM: This is a deceptively simple scene rendered in six shots. We should appreciate how much expository information Fellini supplies to us in the first shot—not from a "master" that tells you everything at once but through skillful staging of actions and interactions of characters that allows us to participate in the *unfolding* of the moment, making what is quite ordinary quite interesting.

- The cut to the second shot allows Fellini a dramatic reveal of Carla's condition. The third shot articulates Guido's genuine concern for Carla.

- What about the fourth shot, the close-up of Carla? It does two jobs. It conveys significance to Carla's question, "Why do you stay with me?" More importantly it allows Fellini to begin to change the dynamics of the scene, for he is well aware of the obligation to keep the narrative thrust alive. To do that he must extricate Guido from his present concern for Carla, but he must do it gracefully and without taking all day. The first step in this journey is the cut to the close-up in which we lose Guido. Then in the next shot we discover that he has already assumed a different position, *having removed himself from his ministrations*. This discovery prepares us for the last shot of the scene, where Guido is totally removed from Carla, physically and psychologically. The urgency of his creative dilemma has once again intruded on the present, forcing him this time to project his thoughts into the future—"What will I say to the Cardinal tomorrow?"—*propelling* us into the next scene *and the next sequence*.

THEME AND ORCHESTRATION OF THE NEXT SEQUENCE

- Although the reliance on theme can get us into trouble if we look at it merely as an abstract, it can be extremely powerful when viewed (as Fellini must have in this sequence) as a matrix that a character lives and breathes, profoundly affecting that character's relationship with others and with the universe itself. The theme I suggest for the following sequence is "the Catholic Consciousness." It pervades each scene of the entire 16-and-one-half minutes of the sequence. It unifies the disparate actions of the sequence and permeates its images, and there is a beginning, middle, and final resolution to the dramatic tension that the theme engenders.
- It is important for a director to *see* an entire sequence before working on individual scenes. Because film takes place in time, this *seeing* must be done *in time*. (This is one of the most difficult things for a novice director to learn, and some don't even try, relying instead on taking care of *time* in the editing room. This is a mistake. The editing process should be looked at always as an enhancement of the director's vision. Yes, a faulty vision might be somewhat salvaged in the editing process, but on the set, rhythms both in action and in camera movements are established that can be very difficult to change significantly.)
- Within the following sequence there are huge tonal changes from one scene to the next that run the spectrum from farcical to profound existential angst—all in 16-and-one-half minutes. Just as in music, these individual sections had to be orchestrated into one overall movement. Transitions are paramount in this melding, and we will take note of many extraordinary examples in this sequence.
- The narrative job of the sequence must be clear in a director's mind because the answer to that question will help to clarify the dramatic arc and emotional journey of your character(s). As has been pointed out many times in this book, the distance the character travels, the individual steps in that journey, and the obstacles that impede progress must all be available to the audience on a moment-to-moment basis.
- In the context of the story so far, what is the job for this sequence? Let's start with Guido's external dilemma, his loss of inspiration. This has driven him deeper and deeper into himself to find answers to the problems of creating a suitable story for his film. He has *consciously* tried to solve the problem through active imagination and memory, even though the dream that started off the film hinted at a much larger problem. In this sequence, Guido uses memory to seek an answer in the innocence of adolescent sexual awakening that brings him into direct conflict with the Church. When Daumier dismisses this memory as having no artistic value, Guido descends back into his now percolating, Catholic-permeated psyche to seek the answer to his problems through fantasy. There, in answer to his confession, "I am unhappy," the Cardinal tells him there is no salvation outside the Church. Of course, this is a position that Guido cannot embrace, leaving him worse off than ever, for in this fantasy he has *articulated to himself* the fact of his profound unhappiness. *We* now understand that this unhappiness goes far beyond whether or not he makes a film. And for the first time, so does Guido.

MEETING WITH THE CARDINAL: The impetus from the last scene is continued with the tracking through the trees. It is the objective narrator's voice, but I don't believe we assign it as such. It acts on us more as an unidentified force pushing us forward into the story.

- The shot of the bearded man is clearly the objective narrator's voice, as is the next shot of Guido. The cut to the Monsignor moving toward the camera as the camera moves toward him is extremely energizing. Here the staging requires the camera to stop, but then it immediately resumes its inexorable journey to the Cardinal, stopping again only when the journey is complete. This extended movement cleans our visual palate before the ensuing static staging for the audience with the Cardinal.
- The Cardinal's stage is revealed in parallel action.
- As soon as Guido realizes that he is not going to get what he needs from the Cardinal, his mind seeks a solution to his problems elsewhere. This time, the legs of a peasant woman precipitate his interior journey. Because this image seems unconnected to the initial images of the school yard, Fellini makes the transition very clear by resorting to the eyeglasses once again, but this time they announce not active imagination, but memory.

MEMORY

This is a *heightened* memory befitting a creative artist. Also, as in the dreams of the mature Guido, Young Guido's memory is both inside and outside his purview, allowing Fellini to render scenes fully, unhindered by the restrictions of Young Guido's direct perception.

SCHOOL YARD: Notice the movement of the authoritarian foreground figure in the first shot: how his turn (revealing his whistle) is choreographed with the entrance of the exuberant schoolboys running in the background. This juxtaposition of authority and exuberance within the same frame instantly hints at the nature of the conflict to follow.

- The Young Guido is introduced in two shots. The first separates him from his peers, making him "special." The second, the high angle with the religious statue in the foreground framing him, does a huge amount of work. It continues the first impression that this boy is somehow different from the other boys, and it places the young Guido squarely inside the pervasiveness of the religious culture in which he has grown up. One more job is shared by the two shots: the strong introduction of the hat and the reintroduction of the cape.

BEACH AND SARAGHINA'S BUNKER: The sea was a symbol of freedom for Fellini. We saw that in the first dream sequence when Guido attempted to escape to it in his flight. It serves the same purpose here.

- Let's look at the shape of the ensuing scene and the dramatic elements that it is built on.
  Mystery (Where are the boys running to?)
  Expectation (An exciting adventure lies ahead.)
  Entrance (Saraghina's face is kept hidden during her entrance into the scene.)
  Preparation (Saraghina collects the admission fee, walks onto the "stage," smooths her dress over her hips, and exposes her shoulders.)
  Dramatic reveal (Saraghina's face is dramatically revealed when she turns toward the camera.)
  EVENT (The dance. It reaches its apex when Saraghina picks up Young Guido.)
  Consequences (Caught in the act by the priests.)
  Aftermath (Punishment. It takes place in the following scenes.)

A minimum of four of these dramatic elements are used time and time again for scenes or sequences whose main element is an *event*—Expectation, Preparation, Event, and Aftermath—providing a template for the event's *dramatic unfolding*.

- Saraghina lifting Guido in the air is the apex of the scene. Dramatically it cannot go beyond this. Hence the cut to the two priests arriving.
- On the next cut, the scene shifts into outright farce, and Fellini acknowledges this by changing styles drastically. He *jump cuts* to Guido being chased by the two priests in the middle of a wide frame. As the chase continues, the motion in the frame is speeded up, reminiscent of so many silent comedy chases. This change in style is so appropriate to the essence of the moment that it requires no prior introduction. (There is a greater license to change style in a comedy than in a drama without the director first setting it up.)
- The staging in the "chase" frame *articulates the progress of the chase*. First the action moves away from the camera, then it moves parallel to it, then it comes directly toward it, breaking this single take into "separate shots."

CATHOLIC SCHOOL: The forward movement in the last take of the previous scene is continued, thrusting the narrative forward into the first scene of this "sequence within a sequence," which is composed of four scenes, each with its own distinct location.

- Courtroom: This scene has extremely formal staging that is appropriate for such weighty proceedings. The "punches-in" to the close-ups of the various accusers articulate the *vehemence* of their attack. Pans link various elements of the scene with one another, keeping us apprised of spatial relationships *as needed*, holding off the spatial resolution of the entire space until the wide shot rendering Guido's exit.
- Classroom: The space is revealed by a combination track and pan, moving first from left to right, then right to left, keeping the frame constantly in motion.
- Dining Hall: The cut to the close-up of the beans being poured on the floor fools us. We assume we are in the classroom. The narrative jump that reveals we are in a new space is energizing, but realize *it is the same shot* that then tracks to reveal the lectern with the reader in the foreground, while at the same time rendering Guido's reluctance to kneel in the background. A lot of narrative work is rendered so seemingly effortlessly that it is easy to overlook the exquisiteness of its design and the economy in which it carries out its narrative function.
- Confessional: An image of death and Guido's reaction to it (in shadow) contextualizes the entire scene, imparting an atmosphere of foreboding to even ambiguous images: the hand closing the curtain and the patterned wall of the inside of the confessional booth. Although we never see Guido's face, it is no surprise to us that he kneels obediently upon leaving the booth.

SARAGHINA'S BUNKER: The transition to this scene is a dissolve from the statue of the Virgin Mary to Saraghina's bunker, juxtaposing the Madonna and the Whore—two categories into which women can be divided according to the perspective that young Guido was immersed in and that still permeates the psyche of the adult Guido.

- Guido's kneeling in front of Saraghina reflects his deep gratitude for the illicit gift she has bestowed on him.
- Saraghina's reveal is delayed. Then when we do see her, she is presented in a much more feminine, even alluring, manner than previously. The white scarf blowing in the sea breeze helps create this softening of her image.

REALITY

RESTAURANT: A dissolve brings us to a comment on the dream by Daumier. It is a bridge scene. Its purpose is to keep Guido from finding any solace in his dream, forcing him to continue the search within himself.

- The transition from the restaurant to the "descent into hell" is, for me, the most impressive transition in all of cinema. It is unexpected, powerful, and momentous in its shifting of gears to another dramatic level. The change in locations occurs on the cut from the female singer to the orchestra. It is not immediately apparent that these are two different venues. (The woman appearing from the bottom of the frame has become a motif at this point.)

STEAM ROOM: This is an imaginative weaving of music, staging, costume (shrouds), location, and imagery, whose dramatic purpose is both metaphorical *and* dramatic. *Metaphor alone, without accompanying dramatic action, is lifeless.*

- The microphone is *planted* as a natural accompaniment of the present action so that it can be gracefully introduced in the fantasy.
- The following fantasy is clearly being generated out of the necessity for Guido to find an answer to his problem. The moment of change from one mode of reality to another is again obscured. It occurs *in part* toward the end of the panning shot of the shrouded clients that follows the two-shot of Guido and Mario, when a female voice-over begins. On the cut to the slight push-in on Guido, we understand that he is generating this voice.
- The cut from Guido's close-up (reality) to the long shot of the steam room (fantasy) is a clear case of cause and effect, and we understand that we are now inhabiting a full-blown fantasy.

FANTASY

- What an imaginative fantasy: both comic and profound. We are introduced to a new character, the stewardess (along with her distinctive voice). There is no logic for her being there, but there is an *emotional authenticity* to it. She is a product of Guido's past, something we now know quite a lot about, and she does not seem foreign to his quest for a spiritual answer. The amalgam of sex and religion and work has become familiar terrain for us in this film. (Think for a moment of how little we knew of the interior life of Alicia and Devlin, even of Truman and Christof, but it was not required for those stories. We did, however, know clearly what they wanted—what objectives they were striving for.) Here we are starting to realize that what we thought Guido wanted—to make a film—is not his main objective, but even he does not yet fully realize this. However, at the end of this fantasy, Guido, and we, will have come much closer to understanding his real conflict. It starts with his admission that he is not happy.
- Guido's journey toward the audience with the Cardinal is brilliantly staged—a complicated, comic choreography rendered in three shots, the first and last "bookending" the middle shot, which introduces Guido's subjective POV (characters look directly into the camera). Why the subjective POV? Because it serves to make the pressure placed on Guido *all the more palpable.* We *feel* the pressure impinging on him because in the middle shot *we are him!*
- There is no logic to the staging for the middle shot. Guido takes a left off of his initial direction, then a right, then another left that turns even sharper left, so that if one were to map out Guido's actual trajectory, we would discover that he is actually returning from where he began. But logic holds no sway here. In fact, we do not keep track of his turns, which are made near impossible to follow because there are no definitive geographical points. Of course Fellini was aware of this. He knew he had this freedom and he used it with relish.
- What does this staging accomplish? By complicating the physical journey, it makes us more acutely aware of the complexities of Guido's interior life.

CARDINAL'S INNER SANCTUM: This scene has powerful, evocative imagery! It is another testimony to Fellini's fertile imagination and his brilliant wedding of poetry and drama.

- Guido himself is absent from this scene, and yet he is fully present. It is because of the window that opened *just for him* and because of his off-screen confession, "I am not happy." When the window closes, we feel that it is closing on Guido's physical presence, and, more importantly, on his hope that the Cardinal would offer a solution that he could embrace.

- The transition to the next scene is subtle but nevertheless quietly dramatic. The dance music from the scene comes up over the tail end of the window closing, a marvelous contrast in tone—an intrusion of the profane on the sacred.

REALITY

PUBLIC SQUARE OF RESORT TOWN: This scene holds a nice surprise. From out of the crowd, Guido's wife Luisa emerges. (She has already made her entrance into the film in the dream sequence at the graveyard, so we know immediately who she is.) Then another surprise: Guido is watching her. The staging that follows does two jobs. It goes a long way to establishing the dynamic relationship between husband and wife, and it allows us some insight into Luisa's psychology. She is nervous—on edge.

- Fellini gives Luisa her own "dance number" to allow us a look at another aspect of her personality. Because of this playfulness, *we like her more*, and we can understand better why Guido is attracted to her.

SPACESHIP SET: This starts with a mystery. Where are we? Then there is a pan to reveal the enormity of the financial investment that has already been made in Guido's film. The detailed shots of the structure only add to our awareness of this.

- In this scene we find Guido's personal and professional lives becoming more entwined, and his growing internal conflict comes more and more into the foreground, as Fellini begins to hasten the job of weaving these two strands into one. Because of the job it has to do, this scene is more narrative in tone than dramatic, but Fellini was still required to create a dramatic tension nevertheless and keep the narrative thrust alive. How did he accomplish this? By realizing that the strongest element *going into* the scene is Guido's discord with his wife, established in the *previous scene*. This discord contextualizes whatever follows it. To make absolutely sure that this tension is carried over into the new scene, Fellini punctuates it with the last two shots of the previous scene in which Guido and Luisa are *sitting apart* in the car. Then, when they arrive at the launching pad, Fellini makes sure that they never appear together in the same frame. Fellini has made this estrangement palpable to us, and it pervades the remainder of the scene.
- Fellini elaborates the crowd climbing *up* the stairs of the tower. This continues to impress upon us the enormity of the project, but it also does something else. The shot panning up the steps sets up a familiar image for the last scene in the film, except then the crowd is streaming *down* the steps.
- In this scene the narrator strays from Guido as much as it has or ever will in the entire film. It is required to do so to provide a stage for the disparaging editorial commentary from the crowd and for the exchange between Luisa and the young man who has a crush on her. Guido cannot be present for these two things to happen. Fellini was aware of this break in the narrative style that he had established, and so he places a shot of Guido standing on the ground below the tower *between the editorial commentary and the exchange between Luisa and the young man*. This shot serves to successfully cover the "breach" in the narrative style.
- What is the young man's dramatic function? To serve as an alternative romantic possibility for Luisa outside of marriage. Unlike her husband, she rejects this possibility.
- Immersed in the physicality of the set, Guido momentarily gains assurance that he will make the film and that he will "put everything in," including the sailor who does a soft-shoe. This sailor has two dramatic functions in this scene. The first is to show that Guido's imagination is percolating. He is continuing to work. But the work is interrupted so easily by the intrusion of the personal—his relationship with his wife—and his ambiguity about that relationship turns to

anger, which is taken out on the sailor (whose second dramatic function is to serve as a barometer of Guido's confusion).

- Guido's immersion in the imaginative possibilities inherent in the set—his continuing to work— is also made clear when Guido looks up toward the top of the tower using his hand to "frame" the image. Yet this moment, too, is intruded upon by his deeper, internal problems, forcing him to admit, "I wanted to make an honest film, no lies, no compromises." But that no longer seems possible because he is "confused." At the moment he has nothing to say, but the scene ends on a note of *possibility*: Rosella tells him he is free, "but he has to choose." This challenge to Guido is echoed in the next shot—the long shot of the tower and the voices calling down from it: "Guido, are you coming up or not?" We understand the deeper meaning of this question: Guido, are you going to make your film?
- The end of this scene marks the *first culmination* of action in Act Two. By holding out the possibility of Guido solving the problem of his film, it is the direct opposite of Act Two's *final culmination*, where Guido announces that there will be no film.

GUIDO'S HOTEL ROOM: The spatial separation between Guido and Luisa continues until the last shot of the scene, which resolves the separation but continues the estrangement through the staging: they turn their backs to each other.

- Luisa stands in front of the billowing curtains that breathe movement into the scene. We are familiar with this area of the room, introduced in the second scene of the film by the nurse coming through these very same curtains.
- Fellini uses the light being turned off by Luisa to change the stage for the new dramatic block that escalates the action.
- The transition to the next scene is from light to dark, modulating the tone once again.

CAFÉ IN THE PUBLIC SQUARE: The pulsing music, the sweeping camera movement, and the fast moving horse-drawn carriage kick the narrative into high gear. We are made to wonder, Who will alight from the carriage? Then we see a wonderfully comic entrance into the scene by Carla.

- As always, Fellini not only chose the perfect location for the scene but then maximized all of its possibilities for creating a dramatic stage with the perfect atmosphere.
- The two tables (Guido's and Carla's) are resolved spatially on a narrative beat: the change in action from acknowledging Carla's presence to defining her character. (As pointed out earlier, *when spatial resolution is resolved with a new shot, it should be wedded to a narrative beat*.)
- The Pinocchio motif returns.
- Guido's change in posture to one of unabashed musing, along with the change in music, announces a new mode of reality.

DAYDREAM

- The track into Carla is the beginning of the daydream.
- Carla and Luisa dancing among the tables dissolves to the large pot on the hearth, which is not an *exact* familiar image, but it *feels* like it is. This is because we have been previously introduced to both the fireplace and the pot in images that are *similar*, and we make the connection. From this image we know where we are, and we are now into a full-blown fantasy.

FANTASY

FARMHOUSE KITCHEN/HAREM FANTASY: This scene is an excellent example of film-time that resembles real time. The actions that occur could never take place in the less than 13 minutes that this scene runs. Yet there is no obvious sense of ellipses—of jumps in time. The scene unfolds with an unhurried rhythm, artfully disguising the compression that is at the heart of film-time.

- As has been pointed out, it is crucial for a director to understand the dramatic shape of a scene, and in all of the dramatic scenes so far, breaking them into dramatic blocks and a fulcrum was sufficient. However, this scene is so rich, so filled with actions that do not conveniently lend themselves to this kind of dramatic "constraint," that we must look for another, "looser" model to organize and *shape* the flow of action. (Without an overall shape in mind before directing a scene, a director will have a slim chance of realizing its full potential.) A model that nicely accommodates this scene is the three-act structure.

FIRST ACT

- This act depicts ordinary life for approximately six minutes. Everything meets Guido's *expectations* for a wonderful evening. Then comes the point of attack (Jacqueline's refusal to go upstairs). This raises the question, Will Guido prevail?
- We have been made familiar with this space (from Guido's childhood memory), which now allows us to participate in the unfolding of the drama without the intrusion of geographic exposition. As mentioned, the first image of the hearth and the kettle is not precisely a familiar image, but it is close enough to resonate as one. Still, there is plenty of exposition to be delivered, and in the very first shot Fellini establishes Luisa, reintroduces the space, and prepares for Guido's entrance from the snow and cold (a metaphor for the harsh reality of the world that he leaves outside of this sanctuary). Those present are introduced, as is their adoring attitude toward Guido, as is the ritual pampering and bath. Fellini then chooses the ideal image for the point of attack to occur: Jacqueline's rebellious entrance, feathers flying, collides with Guido snugly ensconced in his hammock, surrounded by docile women—a collision between Guido's expectation and the reality of the situation. (No different from Alicia's expectation colliding with the reality of Devlin's distrust of her in *Notorious*. The point of attack is most effective when it comes as a surprise to ordinary life/expectations, and it is the director's job to render that surprise/collision so that it has a strong impact on the audience.)
- Jacqueline ascends from the cellar, whose entrance has never been seen by us—an indication that a director has leniency in familiarizing the audience with a space. What are the rules? As mentioned earlier, the only one that makes sense is: *If revealing the geography of a location intrudes upon the action or atmosphere of the moment, don't do it.* Here, too, the cellar steps are barely "read" as a place but more as a condition of Jacqueline's low position in the pecking order of the harem.
- Fellini takes pains to set up the table being *readied for a feast*. Notice in how many shots it is present in the background, and then, just before Jacqueline's emergence, the table locks down the foreground of the tracking shot of Guido being carried in his hammock.
- To enhance the festive atmosphere at the beginning of this first act, a scarf is continually waved in front of the camera. Because this is a fantasy, we never question who it is that is waving this scarf. It's just there. (Does that mean we can do anything we like in a fantasy? No. Even the universe of a fantasy should obey certain parameters *specific to the tone of the film*, and the parameters previously established for Guido's fantasies easily encompass the anonymous scarf waver.)

SECOND ACT

- This act is approximately two minutes and 20 seconds. The second act starts with Saraghina's close-up and her exclamation, "It's not fair!" This rising action is underscored by the music. (Usually the rising action is by the protagonist, but it usually does not mean always. These paradigms are not written in stone, and each creative artist has the license to bend them and, on occasion, to ignore them altogether. The only reason they exist is to aid in telling a story more interestingly *so that the audience will be continually engaged*. In the present scene, the rising action happens to be initiated by someone other than the protagonist, *but it serves the same function*: dramatic escalation. We should also keep in mind that the protagonist and antagonist are one and the same here. It is Guido who is generating the story.)

- Guido does meet the challenge of the rising action against him and succeeds in defeating it.

THIRD ACT

- This act is approximately four-and-one-half minutes. Here we have the consequences of Guido's action. His victory has not made him happy. For the first time he feels that something is wrong in his relationships with women. *But this is a false ending*! Guido cannot accept this. Because he is making up the story, he immediately runs from this conclusion, concocting a new ending, one more to his liking: the obedient wife who "finally understands how things should be."
- This flip-flop in Guido's psychology needs help from the director to make it believable, and Fellini was aware of this. To get Guido gracefully from the first psychological state to the next, Fellini employs a unique piece of staging, coupled with a change in lighting that separates the false ending from the final ending. Watch closely. With Guido sitting at the head of the table, the frame seems to pan right to left to discover Carla and her harp, but in fact the frame does not move (Carla and the harp are rolled into the frame). Then the background behind Carla goes black, setting the stage for an entirely new tone, where Guido is exonerated from all blame.
- At the beginning of this scene, Luisa looks *directly into the camera* and says, "He's such a darling." Here she is speaking to us through the objective narrator. Then, seated at the table, Luisa looks toward Guido, *but not into the camera*, and we read it as Guido's POV. Fellini can move between these two modes of narrative perception with impunity because he has told us from the very beginning, "This is one of the ways I am going to tell my story." So we are not at all surprised and do not consider it to be jarring.
- The ending of the scene is one shot, beautifully choreographed and lit. It starts with a wide shot of the table, moves to a medium close on Luisa, then watches as Luisa's staging turns the frame into a long shot.
- The last image is lit by a spotlight, as was Jacqueline's dance number. We have now seen this motif three times, setting us up for its payoff in the final image of the film.
- The orchestration of this entire scene in the kitchen is extraordinary. Fellini creates a dance between the actors and the camera that takes repeated viewings before its craft can be fully comprehended. It is well worth the trouble. I have more than once said to students that if they could embody the directing craft needed to render this scene, they could direct almost *any* scene. Watch it again and again until the magic falls away, until the strings, controlled by one of the greatest cinematic puppeteers who ever lived, begin to show.

REALITY

MOVIE THEATER AUDITORIUM: It is here that Guido's private and professional lives collide publicly, *forcing* him to leave the auditorium to make one last attempt to invent a story that he can embrace with his whole being.

- The scene begins with Guido talking to Luisa (we see him talking to himself), continuing the fantasy in the farmhouse kitchen until interrupted by Daumier.
- The second shot of the scene reveals Daumier, resolves separation between him and Guido, and informs us that we are in an empty movie theater. Next, Luisa, her sister, and entourage are introduced. Next, the young man who is in love with Luisa. And finally, a man pacing in front of the doorway, waiting, in a shot whose background resolves the spatial separation of

the entire auditorium. This is another nice example of a scene unfolding gracefully, allowing us to participate, to make connections, to be engaged. What else does the beginning of this major scene do? It causes us to anticipate, like the man pacing, the arrival of someone else.

- Daumier's lecturing of Guido can be shot in separation because we know exactly where each character is. When Guido has had enough, he raises his finger, signaling. But for what?

FANTASY

- Fellini does not give us the answer immediately. He makes us wait. He varies the rhythm of the scene by organizing the action into three sentences of descending complexity. In the first shot, a compound sentence with several clauses, a man enters the left side of the frame; then a second man approaches from the right side, revealing a hood that he places over Daumier's head; then both men lead Daumier to the "gallows." The second shot/sentence contains two clauses: a noose is applied, and it is pulled tight. The third shot contains one clause: Daumier is dead.

REALITY

- Guido's finger is still in the air, giving a bookend to the fantasy. (This formal announcing of when one mode of reality ends and another begins will end soon. Reality and fantasy will become mixed, and logic will not matter to our understanding and appreciation of the story.)
- The entrance of the producer and his entourage through the doorway has been anticipated by the man pacing in the very same doorway. It is a grand entrance, signaling the beginning of the *event*.
- Before the lights dim, Fellini uses an over-the-shoulder of Guido to resolve his and the producer's spatial separation.
- The rich tapestry of the screen tests, a testimony to all the work that Guido has put into this project, intercut with the actions and reactions of the audience, the growing pressure on Guido to make some decisions, Guido's argument with Luisa, and finally the entrance of Claudia, and her and Guido's exit from the auditorium, need no comment from me. The dramatic *clash* of images and relationships both on the screen and in the audience speak for themselves. The collision between Guido's personal and professional lives forces him to flee the scene of the accident. The arrival of Claudia gives him the excuse to do that.

However, what we will discover is that *he cannot flee his problem. He can make no decision about casting until he knows what story he wants to tell, and he must find that story tonight!* Who says he must make it tonight? We, the audience. Fellini and his screenwriters knew that. A jolt in the narrative thrust is needed, so the stage is changed and Fellini has Claudia move with alacrity down the stairs of that stage, a bounce in her step, and into her car. *Her momentum supplies momentum to the story*. We don't know where we are going next, but we understand that wherever it is, Guido will come to a decision (exhaust his action) by the end of this night. If the audience knows these things about a story, it makes sense that the director should also.

INTERIOR, CLAUDIA'S CAR: This intimate scene is shot totally in separation until the car comes to a stop. The intimacy is supported by the lighting. Each head floats in a black limbo. Only Guido's eyes are lit. The position of the camera, between Guido and Carla, acknowledges the intimate dynamics—each shot containing the *suggestion* of the other character.

- Fellini starts out with a medium close shot of Guido and then goes in tight and stays there until Claudia throws his question back at him. "How about you? Could you?" Guido's reaction is a narrative beat. The question stumps him momentarily. To make sure that this has a palpable impact on the audience, Fellini articulates this narrative beat with a change in image size (back to the medium close shot).

- Claudia is fully lit and shot in a three-quarters profile, suggesting even more the presence of Guido and *the attention he is paying to her*. (All this from the objective narrator without a hint of a subjective voice or even a POV.) When Guido says, "It's obvious she could be his salvation," Fellini acknowledges the significance of this statement by substantially changing, for the first time, the angle on Claudia to a tighter, full profile. This cut to the new image of Claudia punctuates the importance of what Guido has just said. His optimism here is an extremely important plot point. (Imagine this scene without these last two very small changes, and note how they *significantly* affect the dramatic content. Not everything a director does is pyrotechnic—in fact, most is not.)

COURTYARD OF OLD BUILDING NEAR SPRINGS: A complete and economical introduction of the new location using the car's headlights.

ACTIVE IMAGINATION

- The cut to black from the two-shot outside of the car prepares us for the image of Claudia in the window. As in all of Guido's imaginings concerning Claudia, there is no sound.

REALITY

- Claudia's question, "And then what?" brings us back to reality and suggests a very practical reason for putting Claudia in a black costume: it is a dramatic contrast to her "Woman in White," the possible solution to his film.
- Guido exiting the car is rendered with a sound and a look from Claudia *that carries him away from the car*. His position is confirmed in the next shot, still walking away from the car while putting on his jacket. Claudia is not shown exiting, either. She just appears and we accept it (film-time).
- This is an ideal location for creating the *atmosphere* needed to bring Guido to the conclusion that he does not have a story and will not make a film. It supplies a variety of stages for the different dramatic blocks.
- Guido tells Claudia that there is no part for her. There is no film. There is nothing, nothing at all. This marks the end of the second act. Guido has exhausted his action in relation to the question that was raised at the end of the first act—the external conflict. Will he make a film? The answer is an unequivocal no! But *8½* is not over. The third act is yet to come. Here we will discover, along with Guido, the consequences of his actions, not only in relation to the external conflict but in relation to the main conflict: the internal conflict raging inside of Guido. Can he live an authentic life—a life without a lie?

THIRD ACT

- The third act announces itself with boorish insensitivity to Guido's traumatic discovery that he will not make a film. He is not allowed a moment of reflection but is immediately assaulted by the outside world. It refuses to let him escape the pressure to perform. The images that Fellini chooses—the cars speeding up, their headlights, their noise, the importuning of the passengers—all make Guido's plight visceral for us. (Others might label the next scene as the true beginning of the third act, but in paying strict allegiance to my definition of the job of a third act—consequences of the protagonist's actions—the intrusion of the cars is the harbinger of those consequences.)
- This is another wonderful transition by Fellini. He has used so many ways to get from one scene to another, not merely to get there, but to supply mystery, energy, surprise, and narrative information (the "what" that happened between the scenes). Off of a close-up of Guido at night

watching the producer's car drive off, Fellini cuts to the rear of a car (momentarily we read it as the producer's), but in the next moment we realize that it is the next day and we are at the spaceship set with many other cars, and we appreciate the surprise.

FANTASY OR NIGHTMARE?

SPACESHIP SET/PRESS CONFERENCE: It really doesn't matter to our appreciation of the story what we call this other mode of reality, but for the purpose of this analysis I would come down on the side of nightmare. The urgency of the moment that generated this press conference in Guido's psyche would be greater during the defenselessness of sleep. This is a much more likely place for one to view his own death, and Guido has, in the first scene, demonstrated his propensity for bad dreams. What about the real press conference that the producer promised? It happened, but we never saw it.

- The first shot in this first sequence of the third act is a powerful reveal of the two towers' full majesty, and the large number of cars in the foreground attest to the drawing power of this event. It is no wonder that Guido, in the next two shots, resists attending with all his might. The camera renders Guido's reluctance from the rear, pushing in on him, nudging him inexorably closer to the towers.

- This sequence runs for four-and-one-half minutes and contains 41 shots. The first three shots, mentioned previously, are stylistically consistent with the rest of the film, but on the fourth shot the style becomes more kinetic, in both staging and camera movement. There is a documentary feel due to the frenetic pace of the scene, but the camera is always on a dolly, and the chaotic atmosphere is extremely well designed. A lot of planning went into the choreography of staging and camera. Let's take a closer look at the fourth and fifth shots in this sequence, which introduce us into the frenzied atmosphere and the style that renders it.

- The fourth shot tracks journalists running forward into a medium shot led by the American journalist. *A white veil is wafted in front of the camera*, making the cut to the next shot seamless. This fifth shot of the sequence is an extended take that pans left to right with Guido as he runs from the journalists. The pan continues, tilting up to the band playing then down as Guido moves by and continues left to right, stops, having escaped from the journalists momentarily, then moves from right to left to his wife, passes her, and is again besieged by other journalists. Cut to the sixth shot: *in-your-face* close-ups of journalists (first a pan, then tracking with them as they shout questions at Guido). We believe that this frenzied shot is Guido's POV; then, in the background, Guido himself appears in a wide shot, besieged by another group of journalists. This sudden change of spatial logic is delightful, even thrilling to some of us. At the very least, it is energizing to the story because it was not an arbitrary choice. It was not just Fellini showing off. What this break in logic does is compound the essence of the moment: BESEIGED. The audience must feel this. It must be palpable to them. It must prepare them for the gunshot.

- Every shot so far in Fellini's design for this scene has been a separate camera setup. But now, as was pointed out earlier—when the scene becomes static, when the spatial positioning between characters does not change—camera setups will more likely be broken up into edited shots. A clear example of this occurs on the dais in the exchange between Guido and his producer. Notice in these four shots that the angle on each character contains the spatial dynamics of the other character; that is, the camera is angled *up* at the producer and *down* on Guido. (Fellini stays with the shot looking down on Guido, even when the producer turns away from him. The dynamics no longer exist for this angle, *logically*, but it is more economical to stay with it because it efficiently sets up Guido looking into the image of Luisa in the mirrored image of the table. Again, in the next shot, Fellini violates logic (even nightmare logic) by placing Luisa behind the journalists.

- We have assumed that when Guido was handed something—"It's in your pocket"—that it was a gun, but we haven't seen it. Under the table, Fellini makes sure we do. First its entrance is prepared because of the difficulty Guido has in removing it from his pocket, drawing our attention to it so that the gun needs only a brief reveal to register.
- The image of Guido's mother imploring him not to kill himself is made all the more powerful by the camera pulling away from her, enabling us to feel the finality of his leave-taking.

REALITY

- The low-angle pan looking up at the scaffolding announces the return of reality. It is a desolate image: cables swaying, streamers blowing, the sound of the wind. Defeat. Guido has lost. And this image shouts it out.
- Daumier is revealed nicely, and then, as in the scene on the spa grounds when he was berating Guido about his screenplay, Daumier is given a stage because what he says is important *for us* to hear.
- On the cut from Daumier in the car to Guido outside, we see that Guido is preoccupied. *He is still trying to solve his problem!* But then, with an undeniable finality, a piece of the scaffold comes crashing to the ground, announcing to us, IT'S OVER. There is nothing more to be gained by staying here. Guido knows it. So do we. He gets into the car.
- In the car, Daumier continues his diatribe, but Guido still cannot accept the finality—that it is over. *Neither can we!* We want Guido to *do something!* We are rooting for him! But what can he do? All of these thoughts go through our mind, for *most* of us have an emotional involvement in the outcome of the film. (It is impossible to make a film that everyone will find accessible.) Then, *the move into Guido announces that he has not given up!* It is exhilarating.

IMAGINATION

- There is a distinction here between what I have labeled as active imagination (which Guido used to try and solve the problems of his story) and what occurs now. It is not the same. It no longer comes out of struggle. It is now *inspired*. Intuitive. Creativity on the highest levels. It sweeps the artist along in its power.
- Fellini also acknowledges that something different is going on here in that we are in reality and in Guido's imagination *at the same time*, in the same shot. Guido is being inspired by his muse, and he and we will be surprised. Yes, the artistic imagination was urged into orbit because of Guido's undeniable tenacity, but when in orbit, he has not much control over it. The emotions that are called up cannot be predicted. Guido is totally in the moment, *responding* to his unconscious, *embracing* the raw material being brought forth, *learning* from it, and finally, *giving it form* with his consummate directorial artistry.
- With the entrance of the four clowns and the young Guido playing Nino Rota's music, which will later be augmented by an orchestra, imagination gains complete ascent. No more cutting to Guido in reality. Take note that the band enters a familiar image: the towers.
- The big number, the finale, the event, does not just happen. The stage is first carefully prepared. The participants are gathered. We watch Guido think, *What to do with them?* And we wonder the same. Then Guido's artistry, wedded to his directing craft, takes over, and in one grand, superbly designed extended take, the finale begins.
- This take begins with Guido standing in the circus ring, pondering. Then the band enters the left side of the frame, and he comes alive as a director. The choreography of staging and camera in this one take is worth repeated study. It very much gives the feeling of more than one shot because there is so much variety in the ever-changing image size. Then the grand reveal of the staircase and the swelling of Rota's music with the full orchestra kicking off the parade of all the participants of Guido's life, streaming down from above. This is a wonderful payoff to the end of this intricate and emotionally evocative shot.

- Fellini begins this scene in daylight, but it must go to night to get his final image. He does this gracefully by *preparing* us with the introduction of production lights into the frame even though it is not yet dark. When he jumps the camera behind the dancing circle, it is still daylight, but on the second shot from behind the dancers, set up by a change in music indicating a passage of time, it is night.
- The irising down of the spotlight on the last image pays off and completes that visual motif.

SUMMARY

In the summer of 2000 I gave a lecture in Greece to a group of European writers and directors, and I analyzed this film in much the same way I have done here. When I finished, one of them came up to me. Yes, the lecture was fine, and yes, it was instructive. But what this young film-maker marveled at most was my unabashed enthusiasm for the film. The filmmaker commented on the joy I had, not so much in the story (after all, I have seen the film 50 times or more) but in the demonstration of Fellini's complete command of the directorial craft. This, when wedded to his extraordinary imagination, enabled Fellini to soar to artistic heights that few have yet been able to attain. Without this appreciation and joy of the craft itself—of the nuts and bolts of filmmaking, of the science that supports the art—it is less likely that you will be able to soar yourselves or even have a good time trying.

CHAPTER 18

STYLES AND DRAMATIC STRUCTURES

Films, like literature, painting, music, dance, theater—all art forms—come in many shapes and sizes. This book concentrates on the narrative/dramatic form of film, but obviously, even here there is great variety. In this chapter we will explore some of that variety as it is manifested in a film's style and dramatic structure.

STYLE

As mentioned earlier, there is a subtle difference between style and design, but the difference is worth recognizing. Style can be defined as an *approach* to the visualization of a story, while design can be defined as a *plan*. "Plan" has a clear and unambiguous meaning, and the methodology for such planning is introduced in this book. But what is meant by "approach"? It has a vague connotation in this context, and yet I feel it is the fullest and most inclusive definition of how a director really *works* with style, especially one that is *personal*. The roots of style can be vague, nebulous, tenuous, hazy—as opposed to design, which connotes concreteness, clarity, and intelligibility. Original styles often come from the imagination that rests in the artist's unconscious. A personal style is not something that can be "taught." An original personal style, when revealed, becomes food for fodder and can then be incorporated by future directors in their design.

There are notable exceptions to the genesis of style. In the case of Dogme 95, the handheld and natural light style was dictated by an intellectual idea stemming from a political position. After World War II, the political and intellectual climate in Italy championed the plight of the poor. This, coupled with the lack of lighting equipment, the absence of studios (used as refugee shelters), and the shortage of film stock, led to the movement known as neorealism. These films relied heavily on outdoor locations, the use of nonprofessionals as actors, and the use of long takes. In Jim Jarmuch's *Stranger in Paradise*, the short one-take scenes separated by black leader were dictated by budget constraints. The film was shot on short-ends—leftovers from other productions. In fact, there are many directors who, caught in a time bind, have had to discard a bunch of camera setups from their original design and resort to an extended take, often called a *sequence shot* (a single shot that captures all of the action in the scene either with a fixed camera position or often that relies on staging and camera movement to *articulate* the action). On the other hand, there are directors whose personal style consists of sustained sequence shots.

Setting aside unique situational reasons *outside of the artistic*, the first determinant of style is the requirements of the story being told. A romantic comedy is told differently than a thriller, an action film is told differently than a psychological drama, and for most films this is the overriding consideration. Some directors "invent" a unique style for a specific story. Two clear examples of this are *Natural Born Killers* (Oliver Stone, 1994) and *Fear and Loathing in Las Vegas* (Terry Gilliam, 1998). Some of the elements that Stone uses to convey a hyperreality in this satirical take on society's fascination with cold-blooded murders are cockeyed camera angles, extensive cross cutting between various camera stocks and formats (35 mm color, black-and-white video), the morphing of images, change of camera speeds, manipulation of the image through printing, and animation. The hallucinatory neon colors in the paintings of Robert Yarber influenced Terry Gilliam's visual depiction of the effect of psychedelic drugs on human consciousness. Gilliam and his director of photography, Nicola Pecorini, augmented Yarber's influence by the use of lighting flares coming from no discernable source, colors melting into one another, lighting levels increasing and decreasing during shots, extremely wide angles, and the morphing of shapes and colors.

There is another important factor that can influence style, and this is the director's vision of the universe. This private universe is generated by the culture that the director grew up in and the particular psychological attitudes that culture engendered. Some directors are unabashed yea-sayers—they embrace life—while others are much more reserved in their attitudes. For them, the world might not be such a friendly place. It might even be cold and dangerous. This attitude can permeate a film's style. I've alluded to the difference between Fellini and Bergman and how their attitudes toward the world influenced their styles. At the same time, these attitudes influence the story that each director chooses to tell.

NARRATIVE, DRAMATIC, AND POETIC VISUAL STYLES

The chief characteristic of the narrative visual style is that there is minimal *articulation* of action by the camera. The camera does not emphasize but instead treats all action with a more or less consistent dramatic weight. In the dramatic visual style there is a "punching up" of the action through more frequent articulation of narrative beats, often accompanied by "strong" frames—shots that contain dramatic tension *in and of themselves*. The poetic visual style features lyrical camera movements, sometimes using slow motion, and most always supported by music. Many directors use a combination of the narrative and dramatic styles in the same film, while others, to a lesser extent, weave all three styles together in one film.

THE VARIETY OF DRAMATIC STRUCTURES

The three films we examined earlier, *Notorious*, *The Truman Show*, and *8½*, all had a three-act structure: ordinary life, point of attack, rising action of second act, and consequences of that action in the third act. However, there are other paradigms, the most prevalent being what I call the *umbrella* structure: a paradigm in which multicharacter stories are subsumed under the "umbrella" of theme (*Little Children*, Todd Field, 2006), of spine (*Hanna and Her Sisters*, Woody Allen, 1986), or of location (*Nashville*, Robert Altman, 1975). These three categories are often interrelated in films, but each on its own can serve to unify a film's action. (I hope it has become clear how helpful it is for a director to understand the underlying structure of a screenplay and how this knowledge is crucial in shaping the orchestration of action.)

To explore style and structure, I've chosen 11 disparate films on no particular basis other than differences in outward appearances. Some of them are considered to be classics, all of them have had critical acclaim, and all have engaged a worldwide audience. For this chapter, I suggest that you read my commentary before viewing each film and then again after viewing.

TOKYO STORY, YASUJIRO OZU (1953, JAPAN)

DRAMATIC STRUCTURE

Although the story is organized into what could be labeled a three-act structure, it differs greatly from the three previous films we have analyzed in that there is not a protagonist driving the action of the story. There is no one character that embodies the function of an antagonist. Rather, it is the *universe* that the old couple (we will call them Mother and Father) inhabits that supplies the main action of the film and to which the old couple *react*. (The only significant action they take during the entire film is to leave Tokyo earlier than their children expected.) This larger universe is necessary to tell this story, and it is not only made up of the old couple's children and grandchildren; it is vast enough to encompass a friend's depression, the effects of the recently completed war, and the changing postwar society. The old couple is the vehicle that takes us on our journey into this universe, and they remain the emotional center for the film until almost the end—until Noriko, their dead son's wife, assumes that center position. The reason that we can make this emotional switch so easily is that both Father and Mother wanted Noriko to be happy; in fact, they gave her their permission to seek happiness. This hope of theirs for Noriko's happiness flies in the face of the improbability of it occurring in this film's universe, in which one character asks, "Isn't life disappointing?" and another answers, "I'm afraid it is." Yet against all odds, we root for Noriko's happiness.

The point of attack or inciting incident in the first act occurs when the doctor son tells Mother and Father that he must leave them to tend to a patient. The final extended scene of the first act occurs with Mother and her youngest grandson walking together outside. "By the time you'll be a doctor I wonder where I'll be?" she asks. This scene ends with a long two-shot of them then cuts to Father watching from the house. We now have a "feeling" of what this story is about. We have an emotional involvement with these two characters. We like them. We want them to be happy. The rising action of the second act begins in the beauty parlor and ends with Mother and Noriko exiting Noriko's one-room apartment, leaving the narrator (camera) alone inside. The third act begins in the Tokyo train station.

It is dramaturgically interesting that the consequence of Father and Mother's second act journey—Mother becoming ill—happens off-camera through the reactions of the family. These reactions are in keeping with the theme of the film—the theme is the primary organizing principle in this film—which is hinted at in the film's title. Although the story is grounded in specific characters, at least two of whom we care about very much, it finally transcends their individual lives and expands to encompass the lives of an entire city, of a nation, and ultimately of human existence itself.

STYLE

This film's narrator is the most reserved of any we will encounter among the films talked about in this book. The camera, with very rare exceptions, never moves, and for all but a handful of shots is placed 36 inches above the floor, about the height of an average person sitting on a tatami mat in a Japanese house. Ozu uses the restrictions of the tight quarters in these houses to create powerful geometrical compositions, but it is Ozu's masterful use of the *tableau*—his groupings of characters within a fixed frame—that we should perhaps take greatest note of, for it teaches us volumes about the power and beauty of an economical visual style *when applied to the appropriate story.* (The tableau is basically the same as the master-shot technique of rendering a scene, in which the master is used as a "base" from which the narrator then goes into the scene for articulation. Because of the formal compositions that Ozu employs, and the duration of these "master" shots, and because of their aesthetic force, I make a distinction.)

Only on rare occasions could you consider that Ozu's staging is used to make physical what is going on internally. It is used almost exclusively to render necessary action such as entrances and exits and relevant plot points such as tidying the house in preparation for guests. He delineates dramatic blocks and articulates narrative beats with the camera by changing image size or angles, rarely by putting the camera into motion. Often, within a static frame, dramatic tension is created through the *duration* of simple actions, such as packing for a trip, resting, or kneeling beside a dying mother.

The first shots of the film tell us a few things. Storywise, we learn that we are in a rural setting, and we are introduced to the train, which plays an important role. Stylistically, the static camera is introduced. It is in the first two interior scenes that the other elements of style are introduced, then locked down: camera height, the tableau that has "holes" in it that will be filled by the entrance of a character, the method that the narrator will use to articulate the story (cutting), and very importantly, the pace of the story. I suggest that you look at these first two interior scenes carefully, making sure you understand why Ozu made each cut (narrative beat). You will discover that it is either because he was "framing" a performance beat to make sure that we "got it" (either the dynamic relationships or the psychology or subtext of a line of dialogue or of an action) or because he was introducing a new character or a new dramatic block.

Father and Mother are introduced into the film as a couple in that they occupy the same frame. Every other significant character in the film is introduced separately in their own frame, even though most will initially enter the film in a tableau.

Why such a long time on the old couple packing? Because it helps not only to build the wonderfully warm, dynamic relationship between this couple but also to build expectation.

In separation, Ozu often places his camera right on the axis, which sometimes gives the appearance that characters are looking into the camera. Sometimes the sight lines *are* definitely wrong—grammatically incorrect. I believe these are mistakes, unimportant in the overall effect of this story, and I point them out only because of the nature of this book.

SOME LIKE IT HOT, BILLY WILDER (1959)

DRAMATIC STRUCTURE

This film employs a conventional three-act structure but with one key difference. There are *two active protagonists*: Josephine (Tony Curtis) and Daphne (Jack Lemmon). Although Tony Curtis, because of his scenes with Sugar (Marilyn Monroe), begins to carry more of the dramatic action, it is only a matter of degree, not dramatic function. There are also two separate conflicts: hiding from the mob (exterior) and finding love (interior). When the two conflicts cross paths at the end of the film, there is maximum tension.

The music under the main credits tells us immediately that this is a comedy. There is a wonderful unfolding of the gangster's world before the protagonists' entrance into the film (on the bandstand). This beginning establishes the narrator's ability to go with characters other than our protagonists. The protagonists are treated as one until Sugar is beholden to Daphne for taking the rap for the dropped whiskey flask. Both Daphne and Josephine have their moment on the train with Sugar, but because this story is not about a love triangle, Daphne is edged out of contention quite gracefully and then given her own love complication. The fact that Daphne would agree to go on a date with the millionaire playboy would be hard to swallow in a "real" universe, but with the tone established in this one, we willingly suspend our disbelief, as we do when the yachting clothes—complete with glasses and hat—which fit Josephine perfectly, fall into her/his hands. In comedies, we are given a much broader license in dealing with coincidence.

The ending is open. As an audience we do not require that everything, including Daphne's impending marriage, be tidied up, even though her paramour knows she is a man. For the universe that was created in this story, we are well satisfied. Making any further sense out of things would have intruded on the tone.

STYLE

As in most comedies, Wilder renders the majority of the action in a wide frame—lots of "air." A character's actions are surrounded by ambiance and/or other character's reactions. Close-ups are used sparingly. This prevents the frame from killing the joke by punching it up too sharply—by trying too hard. Keeping the personality of this low-key narrator consistent, Wilder articulates narrative beats, through changes of angle or image size, sparingly. Also, when rendering action he prefers to stage it in sustained takes, rendering it with a fluid camera. An example of this occurs in the first act when we discover our protagonists playing in the band, then again when the camera tilts up from the street to discover our protagonists climbing down the fire escape. Because it is necessary at times for Wilder to make sure that we read certain plot points, the narrator's ability to fragment an action is established early on—for example, the spats, the protagonists walking on heels toward the train, and the whiskey flask strapped to Sugar's leg.

Wilder handles the dual protagonists very craftily. They are introduced in the same frame on the bandstand then are always rendered in the same frame *until* Sugar smiles at Daphne for taking the rap when the whiskey flask falls onto the floor. Daphne is then rendered in separation for the first time. There is a graceful cutting of the umbilical cord here, and one that is absolutely needed for the continuance of this story.

The swish-pans used in getting from Josephine and Sugar on the yacht, to Daphne and the millionaire playboy dancing the tango in the night club, then back again, are effective in tying the two protagonists together. A butt-cut would not have generated the feeling of connectedness between them. Another function of the swish-pan when used as a transition is that it mitigates the expository nature when rendering parallel actions, especially when the two separate actions are not *urgently connected*. (In comedies there is much more of a license to use stylistic anomalies—something that has not been previously introduced or is rendered acceptable due to its *appropriateness to the moment*—than in dramas.)

THE BATTLE OF ALGIERS, GILLO PONTECORVO (1965, FRANCE)

DRAMATIC STRUCTURE

Except for the bookends of Ali-la-Pointe hiding behind the fake wall, the film's structure is based on a chronology of actual events, and that is both its weakness and its strength. Chronology, in and of itself, is not dramatic and might be just the opposite.

There is an and-then-and-then-and-then quality to the film that, if it were fictional, would not engage us very much. It is our belief that the characters in the film actually existed, and acted in the manner they did, that gives the film its power. Just think of the story's power if the characters and events had been rendered in reality—if it had been a cinema verité documentary. It would have been riveting.

Because of the strict adherence to chronology, and even more so, trying to tell the whole story of the conflict from both sides and giving so many characters their rightful acknowledgment, the structure is necessarily fragmented, episodic. Because characters disappear from the film for long periods of time, especially Ali-la-Pointe, who we first assume will be the protagonist, it is difficult for us to gain emotional access to anyone. However, we do have an emotional stake in the F.L.N.'s cause. We want them to win their liberation from the French. Still, I think most of you will find yourselves somewhat removed from events for long stretches of the film. A lot of it, especially the time spent with the French paratrooper colonel, is expository in nature (all of the voice-over in the film is expository) and not dramatically compelling. We are getting facts. Again, *if* it had been a real documentary, *if* this same material had been rendered with the actual French colonel, it would have been fascinating, but a mere re-creation of historical events, no matter how compelling they might have been, falls short of engaging us fully, and the biggest reason for that is because we are outside of the characters' heads. For the most part, we see the surface of things and do not *feel* the inner life of the characters.

However, there are sequences that are constructed with some of the dramatic categories that we have explored earlier, and these sequences are the most suspenseful. Two sequences stick out. The first is when Ali is given the test to shoot the policeman. It is a complete three-act dramatic sequence. Ali is given instructions in the first act. He attempts the assassination in the second, and here there is real dramatic elaboration. The moment is stretched to accommodate and convey all the dramatic tension inherent in the situation. Then in the third act, Ali fires at the policeman and discovers that the gun is empty. During this entire sequence we are totally engaged because we are anticipating, participating in the unfolding, and hoping and fearing. Another sustained sequence that is very effective in creating dramatic tension and emotional involvement—because it too has a beginning, middle, and end—and allows us to *participate in the unfolding* is the women planting bombs.

STYLE

Pontecorvo has done a magnificent job in casting, in staging events (especially the large crowd scenes), and in creating a sense of verisimilitude. His use of the documentary style camera when rendering the actions of the Arabs lends to the overall authenticity. For me, however, the second narrative voice, the "classical" coverage used to cover the French, is jarring. There appears to be no dramatic reason for the two narrative voices, and the second takes us out of the immediacy, the urgency, of the first.

The immediacy, the urgency of a documentary is conveyed by the fact that the narrator does not know what is going to happen next and is therefore not omniscient. The best that the narrator can do is anticipate. This immediacy, this urgency, this never-to-happen-again moment is what Pontecorvo conveys with his camera *even though he knows exactly what is going to happen*. What qualities does this narrator have? First of all it is fluid, ready to go anywhere, handheld. Because it is handheld, the frame "breathes." There is a sense of action "caught on the fly." Out-of-focus shots and less than perfect compositions help to convey this. Because the narrator must often stand outside of a scene, a zoom lens facilitates getting closer. There are no tracks or cranes. The solid base of a tripod is allowed *at appropriate times*.

At the end of the film, the camera becomes more kinetic in style as the Arab population rises up spontaneously. This is conveyed very strongly by Pontecorvo. The camera is *in* the melee. It is swept along by its power. There are more out-of-focus shots and swish-pans. The cutting becomes more jarring, even "ragged." The pictures are not "pretty." What is happening is not pretty. This is a wonderfully rendered sequence and is most likely the reason for the disclaimer at the beginning of the film that no newsreel footage was used in the making of this film.

There is one other narrative voice in this film. It is that of the French colonel's hidden camera. I suggest that it would have been more authentic to have given this camera a distinctive voice—one that was restricted by the obligation to be surreptitious.

There is one subjective voice that is unnecessary and therefore seems arbitrary. It is the French colonel's view through his binoculars.

RED, KRZYSZTOF KIESLOWSKI (1994, POLAND, FRANCE, SWITZERLAND)

DRAMATIC STRUCTURE

This is the last film in a color trilogy, *Blue*, *White*, and *Red*, and is also the last film before Kieslowski's untimely death. It is more narrative (novelistic) in tone and structure than dramatic, focusing on aesthetics and intellectual concerns more than on psychological states, more on ambiguity than on clarity. Even though the main theme of fraternity is clear enough, the harmonics surrounding it suggest a much more complicated universe.

The film does seem to have a classical first act. We have a protagonist, Valentine. We are introduced to her ordinary life: her jealous boyfriend, her neighbor, her job. There is an inciting incident: running over the dog. And there is a question mark raised at the end of the first act: What will happen in the relationship between the Judge and Valentine? The first act ends when Valentine tells the Judge, "Stop breathing," and he answers, "Good idea." The second act begins with Valentine discovering the Judge's spying on his neighbors and begins her rising action in which she eventually forces the Judge to review his behavior, change it, and embrace a new vision of life. But what about Auguste, Valentine's neighbor? How does he fit into the scheme of things? Is he a mirror—a younger version of the Judge? Is his girlfriend's betrayal of him the Judge's girlfriend's betrayal? What is the dramatic or narrative function of Valentine's jealous boyfriend? These questions are left open, as is the larger question that has been raised throughout and comes to a head at the very end of the film. Is Valentine and Auguste's survival due to fate, chance, or magical intervention of the Judge? Here the consequences of Valentine's actions *do not* inevitably lead to the ending *unless* there is fate, magic, or God's intervention due to Valentine's good deeds in reconciling the Judge to life.

Without the clear conflict that we have seen in the other films discussed in this book, without the moment-to-moment psychology of the characters being available to us, and *with* ambiguous happenings and relationships, *Red* still succeeds in engaging us on a very high level. Why? I maintain that it is due to Kieslowski's overriding vision of life that pervades every frame of this film coupled with a consummate cinematic artistry. Let's see if we can discover some of his secrets.

STYLE

Frank Daniel, to whom this book is dedicated, told me that there are some directors whose personal vision is enough to unify the action of a film, and this is certainly true of Kieslowski. How is that vision manifested in this film? First of all by the color red. It is introduced immediately and pervades the entire film. What does it supply? For me, it helps create an atmosphere of disquiet, unease, passion—everything the opposite of calm, pacific, serene, which is what Valentine is striving for. This constant reminder makes us continually aware of the undercurrents flowing throughout this film—it constantly raises the possibility of danger, even death.

In the very first sequence—the telephone call—the objective narrator mimics the speed and distance of the call, supplying urgency and a mysterious relationship that contextualizes the rest of the film. Right away, Kieslowski complicates the mystery by cutting to Auguste (Valentine's neighbor). Did he make the phone call? Right away we must *work* to make sense, and Kieslowski then supplies the clues to allow us to do just that. This intellectual "putting together" of the story's fragmented structure is one of the aesthetic pleasures we derive from this film. Kieslowski keeps us working throughout by coming in on the middle of scenes where we don't know where we are or what is happening. Valentine's photo shoot is an example of this.

Kieslowski layers his story with intrusions of the outside world into ordinary scenes, thereby supplying a constant reminder of the threat lurking out there in a universe that can be dangerous. He does this early on with the helicopter noise invading Valentine's apartment so that she must shut the window to keep it out. Likewise, she must shut the French doors of the theater when the storm forces its way in. There is also the rock through the Judge's window and the glue stuck in Valentine's door. These reminders serve to contextualize the moments they inhabit, resonating within us, deepening the story.

Kieslowski's camera has the freedom to move whenever it likes. This is setup in the first sequence—the long distance phone call—and locked down in Valentine's apartment when the camera moves to the window on her line, "It's spring outside," anticipating her movement into the frame, announcing the narrator's omniscience. The camera/narrator is constantly tying together the chance intersection of lives, usually connecting one character to another with a pan or tracking shot. The camera's freedom extends not only to mimicking the flow of electrical current in a phone wire but to racing after a bowling ball, this latter movement supplying narrative thrust on a transition. The objective camera can comment on the present by showing us the aftermath of the past, as when it pulls back from the Judge as he is telling Valentine that he has turned himself in, and moves urgently to another room to discover the broken bottle on the writing desk.

When Valentine enters the Judge's house a second time, we see her entrance through her subjective POV. She then steps into her subjective POV, turning the shot into the narrator's objective voice. The narrator follows Valentine for a bit, only to leave her and push in on the Judge sitting at his desk. The subjective and objective voices are interchangeable here, physically mirroring one of the underlying themes of the story.

The smallest, seemingly insignificant moments are made pregnant with meaning by the camera's lingering on a character. This is especially true in the camera's attention to Valentine. Because of this attention, we try to get inside her head, but often we do not succeed. Her psychology is not always available to us, and yet, because of the overall atmosphere of the film's universe, we understand *something*, even though we are not able to intellectualize what that is—certainly not at the moment we are experiencing it.

Although Kieslowski's style is more narrative/poetic than dramatic, he uses dramatic elements when they are appropriate to his story, thereby creating palpable suspense. Elaboration is used to bring Valentine to and into the Judge's house the first time when she brings the hurt dog, and again, this stretching of time is used when Auguste climbs up the side of a building and discovers his girlfriend in bed with another man.

Other energizing aspects of Kieslowski's style, structured into the screenplay and finessed through editing, are the disbursement of fragmented narrative information throughout the film, butting up of one image against another, forcing us to make connections *on some level*. Many times these connections are below our level of consciousness, or at least of our ability to understand their meaning, *until later in the film*, when the narrative process is completed.

Kieslowski uses strong reveals, perhaps the strongest being Valentine's face on the billboard with the traffic in the foreground. This is a very nice payoff to a sparse narrative equation consisting of three factors: photo session + selecting from proofs + phone call from photographer = billboard.

SEX, LIES, AND VIDEOTAPE, STEVEN SODERBERGH (1989)

DRAMATIC STRUCTURE

This film is an example of an *umbrella* structure, one where the spine or main action of one of the characters unites the main actions of the other characters. In this case, Ann's spine "covers" her husband John's, her sister Cindy's, and her husband's college friend Graham's. Ann's spine, "to find a solution to her dissatisfaction with her life," is precipitated by sexual dissatisfaction, but that is only symptomatic of a larger problem in her life, as is the case with the other three characters.

Parallel action at the very beginning of the film, along with overlapping dialogue, helps to establish the interconnectedness of these four characters while also giving the narrator license to go with any one of them. (In Woody Allen's *Hannah and Her Sisters*, 1986, the spine of Allen's character, Mickey, serves as the umbrella for the spines of the other characters.)

Within this overriding structure, there is still a three-act organization of action, not for a protagonist, but for *everyone*. (No matter what the structure, action should be precipitated, should escalate, and should have consequences if you want to engage an audience from beginning to end.) The second act begins on the cut to the first video (rising action), and the third act consequences begins with the pan to John from the "snow" on the television monitor after the flashback.

The long taping scene between Ann and Graham is rendered as a flashback, enabling it to be contextualized by John's knowledge and anger. It raises the stakes for the scene. If it had appeared chronologically, this long scene would not have nearly the power it has as a flashback.

STYLE

A lot of directing craft is quietly on display in this spatially static film (people mostly sit and talk, and they talk a lot about the past), and yet there is a constant narrative thrust. This is done for the most part by the objective narrator, in what I call an *eclectic* style. Soderbergh's sentence structure, his rendering of each scene, is determined by the requirements of the scene and not by an overarching aesthetic. This is by no means a criticism; many fine contemporary directors use such a style.

Soderbergh uses a moving camera as well as pronounced articulation through cutting to keep the story lively, continually finding different ways to energize spatially static scenes; but also, when the scene permits, he combines the camera with almost casual, realistic staging that masks its deeper dramatic function. Let's look at some of the specific and varied ways Soderbergh goes about keeping us engaged in this story.

The scene in Ann's living room where Graham and Ann first talk is rendered in what I would call a conventional style, but when Graham *returns* from his first trip to the bathroom, "a false alarm," the camera renders it from a high angle, calling our attention to the strangeness of his behavior. Then when Graham *exits* for the bathroom a second time, the camera punctuates this strange behavior with another high-angle shot, this time of Ann sitting on the couch. It is obvious to us, because of Soderbergh's use of this unambiguous narrative beat, that she is also aware that there is something odd about this guy.

In the dinner scene that follows, Soderbergh uses a moving camera that eventually excludes the husband from the frame for the remainder of the dramatic block, even when he is directly addressed. The last dramatic block for this scene is announced, and then rendered, with a very high angle, imbuing the scene with a feeling of distance between the two men.

Soderbergh never does more than he has to, and in this economy an ordinary scene becomes interesting—for example, Graham and Ann viewing the empty apartment, rendered in one take, using the geometry of the space to help create a sense of narrative movement.

Two scenes illustrate how Soderbergh uses the dramatic ingredients of a scene, along with the possibilities of a specific space, to choreograph staging and camera. In the first, the scene in Cindy's apartment that takes place between her and Ann, Soderbergh keeps the two women separated for an extended period of time, keeping Ann in the foreground of the shot, making physical the internals of their dynamic relationship. In the second scene, when Cindy pays an unexpected visit to Graham's apartment, she remains "glued" to the doorway area, hesitant to advance further. When she does eventually move *into* the room to look at the videotape collection, it announces a huge change in the dynamics—something is going to happen between these two. This is a long scene, and Soderbergh deftly changes the stage for the taping session, then within the session, changes the staging again; Graham gets on the floor, Cindy gets into a semifetal position on the couch. A palpable intimacy is established. Then there is an abrupt cut to Cindy leaving.

Soderbergh also varies the rhythm between scenes. In the scene following the taping session—Cindy finishing having sex with John—the entire scene is rendered in three close-ups.

A wonderful example of psychology changed into behavior that can be photographed occurs when Ann discovers Cindy's earring in the vacuum cleaner. We not only understand her cognitive journey but her emotional journey as well.

SHALL WE DANCE?, MASAYUKI SUO (1996, JAPAN)

DRAMATIC STRUCTURE

Mr. Sugiyama, an accountant, is the protagonist of this film, and Mai, a beautiful dancer, is the antagonist, although this is not a love story because its parameters are larger. To tell this larger story, it is important for the narrator to leave the protagonist, and this ability is set up after the first montage that establishes Mr. Sugiyama's ordinary life. When he leaves for work, the camera stays with his wife and daughter having breakfast.

A three-act structure organizes the action, but because the film develops many subplots with secondary characters, the delineation between the first and second acts is muddy. However, this is no detriment to the story. (The three-act structure is not meant to force the story into an uncomfortable ideal mold, but rather it should serve as a road map for developing action.)

After everyone, including Aoki (the coworker with the wig), has entered the film, the first act ends with the first scene in the dance hall when Mr. Sugiyama tries his hand at social dancing and is defeated. Humiliated, he sits down. The camera holds on him. A question is raised: Will he continue? Rising action in the next scene (Mr. Sugiyama dancing in his pajamas), followed soon thereafter by his wife seeking out a private detective, begins the second act. (This rising action by not only Sugiyama, but also his wife, is why I would designate this the beginning of the second act. Some might wait until Mai turns down Sugiyama for dinner, and she is "rude" to him, raising the same question: Will he continue to dance?)

There is a precredit scene whose purpose is twofold: to frame the film's social climate vis-à-vis dancing and to introduce us to an important location for two of Mai's flashbacks. It is then used as a bookend for the end credits.

Masayuki Suo, the writer/director of this film, uses his knowledge of directing craft to construct the screenplay, fashioning entire sequences out of one-shot scenes. Each image is strong and unambiguous, providing a sense of time passing along with progress in the dance lessons. In fact, the entire film's time is "muddied" so cleverly that its actual duration, one year, is never felt, yet when the actual time is finally mentioned, it seems entirely plausible.

The first culmination of action in the second act occurs when Mr. Sugiyama commits to being Toyoko's partner after she collapses during rehearsals. The final culmination of action in the second act occurs when Mr. Sugiyama, after stepping on Toyoko's dress, watches his wife and daughter leave the dance contest. The third act—consequences of the action of the second act—begins in the Sugiyama's home with a false ending: Mr. Sugiyama gives up dancing. Of course, we know at this moment, or at least we hope, that this is not true. And it turns out not to be so.

We should take note of the two flashbacks that are used here, both generating more interest simply by the fact that they are being told by Mai to Mr. Sugiyama. Her telling is an action that takes place in the present and has an urgent motivation, making the past immediately relevant and not merely expository. We should also note that each character, including Mr. Sugiyama's daughter, is given a dramatic arc.

STYLE

Suo's style is basically narrative, which is to say that for the most part, he renders the action clearly, "framing it" only when dramatically necessary. Because the actors' wants are usually so clear, so externalized, it is most often not necessary for Suo to frame or articulate the essence of a moment. That it not to say that he abdicates responsibility to tell the story engagingly; on the contrary, by using his director's "arsenal" only when the story absolutely requires it, this quiet story is allowed to unfold without the director unnecessarily hyping it. Let's look how some of this arsenal is used.

Suo quickly establishes a familiar image of the dance studio's window from a low angle. This angle serves both the train interior and the exterior station platform.

Some of the secondary characters, especially Sugiyama's daughter, Aoki (the coworker with a wig), and Tanaka (the big guy), have quite oblique entrances into the film. In other words, they subtly enter this quiet film so as not to overwhelm the story. When it is time for them to emerge, to reveal their dramatic function, they are in position. (Toyoko has the most oblique entrance.)

In the first dance lesson, Suo uses Mr. Sugiyama's POV to internalize his infatuation with Mai and his disappointment in having to work with the older teacher. The image of Mai always comes off of a medium close-up of Mr. Sugiyama. This "ordinary" POV sets up the "strong" POV that occurs at the final dance contest, when Mr. Sugiyama's daughter calls out the second time, "Dad!" Sugiyama twists his body around, searching. His POV simulates this movement, swish-panning first one way and then another.

As I pointed out, Suo tells his story "merely" by rendering the action of the characters clearly, but there are a few times in which he dramatically elaborates moments, even an entire scene. The elaboration takes on different guises. For example, he uses slow motion to elaborate the moment when Sugiyama steps on Toyoko's dress. Then, at the party, the final scene of the film, Suo elaborates Mai's choosing her final dance partner of the night. He uses 18 shots to lengthen this wonderful moment. To squeeze out even more drama, Suo jumps the axis between Sugiyama and Mai after the overhead shot. The elaboration ends with Mai's "Shall we dance?"

As mentioned in the section on dramatic structure, Suo's familiarity with the director's craft emboldens his screenplay and his orchestration of the many one-shot scenes, melding Sugiyama's various worlds through the skillful juxtaposition of unambiguous images, edited together with an equally adept sense of rhythm. One montage sequence especially encapsulates Suo's style. It begins with Sugiyama's feet under his desk, practicing—then in the dance hall—then Mai watching him practicing on the train platform—then his wife practicing dance steps from a magazine—then Sugiyama seated in a train, practicing—then in an open space, wearing a back brace, Sugiyama dances with style and grace, watched by two private detectives. Another wonderful sequence employing this graceful style occurs when Mai agrees to coach Sugiyama and Toyoko. The first shot of the sequence is of Sugiyama on a bicycle, coming after Mai's smiling assent to the coaching job. It goes on to elaborate her working with Sugiyama and Toyoko, showing with great economy the progress that is being made. This stylized sequence sets up the first flashback, when Mai was a little girl at Black Pool. The flashback engenders a long, confessional scene between Mai and Sugiyama. This extended sequence derives much of its power from the three distinct but integrated designs that come together in an overarching narrative/dramatic style.

Suo made a simple but important stylistic decision in the shooting of the dance numbers. He knew that he would have to show the dancing in its entirety at times (from head to toe) so that we could fully appreciate it, but he also understood that he would have to fragment it for dramatic and narrative purposes (hands, feet). Both capabilities were introduced in the first dance class.

THE CELEBRATION, THOMAS VINTERBERG (1998, DENMARK)

DRAMATIC STRUCTURE

This story fits quite nicely into the umbrella structure that we saw in *Sex, Lies, and Videotape,* with Christian's main action serving to unify everyone else's. Not only does Christian, the emotional center of this story, thematically unify everyone's action, but he actively initiates and drives the main action of the entire film: to expose the dirty secret that has poisoned the heart of this family.

The film has no distinct division of action into acts, and what might be considered the beginning—the setup—is quite long. What keeps alive the quite considerable narrative thrust that this film exhibits? The first is Christian and the mystery that seems to lie at the heart of his being. The second is the frenetic style of the narrator, which seems to imbue the most ordinary transactions with an urgency and underlying violence. Third, the first part of the film is constantly energized by the parallel action—cutting from one scene to another *before* either scene has ended, causing us to anticipate how scenes will end, while continually weaving the family together, making the fact of family palpable. These abrupt transitions—one scene colliding with another—are like miniexplosions, keeping us off guard. We never know what to expect next. *Within* scenes there are sudden explosions of anger, stopping just short of overt violence. There are no significant plot points during the long arrival at the hotel and the settling in, yet because of these dramatic devices, the narrative thrust never wanes.

After a time in any story, the promise of something happening is not enough. Something must happen, and it does, before one final promise: The father announces dinner, and the camera moves in on Christian, announcing to us that we do not have long to wait for that something to happen. When Christian delivers his speech, a dam breaks in the structure of the story, and plot points spew forth—the chef gives orders to steal the car keys, the sister's black boyfriend arrives, the dead sister's letter is read (the letter itself is a plot point that was introduced earlier, supplying a good amount of suspense). The promise of the long setup is kept.

As in a classical three-act structure, the film ends with the consequences of the film's main action: the family's coming to grips with the awful truth.

A few dramaturgical craft points should be noted. Although the film begins with Christian, it immediately switches its point of view to Michael in the car, announcing straightaway that this narrator has the freedom to roam from one character to another. The dinner scene, which is spatially static, is "broken up" by a fight, a dance, the kitchen, etc., creating a much more interesting dramatic orchestration, breaking up this "set piece" so that each of its "movements" is framed by the event that preceded it.

The other mode of reality that was introduced, Christian's visiting with his dead twin sister, is at first otherworldly, and I feel it works on that level because it comes at an *emotionally appropriate* time, and we accept it. The screenplay then skillfully turns this other world into Christian's dream, but the "reality" of the dead sister stays with us.

STYLE

This film was shot on digital video and transferred to film. Although the style stems from the dictates of Dogme 95, we shall view it apart from any political agenda to see its effect on this story.

The handheld camera is introduced immediately. Its lack of stability is exaggerated. (The camera can be held steadier and framed more accurately, even if it is handheld.) The kinetic camera, the abrupt cuts, and the occasional zoom creates a frenetic, charged atmosphere, even when rendering fairly ordinary actions, imparting a heightened tension that the actions in and of themselves would not have. The style itself promises conflict. It seems to me, however, that this frenetic narrator almost goes over the top at times, but pulls back in time, settling down to render some scenes in a fairly "classical" style. Is there a reason that it changes its style? Yes, and it is a simple one. Some of the scenes do not lend themselves to an emotional interpretation. To render them with a frenetic camera would bend them out of shape.

A scene that does lend itself to an emotional rendering occurs between Michael and his wife when they are looking for his shoes. (Michael is almost always rendered with a frenetic camera, imbuing him with a volatility and possibility of violence.) The camera heightens the discord between husband and wife, making palpable their dynamic relationship.

When the camera becomes wedded to the action, the narrator in the middle of the fray, the staging cannot be used to internalize what is going on (and of course it doesn't need to in these situations because everyone's psychology is immediately available to us). However, there are times when the psychology of a character or characters, or their dynamic relationship, must be conveyed to the audience, and staging is the most efficient and powerful way. A good example of this is in the "shoe" scene. Michael calls a halt in the fighting. Both husband and wife sit on the end of the bed, rendered in a wide two-shot. The shot says "truce." Out of that truce, Michael attacks again, this time sexually.

Vinterberg uses tableaus, especially high shots from the ceiling, to punctuate the ending of scenes, using these shots to nail down the consequences of a scene, or in some cases, to articulate a mood or atmosphere—as in the scene in the dead twin's room, where the uncovering of the furniture is rendered from the high angle.

Vinterberg reveals the geography of the location as needed. Michael running through the hotel to meet with his father not only imparts an urgency to the moment, but it reveals the space, especially the "connectedness" of the various rooms, setting up the same journey that Christian will take later when he returns to the dinner.

The harshness of the light and the graininess of this film, especially noticeable when projected onto a screen, works for this film. It does not work so well for all stories.

THE INSIDER, MICHAEL MANN (1999)

DRAMATIC STRUCTURE

This film inhabits a large universe, frequented by two protagonists and a host of other characters. Perhaps technically, Jeffrey Wigand (Russell Crowe) could be considered Lowell Bergman's (Al Pacino) antagonist, but this appellation seems too limiting, as does the three-act structure, simply because all the action in this multidimensional universe does not fit into such a neat package. As mentioned, in cases like this it is often helpful to think in the broader terms of beginning, middle, and end (as Aristotle suggested), which still offer an organizing principle for action but allow a wider inclusion.

The beginning of the film, the setup, is long and intricate, with a lot of expository information to get out. It ends with the email, "We will kill you," followed immediately by the bullet in the mailbox. Action and plot complications for *both* Bergman and Wigand escalate during the middle of the film. The stakes become higher for both men. The end game for the film, the consequences of all of the action, *for everyone*, begins with Bergman driving in the snow, looking for a new story. Even here, the "cigarette story" is kept alive, symptomatic of one of the key principles at work in this screenplay: keeping all of the balls in the air. This is what keeps the story's *entire* universe alive, even when we go away from a particular character for extended periods of time. The ability to go from one character to another is set up immediately after the Iran sequence with a cut to Wigand leaving his office.

Like *The Battle of Algiers*, this is a true story, but there is a large difference. The former kept a distance—the tone was journalistic—whereas this film invites us into the heads of the characters. We understand their psychology moment by moment, and therefore we gain emotional access to them. That only happens because in fashioning this screenplay, a conscious commitment was made to be emotionally involving, even downright riveting if possible. It began with a basic question that every screenwriter and director must ask himself or herself: What is my story about? The essential answer is that it is about the relationship between Bergman and Wigand. That is the central conflict of this story.

STYLE

Just as the screenplay commits to telling a powerful, emotionally involving story, equally so does the director, Michael Mann. His directing style is what I call "muscular." He grips the audience in a headlock and never lets go. Yes, sometimes he loosens his grip, but only temporarily, letting us catch our breath for a moment. This modulation in the narrator's voice, in the decibel level if compared to an oral storyteller, is wonderfully controlled throughout.

The driving beat of the music and the heavily elaborated driving sequence that opens the film announces immediately that we are in for high drama. The "grabbing" of the ambiance of the street with a documentary-style camera says, "This is real!" It wins us over. "Yes, that must be how it was." This faith in the narrator to tell us the truth carries over into the rest of the film.

Mann pulls out all of the director's tools to tell this story: Aside from the opening elaboration, Mann uses heavy articulation through multiple angles in the following interview scene and jumps the axis to create tension. The narrator has made his presence felt and continues to do so with the use of slow motion to render Wigand leaving his office building, underscored by an eerie music. This same combination is used in the next scene when Wigand enters his home. A dreamlike world is set up, a contrast to Bergman's noisy, "real" universe. Yet the dream state doesn't last for long. Wigand's daughter's asthma attack is rendered with a frenetic, handheld camera, imbuing the moment with extreme urgency.

Mann often uses a "breathing" camera in much "quieter" scenes. Whether it is handheld in some cases or on a steadicam, it imbues the scene with a "roughness" that, when combined with abrupt cuts as found in a documentary, creates urgency. In one such scene, Bergman tries to contact Wigand by fax, then goes to the phone book, finds a number, and makes a call. In another scene, one that does not have an underlying urgency, Mann uses the breathing camera to foreshadow what is about to occur. Wigand's wife is in the kitchen cooking dinner. She hears the computer signal and goes down to the basement to discover on the screen an email, "We will kill you."

Mann modulates his coverage from scene to scene, changing the tone by changing the style in which the scene is rendered. At times he uses a perfectly fluid camera movement to render action. This mixing of styles, never arbitrary—always serving the needs of the particular scene in its relation to the whole story—is akin to the orchestration of a symphony. In fact, Mann's use of music to create atmosphere and emotion is extremely effective.

In the Japanese restaurant, Mann uses heavy articulation—many image changes, again including a jump across the axis to the other side of the room—to call our attention to the depth of the underlying tension in the scene *before* it is revealed in action.

The stylistic device that we are perhaps most aware of is Mann's use of the telephoto lens. It is used from the beginning of the film, gradually making its presence *felt*. It manifests itself in sharply defined images that have either a background or foreground that is out of focus, drawing all the more attention to what is in focus. This fits Mann's close attention to detail—a hand, the rim of Wigand's glasses. These details are not poetic, not metaphors, but the intimacy with which we view them imparts a significance that forces our attention beneath the surface of a scene. At other times our attention is directed from one place to another by racking the focus on the long lenses, another example of how Mann exerts near-total control of our attention.

I don't mean to imply that there is no poetry in this film. There is, and it is a powerful addition to what could have been a high-powered, realistic drama, which it is most of the time. However, Mann transcends this genre by creating at times an ethereal universe, a dreamscape around Wigand. The ambient sound of a scene drops out, otherworldly music takes its place, and the images are often enigmatic, dreamlike, mirroring Wigand's internal dialogue: "This isn't real. What is happening to me just isn't real." The first image at the driving range is an example of this otherworldliness. Mann keeps this dreamscape alive throughout, such as when Wigand invites Bergman to drive with him to his daughter's school. It is raining heavily, and the images of the windshield wipers, combined with the silence, create this atmosphere anew. It occurs again when Wigand is being driven to court with the large police escort. The payoff of this access to Wigand's psychology is the transformation of the mural in his hotel room into a hallucination of his daughter playing. Not only is this crucial to our understanding of Wigand's deep despair, but craftwise it keeps the daughter "alive" for her appearance at the end of the film, proud of her daddy on television.

THE THIN RED LINE, TERRENCE MALICK (1998)

DRAMATIC STRUCTURE

As much as any film we have discussed, and more than most, this film is a product of the personal vision of the artist, writer/director Terrence Malick. This does not mean that I think it is a better film; it simply means that Malick's vision of the universe—the universe that *he* inhabits—permeates the story, and it is both *evident* and *available*.

The story is based on a James Jones novel, and structurally it—the story of Charlie Company in the throes of battle—is what gives the film its movement, its narrative thrust. Take the ridge. Try to stay alive. Try to stay sane. To this, Malick adds another layer, a transcendent layer—some might call it spiritual. It is rendered in a nonlinear narrative form akin to poetry. It is interesting that the colonel, Nick Nolte, mentions the Greek poet Homer and quotes from one of his epic poems, for this is what Malick seems to be striving for here.

The nonlinear element is introduced first, allowing us to become immersed in it before the harder edges of the plot are introduced, and they are introduced quite subtly. We find Witt talking to Sergeant Welsh (Sean Penn). We have no idea that Witt is in the brig of a Navy ship, but we figure it out, and there is an aesthetic pleasure in doing so.

STYLE

The film starts off with the image of a crocodile sliding into the water, followed by images of sunlight and trees. An interior monologue is heard from Witt, a soldier we have yet to meet: "Why does nature violate itself?" *Nature* is at the heart of the thematic unity present here, and *everything* is nature. Malick weaves its imagery throughout the entire film; the trees—especially the trees—birds, sun, moon, an animal, an insect, the natives, the Japanese, the American soldiers. Everyone. Witt asks, "Who are you to live in all these many forms?"

Malick sets up the universe and the narrative/poetic style in which he is going to tell his story early on. The film begins with the poetic images that inform the more straightforward narrative of Charlie Company's mission to clear the island of all Japanese, and these poetic renderings of scenes appear throughout. One memorable poetic phrase begins with flamethrowers, continues with huts burning, wind chimes, a statue of Buddha, and ends with a pan to the night sky.

The action sequences are filmed with consummate artistry and craft. Malick concentrates much of his attention on individuals shot in separation, but he continually ties the separation together in vistas so that we are constantly aware of the whole *when it matters to our appreciation of the story*. At other times he leaves us disoriented when it supplies dramatic tension or imparts a meaning that goes beyond logic.

There is a familiar moving image that Malick uses: the camera pushing ahead on reconnaissance, sometimes across a field, sometimes through a bamboo thicket, sometimes up a hill. This movement is sometimes tied to a subject—a soldier—and we assign it as a subjective POV. Other times this same movement is not assigned to a character and so becomes the objective narrator moving ahead, anticipating. It is this nondistinction between the subjective and objective that of course goes to the heart of this film's theme: There is no difference.

Malick uses a combination of visual poetry and Witt's interior monologue (even though he has been killed) to impart a positive tone to the end of Witt's journey. An image of bright light coming through the trees follows the killing of Witt. Then the freedom of his transformation is captured in the metaphor of swimming. To end the larger story of the film, Malick uses Witt's interior monologue over the faces of Charlie Company: "Oh my soul . . . look out through my eyes at the things you made. All things shine."

IN THE MOOD FOR LOVE, KAR WAI WONG (2001, CHINA)

DRAMATIC STRUCTURE

According to published stories, Mr. Wong worked without a screenplay for this film, meaning that much of the story and structure were discovered in the work with actors and in shooting and reshooting, then orchestrated in the editing. However, this does not alter the fact that the film has a three-act structure with a protagonist and an antagonist. Some have suggested that there are two protagonists and that the culture of the society, and/or ethical restraint on both their parts, is the antagonist. I don't happen to agree, but without arguing the dramaturgical validity of this position, let's proceed to a more relevant question: What is the central conflict of the film? The answer: Will Mr. Chow (Tony Leung Chiu-wai) and Mrs. Chan (Maggie Cheung Man-yuk) become lovers? To that end it is he who *drives the action* of the film by pursuing the object of his desire, and it is she who *resists* his advances. The culture of their society along with their married statuses are without question the overriding component of their circumstance, determining the extent to which they allow themselves to respond to their desire for each other.

On first viewing you might have trouble recognizing the three-act structure that organizes the subtle action of this love story between Mr. Chow and Mrs. Chan, who have moved into rooms in adjoining apartments in 1962 Hong Kong. The extremely cramped living situation along with the frequent absence of their respective spouses slowly, but inexorably, changes the relationship from a rather formal neighborliness, to one of intimate friendship, to that of lovers, platonic or otherwise. This inexorable journey toward love is the main tension of the film—a tension that is supremely palpable. Wong accomplishes this with a stylistic virtuosity that is firmly supported by an underlying dramatic structure.

The Point of Attack (also known as inciting incident) in the first act occurs when Mr. Chow realizes that his wife is having an affair. Then in a dinner with Mrs. Chan, both come to the realization that each of their spouses is having an affair with each other. This betrayal fuels the rising action of the second act, leading to what might be described as a "formal" intimacy, which culminates in an assignation in a hotel room where it seems to me that they make love, although some commentators believe this remains ambiguous. (Mrs. Chan's eyes seem to say "yes" just before she walks off and reaches up to the collar of her dress [to undress?], then in the following scene as they drive home in a taxi, Mr. Chow asks, "Are you all right?")

The two neighbors begin writing together on a martial arts serial, become trapped in Mr. Chow's room for a night and a day because of an all-night mahjong game, preventing Mrs. Chan from returning to her room unnoticed (societal pressure). Here it is apparent that they are in (or have reverted to) a platonic relationship. Mrs. Chan does not want to "become like them," meaning their spouses, but she cannot keep away from Mr. Chow and visits him at the same hotel where he now goes to write. They become a happy "couple," sharing food, the writing, and music, even to Mr. Chow helping Mrs. Chan rehearse an eventual confrontation with her husband concerning his mistress.

When Mrs. Chan's landlady intimates that she is aware of her liaison with Mr. Chow, she stops seeing him. Realizing that Mrs. Chan will never leave her husband, Mr. Chow decides to leave Hong Kong for Singapore, where the third act begins. In an elegant use of a flashback we understand that Mrs. Chan has followed him to Singapore, entered his hotel room, smoked his cigarette, called him at work, then hung up before speaking. Taking her slippers, which she had left behind in his Hong Kong room, she exits his life. Years later, Mr. Chow returns to Hong Kong, visiting the flat where it all began, and discovers, wrongly, that all of the old tenants have left. Unbeknownst to Mr. Chow, Mrs. Chan is now living there with her son. For a moment there is only a doorway separating the two lovers, but it might as well be an ocean. He leaves. The dramatic journey of the film is over, but a coda takes place in the ruins of Angkor Wat. The journey to this ancient sacred place by Mr. Chow is prompted by the need to bury his painful secret while thematically raising this transitory affair to a universal level.

STYLE

Wong uses three intertitles in the film; the last one, being the final image of the film, reads, "He remembers those vanished years. As though looking through a dusty windowpane, the past is something he could see, but not touch. And everything he sees is blurred and indistinct." That might very well be the way we remember much of the film because many images are blurred, indistinct, fleeting, filled with shadows, seen in mirrors, through curtains, or other out-of-focus foreground objects. Wong orchestrates a densely poetic mise-en-scène, combining acting, art direction, lighting, camera, colors, and wardrobe (most notably Mrs. Chan's dresses) into an impressionistic dreamlike landscape in which the characters and their feelings appear as fleeting moments of time. The film's emphasis on the sensuous texture of the image is aided by extensive use of low-light levels and step-printed slow motion, which seems to "float" on the current of evocative music, whether it be a haunting cello or a Nat King Cole love song in French.

The cramped rooms, narrow hallways, and stairwells serve not only as a metaphor for the sexual repression of the society but also as a claustrophobic atmosphere that fosters intimacy. A closed-off frame that effectively changes the aspect ratio of the frame, a motif that is used extensively throughout the film, further emphasizes the spatial geography. Another motif supremely present in many frames is the out-of-focus foreground object. I would include in this motif Wong's extensive use of over-the-shoulder shots. Although the camera is predominately static, many scenes begin with a pan—whether from left, right, above, or below—that comes to rest on the final frame. This quality of the narrator is introduced in the very first shot of the film, panning from pictures on the wall in a hallway, to the back of Mrs. Suen's head, soon to be Mrs. Chan's landlady. To keep the story focused on our two principles, their spouses are shown only from the back, and their voices are only heard off-screen. Another stylistic conceit that serves this purpose is the familiar image rendering Mr. Chan's wife's office in an oval shaped mirror that seems suspended in air. An example of poetic economy is the use of only one exterior location—a street corner. The scarcity of locations leads to the recurrence of many familiar images (the most evocative being the narrow stairway to the noodle shop), each recurrence offering geographical grounding, but more importantly, emotional resonance.

The step-printed slow motion is the film's signature motif, helping to evoke a mood of loneliness and unfulfilled desire. An illustration of the power of this motif occurs in a scene toward the end of the first act, where its narrative job is to convey the inner life of our two principals in preparation for the escalation of their relationship from merely neighbors to something more. The foreground object motif is kept alive in four of the scene's seven shots. This scene is one-and-one-half minutes long and occurs immediately after a scene of Mrs. Chan at work. On the DVD's Chapter Menu, it's entitled "Lonely Hearts":

1. EXT. NOODLE SHOP: Fade up on a tracking shot of a noodle container carried by Mrs. Chan. Continue tracking while panning up with her as she enters the stairway of the noodle shop and begins to descend as Mr. Chow ascends. They barely acknowledge each other as they pass. The shot pans with Mr. Chow as he steps out into the street and exits the frame, which holds on an overhead lamp. It begins to rain, and Mr. Chow reenters the frame seeking shelter.
2. INT. NOODLE SHOP: Mrs. Chan enters into the noodle shop (worker in left foreground) as a second worker crosses in front of her, wiping the frame.
3. EXT. NOODLE SHOP: Standing in the previous frame under the lamp, Mr. Chow dries himself with a handkerchief.

4. INT. NOODLE SHOP: A below-the-eye-line close-up of Mrs. Chan, looking toward the stairway, seemingly disturbed by thoughts of Mr. Chow. (It is possible for an audience to make this interpretation of Mrs. Chan's psychology not only because of the superb acting of Maggie Cheung but also because that psychology is immersed in the palpable atmosphere of yearning that the music and the slow motion have created. It is further aided by the close-up and the staging—Mrs. Chan's turning toward the staircase obscured by the rising steam.) As Mrs. Chan dabs her face with a handkerchief once again, a worker crosses in front, wiping the frame.

5. EXT. NOODLE SHOP: Track left past an exterior wall of the noodle shop to discover Mr. Chow smoking in the stairwell. (It is not unreasonable to conclude that he is waiting for Mrs. Chan.)

6. INT. NOODLE SHOP: A figure in the foreground closes down the frame, focusing our attention on Mrs. Chan; the slight tracking movement to her right elaborates the turmoil of her inner life, and as she looks to the staircase, there is a cut to:

7. EXT. NOODLE SHOP: A slow tracking across the wet pavement as raindrops fall in slow motion.

The next cut is to the interior of the apartment house as Mrs. Chan and Mr. Chow make their way to their respective doors at normal camera speed. Because we have just been privy to their interior lives—their deep yearnings for each other, perhaps below the level of their consciousness—we are not surprised when each one inquires as to the whereabouts of the other's spouse. After this they will go on their first date.

LITTLE CHILDREN, TODD FIELD (2006)

DRAMATIC STRUCTURE

Here is an example of the umbrella structure: novelistic in style with multiple story lines, without a single protagonist to drive the film's action. On the other hand, they all share the same antagonist, internal to each: a deep dissatisfaction with life. The film's spine—its main action—is to search for satisfaction; the want is urgent, overriding reason and good sense, and the individual spines of the principle characters are subsumed under it, providing dramatic unity. The spine of the film goes so far as to subsume the spine of a character from a novel that is discussed in a women's book club, *Madame Bovary*. Sarah, a principle character, describes not only the actions of Madame Bovary but her own as well when she declaims: "Madame Bovary chooses to struggle against being trapped. The hunger for alternative and the refusal to accept a life of unhappiness."

A pretitle sequence contextualizes the film when a television reporter announces the release of a sexual predator into the community. It creates dramatic tension by promising us a "payoff" that concerns this information (because why else would our storyteller give it to us?), and as the characters are introduced, it becomes a promise that the lives of these characters will be affected by this payoff.

In the first act, all of the major characters are introduced along with their particular circumstance, their societal and dynamic relationships, a sense of where they are coming from, and a "smell" as to what we might expect from them. An omniscient voice-over narrator is introduced to supply backstory but equally important to offer insight into a character's psychology. Early in the film the narrator (camera) is given the ability to "jump around"—to leave one character for another. This mobility, when established, even allows the narrator to delve into the past.

The dramatic journey for all four principal characters, Sarah, Brad, Ronnie, and Larry, follow a three-act structure, but because there are four story lines, the acts for each character occur at different times. However, no second act material occurs until all of the first act material is completed, and no third act material occurs until the second act culmination of action happens for all the characters. In the third act, the consequences of each character's actions are resolved in a time frame of a few hours, and the promise made at the beginning of the film that that sexual predator would affect all their lives is delivered.

STYLE

Field deftly creates an atmosphere of mystery and menace in the mixing of images and sounds that preface the start of the film: CHILDREN'S VOICES, CLOCK TICKING over black; fade up on rapid tracking shot of blurry images of trees to reveal a suburban street; cut to a series of shots of clocks, then close-ups of figurines of children, (CLOCK CONTINUING TO TICK, CHIMES UP); crane down shelves filled with figurines of children as (TELEVISION SOUNDS UP); cut to television news filling entire frame, slow pullback from television set to shadowed back of chair, a hand holding a glass is raised for drinking then brought down as the television news continues. The heavy dose of exposition contained in this sequence is made palatable because Field prefaces it with the images and sounds of an ambiguous universe, allowing the unambiguous backstory to grow out of it.

Field is in total control of the director's craft throughout the film, conveying the story through images that are anything but ambiguous. Rather, they are clear and strong, employing a moving camera not only for rendering action but also for articulation of psychology and creating the freedom to use it both as POV for characters as well as articulation by the objective camera. His extensive use of wide-shots to surround the characters with their environment creates a palpable feeling of place, a necessary ingredient to fully appreciating the socioeconomic world they live in. To convey the twists and turns of the psychology of the characters, Field makes liberal use of close-ups for articulation as well as employing slow motion for this purpose, both to elaborate psychology as well as action. Example: It is used early in the first act as a character's (Brad) POV—to "get into his head"—to elaborate his consternation concerning the implications of his son's jester's hat as it is tossed into the air. Later in the first act it is used by the objective camera to render the grace of skateboarder in flight, preparing us for Brad's own leap into space in the third act; the slow motion of his flight raising the question as to its consequences, setting up a cut to him lying unconscious after the jump. Field's use of the POV is expanded when it is assigned to Ronnie's (the sexual predator) view of young bodies underwater. We accept this readily both because POVs have been assigned previously to other characters and because this one is so appropriate to the moment. One stylistic device that has not been introduced earlier and does not fit into the appropriate to the moment category (therefore seeming out of place to me) is the split screen image between Brad's wife and her mother, especially coming as it does quite late in the film.

It is instructive to look at *Little Children* and *In the Mood for Love* back to back, first for the differing dramatic structures supporting each film, each serving to organize *their* story for maximum dramatic impact on an audience, and second, to note the two very different visual styles. Neither story could have been told with the same intensity had they used each other's style. The poetic mise-en-scène of *In the Mood for Love* creates a rich interior life for each of the characters that is made palpable to the audience; we are immersed in it; it is more important than their actions. Had the narrative/dramatic style of *Little Children* been used, the story would have appeared to be trite, being unable to create the rich subtext of emotion that supplies the narrative thrust (rather then overt action). On the other hand, *Little Children* would have suffered from Wong's poetic style as the first rule of storytelling, clarity, would have suffered without Field's dramatic articulation, something virtually absent from *In the Mood for Love*.

CHAPTER 19

WHAT NEXT?

One book on directing, or even a hundred, will not make you a director. But I do hope that this book has empowered you to some extent, has taken some of the mystery out of the filmmaking process, and has given you incentive to proceed full-speed ahead in your own filmmaking career.

You've been given a methodology that I'm sure you will find helpful, if you try it on, but do not hesitate to make it your own. As you become more experienced, some of the written detective work can be discarded—*some*—but not until it becomes second nature to you. Continue to watch films actively, even commercials. Why that cut? Why that camera move? Do I find that actor interesting? One excellent way to continue learning, short of shooting a film, is to delve more deeply into the conceptual aspects of directing (remember, films are first made in your head). Take a scene that seems complicated to you. Watch it a few times. Draw a floor plan. Mark the staging. Figure out each of the camera setups. Determine how each setup was edited into separate shots. Or pick the kind of scene that you don't get a chance to rehearse, such as an action scene. Break down the design into component shots, then put it back together. When you are finished with this deep investigation it is almost as if you had shot the scene yourself—but not quite.

This "not quite" can often seem like a huge obstacle, but I am here to tell you that the next step—picking up a camera and making a movie with actors who speak lines—is not beyond anyone's reach. Not in today's revolutionary world of digital video. But let me go back a bit.

In 1978, Milos Forman and Frank Daniel hired me to teach directing as a full-time assistant professor at Columbia University's Graduate Film Division. Their first directive was to initiate and integrate the use of videotape into the directing curriculum. Until then, Columbia's curriculum relied largely on the teaching of 16 mm technology, as did most film schools in the world. This is symptomatic of what, in the past, was the largest obstacle to learning the directing craft—film. To shoot film requires mastery over a complicated technological world that is expensive, extremely time consuming (waiting for the lab to develop, matching the picture to track, coding the picture and track, the editing process), and ultimately, because of its cost, limits the full exploration of the craft. Pedagogically, the use of videotape and now digital video to teach directing has not only exploded the rate at which filmmaking can be learned, *but it has also become a viable medium for commercial productions.*

BUILDING DIRECTORIAL MUSCLES

Begin making short films: two to five minutes in length. Create an atmosphere: romance, danger, happy, sad. Use music. Move on to create a character that wants something that is difficult to get. Take a bike messenger, a pizza delivery person, a mailman, your brother or sister, or anyone you fancy; have their ordinary life interrupted, creating a dilemma that they have to extract themselves from, like Counterman in *A Piece of Apple Pie*. In these first tentative ventures into the world of film directing it is best to work with nonactors, people you feel comfortable with "directing."

My second-year students at Columbia have had exceptional learning curves in working with actors, staging, and the use of the camera as narrator by directing published one-act plays. One of the solid benefits of working with a play is that it will force you to develop an authorial connection to material that is not your own; to use the detective work set forth in this book to unearth a beat by beat understanding of the text; to unearth character, wants, and actions wedded to those wants, which will supply valuable insights for your work with actors. You will have to sustain a scene for a much longer period of time than is ordinarily the case for a film, and this "heavy lifting" with actors will help develop your muscles in this most experiential area of the directing craft.

Choose a realistic play that has no more than four characters and is contained in one set. If you direct it for a theatrical production, as some of my students have done, it can be extremely instructive in and of itself, but ultimately you should stage it for the camera and shoot and edit it. The actors will be happy to have a tape of their performance, and your *film* directing skills will take a quantum leap. (It is not necessary to get permission from the playwright if the play is not performed in a public venue.)

WRITING FOR THE DIRECTOR

A crucial aspect that was missing from Columbia's directing program when Forman and Daniel came aboard, and from virtually every other film program in the world, was the craft of story development and the writing of the screenplay. This, too, was corrected by having all directors take writing classes. This doesn't mean that every director has to write. It does mean that every director should know how screenplays are put together, and many directors will at some time want to develop their own original story.

I usually begin my first-semester directing workshops by telling students that the biggest problem they will have with their directing will be finding a story. As I do with them I'm going to do with you: encourage each and every one of you to develop your own stories into feature-length screenplays, and I am going to suggest some nonliterary methods for doing so. The aim will be for each of you, if you choose, to develop into a complete cinematic storyteller, even if you do not consider yourself to be a writer.

I assume that you have finished all the other chapters in this book and fully understand them. A cursory reading will not suffice. Nor will a cursory viewing of the films in Part Five. When a real understanding of the conceptual aspects is locked down, your experiential learning will be informed by it and will be markedly more productive.

You will need faith in yourself, and a bit of arrogance, for it takes just that to believe that you can engage strangers with a 90-minute story. It takes even more arrogance to assume that you can earn a living at it. I am not promising you that you can make a living as a director. That's up to you and the world to decide. If that's what you want, start now, and do your very best.

BEGIN THINKING ABOUT YOUR STORY

Not everyone is a writer, but everyone has a unique, even compelling story somewhere inside of him or her. Perhaps, when the imagination is primed, there will be other stories as well. The trick is to dig them out.

The writer/director Paul Schraeder (*Taxi Driver*, 1976) told his writing workshop at Columbia that screenwriting is not writing but *concocting*. Approaching your story this way can make it seem a lot less daunting. Who is my character and what does she want? What are the obstacles? What happens next? So much work can be done without ever writing a word.

For the past eight years I have been teaching a two-week script development workshop in Europe. Each student in a class of six must first present their story orally to the entire class. Even if a screenplay has already been written, and more so if it has not, this oral presentation will immediately disclose holes in the story, underdeveloped characters, lack of action. More importantly, it can disclose whether or not the premise of the story, even if it is underdeveloped, has a *potential* for a compelling film.

Schraeder let his class in on the way he begins to write a screenplay. He doesn't write (and this is a guy who has been extremely successful at his craft) until he can *tell* his story orally for 45 minutes. He'll start out with an idea. Maybe he told it to a guy sitting next to him on a plane, or in a bar, or a friend. The listener will soon indicate, nonverbally, whether the story is of interest or when it begins to flag. You can see it in someone's eyes when they lose interest. Okay, fine. Back to concocting. Invent another plot point. Introduce another character. Find another listener. Start the process again and add more details, more complications, until you can evoke the entire story—beginning, middle, and end.

Before beginning this process, it is helpful to know that all stories begin from character, circumstance, or theme. That is, the seed of the story comes from one of the three. In some of the films of Part Five we can see their likely genesis: *8½* with character, *The Truman Show* with circumstance, and *Red* with theme.

Do you have an interesting character, circumstance, or theme you would like to explore? You have some vague ideas. Okay, here's a suggestion that might make your concocting a bit easier. Begin with an event: a birthday party, anniversary, funeral, or graduation. I remember a Christmas as a little boy when my uncle fell into our Christmas tree. Is that an inciting incident? Is my uncle a good character? Was I different when I went to bed that night?

Go back into your own life. Spend some time there. Go into your fears. Your joys. This is a time to be both patient and active. You can jot down what seems interesting so you won't forget. Make no decisions. Work at least 20 minutes a day on this. Every day. Become clearer on the essence of your character's dilemma. If you are beginning with circumstance, ask yourself, What characters do I need to "people" this circumstance? If you are starting with theme, what characters or circumstance would be most helpful in exploring it? (Theme is the most "dangerous" to use as a starting point for your story because it can easily lead to a polemical argument. It works best in the inexperienced writer's hands if it is used in the latter stages of story development to provide illumination for character and circumstance.)

To keep the budget of your digital feature to an absolute minimum, your story should not have elephants in it or require the Russian Army. Rather, it should have a small cast with minimal location requirements—locations that are available to you, such as your apartment, your parents' house, a friend's gas station. The best model for that kind of location economy in the films we have looked at in this book is *Sex, Lies, and Videotape*. But I do not want this to be too much of a restriction on your imagination. Over the years my students have constantly surprised me with wonderful locations that they have secured for little or no money.

It is a good idea to read a book or two on screenwriting or take a writing workshop. When this is combined with some active knowledge of and experience in directing, it can be very helpful. Film is not literature, and a full understanding of the plasticity of the medium is necessary to tell a good film story. This is very difficult for most people to get from a book. However, a good knowledge of structure, character, and plot development—all the things that good screenwriting classes and books can impart—*is very important*. The book I would suggest is *Story Sense* by Paul Lucey.

CONCOCTING YOUR FEATURE SCREENPLAY

Don't agonize too long over what story you are going to tell. Commit. It is better to shoot something very soon than to waste years making sure. You can never be sure. Within a month you should be able to come up with at least the beginnings of a story. You're not sure what will happen, but what you are sure of is that the story contains potential, possibilities for growth. Now what most writing programs will tell you is to go home and write. Okay, it might take a year, or five, but that's what writing is. It's lonely.

Yes, it is lonely. And maybe you realize you are not a writer. You're a director, but you still do not have a story to shoot. What's more, you're not *really* a director because you haven't directed much of anything, if anything. But you have read this book, so you understand quite a bit of what is required of a director, and you believe strongly that you could do it, and would do it well, if you only had a story. Well, my friend, that half-formed story inside of you could be just what you're looking for.

I tried an experiment one semester. I invited six very good students in Columbia's film program to invent a story with me. I gave a very clear circumstance. That's all we began with. Then each of us developed a character. In 12 meetings from two to three hours, with homework in between, we came up with a complete story with motivations and dynamic relationships and had sketched the big scenes and sequences—in short, we were ready to start writing. What if you still don't feel confident in writing the "big" scenes or creating a memorable character—the meat and potatoes of what a writer is supposed to do? Try the following.

"WRITING" SCENES WITH ACTORS

While shooting a documentary on John Cassavetes while he was directing and acting in *Husbands* (1970), I witnessed him writing a scene with actors. The scene was to take place in a bar, but it had not yet been written. In the middle of a hotel conference room, Cassavetes gave Peter Falk and Ben Gazzara the circumstances of the scene and what was supposed to happen *to advance the story*. Then a tape recorder was turned on, and the three actors began to improvise, stopping to regroup if Cassavetes thought they were straying from the job of the scene or were out of character or if he had a suggestion to offer. They would begin again, moving forward from the beginning, to the middle, to the climax of the scene. Of course it was rough. It is nearly impossible, no matter how talented an actor is, to improvise a sustained dramatic scene. That was not at all the intention. The improvisation was to be only a *sketch* of the scene. A transcript was made of the tape, and then that transcript was edited and added to—crafted by Cassavetes—until he was satisfied. Yet still, in the actual shooting of the scene, Cassavetes allowed for more invention by the actors. Each actor was given license to improvise further. To make sure he could cut this together, Cassavetes ran two cameras simultaneously.

I am not encouraging you to work without locking down a scene *before* shooting. It is difficult to get specificity with staging and camera if there is no solid script, and even with the best improvisers, you often can see them "fishing" for the next line. What I am encouraging you to do is to explore your story with your friends, colleagues, and actors. Fantastic things can come out of this kind of collaboration.

SHOOTING YOUR FILM BEFORE YOU FINISH WRITING IT

While we're discussing this writing business, don't forget everything you have learned in this book about the director's POV in approaching a story. And don't forget something else. The reasons we are going on this journey are twofold: to get you an original screenplay that will engage an audience with a story that resonates within you, and more importantly, to give you what you need—a lot more experience in directing actors and camera. So pick a scene that you feel very sure must be in your film—say, the first meeting between the two characters in a romantic comedy. Work with the actors to get a scene on paper, then stage it and shoot it. See if it works when edited.

Depending on what stage you've reached in this process, it is a good idea to think of some of these explorations as being realized fully enough to actually go into the finished film. Thinking this way, of course, imparts urgency and a reality for the actors *and for you.*

THE FINAL SCRIPT

Mike Leigh, the English director of *Secrets and Lies* (1996) and *Vera Drake* (2004), works on developing a screenplay through improvisations with his actors over a long period of time, yet it is possible for to you make your entire film without ever having a completed screenplay. I realize my colleagues might consider this heresy, but what is the difference between making a film this way and writing a novel as a serial, as Dostoyevsky did with many of his novels, including *Crime and Punishment*? Of course, he had an overall view of his story, but he did not have every scene worked out. This is precisely the kind of creative possibility that the digital revolution brings to filmmaking. What starts out as a necessity—for Dostoyevsky it was earning a living, for you it is finding a worthwhile story to tell while learning the directing craft—might lead to something quite exciting.

SHOOTING WITHOUT A SCREENPLAY?

I served as a cameraman for two of Norman Mailer's films, *Beyond the Law* (1968) and *Maidstone* (1969). Both films were made without scripts. What Mailer did was assemble a group of actors and nonactors, give them a character and a want, and place them in a circumstance. Mailer himself acted in both films. There were absolutely brilliant *moments* in both films, but the dramaturgy needed to organize the action of a *complete* story was missing, so the final outcome was ultimately disappointing.

Each of these films was shot in under a week, preventing Mailer from stepping back, assessing what he had, what he still needed—preventing him from injecting his considerable narrative skills into the process. He was able to accomplish some of that in the editing, but without the necessary raw material, he was of course severely limited. Still, what *was* accomplished by Mailer points to a creative process that, with orchestration by a director, could lead to a more complete and satisfying outcome.

QUESTIONS DIRECTORS SHOULD ASK ABOUT THEIR SCREENPLAYS

The following are questions that directors should ask about their screenplays:

- What precisely is the protagonist's predicament, and is it the *stuff of drama*?
- What is the *main tension* of your story?
- At what point does the audience gain emotional access to your film? Or does it?
- Why today? Why begin your film at this point?
- Are the circumstances clear to you? Are they imbued in the characters?
- Are your characters clear? Interesting?
- Is there an emotional consistency to your characters?
- Does each of your characters deserve to be in your film? What are their dramatic functions?
- What is the character's arc–journey? Is it psychological, dramatic, spiritual?
- Are your characters' wants clear, strong, urgent—life and death? Can you make it more difficult for him/her? Can you raise the stakes?

- Are your characters' wants opposed by obstacles?
- Are your characters' actions in service of their wants?
- Is the dialogue action or talk?
- Have you written performances for your characters? Do they have something to do all the time?
- Do you set up the proper tone at the beginning of the film (permission to laugh in a comedy)?
- Have you explored the dynamics of your transitions, such as the use of contrasts—fast/slow, light/dark, loud/soft, etc.? The "what" that happens between the cuts?
- Do your characters have an entrance into your film? An exit?
- Does your film unfold? Does it allow the audience to actively participate?
- Have you made use of question marks? What will happen next? (Questions create suspense.)
- Have you made maximum use of locations?
- Have you taken into account the power of the film image? What does the shot tell you? Or the moments of just looking at your character—letting them be?
- Have you created the atmosphere for your story to happen in? Romance, suspense, supernatural, etc.?
- Have you set up the required universe for your story to happen in (e.g., elephants can fly)?
- Have you planted when necessary (clues, props)?
- Have you prepared the audience for something that will happen in the future so that when it happens it will be accepted?
- Have you made sure that there are no emotional or dramatic U-turns taking place off-camera?
- Are you working with expectation?
- Do you show aftermath? (The result of realizing or failing to realize the expectation.)
- Is the narrative thrust kept alive from scene to scene?
- Is there moment-to-moment reality? If not, do you have a reason?
- Do your characters exhibit credible human behavior? (Idiosyncratic behavior—behavior that is not wedded to character, circumstance, and wants—is not interesting.)
- Can everything that happens to or between characters be made available to the audience when transferred to the screen?
- Does everything you have set in motion at the beginning lead to an ending that is inevitable?

CONCLUSION

If you enter on this exciting journey with a great amount of passion, a fair amount of patience, some free time, and a few thousand dollars, it is possible that you can have a feature film "in the can" within a year or two. Will it be any good? Will it make money? Will it win first prize at the Sundance Film Festival? I don't know. But in my dealings with students, I am continually reminded of Francis Ford Coppola's prediction about what the advent of video recorders would mean: "Suddenly, one day, some little fat girl in Ohio is gonna be the new Mozart and make a beautiful film with her father's camera, and for once the so called professionalism about movies will be destroyed forever, and it will really become an art form." Today that little girl is running around with a digital video camera.

I wish you the best of luck!

BIBLIOGRAPHY

Aristotle, *Aristotle's Poetics*, Hill and Wang Publishing, 1961.

Bare, Richard L., *The Film Director: A Practical Guide to Motion Picture and Television Techniques*, Hungry Minds, Inc., 1973.

Baxter, John, *Fellini*, St. Martin's Press, 1994.

Clurman, Harold, *On Directing*, Macmillan, 1972.

Cole, Toby, and Helen Krich Chinoy, *Directors on Directing: A Source of the Modern Theatre*, Pearson Allyn & Bacon, 1963.

Dmytryk, Edward, *On Screen Directing*, Focal Press, 1984.

Eisenstein, Sergei M., *On the Composition of the Short Fiction Scenario*, Heinemann, 1989.

Kurosawa, Akira, *Something Like an Autobiography*, Vintage, 1983.

Lucey, Paul, *Story Sense: A Screenwriter's Guide for Film and Television*, McGraw-Hill, 1996.

Lumet, Sydney, *Making Movies*, Vintage, Reprint Edition, 1996.

Rosenblum, Ralph, *When the Shooting Stops: Inside a Motion Picture Cutting Room*, Viking Press, 1979.

Scharff, Stefan, *The Elements of Cinema: Towards a Theory of Cinesthetic Impact,* Columbia University Press, 1982.

Tolstoy, Leo, *What Is Art?*, Penguin Classics, 1995.

van Gogh, Vincent, *Dear Theo: The Autobiography of Vincent van Gogh*, Plume, Reprint Edition, 1995.

Young, Jeff, *Kazan, The Master Director Discusses His Films: Interviews With Elia Kazan*, Newmarket Press, 1999.

INDEX

Page references followed by "f" denote figures